The Patriarch, Caldwell & Company, and Me, Shirley

The Patriarch, Caldwell & Company, and Me, Shirley

BY

SHIRLEY CALDWELL-PATTERSON

CHURCHILL/BLACK
2021

COPYRIGHT © 2021
DAVID PATTERSON

ALL RIGHTS RESERVED

ISBN 978-0-578-53803-7

Edited by William M. Akers
Line Editing by W.M. Akers

Book Design by
John Balkwill, Lumino Press

Cover Design by
Locomotion Creative, Nashville

TYPESET IN ADOBE GARAMOND

PRINTED IN THE USA

Churchill/Black
Nashville, Tennessee

*From the hearthstone and fireside tales comes
the warp and woof of history.*

BARBARA TUCHMAN
Practicing History

*To the Supreme Power of the Universe
we appeal for the good will and wisdom in
our remembering that while our lives
are but watches in the night.*

*Make us ever mindful of the generations that
follow us and their just claim to this good earth.*

LUCIUS E. BURCH, JR.

In Gratitude

I DEDICATE THIS EFFORT OF THE LAST NINE years of my rather extraordinary life first to my grandfather, James Erwin Caldwell, who came to Nashville alone with seven dollars and twenty cents in his pocket at age fifteen. He thrived by following his own instruction to his sons to "look about you for opportunities where you can furnish the needs of people at a cost that the greatest number can afford." To the rest of us he reminded that it was we who were responsible for bringing the South back to its own and to make amends for the vileness of slavery in every way that we could.

To Ellen Thomas and Meredith Caldwell, my mother and father, I am beholden for an infinity of life, liberty, the pursuit of happiness and my education.

And most certainly to Lucius Burch, my very best friend, my gratitude is endless. He finally, at the tender age of some fifty years, took me on to know the world as few see it, to sleep on the ground and build a fire in the snow tucked in the mountains from Olympus via South America to our own Alaska, to catch trout and bonefish on a 6/7 rod with flies from the size of gnats to mayflies. But best of all, he showed me how to do things, know things that I needed, and looked me in the eye.

Thank You

To Ma May and Papa and the land that made us into a family, for letting us know who we are in your 1923 books, *Little Girl of the Confederacy* and *Recollections of a Lifetime*, where you never let us wonder why, and let us know what we should do and what we should leave undone. Though we may be more amiss in commission than omission, we try—not as successfully as you but to some degree we do see above the eaves of our own barns and stand for justice as we conceive it. May we never offend your household gods, but may we each follow our own hearts toward what we think of as the useful and the good.

To Donald Davidson, my creative writing professor at Vanderbilt who kept saying, "Shirley, you write well, but why don't you write about what you know?" Here it is, Sir, at long last.

To those few who said "keep writing"—to Will and niece Cissy Akers, and Elizabeth Queener during the many years, to Lucius Burch for his pushing, shoving and flattery, and to my children who are silent but patient—I think.

Special thanks go forth to my young friend, Hot Shot, who appears at tight times, and to Stavros Mykelis, who disappeared long ago.

My Simplified Family Tree

My grandfather, James E. Caldwell (Papa)
married my grandmother,
May Winston (Ma May) in 1875.

They had 10 children.
Among them, my father, Meredith Caldwell (Daddy)
and Rogers Clark Caldwell (Uncle / Uncle Rogers).

Uncle married Margaret Trousdale (Aunt Margaret).
They had no children.

Meredith (Daddy) married Ellen Thomas (Mama).
They had four children:
Meredith Caldwell, Jr. (Brother),
Shirley Caldwell-Patterson (me),
Allison Caldwell Byrd (Allison),
and Ellen Thomas Caldwell (Ellen).

Meredith Caldwell, Jr. (Brother) had five children,
one of whom is Cissy Caldwell Akers,
married to Will Akers.

I married David G. Patterson and we had two children:
David G. Patterson, Jr. (Son David)
and Sheppard Patterson Speer.

Son David married Elizabeth Bethea (Libby)
and they have one daughter, Bethea, now Bethea Schoenfeld,
married to Richard Schoenfeld.

Sheppard Patterson married Earling Speer
and they have one child, Meredith Speer.
She married Peter Gardner and had two children,
daughter Meredith Gardner
and son Griffin Gardner, my great grandchildren.

CONTENTS

I
CALDWELL FAMILY

1.
THE PATRIARCH

The War, and the Aftermath	18
A Start in Business	23
Longview	26
The Telephone	34
A New Era in the Telephone	40
Changing Business	42
Some Men I Have Known	44

2.
THE MATRIARCH

She Who Got Things Done	38
Christmas Dinner	53
Longview at My Coming	56
Pro Bono Publica	59
The Peace Monument	61
Death of the Youngest Child	65

3.
THIS CHILD'S "LONGVIEW"

Life at Longview	71

II
CALDWELL & COMPANY

Rogers Clark Caldwell	85
THE ROGERS CALDWELL STORY *Excerpts from The Tennessean, 1963*	90

THE INTERVIEWS

Tommy Goodloe	100
Frank Burkholder	108
John Seigenthaler	113
Sam Fleming	130
Jack Norman	138
Luke Lea, Jr.	144
Wentworth Caldwell	152
Ross Evans	160
Robert Lee Davis, Jr.	169
Ewing "Commodore" Bradford	180
Overton Ward	184
Sydney McAlister	190
Ed Nelson	195
Peter Taylor	198
Wilbur Creighton, Jr.	200
Libby Zerfoss Fryer	206
May Buntin Murray, then Hill	212
Shirley Caldwell-Patterson	219
Aunt Margaret	232
John Wilson Thomas, Jr.	236

III
AND ME, SHIRLEY

Us Chillun	241
Margaret (Dillie) Duncan	248
Spence School	250
Belle Meade	256
Vanderbilt	264
Wedding at Belle Meade	266
Domesticity	269
Nashville Union Stock Yards	274
Something Else I	281
Winged Victory of Samothrace	289
Something Else II	291
Something Else III	299
Hie Thee to the Mountains	305
Night Flight	310
The Two Nights that Bracketed the Full Moon	311
Heraklion	314
Hagios Nikolaos	315
The American School of Classical Studies	321
Cabo San Lucas	325
Good Things One After Another	330
Self Reliance or Else	335
Role of Middle-Aged Archaeologist	337
Variations on Many Themes 1971 - 1973	339
Monday, November 6, 1973	348
Not Too Late to Seek a Newer World	352
Quantas Airlines	354
New Zealand	355

Sheep Station	360
Australia	362
Al-Sumut	363
Williams Lake	363
Kleena Kleene	364
Bella Coola	366
Tennesse, the Beautiful	367
Tongariro River	370
Horses, Hitches and Rocky Trails	378
A Long Time	381
South America Bound	389
Westward Ho!	393
Big Ap	399
Return to the Malleo	402
Then Summer was A Comin In	408
My Horse Joker	410
Lift Up Thine Eyes	413
Bliss Meadows	417
Tel Anafa	420
Loose the Hounds of Change 1969-1973	423
Hawks Rest	425
"Hello The Camp!"	428
August in the Wind River Range	429
Dinwoody Glacier	432
October's Bright Blue Weather	434
Spider Silk	437
Rage, Rage Against the Dying of the Light	445
Mushing On	446

IV
CAST A COLD EYE ON LIFE, ON DEATH

Whither Away	469
Yuletide Was A'Comin In	475
Spring 1997	479
Epilogue	482
Appendix	487

ADDITIONAL VOICES

David Patterson	495
Sheppard Patterson Speer	497
Meredith Speer Gardner	497
Meredith Caldwell, III	498
Cissy Caldwell Akers	499
Thomas Byrd	502
Andrew W. Byrd	503
Paul Sloan	504
Joe McCarty	505
Charlie Newman	507
John Neel	508
Vic Scoggin	508
Bill Forrester	510
Wendy Smith	512
Margo Farnsworth	513
Shirley Caldwell-Patterson 1919-2016	517
EDITOR'S NOTE	521

I
CALDWELL FAMILY

*The father got the land.
Without the land,
there would have been no family.*

FERROL SAMS
Run with the Horsemen

My Grandfather, James E. Caldwell

I.

The Patriarch

JAMES ERWIN CALDWELL FOUNDED HIS CLAN IN Nashville and kept it there through difficult times, including the Depression and worse. Difficult times were no strangers; nor would they ever be.

According to his *Recollections of a Lifetime*, privately published in 1923, he was born in Memphis, where his father and mother, Alexander, a private banker, and Matilda Watson Sheppard, were early settlers. Soon after his birth in 1854, due to his father's failing health, they moved to Leflore County, Mississippi, with some fifty slaves to improve their 2,000 acre cotton plantation at Sheppardtown on the Yazoo River near her brother, Charles Sheppard, a prominent lawyer at Carrollton. Not long after their arrival, his father died and his mother, a widow at 35 years with six children, carried on the management of the plantation with the overseer, Brock.

The Sheppards were Scotch-Irish Presbyterians from Portadown, Province of Ulster in Northern Ireland, who came to Richmond. Matilda was a lineal descendant of Thomas Wentworth, Earl of Stafford, Chancellor of the Exchequer and Deputy of Ireland under Charles I. When Charles' reign began to falter, he called Wentworth to London to take charge of the government finances. Wentworth's wife tried to prevent him from accepting, but he felt it was his duty to obey. In the civil war that followed, he was executed by Oliver Cromwell.

Baron Watson of Rockingham County, England, married Lady Wentworth, Thomas Wentworth's daughter, and from their marriage came the forebears of Papa's mother. His Grandmother Sheppard and her brothers were cousins and intimate with Robert Emmet, the Irish patriot of the Insurrection. When they came to visit America, they did not expect to remain, but were so taken with the country that they never left. After the death of his grandfather, Papa's grandmother moved from Richmond to Nashville so that Papa's mother and Uncle Charles could benefit from the schools, the Female Academy and the University of Nashville, from which they graduated.

Papa's story continues in his book with the spring of 1863 when, in preparation for the attack on Vicksburg, General Grant sent gunboats up the Yazoo River.

from Recollections of a Lifetime, *by James Erwin Caldwell*

THE WAR, AND THE AFTERMATH

Perfect panic raged among the people, and, as they neared our place, preparations were made to leave.1 It was indeed an exodus. The family was packed in the carriage, the Negroes in the wagons, and so the whole cavalcade put out just before dark back into the swamps and forests with water standing over the narrow dirt roads. Yes, dark, ominous, black night with mud and slush at every turn of the wheel. As we got perhaps a mile back from the river, the smoke from the chimneys of the gunboats could be seen, and they soon came into full view just as dark came on; then such a sight as only the storming of Sebastopol could equal. About two miles above, the Confederates had thrown two Mississippi River steamboats across the river and set them afire to obstruct the channel that the gunboats could not pass. A regiment of artillery opened fire, which was returned by the gunboats, all going on in full view and sound. It was terrible and wonderful—the burning boats lighted up the very skies, there was the shrieking of shells bursting high up in the air, and the booming of cannons. While all this was going on just behind us, in front somebody had set fire to a big cotton warehouse to keep it from falling into the hands of the enemy. So the terror was complete.

With great fireworks going on all around us, on we pushed, splash, splash, through water and mud, all night long. To add to such an awful

---

1 This is Shirley's transcription from James E.'s book. It is not 100% accurate. –Ed.

experience, it was augmented by the grief and terror of my sister, Mary, whose new husband was with his company in the midst of the fighting. Of course, she could see nothing but his death and destruction. So, as I say, in the midst of it all we traveled the whole night through. At times it seemed that the carriage would go out of sight in the mud holes. It might be asked where we were going; we were just getting away from those awful gunboats.

I have, in my mature years, tried to visualize what must have gone on in my dear mother's feeling; she, a widowed woman with six children and a caravan of slaves, had the whole responsibility resting on her. Such resolution and heroism could not be surpassed. In the midst of all and the tears of anguish of my sister, she sat supreme, not a moan nor a tear from her.

He continues the harrowing account of her establishing authority at daybreak when they stopped to prepare breakfast for fifty plus.

She had been warned by the carriage driver, Jim Sheppard, that there was trouble among the slaves, that mutiny was brewing, and statements being made that they were going no farther, and perhaps other threats. Of course, some fifty darkies, one-third of them being big, strapping men, with a widowed woman with three daughters just coming of age and three little boys, the oldest of whom was twelve, presented a fearful possibility. My mother met the situation like a lioness. She went into the gathering of those people, seeking out the ringleader, she drew from the pocket of her dress a revolver which she pointed at the man, and told him to move when and as she said, or she would blow his head off. The victory was complete, and never again through those long, trying years was there the slightest trouble.

We exiles made for the hills east of the river, and after wandering the wilderness for a few days, we hung up near a dilapidated little village called Blackhawk. Here we found some of our old neighbors who had preceded us and we rented a place some three miles back where it was supposed that no soldiers would ever come. Indeed the country was so poor that a crow would have to take his provisions with him.

We lived there cut off until the end of the war in poverty: no salt, no sugar, no coffee, no cloth for clothes, no anything except the corn, peas, and "yaller yams" that the poor soil would provide. My mother kept rigid family discipline. The meals were regular and punctual, the school hours never interrupted, nor morning prayers.

With the end of the war, the cavalcade made its way back to the plantation but use of it was impossible—her money was worthless, fields overgrown and labor erratic. The ensuing odyssey back to Memphis and then to Franklin was full of woe, the deaths of children, and yellow fever that took whole families.

During that year of 1865 and those long, lean, hungry years following, and they were full ten in number, there was not the slightest sympathy extended or aid offered from the world towards the destitute and utterly poverty stricken people of the country. Modern history can give no account of such a tragedy. A masterful, dominating people accustomed to wealth, luxury and dominion reduced to penury and deprived of all civil rights and with no vote or voice in the government; all such privileges put into hands of their erstwhile slaves, a people of alien blood, without education whatever, and no semblance of experience in government. Not only was no sympathy offered, but curses and imprecations were hurled at us from all over the world. Europeans joined with the North to pillage and profiteer off the country.

Yes, we people of the South had to, and did, get up on our own feet and work out our own salvation in poverty, hunger and dirt. Yes, slavery was an awful mistake, a great crime, a crime that a warm-hearted chivalrous people had grown into unaware. Such is the power of training through several generations. That mistake and great crime had to be atoned for, and for more than fifty years, we of the South are still paying on that debt, and the end is not yet in sight.

Toward late 1864, the country having fallen into Federal hands, all hostilities were at an end. Many of the planters returned to their homes and resumed operations. My brother and I frequently went back to our plantation, staying for a day or two, sleeping in the house and getting our meals with old Uncle Randal who was a trusty left to take care of the house and such stock that was left.

My brother, Charles, and I discovered that the Negroes were quite ready to spend their money, and they all wanted tobacco. So we rummaged around the two or three stores in Blackhawk, and, with a little money borrowed from our mother, invested in tobacco and cheap unbleached cloth, and took it back to the Swamp, as the river country was called.

The stuff sold like hot cakes at almost any price we asked. So we made regular trips back and forth as the trade flourished. All was carried on in Confederate money which we were advised was the only patriotic thing to do.

The following spring we moved back to the plantation and our business came to an end. We had made a little more than $1,000, all in Confederate bills which were worth nothing. That was a lesson in finance to me. I have never since seen any money too good or too well safeguarded.

Some of the trips into the Swamp were eventful. The distance was about forty miles and was made on mule back. Both mules were old and slow, and I had only a semblance of a saddle so I sometimes rode bareback with "my stock" in a sack thrown across the mule back behind me.

As I look back, I wonder how our mother ever allowed us to make such trips—I was only ten years old and brother Charles was thirteen. The road down from the hills had long stretches of gloomy woods and quicksand at a time when the country was full of prowling men from both armies and runaway slaves, but it stimulated self-reliance. When I was ten years old I felt as fully grown and able to take care of myself as I have ever been.

Peace was declared and it was in the spring of 1865 when we returned home. Everything was so changed. Landowners had no capital with which to carry on the planting; their money was worthless. The rich land left uncultivated for some years had grown over and required much work to put in order. The Negroes now had no money and could not comprehend what freedom meant.

Then there came down the river two brothers of ample means named Clark with a boatload of implements, equipment and provisions. They contracted with my mother to rent and run the plantation and we were much encouraged with the prospect. In 1866 we moved to Oxford, Mississippi, where I attended my first school. In a two-room schoolhouse about fifteen feet square, I first saw how boys were taught in classes. I was at neither the top nor the bottom, but the thing that I really remember was the novelty of the swimming pond nearby. I did not exert myself very much

The Clark brothers who had come so bravely down made a complete failure. The Negroes ate up much of their supplies and did little or no work. As summer came they were taken with chills and fever and by

August moved back to Ohio leaving my mother to extricate herself from the wreck. I have always recalled the experience when I hear northern people giving advice to the South.

We then returned to Memphis which is now [in 1923] beautiful, but at that time conditions were deplorable. It had been used by Grant as a main commissary depot and all sanitary work was neglected. At the corner of Main Street and Front Row, the very heart of the city, I saw a pair of old boots upside down in the mud as though a man had gone in headfirst. Nearby was a sign reading "NO BOTTOM."

City life did not agree with me. By summer, I was in a deplorable condition and the danger of yellow fever was reason for desiring a change. My father's nephew, Mr. William Rossier, a Presbyterian minister, lived in Franklin, Tennessee. His wife had just died in childbirth, and he wrote to my mother asking her to come to take charge of his house, which fitted her desire to get out of Memphis. We left in July 1867 just before the outbreak of the fever which took every member of a neighboring family.

Middle Tennessee was so different from Mississippi's rich bottomland that I was, at first, disappointed. However, when reaching Franklin with its beautiful running streams and green pastures, I quickly changed. My mother never mentioned our poverty, which at that time had reached its height. The Clark brothers' failure had stopped any vestige of ready money and the sale of the plantation would not have paid for the taxes that had been levied against it.

We all worked, and among my duties was to keep the woodpile full. The winter of 1867 was rough and cold, and at one point I let the wood pile get low. I ventured out with the cart and horse to the woods lot atop Ropers Knob. When I got my load and started down, the cart slipped on the edge of an icy rock and spilled down the hillside. Fortunately, I was walking and was not injured. As I stood there on that bleak, desolate hillside with the temperature at zero, ice afoot, wind like a knife, I looked down at that house with no wood. Out on that great desert of frozen landscape, all the beauty disappeared and perfect terror seized upon me. The thought flashed through my mind—Must we all freeze to death and perish utterly?

Then the blood of my Scottish ancestors who had, from generation to generation, faced just such conditions on the hillsides of Scotland came to my rescue. I summoned my courage, looked out on the forlorn prospects, and soliloquized that there must be some way out, and I resolved to find it.

I did find the way out: I found better things in the world, and, above all, I found that the way that leads to them, which I never learned from books or school, lies along highway of industry, good morals and frugality. WORK AND SAVE—that is the universal cure for hard times which come to man.

A Start in Business

So it came to pass that on September 15, 1870 within three days of my sixteenth birthday, I left forever my mother's roof except as a visitor. I landed in Nashville presumably to go to school. I presented myself for matriculation at the University of Nashville from which my mother's brothers had graduated many years before. It was conducted as a military school under the direction of two distinguished Confederate generals. I had no trouble passing the examination for entrance, but said to them that I had seen as much of the military as I cared for, and asked if I could board outside and attend classes and lectures. They conferred and then replied that that was impossible to arrange. So we parted.

I procured board with Mrs. Mizell on Cherry Street, and opened an account at the Fourth National Bank with the $75 money order from my mother from a little fund arising from the estate of my father's mother. I entered Bryant and Stratton Business School, and in due course, told my mother what I had done. So great was her desire that I have college training that, when she received my letter, her reply was full of bitter disappointment. She urged that, if I were not going to the University, I come home and resume the work that I had had in Franklin.

I had launched my boat, and was not going back. With the $75, I made it through two months. Then I was offered and accepted a position as bookkeeper for a wholesale and retail grocery store on Broad Street at $40 a month. I slept in a room on the second floor of the store and continued to take my meals with Mrs. Mizell.

No surroundings could have been more trying and no temptation greater. I had to pass rows of whiskey barrels to get to my room just across the street from a variety theater and dance hall which was the toughest joint on earth. Nashville was overrun with every kind of tough element during the war, male and female, and a great number of them were still hanging on. Drinking, gambling and every known sort of immorality were practiced in full view out my window. It was a wide open town.

Alongside the whisky barrels at my door was a pile of books, the contents of some library dumped there for safekeeping. Among them I noticed a handsome copy of Milton's "Paradise Lost" and "Paradise Regained." I was first attracted by the beauty of the binding, but after opening, the beauty of the language and word painting captivated me entirely. The influence of Milton, long since dead, exercised a direct and powerful effect on that boy. Toward the end of the volume, in the short crisp sentence "In vanquishing temptation, Paradise is regained." I found the whole story—the Ten Commandments comprehended.

I thus started out on the real journey of life with the merest smattering of education obtained from schools, all told, not much over two years. Such schooling that I had was that taught by my mother, but I did have a liberal education in life and the ways of the world.

I made friends and acquaintances rapidly, and soon was in the midst of choicest social circles. I attended church regularly, not just because I was so religiously inclined, but because I was bound to meet some, or many, attractive young ladies. I spent my money carefully, but sufficient for a Prince Albert coat and a high top hat for Sundays.

Man is a gregarious animal, and needs to have his manners and social side carefully and fully developed. At one of the first little dinner parties which I attended that winter, the hostess started to carve the turkey. Without hesitation, I requested that she allow me to relieve her of the task which she readily granted. I was thoroughly trained and accustomed to carve at the table, and, when it was seen that I could and did the service with ease, I was showered with compliments, and my reputation was made in the mothers' circles. I am sure that I presented the appearance of a novel and fresh fish to those dear old ladies. From the surprise and admiration manifested by the company, I realized for the first time that it was an unusual act. Reputation can rest upon small circumstance if it serves to give an insight into good manners and good breeding.

The following spring, I secured a position as bookkeeper in the First National Bank at a salary of $125 a month. I was greatly elated, and felt rich for the first and only time in my life. But after a few days I realized I had made a mistake. There was no harmony among the men, and I was aware of a disagreeable state of affairs. Within a few days I reapplied for my old still unfilled job, but Mr. McLean declined by saying that there was no use taking me back, that surely I would be offered a better job soon and be gone. So I was out on the street. But I was offered a position with another grocer within a week at the same salary as the bank.

The panic of 1873 was terrific, banks were suspended, cholera raged and merchants failed in all directions. All my friends left town and I was left very much alone. The early part of the season had been very dry, but good rains came in July which caused a great demand for millet seed. Our house did not handle such goods, but took orders which were filled by buying from regular dealers. Handed a batch of orders, I made the rounds and found only two firms which had any on hand. I concluded that it would be a safe speculation, and bought all they had, giving instruction to fill the orders that I had and to send the balance to a warehouse to my personal account. The very next day, both houses, getting orders, found that I had all that were to be had, and paid me twice as much as I had paid the day before. With this neat sum, I began my first "banking" by buying notes.

A close friend, Frank Harding, clerked for Mr. French who came from Baltimore at the close of the war and bought a quantity of junk from the government—wagons, carts, harness and so forth. As he had no previous business training or talent, after selling his real bargains, he began to fall behind, and to complain of his troubles. He said that, if he could get enough money to get out of town, he would turn over his business to anyone who would take over his debts. I asked him to make a list of his indebtedness, and let me have a look at it. He did so, and the amount was quite small as compared with his stock. I traded with him by taking assignment of his business in consideration of my assuming his debts as enumerated. I gave him less than $100 with which he turned over his store to me, and left town. I became a wholesale merchant at twenty years of age.

I put Harding in charge, urging him to press sales as rapidly as possible, which he did efficiently, and I kept my own work. Within days, creditors began to show up with claims not embraced on my list. I knew trouble was coming, and so did his creditors. I was in possession of a valid bill of sale. And besides I was under age, a minor, and hence a lawsuit was impractical. I declined to pay any of them, but continued to sell goods at a lively rate. Their lawyers swarmed about me, some pleading, most threatening. After a few days of wrangling, they made me a proposition—

that I would keep the money and accounts for all I had sold, and turn the remainder over to them. I accepted. It left me with a neat sum that, with my seed money, gave me my real start.

The hand of Fate reached out one evening when Harding and I went with Miss Horton and Miss McCrory to visit friends of theirs, Miss Ellen Winston and her sister, Miss May, whom I had not met. As soon as I laid eyes on her, I realized that fate had laid hand on me and I was not inclined to remove it. So it came to pass that I, a fatherless boy, and she, a motherless girl, found ourselves tossed together by chance, destined to make the voyage of life together. We were so happy, and so poor.

Our year of courtship was one of perfect joy and delight; our first year of marriage was one of sickness and sorrow.

Longview

A few weeks after our marriage, the house where I was employed, having met heavy losses beginning with the panic of 1873, closed its doors. Sam Murphy, its largest creditor, blamed me violently for not telling him of the condition, and thereby saving his debt. I explained that such a course would have been reprehensible on my part. I was then given a position with the house next door. Within a few weeks I became very ill with inflammatory rheumatism and was confined to my bed for several weeks. While still in a crippled condition, I was fired because Sam Murphy demanded they discharge me and replace me with one of his choosing.

Yes, I was bodily fired, with my young wife to support, and just able to creep around after a severe illness. As it could not be made public the cause for discharging me, it left me under a cloud. I had absolutely no one to look to for assistance or advice. While I was thus without employment, my wife was taken ill with a lingering fever from which she hovered between life and death for many days. I drank the very dregs of bitterness and anguish. Gradually she grew better, hope returned, and finally, good health.

About that time, I purchased, with the last remnant of my little fortune, an interest in Mr. W.C. Nelson's fire insurance business, the firm being named Nelson & Caldwell. The first customer I secured wanted $500 of insurance on his residence on Wharf Avenue. So I walked out

James E. and Ma May

there to look the risk over. It was a warm day, May 14, 1876 and the distance fully a mile. The premium was $5.00 and the commission thereon 75 cents; I walked two miles for the first thirty seven cents that I made in business of my own.

I was very fond of the insurance business, and found it splendid commercial training; indeed, all commerce, including banking, rests on the insurance business. It gave me a wide acquaintance with businessmen and taught insight into the workings of all sorts of business that has been of great value to me.

The recollection of my humiliation over being discharged caused me to hold my insurance office as my personal property in which I could employ my sons and grandsons without asking such favors of my friends. More importantly, if I ever found my connection with any corporation unpleasant, I would always have a business of my own to fall back on.

While actively engaged in said fire insurance, I organized and built the first streetcar line to Glendale Park and the Waverly Land Company's suburb. It was chartered as a regular steam railroad and pulled from one to three coaches. Up until that time streetcars were pulled by small mules. Therefore when it opened with engines running at twenty miles an hour with open cars in summer and warm ones in winter and with Glendale

Longview Christmas 1894

TOP ROW (LEFT TO RIGHT)
Belle Morgan, Clara Allison, Annie Allison, James E. Caldwell, Matilda Sheppard Caldwell, Charles S. Caldwell, Annie Foster Caldwell

SECOND ROW
Elsie Caldwell, Maggie Winston Caldwell, baby Dandridge Caldwell, May Winston Caldwell, Louise F. Caldwell

THIRD ROW
James E. Caldwell, Jr., baby Harold Pendleton Caldwell, Alexander S. Caldwell, Jr., Charles Winston Caldwell, Charles Sheppard Caldwell, John F. Caldwell

FOURTH ROW
William Underwood Caldwell, Shirley Caldwell, Turner Foster Caldwell

BOTTOM ROW
Houston Watson Caldwell, William Dake Caldwell, Winston S. Caldwell, Rogers Clark Caldwell, Meredith Caldwell, Randolph Foster Caldwell, Erwin Foster Caldwell, Jere Witherspoon Caldwell

Park and its amusement buildings, the people literally swamped the road. They so packed the cars that the boys actually rode on the roofs.

I had charge for a year then sold it to be included as a part of the city system. This caused the use of horse cars to be abandoned and the city system to be electrified.

Our first darling child, whom his mother named for me, was born in 1876. Joy turned to grief when he hovered between life and death for nearly a year. Within two months thereafter a beautiful little sister came to keep him company.

My family was then too large to handle where we were, so we set up housekeeping in a house I bought on Vine Street. My dear younger brother Alexander, just graduated from Southwestern University in Clarksville, came to live with us. My wife's sister Miss Maggie was a frequent visitor, and, after a pretty romance of a year or two, they were married and remained with us. Soon my wife's sister, Miss Ellen Winston, came. The kitchen garden in the back I worked myself, and we owned a cow and a horse and buggy. We were never happier, but had to watch every penny.

Perhaps great love for the country brought the conviction that we could not bring up our babies in the city. A place offered for sale on the Franklin Pike attracted us most. The original place, consisting of 2,000 acres, a four-room, one story brick cottage with a one room brick office in the rear garden and large smoke house, was built prior to 1840 by Laura Sevier, daughter of John Sevier, Tennessee's first governor, and her husband Henry Norvell.

The land was badly used, the house small, plain and dilapidated but well located and had a fine stream with a picturesque springhouse at its side. Above all, the owners were willing to sell on a long-term basis without a cash down payment.

Centered on the battlefield of the Battle of Nashville, it was named Hood's Waste because his army camped there for some weeks and cut all of the trees for firewood. Army trains had cut roads across the upland during heavy fighting and caused the topsoil to wash so badly that no vegetation would sprout and the creek bottom so soggy and sour that only foul weeds would grow. Nothing can better illustrate the underlying value and possibilities of the land of Middle Tennessee than that demonstrated on this place. But I was 24 years of age and had moved sixteen times. The only place that I felt like home was the plantation on the Yazoo, and I longed

Longview

for a place to feel like that again and from which I would never move again until death.

I put the title to the place, renamed Longview in a permanent trust for my wife in such a way that, if anything befell me, she would always have a roof over her and our children's heads. That gave me more satisfaction than any transaction of my life.

Here moved in, not only my wife and I with two babies, but my brother Alexander, and my wife's sister, Miss Ellen Winston, and very soon my darling mother who lived with us until her death, quite twenty years later. Also my wife's younger sister, Maggie was with us for some time, and my brother Charles and his wife for a year.

Papa's love and admiration for his mother was so pervasive that I named my own daughter, Sheppard, for her—without the Matilda, a name out of fashion at the time. He speaks of her constantly in the early part of his book, but she is seldom mentioned after she had to move to Longview.

Think of that powerful woman who took her six young children away from their home to feed, house and educate in the wilderness for safety's sake during wartime and to provide for the slaves who remained when the others moved on. Think of her life in the growing establishment ruled by another strong woman, wife to her youngest son. Is it surprising that the only thing I ever heard of her except praise from Papa was from Cousin Edith, who said she was the meanest woman she ever knew?

However, there is a story about her that stands me in good stead. Every morning when she rose, she washed her hair until one day she was unable to do it herself without help. She then gave orders that she not be disturbed, withdrew to her room and closed the door. Three days later she was dead. I only hope I can do the same when my turn comes.

The following *Notes on Family History*,[2] dated October 15, 1889, is the only written record I could find on her:

The present generation is giving much attention to genealogy. A strong desire seems to have sprung forth to unfold the links of the chain which bind the individual of the present with the generations gone before. Therefore, at the request of my son, the following facts are written.

It is a matter of history that, during the reign of Charles I, the property belonging to the native Irish in the Province of Ulster was confiscated and given to favorites in England and Scotland. Here begins the history of the Watsons in Ireland. Baron Watson of Rockingham County in England married Lady Wentworth, daughter of the Earl of Strafford who had been made the Deputy of Ireland. One branch of the family chose to retain the maternal name of Wentworth and named his son, Watson Wentworth and from whom the Wentworths descend.

My mother was the daughter of John Watson, Esq., a country gentleman, whose estate was near Portadown, in Ulster. He was father of five children, two sons and three daughters. His wife died when my mother was quite young. He never married again, but being of social temperament, I heard my mother speak frequently of the house parties they had.

My mother's brothers were educated in the law, and, after the rebellion in Ireland in which Robert Emmet, their cousin, was hanged, they immigrated to the United States.

My father died when I was quite young, and I remember but little of him. He is a picture to me of a very large man who wore long stockings, knee pants and the front of his shirt finished with a broad ruffle on each side which was pleated and laid over one another secured by a pin.

---

[2] The location of these notes and from whence they came are, sadly, lost to the mists of time. —Ed.

The interest in genealogy which is such a prominent feature of the present generation did not then exist. It seemed to be accepted as a fact that ladies and gentlemen were descended from gentlemen and ladies.

In Recollections of a Lifetime, *Papa continues:*

My wife was as frugal and industrious as possible, making and mending children's clothes, putting up preserves, pickles and such like, not leaving the place for weeks on end. I used a horse and buggy in trips to and from my business, and, being very fond of horses, always had a good one. I made the payment on the place promptly on the day it was due, but it was work, work, work, and save, save, save for seven long years. In addition to paying for the place, there were doctors' bills, servants' wages, food and clothing. The strain was so great that my health gave way, and I was months in dragging back. Life has been pleasant to me, but I would not accept renewal if possible.

Yes, Longview was Home, and will be until the end. Here eight of our ten children were born, eight growing to maturity. From here six went out in marriage, and four went out in death, three grown men within eighteen months of each other, William Underwood, Shirley and James E. Jr. in order named, and long prior to them, two darling little girls. On the day we buried the first, little Margaret, little May came to take her place. They both died in my arms—their darling mother could not bear the agony. My wife and I were mates in misery. Those who have buried infants always have young children.

Longview has long been held out as a home for children, to come to when and as they please, any time, day or night, and to ensure that there was always an extra bed and an extra plate at the table.

For me he was an icon held by the rest of the family, but he was really my icon. It was he alone who commented on the fine row of calluses at the base of my fingers that I cultivated each summer. One day as I waited to wash my hands for lunch in the "wet-room" at the back door, he summoned me to the basin. As he soaped my hands, he turned them over, rubbed a finger across my pride and joy, and said, "Goodness, daughter, what is it that you do?"

If or when things were not going quite right, I could go through the glass conservatory where the tree-sized poinsettias thrived, and stand at the glass doors

James E. as a Young Man

to his study. When he saw me, he rose, opened the door, and we bade each other good day. Seated on either side of the hearth, we briefly discussed the weather and how the crops and flowers fared. He asked no questions other than how I was getting on. Then it was my turn, but by then sometimes I had forgotten why I had come. If things were really serious, I would state my problem; he listened, nodded and looked me in the eyes until I finished. After a few moments of pondering, he would lift the book beside him to slowly leaf through and stop. He spoke a few words on the troubles of man, and then read from the book a brief passage. By then the world had brightened, and I was ready to leave, confident with him that Emerson's words on self reliance were true.

He was a man of routine. He had a schedule that suited him, and was seldom, that I knew of, asked to do anything that he did not devise for himself. But I felt he had a special place in his heart for me, for he did for me peculiar things he never did for anyone else. When we walked to the barn together if no one was looking he even let me hold his hand.

The Tennessee State Fair was a weeklong affair each fall. The horse shows were held in the evenings in the great coliseum of bright lights and a big brass band that played Sousa marches con brio. This was the high time of my life; cold September nights with a full harvest moon still bring back flashes of the excitement.

Included in the classes was the Parent and Child Ride, in which I had never shown until Mama asked Papa, and he agreed. At his horse's running walk and my Jack of Hearts' fastest rack, we entered the wide gates to the arena, side by side, to the clash of cymbals, and the whistling started. He was dressed in his farm riding clothes and I in my black formal habit with high top hat, short white kid gloves turned back properly at the wrist, and gardenia pinned to my lapel. His horse and my pony were almost identical—dark bays with lush black manes and sweeping tails. The difference was that I and my pony were less than half his size. Round and round we went at top speed, passing the more sedate couples as if they were tethered. Victory was ours—hands down. The judge handed me the blue ribbon and gave the trophy to Papa. Charley Hatchery attached the ribbon to Jack's brow-band and Papa handed the trophy to me. We circled the ring again at a speed that only my adrenalin could take us. Then back into the night. There was Mama waiting for us as I knew she would be, looking her most gorgeous. And I tell you—she was one good looking lady.

In Recollections of a Lifetime, *Papa continues:*

THE TELEPHONE

The telephone had been patented for some years, but had attracted no special attention. It had been started in Nashville in a crude way with a little central office switchboard, and wires strung on housetops and trees. The service was not such as to inspire confidence. A few years later, about 1883, some party from Evanston, Illinois, had chartered under the name of the Cumberland Telephone and Telegraph Company with properties in Evanston, Nashville and Memphis.

I did not make a point of going to my office on Sunday, but some expected letter caused me to make this exception. I went to my office which adjoined the Western Union Telegraph office. As I got out of my buggy, the local manager told me they were going to experiment with the telephone over their wires to Evanston. He asked if I would like to join them. I accepted, and had my turn to talk. It was during that talk that the possibility of the thing came to me. In my imagination I could see what a wonderful thing it would be to connect every town and house with each other. That picture got in my brain there, and never got out.

A Mr. Babcock, the leading spirit in the movement, soon realized my interest, and made it convenient to see me frequently. I could see that he was only building his business for speculation. Sure enough, in a few months, pleading poor health, he offered to sell. I readily interested a group of friends and effected a purchase.

Mr. Oscar Noel who made his headquarters at my office was made president and general manager, and Mr. I.T. Rhea and I formed the executive committee with him. Mr. Noel was well on in years, being quite sixty-five. He had been successful as a grocery merchant, but had disposed of all of those interests, and determined to retire. But he went into this new scheme with alacrity.

Soon thereafter I conceived the notion of building a streetcar line to Glendale Park, and, in order to carry that through, I sold my interest in the Telephone Company. For some time I was out of touch. In the meantime, the telephone business did not thrive. Friction built up, and Mr. Noel sold out to his partners. Maintenance was neglected and the plant became dilapidated.

I sold my streetcar venture, was giving my full time to my insurance office, and was very content. While there was discord and dissatisfaction in the Telephone Company, I was on friendly terms with all of them. They made overture to me to come back into the company and assume the management, but I gave then to understand that I would not, under any circumstances, give up my insurance business. It was accordingly arranged that I buy a block of stock, be president and general manager, would have a free hand to select my subordinates, and to give such time to the organization as I should choose.

Thus I came to find myself saddled with a run-down, thoroughly discredited concern, committed to the management of a business that had gone steadily down under each new management. There were three different administrations in five years, and, at the time I took charge, the directors were endorsers on a note for $5,000 made to meet the payroll, and a very large outstanding indebtedness to the manufacturers of material and supplies and for rental and royalties. Such is the power of faith and imagination. I never could get out of my head the impression formed while talking over that line to Evanston.

I had witnessed with disgust the trouble and interference of the legislature, city authorities, labor unions and the newspapers were giving the railroads, telegraph and other public utilities, and had promised myself that, under no circumstances, would I get into the management of any such business. Yet here I was getting into the kind that would touch the nerve of every man and woman, child and chick, and therefore invite and have to bear the brunt of the worst sort of such attacks. But at the time the telephone business was so poor that it had not attracted the attention of these worthies, and I fancied that it would be immune from such troubles.

My first look-in was a sad affair. Memphis was the only bright spot. Mr. Leland Hume, just out of school, had demonstrated his ability and trustworthiness, so I brought him to Nashville as assistant general manager. No history of the Cumberland Telephone and Telegraph Company could ever be written without Mr. Hume's name writ large and high at the top of the page.

Within ten days after my election as president, I was taken desperately ill. It was thought that a serious operation might be necessary, but that was avoided. My embarkation was as gloomy and discouraging as possible. In addition to indebtedness to the bank and sundry floating amounts, there was an accumulation due to the parent company, the American Bell Telephone Company in Boston. They let it be understood that they wanted their money, and used language that could not be misunderstood. Soon it was found that the bookkeeper had absconded with a large sum, but it all was recovered, part from the surety company which had made the bond, and the balance was paid. The controversy with American Bell Telephone Company and myself grew heated and was rapidly approaching the courthouse when their attorney suggested that I go to Boston and confer with Mr. John E. Hudson, the president.

I did so, and we came to a perfectly satisfactory conclusion. From that hour until the day of his death, we were warm personal friends. I consider him a born aristocrat, and of all the prominent men I have known over the past forty years, I consider him the greatest of them all.

Time and circumstance have done their work on my mind, so I shall not do more than record events as they recur to me.

After getting matters adjusted in Boston and the shortage in the treasury straightened out, I began to look into and form some opinion about telephone art. So in October, 1891, Mr. Hume and I made a trip to find out what was to be seen and learned in the North and East. Our journey was made to Buffalo, with a stopover in Niagara Falls, then to Montreal where two rival companies were struggling for mastery, thence to Boston, New York and Washington. The only thing we learned was that all were groping in the dark. We met many who were cocksure that they knew everything they were ever likely to know, but no two agreed.

The parent company was struggling to maintain its patents, and test new instruments, switchboards, and mechanical appliances, but as to how to build the system, what prices to make for service, how to convince the public to make use of the implement, how to induce capital, no one had any sort of sensible suggestions. It is impossible for people now living when its use has become universal to realize how difficult it was to introduce it and get people to use it. Such is the force of habit. That generation was accustomed to a slower pace, to use the mail, couriers carrying messages and the telegraph. We had to cater to the whims and idiosyncrasies of the public.

Poverty was one of our great protectors. The company had no credit, and we, the new owners, had no more money to put in. So we had to make do with what we had, and wrack our brains for solutions to the problems. I had no pride of opinion to vindicate, no pet theories to work out. I went into the business not for employment or position; I had both. I went because I had faith that it was to be the best business of its day and generation, and that I could make money out of it.

For years we studied and experimented with prices, making every effort to make them within the reach of the broadest human strata, below which no competitor could go. At no time did I ever presume on patent protection, but built the structure as economically and as permanent as possible to curtail operating expense—to make the dollar go as far as possible, and reward the capital invested as liberally as we could to ensure a constant supply. How well it succeeded is generally known. We started with a half dozen exchanges, a total of about 4,000 subscribers, a few scattered, ragged toll lines in worn-out condition, and a capital of $1,100,000. When I retired from active management, the system embraced Kentucky, Tennessee, Mississippi, Louisiana, southern parts of Illinois and Indiana including the river cities of Louisville, Memphis, Nashville and New Orleans together had more than 100,000 subscribers, and a paid up capital of quite $20,000,000, which paid a regular quarterly dividend. The company's credit in national money markets was as high and well known as any public utility in the United States, and its stock sold on the Boston market at over $150.

I had the greatest faith in the long distance service and pressed without relaxation. Our first ambitious move in that direction was the building of a first class line from Nashville to Evansville, Indiana. Mr. Hume and I literally walked on foot every mile of that territory and negotiated for a private right-of-way. I wanted to know how the country people, and especially the farmers, would look upon such a proposition. We found on a clear and honest presentation of the facts that they made no objections, but readily gave the right-of-way free of charge. We secured 150 miles at a cost of not much over $500. It also gave us a personal insight and practical knowledge that was of incalculable value in the years to come.

We finished our venture through to Evansville and it was highly reassuring. We hesitated no longer, and made application to American Bell for a permit to build on from Evansville to Louisville. The application brought a request for me to come to Boston. There I met for the first time Mr. E.J. Hall, vice president of the American Telephone and Telegraph Company, then known as the Long Line Company and which was owned outright by American Bell Telephone Company for the purpose of connecting all of the local operating companies.

Mr. Hall and Mr. Hudson and I discussed our application. And they explained that it was their intention to build the said line themselves, and we went into a wide range of plans to do so.

My dear friend, Mr. E.M. Barton, president of Western Electric, was largely interested in the Great Southern Telephone Company, covering the territory of Mississippi and Louisiana. It was not going well, and I was invited to come on the board of directors, which met in New Orleans.

He was much discouraged and suggested a sale of Great Southern to the Cumberland Company which was done.

It was impossible to raise enough money to meet the combined necessities through the sale of additional capital stock. At the suggestion of Mr. G.G. Hubbard (the father of Mrs. Alexander Graham Bell), recourse was had to a bond issue of $1,000,000, a rather staggering proposition at the time. I recall the amused and incredulous expression that came over the faces of bankers and brokers in New York, the idea of bonding a flimsy, perishable structure of poles and wire appeared to them as absurd. But I met an unexpected ally in Mr. Wolverton, the president of the Gamewell Fire Alarm Telegraph Company. He had become attracted to the proposition through Mr. Cutler, the president of the New York Telephone Company, and with a few of his friends took one half of the issue. Within two weeks I placed the other half with a bond house in Boston. It was the first substantial sum of money to go into the telephone business south of the Ohio River. It attracted some attention. Within six months the price of Cumberland went to par and never sold below par thereafter.

Within a short time the Cumberland bought, for cash, the Ohio Valley Telephone Company, which included Louisville and surrounding counties. Soon the East Tennessee Telephone was purchased, which included Knoxville, Chattanooga, Lexington and the bluegrass country of Kentucky. This rounded out the territory of Tennessee, Kentucky, Mississippi, Louisiana and the southern counties of Illinois and Indiana. It made a strong appeal to the imagination to provide that inland empire with the modern wire service which would require millions of dollars. Could it be done with headquarters in the South? It was done, and for many years Nashville directed both the local and long distance for its larger rivals, *viz.*, Louisville, Memphis and New Orleans.

When we built the trunk line from Memphis to New Orleans and reached the marshes north of Lake Pontchartrain, the right-of-way, fifty feet wide, cut through the jungle. Men worked in from one to three feet of water all of the time with the ever-swarming mosquitoes and buffalo gnats and finally the yellow fever. No men ever displayed more grit and courage.

A New Era in the Telephone

Mr. Hudson died very suddenly. He was a hearty man, really in the prime of his life, and, hence, no thought had been given as to his successor. Consequently, some time elapsed before one was chosen.

The American Telephone and Telegraph Company (AT&T) was originally owned by the American Bell Telephone Company. It was organized to develop the inter-connecting lines among the various operating companies. Ultimately all of the assets of American Bell were transferred and retired from business. Through this process, AT&T became the owner of stock in all operating companies, and the actual majority in many including our Cumberland Company. Therefore whoever was president of AT&T was virtually the controlling stockholder in the companies. Mr. Vail, who succeeded Mr. Hudson had to be consulted on all matters requiring a vote of the stockholders, and could elect the board of directors.

I decided to sell my stock for Cumberland Company's first mortgage bonds, with the right reserved that each and every stockholder would receive the same if they so desired. I met with Mr. Vail, and as if by mutual consent we moved toward the trade.

As I signed the papers and stepped from his office, the realization came over me that I no longer was the president of a company that for twenty-one years I had labored so untiringly, and for which I had a great deal of sentiment and true attachment. It cast a gloom over me. But I was placed where I must choose either to get out or submit to dictation. The various regulating bureaus and commissions which have beset the business would have run me mad. Such is the hand of fate and the wheel of fortune.

Soon I received a telegram from Mr. Vail suggesting that I consider transferring my telephone investment in Cumberland bonds into AT&T stock. He made me a very profitable offer, and invited me to become chairman of the board of directors of the Cumberland Company, all of which was entirely in harmony with my inclinations, and so the matter was arranged and all plans were carried out smoothly.

The new operating officers were elected and the headquarters moved to Atlanta. The community of Nashville gazed at that event with surprise and resentment. Yes, a great commercial tragedy had taken place. Rates were lowered in all the large cities, and rebates amounting to the hundreds of thousands were made. All litigation discontinued, and the newspapers and politicians applauded.

Within a short time dividends were reduced, and in a few years discontinued altogether. Every effort was made to restore rates in order to prevent the company from becoming embarrassed and unable to meet the growth and give service. I had supposed from Mr. Vail's action on asking me to become the chairman of the board and to interest myself largely in the stock of AT&T that he planned to make some active use of me. I quickly discovered that he merely intended to treat me as he had others, by giving me an office and continuing my compensation, but refer no matters to me, expecting me to wither.

However, circumstances were shaping rapidly in other directions. I was much the largest stockholder in the Fourth National Bank in which I had been a director for many years, indeed since I was twenty-four years old. Mr. Samuel Keith, the president, died, and Mr. Watts, president of the First National Bank received and accepted a very flattering offer to be president of the Third National Bank of St. Louis. Just as soon as he decided to go to St. Louis, he and his associates importuned me to bring about a consolidation of the Fourth and First National Banks and take charge as president.

Notwithstanding the bank consolidation, I still retained my stock holdings in AT&T, and so gave much thought to the telephone business. Information seems to flow naturally through banks, and so I came into possession of a forecast of the intention of the Attorney General of the United States to break up Mr. Vail's plans for the Western Union Telegraph Company. I wrote to him of what I knew twice. As he gave no heed to the letters and showed no intention of changing course, I was so uneasy that I sold my entire holdings.

Sure enough, the Government did take action and forced Mr. Vail to retire from the presidency of Western Union and sell the stock therein which had been acquired from the Gould estate and entailed a cruel loss.

Changing Business

I had witnessed the trials of the panics of 1871 and 1893 which closed the doors of every bank in Nashville except the Fourth National, of which I was a director. I did not forget the terrible responsibilities which fell on the shoulders of chief bank officers, and had promised myself that, under no circumstances, would I ever accept such a position. But it was put in such a plausible, flattering manner, and with so many assurances of support, that I yielded.

James E. the banker

The consolidation took effect on June 1, 1912, and I was made president thereof. This was just five months after my retirement from the Cumberland Company. The combination under the name of the Fourth and First National Bank was easily the largest national bank in the South. So, instead of an office of ease and indolence which it seemed I was to fill, I found myself engaged in a new business, for me, and a most exacting one. I wondered why a man in his senses would assume such a responsibility, having in charge of the vast savings and funds of thousands of people, literally standing in the breech where, if failure comes, nothing is left but contempt or death.

I went into the banking business from a different motive from the other businesses which I had followed. At 58 years of age I had sounded the depths and shoals of commerce, and my curiosity concerning it and the affairs of the world were fully gratified. I think I can truthfully say that I was actuated solely by the motive of occupation. I did not think that I could possibly be content to quit commerce, which was to me a fascinating game.

While all business depends, more or less, on confidence for its success, to banking that is its sole dependence. A friend of mine who runs a bank in a small town once said, "The banking business is about 10% cash and 90% confidence." Through banks flows all the gossip of the community; this is necessary as it bears directly upon credit. The connection between correct living and credit is intimate. It is the last business that should be engaged in with the hope and intention of acquiring a personal fortune. The chief executive officer of a commercial bank should be so circumstanced as to be beyond pressing needs or being overmastered with a longing for personal riches.

There follows a detailed discussion of the Federal Reserve Act, the gold standard and other banking subjects which are afield from this story and from me. For those who have this special interest, I refer you to his book.

This is where Papa was when his book was published, but he had another twenty years to live until he died in 1944.

Some Men I Have Known

Mr. J.P. Morgan was easily the leader of finance in this country during his lifetime; I met him first under unusual circumstances. Governor James D. Porter was president of the Peabody Normal School of Nashville, and also a member of the George Peabody Fund. He had been very active and effective in securing favorable action by the board in appropriating $1,000,000 of said funds as an endowment for an institution to be located in Nashville under the name of the George Peabody College for Teachers, but after securing the appropriation, some dispute arose as to the final location whether in south Nashville or contiguous to Vanderbilt University. In some way Governor Porter offended Mr. Morgan, who was a member of said board and treasurer thereof, and, in consequence of that offense, Mr. Morgan seemed determined to prevent the appropriation from being paid. The matter dragged on for years.

Mr. John Vertrees, who had been looking after the legal matters in chartering the college, came to my office and explained to me the troubles. He said that unless some influence could be brought to bear on Mr. Morgan, Nashville would certainly lose Peabody College. He asked if I knew Mr. Morgan or could aid in the matter in any way. I replied that I did not know Mr. Morgan, but that I was going to New York the next day and felt confident that I could secure an interview with him, and do the best I could to help the matter out.

I had planned to take my wife and three youngest sons, Rogers, Meredith and Dandridge to the opera. So the day I arrived, I contacted Mr. Henry Davidson, one of Mr. Morgan's partners, who arranged an interview that afternoon. I took the boys with me, explaining to them that they were to have an opportunity of seeing the greatest man in New York. Mr. Morgan's private office had a clear glass partition that separated it from the reception room. When I entered with the three boys, it seemed to arrest his attention and excite his interest at once, but when I indicated what I wanted to talk about, he went into a perfect rage, referring to his trouble with Governor Porter, and that the newspaper in Nashville had made slanderous references to him, etc. It was plain to see that he had made up his mind to defeat the whole thing.

I did not try to stop him from ventilating his mind, nor could have done so had I tried, but while he was delivering his opinion it gave me time to study him. He had a striking personality. A born patrician of a little above medium size, he had a most remarkable pair of eyes, but was afflicted with a peculiar growth on his nose which greatly disfigured him. I made myself a most patient, polite and attentive listener while he abused Governor Porter and everybody in Nashville. I let him continue without uttering a word or showing the least impatience; indeed, I was too highly entertained and too much absorbed in studying him to wish to interrupt or bring him to a close.

So he ventilated his pent-up feeling for quite ten minutes without a pause, and when he came to finish, with sort of a jerk, he asked at rapid fire, "Now tell me who you are, and what interest you have in this matter, and are those three boys sitting out in the lobby your sons?"

I explained who I was, the business I was engaged in, and acknowledged the parentage of my three boys with some pride. Then I remarked that I was sorry to hear the indictment of the people of Nashville, etc. I said in as winning a voice as I could muster, "Mr. Morgan, you know that a very eminent man has said that you cannot indict a whole community. Nashville has some unworthy people, indeed some very bad ones as every other place, but that it was above average in culture and refinement, and had many people whose friendship you would value if you knew them." I added that there was no place where the funds would be more highly valued, more zealously guarded or bear more fruit than at Nashville. I said no more.

He changed into the kindliest voice and, without any hesitation, said, "I will turn that money over to you, but never to Governor Porter." He asked if I could meet him in Washington two days hence where the Board of Trustees was to meet, and that he would have them say their last words, and he would turn over the $1,000,000 to me.

That necessitated cutting our stay in New York shorter than we planned which caused the indignation of my wife in eliminating the object of our visit.

My meeting with the board of trustees of the George Peabody estate was memorable. Mr. Morgan, who was then an old man, was quite the youngest looking member. The meeting was presided over by Judge James Fuller, the then Chief Justice of the Supreme Court. Another member was Mr. Joseph Choate for whom the school is named. It was a meeting of patriarchs. Judge J.M. Dickinson, a Nashvillian who was present as one of the trustees for the George Peabody College for Teachers, was then Secretary of War in President Taft's Cabinet and was making his home in Washington.

Someone made the suggestion that I was from Nashville and might have something to say. Governor Porter arose and expressed an objection to my being heard as I was a member of neither board. Mr. Morgan stated that I had come at his invitation, and it was entirely in order in my being present. Mr. Choate rose to his feet, and addressing the Chief Justice in a most princely style moved and put to a formal vote, that I be invited to make any statement about the matter that I might desire. The motion passed unanimously except for Governor Porter. I made a short talk, such as seemed to me pertinent, and then sat down.

After that I saw Mr. Morgan often, once at his home where he had a most interesting library. Sometime after that he went to Egypt in quest for health. I wrote to him in Alexandria of the further pressing needs of Peabody College; he responded with a gift of $1,500,000. He never returned to America alive; he died a short time thereafter in Italy.

Mr. Morgan was not as rich as many others, but he made it easily and spent it lavishly, not in lavish living but in public ways. I think his reputation lay in his absolute integrity. He was trusted and seemed to control the money of the world. I remember vividly how he replenished the Treasury of the United States during the panic of 1893 to restore the credit of the Government, and arrested the panic. I can think that Mr. Emerson had this man in mind when he wrote the following words:

"It is natural to believe in great men. . . . The world is upheld by the veracity of great men. They make the earth wholesome. The race goes with them on their credit. The gods of fable are the shining moments of great men."

My Grandmother, May Winston Caldwell

2.
The Matriarch

MAY WINSTON CALDWELL, CO-FOUNDER OF THIS Caldwell clan, was the younger daughter of Charles Winston, a Nashville physician who was among the founders of the Medical College of the University of Nashville and served as its first president. He came at an early date from Kentucky where he had married Ann Rogers, an aunt of George Rogers Clark of Revolutionary War fame. She was also, to my own heart's delight, an aunt of William Clark, of the Lewis and Clark Expedition who preceded me in the joy of exploring the northern Rocky Mountains on foot and horseback by about a hundred and fifty years.

Here's how the lineage goes according to a series of authenticated documents that rest in my much-worn gilt box:

> WILLIAM DE PERCY married
> EMMA DE PORTE the Saxon lady whose lands had been granted his (after the Battle of Hastings of the Norman Conquest, 1066). The old chronicle says, "He wedded her that was the very heir to them for his conscience." He died near Jerusalem in the First Crusade.
> THEIR ELDEST SON
>
> ALFRED DE PERCY SECOND BARON married
> EMMA daughter of Gilbert de Ghent, son of Baldwin, Earl of Flanders, brother of Queen Maud, wife of William the Conqueror.
> THEIR SON
>
> WILLIAM DE PERCY married
> ALICE DE TUNBRIDGE daughter of Lord Clare. They left two daughters. Lady Maud died and left her great fortune to

HER SISTER
LADY AGNES DE PERCY married
JOSCLINE OF LOUVAINSON OF GODFREY, Duke of Louvain and Count of Brabant, descended from the Emperor Charlemagne. In spite of his high descent, the proud heiress would not consent to wed him unless he took the name of Percy.
THEIR ELDEST SON

HENRY DE PERCY married
ISABELLE daughter of Adam de Brus, Lord of Skelton.
THEIR SON

WILLIAM DE PERCY married (second time)
ELENA daughter of Ingelram Balliol, died 1245,
THEIR SON

HENRY DE PERCY, Ninth feudal Lord and First Baron Percy of Alnwick, Parliament 1299-1315, married
ELEANOR PLANTAGENET,
THEIR ELDEST SON

HENRY DE PERCY, Second Lord Percy of Alnwick, in Parliament 1322-1351, married
IDONE a daughter of Lord Clifford,
THEIR DAUGHTER

MAUD DE PERCY married
SIR JOHN DE NEVILLE Third Baron Neville of Raby, in Parliament 1368-1388,
THEIR SON

RALPH DE NEVILLE, Fourth Baron of Neville of Raby, First Earl of Westmoreland, Knight of the Garter, in Parliament 1388-1396, married
JOAN DE BEAUFORD second daughter of John of Gaunt, son of Edward III, King of England and his wife Philippi of Hainault, descendent of Charlemagne.
THEIR SIXTH SON
SIR EDWARD DE NEVILLE married
LADY ELIZABETH BEAUCHAMP,

THEIR SON
SIR GEORGE NEVILLE married
MARGARET FENNE,
THEIR SON

SIR EDWARD NEVILLE married
Eleanor, Lady Scrope,
THEIR SON

EDWARD NEVILLE married
CATHERINE BROME,
THEIR SON

EDWARD NEVILLE married
RACHEL LENAR,
THEIR SON

HENRY NEVILLE married
Katherine daughter of Lord Vaux of Harrowden,
THEIR SON

GEORGE NEVILLE married
MARY GIFFORD,
THEIR YOUNGEST CHILD

URSULA NEVILLE married
SIR WARHAM ST. LEGER of Ulcombe,
THEIR YOUNGEST DAUGHTER

URSULA NEVILLE married
REV. DANIEL HORSMANDEN,
THEIR ELDEST SON

COL. WARHAM HORSMANDEN married
MARY NEVILLE,
THEIR DAUGHTER

MARY HORSMANDEN married
COL. WILLIAM BYRD I,
THEIR DAUGHTER

Mary (Maria) Byrd married, (1716)
John Rogers
their son

George Rogers married (12/16/1754) Francis Pollard. (His sister Ann Rogers married John Clark, to parent Frances Pollard their son, Gen. George Rogers Clark, the Revolutionary War "Hero of Vincennes" and Capt. William Clark of the Lewis and Clark Expedition)
their son

Edmund Rogers married (1/27/1809)
Mary Shirley,
their daughter

Ann Brown Rogers married (9/6/1836)
Dr. Charles K. Winston,
their daughter

May Winston married (10/12/1875)
James Erwin Caldwell

She Who Got Things Done

Ma May upheld her vow of "for richer, for poorer, in sickness and in health, until death do us part," under conditions that would challenge heads of state. She gave birth to ten children at two years intervals for twenty years, nursed the ones who lived and mourned the ones who died, and ran a household of awesome size. There were few hitches, although one memorable one came the day she heard louder than usual noises downstairs. She leaned over the banister and called out, "Whatever you boys are doing, stop." It was then that she saw the ponies in the front hall.

She was a power for the useful and the good in a society still under the shadow of the Civil War and Reconstruction. But she did not do it alone. Her older sister, Edmonia, was "a lady of education and artistic bent, never married, but who made her sister's children her own." She came soon after their marriage and father's death and remained until her own death. Her common sense and great love of children made her a perfect second-in-command.

To me Ma May was as much a picture as a person; I see her at her desk writing. Even when she lifted her head, smiled, petted my hand, enquired and fulfilled my needs, in her mind she was writing. There was little displayed affection, and as to baby-talk—heavens no. But good humor and tolerance for such things as allowing roller-skating in the attic were never in doubt.

She was a lady of habit. When I trotted down the path from home early, and she and Tom, the gardener, were at work in the flower garden, she handed me an extra trowel from her basket. I sat beside her and was shown what to do and what not to do. When she stooped to the ground in her ankle length white voile dress, white cotton gloves and wide straw hat, she was not playing; she was laying on the strokes of an art piece. Papa was a farmer, she a gardener—both with equal ardor and skill.

At about ten o'clock, she clipped the daily flowers and was off to the big kitchen pantry where she and Alicia, the downstairs maid, arranged them for the house. After that she was upstairs to bathe and dress for the day. Exactly what she did then I didn't know; she went her way, I mine.

On reaching high-chair age, each in the long string of grandchildren took their place to her left at the dinner table. Before anything else was served, the child was given a small plate of the soft inside of hot water cornbread mashed with clear gravy. The crisp outside could be waved about in small clenched fist or gnawed—excellent for teething. This rite came with soft words of cheer and praise. When you were left to your own devices, she reached and laid her hand on Papa's who always sat to her right. It says something that this slight gesture is remembered so clearly this almost ninety years later.

Christmas Dinner

From 1880 to 1945, Ma May always gave Christmas dinner. It was indeed a feast day, with 24 at the table plus two drop leaf tables each accommodating eight small children with their nurses. No presents were exchanged except from Papa who had a roll of new one dollar bills that he peeled off to the crush of small ones whom he addressed as either Daughter or Son. I wonder if he knew all of our names, or noticed who were repeats. The only Christmas tree was a twelve-foot cedar, undecorated except for real candles, which stood in the upstairs nursery on the hearth with a bucket of sand nearby in case it caught fire.

We arrived at one o'clock, not 1:10. No alcohol was served, and smoking was not only outside but beyond the garden wall. People gathered in intimate groups in front of the three open fires. The men and maturing boys filled Papa's study to talk of men things. In the sitting room were the more sedate ladies, and in the hearth alcove of the great front hall there was gossip, laughter and an occasional curious man wanting to know the latest.

Ma May entertained the mass of children by the grand piano, next to which stood an American flag on a brass standard and a half life-size statue of Uncle Dan in his World War I uniform. She played Christmas carols to dubious singing. When dinner was announced at two o'clock she broke into "Dixie," and in a line, we marched with knees high to our places.

The dining room was spread with white linen damask and epergnes of fruit linked together by silver pheasants on a streamer of almonds, pecans, and black walnuts—all still in their shells—raisins in bunches on their stems, and holly. There were compotes of celery, olives and pickled peaches which had seasoned in the storeroom since summer. The ladies in their Christmas colors blossomed—my Mama was the grandest—among the dark-suited men of all ages. You sat wherever you pleased or, if you were slow, wherever was left. Ma May sat at the head of the table, with Papa to her right and the highchair of the youngest at her left, each receiving her equal attention.

Oyster soup of pure cream and much butter was the waiting first course. Then strong-armed housemen—Leland and Aunt Elsie's John Smiley—brought in the two biggest turkeys which had summered with the guineas in the side yard. (What happened to guineas? Most farms raised them as watchdogs—like the geese which saved Rome—and to eat like chickens, but much better.) With steam rising, decked with holly and smelling of Christmas, one went to each end of the table where stood my father and Uncle Rogers whetting their carving knives for the fray. I knew my Daddy was the best because his were sliced perfectly and Uncle chunked his.

Children were served first, and then the procession began. Platters of baked country ham from Rock Rest (Aunt Elsie's farm in Robertson County), spice-round, cauliflower with Hollandaise, macaroni with sharp Cheddar and sweet potatoes crested with marshmallows—what else I don't remember; these were my favorites. Then desserts: charlotte russe and wine jelly were passed, but Ma May served the plum pudding herself. The sherry for the charlotte, brandy for the pudding and Sauternes for the wine jelly were the only alcohols that ever knowingly made it into the house.

No coffee, and by then it was dusk and homing time.

This rite was not limited to Christmas, but, on a somewhat smaller scale, took place every Sunday, except the first of the month when we went to our house, Aunt Elsie's or Uncle Rogers'. First we made cockade hats out of the morning newspaper, then marched round and round, singing "Onward Christian Soldiers" or just stomping to Sousa marches. But when Leland announced dinner, and "Oh, I wish I was in the land of cotton, old times there are not forgotten. Look away, look away, Dixieland" rang out, our voices were assured as into the dining room we marched.

Sometime before 1925, left to right

Meredith Caldwell, Sr., Shirley Caldwell, Ellen Thomas Caldwell,
Anne Nichols Caldwell, Wentworth Caldwell Sr., Unknown,
May Winston Caldwell, Tom Buntin, Betty Buntin, Nurse,
Elizabeth Keith Caldwell, Jim Caldwell, Keith Caldwell,
Nurse holding baby: Allison Caldwell?, Standing: James E. Caldwell,
Edie Caldwell, Elsie Caldwell, Meredith Caldwell, Jr,
May Buntin, Elsie Caldwell Buntin, Charles Caldwell,
Margaret Trousdale Caldwell, Louise Caldwell,
Nichols Watson Caldwell, Dan Caldwell, Rogers Clark Caldwell

Longview at My Coming

Longview at my coming was some thousand acres of land added to the original homestead. The devastation from the Battle of Nashville only a few years earlier was healed, but the land still required care. No row-crops were planted, and the grass behind most of the mowers was left for mulch. But some went to fill the haylofts for the milk-cows, horses, mules and the brave horned Hereford bulls fattening in their separate paddocks, awaiting their return to the herd at Elysian Fields at breeding time. The smell of barns with hay in the loft evermore seizes my heart with joy.

The house grew as Papa prospered and eight more children were born. Two additions were made, and by 1906 it was called a Beaux Arts mansion in an old newspaper clipping. Exactly what that means, I don't know, but it followed Frank Lloyd Wright's advice of growing from the inside out to fit its needs. Then the outside was designed in proportion and according to current taste.

Bedrooms and baths were added upstairs. Downstairs the very large dining room opened on a bigger "front hall," which was actually a reception room with a side music room. With or without the wide doors thrown open to the adjoining two-story glass-roofed conservancy, two or three hundred people could easily be received. And they were received, when he was developing the telephone company and the bank or when Ma May was up to her good business. After the Depression, it was the still growing family who swarmed the halls.

The façade consisted of a two-story portico supported by four fluted columns with Ionic capitals, and approached by steps extending the entire length. The openings in the cream-colored stucco walls were French doors with arched fanlights. Upstairs they were faced with narrow iron balconies, and inside were left undraped for the light to pour through. A long porch extending from the entry around to Papa's study was much used as summer sitting room with white wicker furniture and the smell of trellised yellow climbing roses.

The music room, with walls of crimson silk damask, stately gold pier mirrors and little gilded chairs with red velvet cushions was the only part that I remember not being used by someone every day.

To maintain the establishment called for a web of servants; most lived in cottages on the place. The others came and went to town on the trolley running through the property that Papa had had built for this purpose, and as access to Glendale Park and the Waverly area as Nashville expanded.

The center of the web was Cook Ora, who lived in the back yard with her young granddaughter, Margaret (for years Sister Allison's best playmate), in a building that contained their rooms, a one-car garage for Aunt Anne's Model A Ford and the milkhouse. Cook was a permanent presence—big, not fat, one blind eye, quiet unless riled—who ruled her kitchen with little nonsense from the young or anybody else. Well she might, because she fed this collection of at least fifteen people three meals every day except Sunday and Thursday night, and fed them well. Three Sundays each month the number at least tripled with the coming of the clan.

Next to her house was the playhouse of two small rooms built mainly for the assemblage of girls. One room had a small cast-iron wood-burning stove used mainly for frying eggs. The smell of eggs frying in butter, the stomping of feet and rowdy singing of "Fe, fi, fo, fum, I smell the blood of an Englishman, and be he live or be he dead, I'll grind his bones to make my bread" would bring the most macho of boy cousins stooping through the low doorway looking hopeful.

The milk house was the domain of Bob Covington, who tended the herd of Holsteins. Here he put the milk through the separator to get the cream, to churn the butter and get the buttermilk. Looking back, Bob must have been a lonely man. Almost every night I could hear him waiting for the trolley down the lane, playing his harmonica and singing, "Lost John, put him in the pen. Lost John's done gone again," over and over. It sounded so sad; all I could do was burrow further down in my covers.

Then there was Leland, the chauffeur, of much Indian blood—tall, aquiline featured, copper colored. His quarters were over the garage which had been the carriage house, but now housed the big black Packard, and my very fancy show buggy. He drove only Ma May and Papa unless something else, like Sunday school, could be included as a back haul. He waited on the table, did the heavy cleaning, and, from the goodness of his heart in winter, poured kettles of hot water on the snow, which froze hard into a super-fine sled chute down the hill in the front yard. At the bottom where the sled hit the soft snow, it would usually flip over and pitched us further down the hill almost into the creek. Absolutely splendid!

Full Knee Deep Lies the Winter Snow at Longview

Tom Weakfall and his two romantically named daughters, Lethe (one of the five rivers of Hades) and Alicia, had the cottage atop the rise beyond the barns, next to the Indian burial ground. This site was easily identified by the rows of upright stones of the box graves exposed by the eroded soil. On the brow of the hill the dissolving remnants of breastworks facing Nashville produced an occasional minié ball, one of which I found and soon lost.

Tom was a thin, frail looking man who disappeared from time to time. Methinks that's the only way he could have gotten all his work done; he was the gardener. To tend some acres of vegetables and a formal flower garden is no small thing, but it got done. Lethe and Alicia were the upstairs and downstairs maids, waited on the table, and helped Ma May arrange the summer flowers which filled the house.

Lucille, the laundress, lived in town. Like Tom and most everybody else, her workload was prodigious. Think of it: for starters, the damask table cloths and napkins for a table seating 24 people, then sheets for seven adults plus the rest—without a washing machine or dryer other than the sun, I cannot imagine how it got done, but it did.

Charley Hatcher was a *café-au-lait*, thin, wiry horse genius. Uncle Rogers sent him to look after Elsie's, May's and my ponies and horses. He would saddle the riding ponies, and, armed with sandwiches, off we went for most of the day. After getting us out of his way, he exercised Elsie's two, my two and May Buntin's one show ponies on a lunge line. Then he set about saddle soaping the bridles and saddles and polishing the metal trappings. That tack room must have glowed in the dark.

Occasionally he would pull my show buggy out of the garage to clean. He used Vaseline on the black patent leather body and a whisk broom for the crimson seat cover and carpet. The bright red wheel spokes were inspected, axles oiled and then, re-covered with its tarp, replaced to await the fall when the shows would start. Back in the tack room, he took the harness from its soft storage bag, saddle soaped the leathers, and polished the brass fittings 'til they gleamed like gold. It was a museum-like toy which he tended with great care.

Charley was a man I envied. When we traveled hither and thither to horse shows, there were the trains. In a private boxcar, however many horses, usually four, that were to be shown (Cousin Elsie frequently went with us) were separated by low barriers of straw bales. In between was open space where the bales of hay and feed sacks were stashed. Propped against the side were the lyre-shaped shafts of my still shrouded but soon-to-be-used buggy. There were bales of hay for seats and a stack of blankets to be laid on the shiny new straw for beds. The second bed was for Slim, Uncle's farrier, who liked to travel. Such luxury and excitement has rarely again faced me. I begged in vain to be allowed to ride with them, but Mama, Elsie and I had to make do with the sedate drawing room in the Pullman.

Pro Bono Publica

Echoing what Papa said about the people of the South having to work out their own salvation, Ma May was a busy lady. She helped organize at least two ladies' groups to examine issues of the day and to read and discuss books: the Query Club and the Review Club. Both are still active. She was heavy into garden clubs, and Daughters of the American Revolution, Polk Memorial and the Ladies Battlefield Association were musts. In 1911 she published *Historic and Beautiful Homes and Gardens Near Nashville*, which is still sought by collectors, and is a rare example of a book which had colored pictures at this early time.

When she entertained these ladies at afternoon tea, we granddaughters dressed in our frilliest, smiled, and served little sandwiches and petit fours. I took a dim view of such, and spent most of my time behind the screen in the dining room, gorging on the little cheese wonders that Cook Ora made—thin, crisp, sharp Cheddar wheels made in something that looked like a shrunken tennis racket. There were advantages in being the youngest and smallest—it gave me choices.

Many years ago when the Federal Government considered Fort Negley of enough historic importance to restore, the engineer in charge called Ma May saying he had been in Nashville for some time and could find nothing about the old fort. She had the map of the city as it was during the war together with a working plan that any engineer could follow and a picture of the interior—all of which had been sent to her from the War Department in Washington at the request of Senator Tyson.

She knew the fort well, as she recounted in *A Chapter from the Life of a Little Girl of the Confederacy*: "When Nashville fell into the hands of the Union forces, Fort Negley was soon underway, and the spoiler's ax could be heard as he cut down the monarchs of the forest, and our beautiful woods were no more. In its place there arose what, to our children's fancy, appeared to be a robber baron's castle.

"My chief reason for being interested, for the last twenty five years, in the restoration of Fort Negley is because it is a picturesque, historical landmark and interesting as a relic of obsolete warfare."

I have never been to Fort Negley; it concerns me why. To me it is still a dusty hillside of scruffy trees and ugly stone gateway over there somewhere to the right on my way to Ward-Belmont from home on Caldwell Lane. To my grandmother it was a relic of obsolete warfare. To the Union Army, determined to hold Nashville because of its importance as source of supplies by river and rail to the South, it was worth the huge cost of the four acres of fortification and earthworks.

Methinks it says much of our teaching of history, especially to the very young. Broad strokes of dates, generals and killings are hard to swallow and worse to digest. Think of what I might have absorbed had I been taken on a spring morning to stand on McCloud's hill, looking south at the rolling green hills toward Franklin and been told the story. How close we are, fingertips away, to our past. Why does it tend to join in importance the Trojan War or Noah's flood?

The Peace Monument

Her most lasting achievement was as president of the Ladies Battlefield Association at a time when lingering feelings of animosity still hovered in those who had survived the Civil War and Reconstruction. She was much involved in every phase of the Peace Monument's design and erection.

The Peace Monument at its original location on Franklin Road
PHOTO COURTESY OF TENNESSEE STATE LIBRARY AND ARCHIVES

This is what Ma May wrote:

A monument like this, standing on such memories, mixes with surrounding nature by day with changing season, by night the stars roll over it gladly—becomes a sentiment, a poet, a prophet, an orator to every passerby.

The monument overlooking the Battlefield of Nashville was located on the Franklin Pike, three miles from the city. It carries a beautiful symbolism as follows: At the base of the tall shaft a group of bronze figures—two rearing steeds, held in check by a youth—symbolize the North and the South, once separated, but now held together by the younger generation of the World War. The youth with the South at his right, and the North at his left, is facing the east and moves forward toward the dawn and the rising sun.

To the sculptor, Mr. Moretti, is due much credit for the message he has given. He has told the story of the past, interpreted the spirit of the present, and, for a moment, caught a glimpse of the future. In the glorified face of the Youth in his magnificently modeled body, he has expressed the idealism and the strength of the reunited America—the new America which is the most potent unit in the world today for peace, justice and liberty.

The funds were contributed by patriotic citizens of Tennessee and many other states, both North and South. The monument was executed in Florence, Italy. The shaft and angel are of Carrara marble and the bronze figures at the base were made from an Austrian cannon near the spot where Cellini cast his famous Perseus.

The day it was dedicated, I was so small as to be allowed on its base while the black-hatted ladies and bewhiskered gentlemen spoke. All around the open country of cool breeze, waving grass and the sensual feel of my fingers rubbing the polished marble kept me still. When I looked up, there was heaven of an angel, horses and swirling folds of bronze and stone. I laid on my back at leisure while the voices rolled on.

Today what is left of this monument after its original site was sliced to pieces by interstate mazes is on a little known greensward off Granny White Pike. Care by a handful of people saw to it that it still stands on a quiet part of the battlefield, lovingly restored.

The original official recommendation was that it be placed on an overpass of Interstate 440—it makes the blood run cold.

Moretti's plaster model of Peace Monument statue
PHOTO COURTESY OF TENNESSEE STATE LIBRARY AND ARCHIVES

To consider what she accomplished makes me grateful for the pattern she set—not just for the adage "to whom much is given, much is expected" but the joy, the fun of getting things done that need doing—things of more import than self. Once upon a time I picked up a paper on Ma May's desk—a Federal army police report commenting on various notable Nashvillians during the Occupation. The name of the owner of a nearby farm caught my eye; it said "that he could not see above the eaves of his own barn." I did not want that said of me.

The strain follows to my children: daughter Sheppard heads the Florida Psychoanalytic Foundation, granddaughter Meredith serves on the Orlando Museum of Arts' Board of Directors, and granddaughter Bethea has a sizable list from her school and church work. As for me, I proudly have a Presidential Citation instead of a police report.

Ma May at the Dedication
PHOTO COURTESY OF TENNESSEE STATE LIBRARY AND ARCHIVES

Death of the Youngest Child

It is wistful to read of her youngest son, Dandridge, who died in the flu epidemic of 1918 in a military hospital. Here is what Papa had to say in his book:

When I approached young manhood, and looked out over the commercial field, the Civil War had been ended but a few years, and poverty and desolation covered the horizon. I had lived through those years, and the horror and destruction of it all was familiar. I thought that I should never see another war, that surely the world had grown too wise to employ that means to settle disputes.

On August 1st, 1914, when the explosion took place in Europe, it did not seem remotely possible that this country would be involved. We witnessed the performance as spectators in a grandstand. But the sinking of the Lusitania produced a sensation, and a considerable party was formed advocating our active resentment of the act. However, President Wilson was clearly opposed thereto, and his second election campaign was made on the slogan of keeping us out of war. Yet the Germans, instead of avoiding acts calculated to arouse public resentment, increased the pressure until the President could not withstand the pressure. So on April 1st, 1917, the Congress declared war.

We had three sons of draft age, and seven nephews. Four of our nephews were included in the first call, but none of our own sons. Rogers and Meredith took it philosophically and refused to be alarmed, stating that they would wait until called, which they never were. Dandridge could not rest and enlisted, passed the examination, and was assigned to the officers' training quarters at Camp Taylor in Louisville, Kentucky, August 28, 1918.

On September 26 I received a telegram from him saying, "I have turned up with the flu; have Dr. Glasgow look me up." My wife and I went to Louisville by the night train, taking with us a trained nurse. The next morning we went right out to the camp. Such a scene! A vast line of hastily built frame structures, miles on miles; men in uniform coming and going, great throngs of idlers, men, women, boys and girls hanging around all the approaches, army truck moving to and fro, many loaded with empty caskets, and some going away filled.

We finally reached the Y.M.C.A. hostess house where the proper intelligence officer could be found. But the scene in that house made the blood run cold—a perfect jam of panic-stricken fathers and mothers seeking their loved ones, as we were, who had been stricken down with the influenza epidemic. Everyone was required to wear a white mask to protect from contaminating the inmates; the effect produced was terrible.

After driving around through many rows of barracks, we finally found our son on the second floor of a temporary emergency hospital. We were much relieved as Dandridge did not seem very sick. Feeling so well satisfied, I returned home, but my wife and the nurse remained. A few hours after I got home, I was called on long distance, and my wife told me that pneumonia had developed, and that he was being transferred to the base hospital.

I returned at once, and from our hotel rooms in Louisville, we went out every morning. Day after day, the fight went on for a month. The strain and anxiety cannot be described in words, and neither can the scenes where hundreds, indeed, thousands of boys from all parts of the country and in every stage of suffering were grouped, groaning with pain and raving in delirium. Their looks of fright and despair, the anxious faces of throngs of parents gave evidence of hope departed. The poor lone mothers faithful till death, the Red Cross nurses clad in white flitted silently in every direction, the drawing of a white screen around the little beds indicated that the occupant had found his final rest. From the rear of the wing passed out the filled coffins.

At the officers' headquarters, a line of new recruits, young boys in their civilian clothes, entered and were assigned. Their expressions showed a strange awe as though they apprehended a danger but knew not what or where. It presented to me the appearance of the livestock as it is started in the alley that leads to the slaughtering platform in a great packing plant. At times I wonder if God Himself were dead and utter chaos was to reign on earth.

It seemed to me that, with that epidemic raging, they would better take no new inmates and scatter those on hand. I tried in every way to remove my son and bring him home, but the officers seemed made of stone, paying no more attention to my entreaties than a horse would.

They appeared unmoved at the sickness, suffering and death as they did to the smoke from the chimney-tops. They were trained for killing—which I realized is what war does and means.

Occasionally Dandridge would rally, which would inspire hope. When the pneumonia subsided, meningitis appeared, and the contest was unequal as his strength was gone too far to cope. One night, when it seemed it might be his last, I was with him. It was raining, and the cold wind was blowing, which, with the rumbling of trucks, the passing of couriers on motorcycles, the terrible suspense, with sickness, suffering and death all around, made sleep impossible.

On October 28th, 1918, just one month after being taken sick, our youngest, and our baby boy succumbed. I sat by his bed through the night when it seemed that every breath would be his last. These lines from Hood coursed through my brain:

> We watched his breathing through the night,
> His breathing soft and low,
> As at his breast the wave of life
> Kept heaving to and fro.
>
> But when the morn came dim and sad,
> And chill with early showers,
> His quiet eyelids closed—he had
> Another morn than ours.

With his hand resting in mine, the last breath came, and, as I looked at his placid face and magnificent brow, my knees gave way. I sank down by his bed, and the white screen was placed around us. The sentry at the door of the ward was humming "Keep the home fires burning," and, from the window came singing, "I shall see Him face to face." I could not rise.

I could not go immediately back to the hotel and break that last fatal news to his mother. She had become so weak at the long vigil that she could not come out. I wandered in an open field close by the hospital where I could be out of sight of man, if only for a few minutes.

My dear son Charles, always great in an emergency, took charge of his brother's remains, and stayed right by the body to prevent its being exchanged for some other, as had occurred on several occasions.

Poets write about war and warriors, and women hurrah men into war, but what I have written here is only a part of war. President Wilson stated it exactly: "I do not need to draw for you a picture of how the burden has been thrown back from the front on the older men, upon women, upon children, upon the homes of the civilized world, how the real strain of the war has come where the eyes of the Government could not reach, but where the heart of humanity beats."

One of the Greek philosophers, seeing a friend in great distress over the loss of his son, said to him, "Why do you weep, seeing that it can do no good?" The friend replied, "That is the very reason why I do."

Doctors, nurses and men are the merest shadows when confronting death. I now realize that I had no right to be startled at his death. It seems the most natural event. His fine organization demanded it and nature yielded. He was born for the future.

Me in Formal Riding Attire

3.
This Child's "Longview"

LIFE AT LONGVIEW

To try to describe "Longview" is to try to describe the face of one's beloved. To do it at all, I'll just start and see what happens:

This home was named for the sweeping view down to the rose-covered stone wall and front gate. It cornered on the Franklin Pike and Caldwell Lane. Until World War II this was all open country—a series of interlocking farms, each with its own great house and handsome stone springhouse. East across Franklin Pike was Overton land of "Travelers Rest," soon split among the second and third generations—the Dickinson's "Hundred Oaks," Lea's "Lealand," Thompson's "Glen Leven," and unnamed homes for Coltons and Ewings. Further south came Papa's working farm, "Elysian Fields" (in Greek mythology where good souls go after death). West of Franklin Road was the Kirkland's "Oak Hill" (now the First Presbyterian Church). Further west was Noel land on both sides of Granny White Pike, split among three sons, William, John and Oscar, whose wife, Miss Jeanette, was the granddaughter of Adelicia Acklen Franklin of not very far away "Belmont."

Across the lane were the houses of Cousin Winston, with wife and three children. Aunt Maggie, Ma May's younger sister and widow of Alexander, Papa's younger brother, was next, then Cousin Harold with wife and three children. A bit further lived Cousin Houston with wife and three. If it takes a village to raise children, we were ready. I once counted our number: within a two mile radius, there were over 35 kin, some as close as double second cousins.

Uncle Charley moved back to Longview with his two daughters, Edith and Elsie, after his wife died in childbirth. We moved into their pleasant four-bedroom house which faced the back of the garden at about the distance of a football field. I was three, at the dawn of remembering, but the magnetism of Longview was not far off. On my first spend-the-night, I gleefully stuffed a small suitcase with my baby pillow, and went trotting beside Daddy down through the garden. I must have been a mere nothing at the time because I had to sleep in the little bed at the foot of Ma May and Papa's. But soon I graduated to share cousin Elsie's room for many years to come.

Home was good enough after dark, but, for days, it was Longview's barns for cats with kittens, cows, bulls, an irritable goat that was supposed to pull a small cart but refused, mules, horses and ponies. And one of those was mine! Dixie, barrel shaped as Shetlands are, had no saddle—none could stay on her back without creeping up around her neck. I rode bareback, hanging onto her thick black mane and gripping with my knees. It was just Elsie and me, exploring and re-exploring the gentle hills and hollows.

On Saturdays, bands of city kin, boys and girls, arrived. Brown's creek had holes deep enough to think you were swimming. Battles of Yankees and Rebels were fought around the barns with flying corncobs and cane lances; sometimes iodine was called for. When action got too scary, I circled the garage and retreated unseen to the house, upstairs to Edith's room where she read aloud to me. Eight years my elder, she was pretty, prim and bookish. And besides, there was one turkey gobbler among the flock that cropped at will around the house which, when he saw her outside, chased her with much flapping of wings and raucous gobbling until she retreated. She read the likes of the *Three Musketeers*, *Ivanhoe*, *Scottish Chieftains* and poetry, particularly "The Lady of the Lake." Longfellow's "Children's Hour" described her perfectly: "There was grave Alice, laughing Alegra and Edith with golden hair." Edith's hair was twenty four carat; the rest of us were mouse-brown.

When I turned seven, there was another pony with a fine English saddle. With it came an early career of showing in horse shows that eventually took Mama and me as far afield as Louisville, Chicago, Kansas City, Augusta, and, the top of the heap, Devon, Pennsylvania. We did well. I was small for my age but dressed for the occasion, and, since the competition was frequently shown by professionals, was an anomaly. Mine were two fine, perfectly trained, small horses. Mama saw to that.

While we're here, let me tell you about horse shows. They started when I was five in Blowing Rock, North Carolina, where we summered for several years. The Mayview Manor clung to the side of Grandfather

Mountain with three or four stories of guest rooms above ground level. The downstairs dining room, approached from the lobby down a great curving stairway, seemed suspended in air with full view of the valley. This belonged to ladies in gem-colored gowns and gentlemen in evening dress. It smelled of cedar from the shakes that cover such places in those mountains and the brewings from the kitchen which were certainly not oatmeal. Its glamour may have been exaggerated by my only being invited for dessert. After supper taken in the children's dining room, which did smell of oatmeal and housed lesser beings, I alone of the young was invited into this well of gaiety to select the ripest peach from the fruit basket and have my own plate of meringues. Prissy me.

Up the road was the playground where days were passed with my still suckling sister, Allison, and Lula, her nurse. Near the end of one summer Mr. Tate, an equestrian hero for whom my doll was named, put on a horse show for the hotel guests. Mama decided that was what I wanted to do (she seems to have done this for most of my life and was always right), so for a few days she led me around inside the show ring and convinced me that I was having a good time. Come the big day, she led my beast into the ring and disappeared. There I was—kicking, kicking; the pony was eating, eating grass. He would not stir.

In the fall with my Dixie, the career was off to a slow start. I rode almost all day, every day, as I grew big enough for my legs not to stick straight out, but fell properly to the sides. Then, at seven, Mama thought again I was ready; there appeared a pony named Jack of Hearts, straight from Valhalla. No fuzzy barrel he, but a miniature (less than 48 inches high at the withers) perfect American Saddle Horse—dark bay, with lush black mane and tail sweeping the ground. He was fully trained, but I was a chore for Mama and Charley Hatcher. It was sit up straight, grip with your knees, heels down, toes in, elbows in, hands together, chin parallel to the ground—almost every afternoon. The undivided attention of those two, plus the wonder of being a part of this sleek beast, was splendid.

By September and Fair time, I sat on Jack outside the coliseum, dressed in a black formal show habit—sat and shivered. Charley and Mama stood beside us with her hand on the bit to keep him still while we waited our turn. The bright lights poured from the great open doors and the band played. I shook so hard that Mama took off her fur coat and threw it over my shoulders—it smelled of Patou's "Joy." Nothing was ever so exciting until I reached puberty.

Then it was time—we entered at a fast trot as told, and kept to the right against the rail until told to reverse. Jack was a pro, and I was willing. Then it was time to line up in the center for the judging. Charley was there waiting at the end of the line—separated several feet from the others—violating my seven-year-old's urge to cluster with the crowd. When the judges came, Charley waved his hat for Jack to prick up his ears, and held his bit when he started to rear on his two hind legs—his disconcerting habit when things got confusing. Then came the wait for the judging. When my number was called, Charley ran beside us to the judges' stand. With the presentation of the trophy, he stepped back and let loose of the bit, Jack reared straight up; I slid off his back still clutching the biggest silver trophy in the world. The audience whooped with laughter. Charley picked me up, brushed some of the tanbark off, set me back in the saddle, and off we trotted with Charley running alongside, whooping.

Life at Longview was scheduled around Papa. Leland drove him to his office early and brought him home in time for a quick nap stretched on the floor in front of the fireplace. Dinner was at two o'clock, not 2:10; you were expected to be on time, with hands washed. If I slid in late, nothing was said, but there was silence, and he looked straight at me; it didn't take long to learn that "punctuality is the courtesy of kings."

After dinner and changing to his farm clothes, he walked to the barn, mounted his saddled horse and set off on the miles to his working farm. If Elsie were not around to see, when we walked to the barn I held his hand. Public display of affection was rare.

Sometimes I rode with him, single file, down Franklin Pike. His plantation horse, forerunner of the Tennessee walking horse, moved at a smooth running walk at a pace that my pony was pressed to keep up with at a canter. Turning in at the stone gateposts (they are still there) to Elysian Fields, he beckoned me to his side, and we talked. We spoke of horses—he of their dependability, the advisability of having a good one, not a nag, and I of how beautiful they are. After he got my attention, he spoke of caring for the land by crop rotation and natural fertilizer, explaining which years to lie fallow. Looking over the herd of registered Herefords, he talked of cattle breeds, when and why one was preferable to another. He

asked my opinions as we talked, spoke of the evils of smoking, and why he continued to grow large crops of tobacco as the best assurance that the farm would prosper even in drought. And he told me, "The only way to be sure of leaving your children anything is in land."

These words were prescient; at the moment he was one of the wealthy men of the south, his land was incidental, but it was also at the brink of probably the greatest national depression. He was right. Years later the price of land soared; he did take good care of his mass of offsprings. Best of all, he lived long enough to know that his difficult life dedicated to the well-being of his family had, in many ways, succeeded.

I didn't go very often because he took so long that I got tired and frequently cold before we got back to Longview near dark. He knew exactly where each farming activity was and the name of every worker. When he bought all the adjacent farms available, the owners were given the choice of remaining in their houses to work the same land. Most did. We visited them all, and they talked and talked—boring. But when we neared home, we went by the springhouse, the beautiful Gothic façade of trimmed field stones built into the hillside that housed the precious source of pure water, which was once the house's sole source of refrigeration. He took a dipper from his saddlebag, and, without dismounting, reached into the spring to hand me a drink, then one for himself. I am grateful these many years later, to still have such a memory.

When we finally got home, there was tea with Ma May in her sitting room—uncolored Japan, and buttered toasted crackers. That the tea was green was no accident, but an incidence of foresight leading straight to today.

Both Papa and Ma May were wartime children, which left their health fragile from what was called inflammatory rheumatism and weak lungs. At some time after he was not so pushed just to keep bread on the table, they went to Dr. Kellogg's (of cornflakes fame) Sanatorium in Battle Creek, Michigan. They brought home a regime of exercise, exercise, exercise, no smoking, no alcohol, no coffee, little red meat—only the chickens, turkeys, guineas, lambs and eggs produced at home—vegetables and fruit aplenty, nuts, whole grain cereal and green tea, summer and winter. It worked; through the next three generations and beyond, most of their offspring are tall, lean and fairly tough. I never remember either of them being sick even into her eighty some odd years and his ninety-three. Both of their minds remained sharp as they aged, except for Papa's last days.

About six weeks before he died, he slipped to the long ago. He believed that now, 85 years later, the time had come to go home—to the plantation on the Yazoo. But Edith, whom he fully recognized as his granddaughter, was doing nothing to get ready. He knew that she had kept house for him since Ma May's death, but she refused to pack. His frustration was piteous.

The last time I remember of seeing him alive was one Saturday evening when husband David and I went to call. We went in through the back door to Ma May's brightly lighted sitting room. The rest of the great house was dark and so quiet. He sat at a card table, playing solitaire with a small radio at his side tuned to the Grand Ole Opry. There he was—immaculate in his black Prince Albert coat, starched white shirt, high stiff collar and trimmed white beard. He looked so elegant that I told him, "Oh, Papa, you just look so splendid." With a big smile he said, "Thank you, Daughter, my creditors demand it."

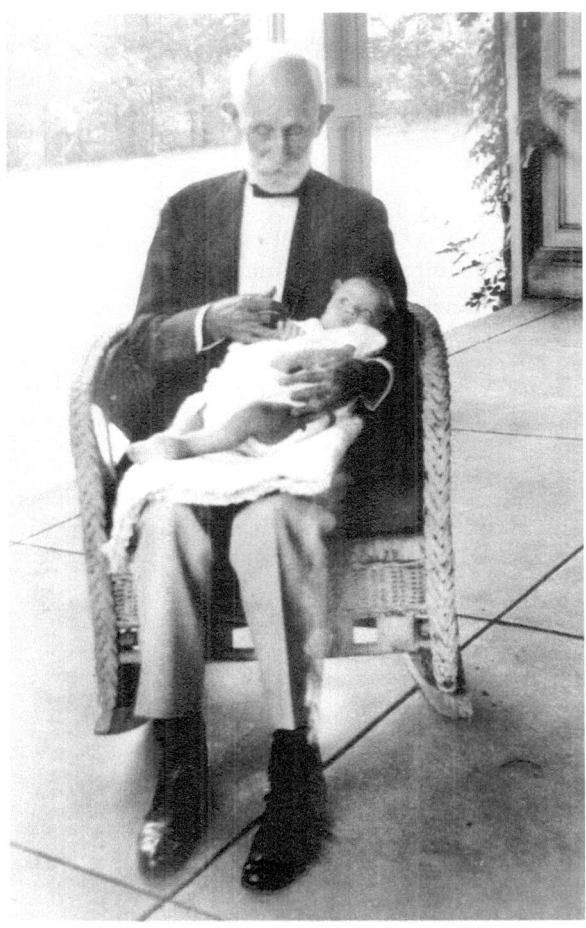

James E. and Son David, 1943

Your garden, Ma May, is a lovely place,
Old-fashioned, full blossoming and fair.
Can anything equal its beauty
The blossoming peach and the pear?

Your garden, Ma May, is a joyous place,
And children chase butterflies there.
Sometime don't you dream of Margaret and May
With the sun and the wind in their hair?

Your garden, Ma May, is a sacred place—
So peaceful, restful, how rare.
Is it because some spirit flower
Blooms in the scented air?
E.T.C.

Among my remaining yellowed newspaper clippings is this poem by Mama, Ellen Thomas Caldwell, who tended to keep her feelings to herself. She, who was born a couple of generations too soon when ladies were expected to be just that, was avant-garde. She let me wear Brother's last year's khaki shorts and skirts, go barefooted all summer, taught me to swim and, with swarms of other young, to play poker—draw and five card stud, nothing wild, for ivory chips. She drove herself, and, being of a railroad family, even knew how and did run the locomotive of her father's and grandfather's private "Little General" with its living and dining cars and caboose. In summer, it parked on a Trace Creek siding for family days of fishing.

My daily run to Longview was out the front door, across the lawn, through the iron gates (always leave gates behind you as you found them) and down the long gravel walkway bordered by low blossoming shrubs and peonies. To the left was the fenced kitchen garden, which started with some fifty yards of buttercups, the familial name for daffodils, and narcissus of such varieties that they successively bloomed from early spring into July. These were for cutting by anyone with the urge. Next came hilled rows of asparagus, my father's delight. Every late afternoon during the season he took me by the hand, and, armed with a long butcher knife, spied out the green tips just breaking the surface, plunged the knife in some eight inches down the side of the hills, and carefully pulled the pale treasures out for supper, to be awash in butter.

Next rows of Hickory King corn were planted and replanted so that ears ripened all summer. Intertwined were climbing beans of all sorts snaking up the stalks. Following were the usual vegetables—okra, onions, carrots, Irish and sweet potatoes, peas, and a large swath of turnip greens for the winter. At the end were the rows of tomatoes, staked with cane cut from a small brake nearby, as were the rows of sweet peas in all of their delicate colors and glorious smells.

The transition between the vegetable and flower garden was an ancient white oak standing in a clipped greensward, with its iron garden bench and a huge semi-circular bed of lilies-of-the-valley. There started the high stucco wall, of the same texture and color as the house, which bound the flower garden on three sides. The center was a simple round fountain where water gurgled all of the time. Following its curve were four stone benches and, radiating out were precise beds bordered with old brick set at the diagonal and separated by walkways of raked gravel. The flowers were selected to bloom from first spring until after frost. First were the hyacinths ("If thou hast two loaves of bread, sell one and buy hyacinths for thy soul."), snowbells, and early daffodils. Next came the tulips, in their Easter-egg colors, and peonies preceding the lilies—from the fragrant Easters, through the Lemons, to the black-spotted orange Tigers. Poppies as big as two closed fists fluttered in masses. And roses, roses, roses—from pale pink and white climbers on the arbors to the bush roses of astonishing color and shape, held at perfect posture by hidden cane supports, blooming all summer and well into cold weather to accompany the dahlias and asters. There was a row of tomatoes along the north wall, left from the days when tomatoes were admired for their red globes but thought to be poisonous.

Inset in the front wall between two ornamental iron garden gates was a low, windowless stone hut with walls studded with moss and maidenhair fern that seemed to have sprouted from the earth. This was the potato cellar which housed root vegetables for winter. It had a heavy wooden door, opened with a key the size of a big fork. The steps went straight down some eight feet to a trimmed pit of earthen walls and floor. It was always kept locked, and I almost never went all the way in. Elsie said there were snakes. But it was cool in summer and warm in winter, and smelled promising.

Memory of Ma May's garden, other than as a place of earthly delight, recalls one Sunday during World War II when Papa and I sat together on one of the stone benches. I asked why he did not seem very concerned about Brother being in Burma, and Keith and Dan off at sea. He turned to look straight at me, and said, "Daughter, when you have lived through the Civil War, nothing seems very crucial."

When morning rain or cold drove me inside, Ma May was usually seated at her desk, writing, always writing. She would look up, smile, bid me good morning and ask if I had breakfast. If not, she sent me off to the kitchen where, if I didn't look like I was going to loiter overlong, Cook Ora would slather butter on a large piece of thin sliced, toasted French bread, sprinkle it with sugar and a glass of milk, and direct me to a seat at the side kitchen table. One did not dawdle. She had the weight of seven "house folks" and nine servants on her shoulders for seven days a week.

The attic was Elsie and I's destination of choice. It wasn't something tucked under the eaves, but a third story as big as a ball room, with wood floors perfect for roller-skating; the noise was never mentioned. There was also a trestle table some ten feet long stacked high with old copies of the *Illustrated London News*, a large format, slick magazine with gorgeous colored pictures. We spent hours choosing which to cut out and put in scrapbooks. The one I remember was full page—a lady riding sidesaddle on her splendid hunter dressed in black, with a derby just like mine except that hers has a veil. With her groom behind her, they are returning from a hunt through a forest of very straight trees in the orange of sunset. Handling those magazines, and cutting out choice pictures for my very own, made me an Anglophile long before I knew what one was.

Then there was Aunt Anne, widow of my Uncle Jim whom I never knew. She was a permanent fixture, who taught Elsie and me to play three-handed bridge, and occasionally took us to town in her prim electric car to the picture show. One day she reprimanded me for eating crackers and making crumbs in the sitting room, saying, "Shirley, you are making such a mess, I bet you don't do that at home."

"No, ma'am, that's why I come down here."

Of course in summer, Cousin Annie, Principal of the Day School at Ward-Belmont, came to stay, read aloud long and exciting books every night, and told us about Paris so lovingly that I became an instant Francophile as well.

Let me not forget the asphalt tennis court which required no maintenance but was ever ready for all lucky enough to have or could borrow a tennis racket and, at least, one ball. Then there was the office in the back yard which housed the Ping-Pong table, which was the site of whooping and hollering: "Death to the loser!" Nearby was the well-worn ring for marbles or mumble-peg. Breathes there a soul of less than seventy years who knows that game of skill, played with an open pocket knife, where failure called for pulling the short wooden peg from the earth by the front teeth?

If you were ever bored, it was your own fault.

11
CALDWELL & COMPANY

*The secret of happiness is freedom;
the secret of freedom is a brave heart.*

Pericles

Rogers Clark Caldwell

Rogers Clark Caldwell, my uncle, was born in 1891, the eighth child of two people who, as young children, survived the trauma of war and the humiliation of defeat and Reconstruction.

His beloved mother's was the lighter load. The Union occupation of Nashville was relatively benevolent—it was easier to control this vital center of river and rail transportation if the locals were docile. Her father, as a physician, was even given protection. She tells how,1 when he was called out at night, two armed guards were sent to escort him or he might never have returned.

She also tells us: "I so often think of the tragedy and sad awakening of the young girls of that period in finding their young men friends marching away in their lovely uniforms to the strains of 'The Girl I Left behind Me.' It is no wonder, in their bereft state of mind, that many fell under the spell and charm of the Union soldiers and some even gave them their hearts and hand in marriage. Life without romance is dull indeed.

"I remember one morning seeing a Federal officer come dashing down the street on his horse shouting, 'Get in the house, get in the house. The battle may start any minute, and your children are in danger.' We were much impressed, but too young to know that the Union officer was General Thomas, the ranking federal officer who came from Virginia but stood for the Union because of his Yankee wife."

Rogers' father's load was extreme—the loss of home and land, utter poverty, scarcity of food for a growing boy which left his health fragile, lack of opportunity of formal education, and the weight of knowing that he must be a factor in restoring civilization to his homeland, the South.

In *Recollections of a Lifetime*, he wrote: "When Nashville fell into the hands of Federal troops after the battle of Fort Donelson, we heard nothing from my sister Letitia who was at school in Nashville, there living with my aunt, Mrs. Margaret Erwin. Finally my mother could bear the suspense no longer. With my brother Charles, they made their way to Memphis on mule back, from there they went by boat to Louisville, and thence through military lines by rail to Nashville.

1 In *A Chapter from the Life of a Little Girl of the Confederacy* by Mrs. James E. Caldwell née May Winston.

"While my sister was thus cut off, her cousin married a Federal officer from Wisconsin. They made quite a bridal trip to New York and Washington taking with them my sister. Of course, it was a great treat for her and she could talk of nothing else for months. She had just returned when my mother arrived; the trip home was started at once.

"Soon thereafter our greatest sorrow and misfortune occurred. My youngest sister, Harriet, was taken sick with inflammatory rheumatism, suffered agony for weeks, and passed away. Bear in mind, we had no undertaker and none of customary means for burial. A plain pine box coffin was made for her.

"My father was buried in Elmwood Cemetery in Memphis, and there my mother determined to take her remains. I have never been, to this day, able to remember without tears my darling mother with her little son as they set out on this mournful journey. I stood at the gate, looking through the slats, watching that wagon move off down the lonely road into the woods with that pine box and Brother her sole companion. With her scant, plain, black robes, looking straight out at her fate, she drove off giving no vent to her feelings. On to Memphis they went through hostile and friendly armies, and there interred those precious remains of that young girl by her father. There they slept undisturbed through the long, horrible years to come."

As late as the early 1900s, as Uncle grew to manhood, the South was an agrarian culture whose agriculture was still in ruins—little dependable labor, few decent roads or transportation (freight rates were higher in the South than elsewhere until after World War II), little communication or electricity, little or no rural schools or medical facilities. Above all, there was no capital to get any of these. Like a third world country, the only hope for progress lay in the few towns on navigable rivers or railroads such as Nashville.

So here came Uncle Rogers, a young man in an increasingly affluent family, full of energy, optimism and ambition. In 1910 at nineteen, after two years at Vanderbilt he dropped out to work at Papa's insurance company, where he dealt mainly in surety bonds. In 1917 at twenty-six, he determined to open his own municipal bond house, Caldwell & Company, which in thirteen years became the largest investment banking house the South had ever had.

It started under ideal conditions. The need for the original concept—to make available to rural communities the capital for infrastructure—was all too visible. The money was in the North, but it had not come south for a variety of reasons. The South had a poor credit record, especially during the Reconstruction years, and large bond dealers did not deal in the small denominations that rural borrowers needed.

Courtesy of Kermit C. Stengel, Jr. Collection

The solution followed Papa's formula: "recognize the need, provide a solution of permanent value affordable to the broadest range of customers at a price where competition is discouraged." Caldwell & Company provided the solution by buying large bonds, then dividing them into smaller units as were convenient to potential customers. A 5% fee was charged to procure bonds. All of the proceeds were not needed at once but incrementally, as work progressed. The Bank of Tennessee, a private bank belonging solely to Caldwell & Company, was formed to hold the as yet unneeded funds, if the purchaser wished, at 7% interest, which was slightly higher than usual. The deposited money, as in any bank, was used, not simply held.

Courtesy of Kermit C. Stengel, Jr. Collection

As Dickens opens his *Tale of Two Cities*, "It was the best of times, it was the worst of times." So it was for Uncle. With the end of World War I, the South began a period of extraordinary growth. There is reason to believe that Caldwell & Company was in no small part a cause.

Twelve years later, in the fall of 1929, came the stock market crash and the resulting Great Depression. One year later, in the fall of 1930, Caldwell & Company was declared bankrupt, and Uncle was indicted. At thirty-nine, with about half of his life still ahead, how did one man handle all this?

I was ten years old and felt little or no change—the ponies were still in the barn, Mama and Daddy were just as loving, and we never spoke of the trouble. Later, I did not read John Berry McFerrin's *Caldwell and Company*; I simply did not want my image of family tarnished in any way. It is arresting that I should not have had more faith in what I thought to be good.

The interviews in this section were taped from 1988 to 1990 by Will Akers, husband of my niece Cissy, whom I thank from the bottom of my heart. As I transcribed them, there was so much repetition that I omitted some of the text but did not edit except to replace with pronouns a few names when unflattering remarks were made. These many years later it can hardly make any difference except to Uncle—and to me.

Instead of starting with my describing Uncle, I give here excerpts from the 1963 Nashville *Tennessean* supplement by George Barker. How accurate they are, I know not, but they are more objective than I could be—I was a child and Uncle Rogers was just another uncle.

S C P

The Rogers Caldwell Story
by George Barker

In the 1920s Rogers Caldwell was the biggest wheel in the south. His name meant horses, beautiful women, lavish parties and visiting ambassadors. It meant Derby Day in Louisville and Palm Beach in January. But most of all it meant a hell-for-leather sort of personal wheeling and dealing in high finance which the South had never seen before or since...

In the 1930s, when almost everybody was broke, Caldwell's name meant something else. He was probably the most hated man in Tennessee. When school teachers weren't being paid because there were no state funds to pay them, they thought of Rogers Caldwell. When banks closed and mills shut down and workers' children went hungry, there was talk of Rogers Caldwell.

And when a rich man decided he did not have the courage to face life as a poor man, Caldwell was the man some people blamed when they read the suicide report. "People blamed Herbert Hoover for the depression in a general, impersonal way," one old-timer said. "With Caldwell it was different—he was right here with us. We could blame him personally."

He was indicted on three counts. The crumbling was front page news all over the county and, as he says, "The papers gave the stories big headlines, but they never seemed to have much room when I was cleared."

Caldwell said nothing publicly. He was, and remains, timid about personal publicity and maintains an almost obsessive dislike for being photographed. He agreed to this request for a series of interviews as a contribution to public insight into dramatic events of history at a time when he had had a tremendous impact. Caldwell had no wish to "tell all." And he stipulated that he would not speak unkindly of anyone. When the interviewing was done, Caldwell was still clothed lightly in an air of mystery that accentuates the adventure.

He lives alone. His wife, a beautiful woman of great charm who was as much in command at a seated dinner for 150 honoring a Russian prince or a British ambassador as she was aboard a horse, died two years ago.

Caldwell spends a few hours each morning at his office at the Nashville Union Stock Yards, a family property, where he handles paperwork in connection with the estate of his late father and keeping up his correspondence. He admits that he doesn't work very hard, and gets home in time for lunch, which he seldom eats alone.

Luncheons at his house have become a forum for emerging and established leaders of this area. Every Saturday finds a dozen or so sitting around the big dining room table eating, joking, pontificating—bankers, teachers, writers, politicians, doctors, lawyers, newspapermen. Caldwell listens more than he talks. He smiles a lot. He does not play the old soldier nor does he regale his friends with stories of the brave campaigns of yesteryear. His interest is "now" and "tomorrow."

A shy man with intense dark eyes, a large nose, gray wispy hair, he has the perpetual look of just having shaved. He keeps his tie tucked into his shirt about two buttons down. "I don't want to be stepping on it," he smiles. He has a broad sense of humor and an almost cosmic array of information drawn from newspapers, books and any other printed word that come before him. He goes through the stuff like a bonfire. When he laughs, his eyes close and his conversation sparkles with humor.

There is a tendency on Union Street to speak of Rogers Caldwell in the past tense as if he were gone. "The one who lives out in Franklin and the one of the 1920s are two different men," one Union Streeter said, "You never see him down here watching the stock quotations or having lunch with the men in investments. We only see each other at funerals nowadays. In the old days he was everywhere."

In 1910 he made his debut in the business world with a lot of rich-boy nerve and a dead-pan kind of sincere charm. By 1930 he had used it to build himself a financial empire which controlled a half-dozen insurance companies, about 75 banks, three metropolitan newspapers, and a score of other enterprises including hotels, department stores, textile mills, mines, real estate and oil companies and the Nashville Vols.

Everything—except the Vols, of course—was making money. The whole caboodle was worth about $650 million in 1929. Today it would probably be worth about five billion.

His basic business was selling municipal bonds. If a town needed a million dollars to build sewers, schools or street lights, he would get it for them. He lured about $100 million of fresh money into the South each year. The money he attracted left its mark on the land that can still be seen today. He, more than anyone, made Nashville the Wall Street of the South.

Rogers was a mild-mannered little boy who learned quickly to stay out of fist fights because he lost too often. His life at the 1,500-acre Longview estate on Franklin Pike was idyllic, there were plenty of boys to play with—there were six brothers—and ponies to ride even to his school at Robertson Academy some six miles down the pike.

He enrolled at Vanderbilt in 1908 and quickly distinguished himself as a ferocious all-night poker player and disinterested student. In his second year, he walked off campus and into his father's office. "I had always been obsessed with the idea I could be a good businessman since, at 13, I made a killing selling ice-water to railroad workers camped on our farm property."[2]

Instead he was sent off on a grand tour of Europe and North Africa. But a few weeks later he was back in town looking over his father's shoulder and, in 1910, it was agreed that he take over the family's small insurance company.

This is the time of survey-conscious, university-trained experts who can tell you it won't work. But yesterday belonged to the man who was willing to scratch and sweat bullets to make it work. Rogers Clark Caldwell was one of those. He was young, smart, daring and had magic with money. In 1920, at 30 years of age, he was a millionaire at a time there were few in the South. He was idolized as a true financial genius netting about two and a half million a year and not quite sure what he did have.

Just past 40, he didn't have any, and was scorned with the scorn reserved for fallen idols. "I remember the first taste of it very well," Caldwell says, "it was October of 1930 and Margaret and I were giving a dinner party. Col. Robert McCormick of the Chicago Tribune was one of the guests. I had lost two million dollars that day. When you are giving a dinner party, you don't want to disconcert friends with your troubles. But, I'll tell you, losing two million dollars in one day is disconcerting. I knew it was the beginning of the slide and I wasn't sure there was any way I could stop it. I was not prepared for it."

And it came. Within a week of the fateful dinner, his company collapsed and triggered the start of the Depression in Tennessee. Popular history has given the tag of "The Crash" to the collapse of Wall Street investment houses in 1929. Some of the more perceptive financiers around here will tell you that the crash of the Caldwell empire in November of 1930, while due in part to Wall Street, had more significant effect on

---

[2] As another example of apples not falling far from the tree, at the age of eight, my granddaughter, Meredith Speer, did well selling water to the runners who raced through her home town of Aspen, Colorado. She hired a six-year-old boy to dispense the water; she handled the cash.

Tennessee and the South.

For one thing, the state lost most of the several million dollars it had on deposit in Caldwell's Bank of Tennessee. Add to it the effect of the closing of his mills, shops and scores of banks and business houses across the south, and you begin to have an idea of the scope of the disaster.

"You might say that Caldwell was technically but not morally at fault," one Nashville banker says today. "I don't think his integrity was ever doubted by those who knew the score. Look at it this way: say I give you a ten dollar bill to give to Joe Jones. You put it is your wallet, but before you see Jones, you lose the wallet. You no longer have my ten. Does that make you a crook?"

The sinking ended forever the most audacious 15 years of financial empire building the South has ever seen. From the first, it had been pretty much of a one-man show. In the beginning there was Rogers installed in his father's insurance company. When there was a disagreement between the two over the risk factor of the bond business, he moved out and rented a little office on Union Street.

Southern municipal bonds had been regarded with suspicion by Northern financiers since the Reconstruction, and Southern financiers didn't think much of them either. They were hard to sell; he had the field virtually to himself. But within a couple of days of opening his own office, he had an offer-to-buy from a Chicago bank. But then news of the sinking of the Lusitania and the possibility of war sank the deal. "I decided right then that I would get in a position where no one would ever be able again to withdrawn a bid on me."

He started hiring hustling young men—when the company was at its peak with some 200 employees, only half a dozen were above 40 years old. To say that Caldwell cleaned up in the boom that followed World War I misses the mark. He is one of the big reasons the boom boomed.

The South was ready to expand in all directions. Towns, counties, manufacturing firms all needed money and Caldwell got it for them—most from the North and Midwest. The method was basically simple: He would buy the bonds and, by dint of advertising and promotion, sell them for from 1 to 5% more than he paid. Once in a while he couldn't sell what he bought, so he kept it for himself, thus collecting pieces of companies.

It is hard to imagine the bitterness of the early 1930s. It is true that unemployed men sold apples on the street corners to fend off starvation, and what they couldn't sell, they ate. Poverty was virtually universal, and there was not much to do about it but to identify the cause of pain. In the South, the most convenient target was the man who had the most money.

Because he had most to lose, he might have been considered the greatest victim, but this fact was lost in the public impression created by his enemies as the chief cause of the crash.

There was one other man during the era who compared with Rogers in dash and boldness. That was Col. Luke Lea, a former Senator, World War I hero and owner of the Nashville *Tennessean*. Although Lea was much older, they knew each other well, were neighbors, had served on the city park board, and they became partners. The move put Rogers firmly into the field of controversial politics.

"Col. Lea wanted me to help finance his expansion in the newspaper field." Caldwell says, "I studied the idea and it seemed sound." They bought the Memphis *Commercial Appeal*, the Knoxville *Journal* and came within a whisker of the Atlanta *Constitution* and the Kansas City *Star*.

Caldwell "bought" something else he hadn't bargained for—Col. Lea's political enemies. But he went with his eyes open and was not afraid of a fight. Lea backed Gov. Henry Horton's administration, but Horton's opponents found Caldwell's millions a perfect target.

He today declares there was never any dark conspiracy on his or Lea's part "to run the government." But he does admit, with surprising candor, some behind-the-scenes manipulations that followed the death of Senator Lawrence Tyson to elect William Brock, the Chattanooga candy maker, to fill the term, and then Cordell Hull in the next election.

The state administration which succeeded Horton was hostile and sought retribution by deciding that Brentwood House would make a splendid governor's mansion. To "satisfy certain state and federal judgments" against him, the state took over "Caldwell's Hermitage," but it took about 25 years to do it. "They had to pass some new laws to do it, but they finally succeeded," he says. "They thought they could sell it but they couldn't. The title is still clouded by a lot of legal uncertainties. That's why they decided to just go on and use it." Today it is known as the Ellington Agricultural Center.

In June, 1957, they left the place, and the state sanctioned an auction of furnishing not needed for their new place in Franklin or given to Belle Meade Mansion. They were permitted to keep half of the proceeds. Today he is surrounded by huge paintings and furniture not put up for sale.

Brentwood House

The reason for this leniency was, as quite commonplace at the time, that household goods were the legal property of the wife.

"I'm convinced that it all worked out for the best," he says. "If I had the farm today, I couldn't take care of it. Margaret and I have no children and it would irritate me not to be able to run it in my lame condition."

He treats the millions of dollars that were and the billions that might have been as if they are ghosts that have vanished. If they haunt him, he doesn't show it.

"I have had a very eventful life and I wouldn't trade a single hour of it. It's been a great drama, you might say. Sometimes I wake in the middle of night and think of all that might have happened and think, 'My God, I'm lucky it turned out this way.' Maybe it's like Napoleon said—'he who can see from the beginning whither he is going, will not go far.'" There is no regret in Caldwell's words. There's an implication that what happened—from start to finish—was inevitable. "I guess," Caldwell says, "if I were a young fellow starting out today, I would do the same things over again. It can still be done, you know. My gosh, everything is still waiting for the young man who wants to get ahead. It always is!"

His friends said of him, "I never knew any man with a greater capacity to forgive his enemies than Rogers."

"I'll say this, if I lost the fortune he did and the potential he had, and the place in the business world he held—if I had lost my home and my farm and my wife had died recently as his did—I'll tell you, I'm afraid I couldn't muster one half the dignity, poise, good humor and gentility that man has. I would be a cranky old grouch, as would most of us."

"I don't think Rogers has ever been happier than he is right now. He rounds up his great-nephews and their buddies about every week or so and drives them somewhere for lunch or dinner. Sometimes he drives them all up to Miss Clara's Restaurant at Sewanee. He'll drive anywhere so long as he can get back by nightfall."

Down on Union Street, in a hushed and carpeted office located above the clamor of commerce, a former Caldwell lieutenant tells you, "off the record," about the South's most serious loss of the Depression. "It wasn't the millions Caldwell almost had or the billions he would have made," the man says. "When Caldwell & Company went down, Rogers Caldwell went down with it. He never came back. That's our real loss—he was a genius."

Uncle and Son David

The Interviews

I grew up in Nashville and heard stories about Rogers Caldwell and his business enterprises all my life. When I married Cissy Caldwell, I began to hear of her Uncle Rogers from a more personal angle. As a writer, I'm interested in fascinating characters and Mr. Caldwell was one of the most interesting.

In 1998 I decided to write a play about him and his financial empire and, because I knew next to nothing of my subject, I embarked on the research trail. People in Nashville had vivid memories of Mr. Caldwell and many of his former employees were alive and well. It was a fascinating journey that took me to many quiet parlors, club dining rooms, and more than one busy elderly man's office. I am pleased that those interviews have at last found the light of day.

I learned a lot about my hometown, about business, about living a long time, about Mr. Caldwell, and about the people I spoke with who are gone now. They certainly taught me that to stick around, one better have something to do!

The play has yet to be produced, but you never know. Maybe one of these days, I'll tuck in and do a rewrite.

Because the Caldwell & Company interviews triggered Shirley to write this book, I, you and the world at large are better off because I had the idea to write something based on my wife's great uncle.

It has been my enormous pleasure to have edited Shirley's book. With each read, her achievement has grown on me. She is one of the finest writers I have ever read. With her elegant, smooth, compelling prose, staggering recall of details and a second-to-none gift of storytelling, I wish she had written ten books.

William M. Akers

Tommy Goodloe

With Dewitt Carter and Ed Heitzberg, one of the vice-presidents of Caldwell & Company. He later co-founded Equitable Securities, which was composed of many ex-Caldwell & Company employees. He was a close friend, and brother-in-law of my cousin, May Buntin.

In 1925, Rogers bought Hourless at the August Belmont dispersal sale in Kentucky. Tell me about that horse.

[Rogers Caldwell] liked to have people around all the time. Had people living in his home; an old British Cavalry officer named Colonel Dickinson lived there for about two years just as a guest. He rode some horses around there, but Rogers finally had to tell him to leave. It wasn't too long after he left that the main stud horse died. There was some suspicion that the old boy was feeding him a little strychnine. It was a great horse, a stallion named Hourless.

If true, it must have been a lot. Small amounts of strychnine as a medicinal at that pre-penicillin time were not unusual. I know because, as a scrawny, mouse-brown-haired child who preferred the barn to the house and ate nothing but bacon and tomato sandwiches and pork and beans, I was given a thick, brown, evil concoction called "iron, quinine and strychnine" to buck me up. It must have worked; I'm still here.

He had a man work for him named Albert Philips who worked there all his life; don't think he ever got off the place once. They called him Home Boy and Rogers was very fond of him.

[Philips] is buried in one of the paddocks. I can only hope that it is next to Hourless that is also buried in one. He was so attached to that great horse that he slept in his stall every night instead of in his own cabin.

How much land did he own?

Well, there was about two thousand acres in total. I'd say probably seven hundred acres were Rogers' and the balance belonged to his father.3

---

3 The full acreage belonged to Papa. Uncle had just built his house on family property which was later the source of twenty-five years of legal battles.

What happened to his father's land? Do you think the state got it?
No. I don't think the state got it. It was in his name, James E. Caldwell. Rogers had nothing to do with that. No, the state did not get that property.4

I wonder where that all went.
Of course, Rogers had to have something to live on all those years. I imagine his father... I really don't know about any of that. That's just speculation.5

Why do you think Rogers never made it back?
The reason he never made it back was that he had lost his credit. The local banking circles were taken over by adversaries of his father, the family you might say. His credit status—what he had been doing in the twenties—buying these companies and borrowing money from the banks, simply was not there anymore. You've got to have credit to do any good, particularly in the investment business.

How did that affect him?
He worked on various deals, but never could hit on something to spark it off. I'm sure it concerned him, but you would never know it.

Who were his really close friends?
He had a lot of friends. I don't think you could just pick you any four or five. He kept a horse out there for Porter Lewis, old big gray horse named Bobby. Porter was quite a character around town—an insurance salesman, big guy, known as the keeper of the wine cellar.

---

4 Those 2,000 acres were farmed. I remember the summer of 1937 when the tobacco crop, all Burley and sixty-seven acres of it, was well above my head. During World War II, the crop was harvested by German war prisoners held in Tullahoma. They were bused in every day, paid the going wage, and overseen by their own officers. It was interesting to ride out to watch them—their precision was astonishing, and they were a gorgeous bunch of men. Uncle didn't know exactly what to do about the officers, so he just invited them to lunch every day.

5 Papa Caldwell lived until 1944, about which time the farming stopped, but cattle were fattened for market well after. The interstate highway system was buying rights-of-way so the land remaining, after the state took Brentwood House, was sold and the heirs, of whom I am one, got the money.

On the day that the company closed, what actually happened? Where were you?

I don't remember exactly. You know the news on these things travels pretty fast. When Caldwell had not refinanced his loans, and they came due, that was the crux. Then people began coming in to seize collateral, all that kind of stuff, to pay off the loans. When his credit was cut off, he had to close.

Did he and Dewitt Carter have anything to do with each other after the trial?

I don't think so. No, they didn't.

They had been good friends before, hadn't they?

Yeah. Long time.

Why did Mr. Carter give the evidence he did?

I don't know except if he had not received the authority and response that he had requested, he was mad.

You have read the *Caldwell and Company* book.6 What would you ask the author if you saw him?

I'd ask him why he didn't bring out the real crux of the financial structure of the company. It was set up with all the assets required and all the money borrowed on thirty or sixty day bank loans. Rogers had money borrowed from Texas to New England; that was fundamental when the market crashed on top of that financial concept. He had a holding company where all the stocks were held. Of course, he controlled the holding company. He had the public in for a half or two-thirds, but he still had control.

Why did he do that?

Well, as I told you before, he was trying to do that right when the market failed. I was in New York working on an associated life deal that would have encompassed all his life insurance business in a holding company. If the market had lasted until he could have sold out fifty percent interest; he wouldn't have had this market support situation.

---

6 *Caldwell and Company* was written by John Berry McFerrin as his doctoral thesis at the University of Florida. When I interviewed him, he said the only change he'd make in the book was that he'd be harder on Mr. Caldwell .—Ed.

I think that's the most important thing that most writers haven't pointed was the way the company was structured. It should have been on stock ownership rather than sixty-to-ninety day paper. Just like you gamble going into the market buying a lot of stuff. If you buy a 100%, and the value goes down—you are in the soup. You put a whole company on that basis; it's the same thing, just larger.

I told you earlier that he was an inveterate bull; he never looked back, always looking forward.

It must have bothered him, but no one really knew?

I don't think so. Of course, it bothered him in the later days when he realized that he had so much trouble supporting these markets on the stock he had on collateral on thirty-to-sixty day bank loans. I think he was worried then.

If the Bank of Kentucky deal had stood up, he would have weathered the storm, in my opinion. He had a lot of Caldwell & Company stock that had to be converted to money. But then the market for the stock dried up on the Bank of Kentucky. If he could have sold that stock, he could have taken care of his own bank loans, and gone on down the road. But he was caught in the same thing the Bank of Kentucky was caught up in. The market on both of the stocks caused the demise of both of them—almost simultaneously.

Was it pretty obvious at the time it happened?

I don't think so. I think Rogers had great hope that he could sell enough of these stocks to pay off his bank loans. He never wanted to sell off the insurance companies that he had an interest in, but that would have obviated any liquidation sale. I don't mean that would have solved all his problems. He would have had to reduce his expenses—overhead, that kind of stuff.

There was a memo in that book from Carter that indicated that the company was not very tightly run.

That's probably true. I don't think that company was as organized like they are today. It changed so rapidly, expanded so rapidly; I think it got rather out of hand.

What did Rogers do every day for the company?
He was primarily interested in borrowing money and buying companies. He got into politics too—Luke Lea and Henry Horton.

Did that get him prejudiced against in the city?
Well, Luke Lea had a pretty fast finality to his undertakings. Of course, that was before Rogers had any trouble. I don't know what that was all about. But they caught him over in Jamestown for kiting some collateral in an Asheville bank.

That didn't help their relationship. I don't know whether that rubbed off on Rogers. But Rogers was associated with Lea in buying newspapers—the *Commercial Appeal* in Memphis, the *Knoxville Journal*, the *Tennessean*.

He and Rogers were similar in only one respect: they were both inveterate bulls. I think he was overextended on a personal basis, and much as Rogers was on a company basis.

Did Rogers have any money of his own or was it all in the company?
Everything he had was in the company as far as I know. He did have his horses. But he didn't get out of anything with any money.

What was the mood like in Nashville when Rogers went under? Was everyone scared? Angry?
Well, there were a lot of things—banks failing and such—beside Caldwell. It was a very unsettled time in the financial world, a sort of general collapse of all the markets.

Was there any sort of panic on the streets after Caldwell collapsed?
I don't think so. Of course, he'd sold a lot of stocks to the public. Some of them worked out all right, some lost. But most anything you had at that period lost money.

Who was his biggest enemy?
Probably the American Bank, but that would have been with the Fourth and First Bank; they were competitors. I don't know that Rogers had any enemies. The American had been in on the Missouri State deal; Rogers

bought them out.

Do you know why it was so important to him to hang on to Brentwood House?

He built that house, he loved it—everything about it, and Albert Phillips was buried there.[7]

Did you go to the trial?

No, I didn't go.

What was Nashville like when he finally came to trial? Were people for or against him?

Some of both. Some of the people who had lost money in the Fourth and First Bank stock were pretty troubled too. Some blamed that on Rogers on account of the loans he had over there. His failure triggered the takeover of that bank by the American Bank. No question about that.

What about the Bank of Tennessee?

It was an unusual structure. It was a privately owned bank, chartered

---

[7] This question saddens me; it reflects the detachment of later generations from a sense of place. Certainly Uncle loved this great house, which he had created. It was and is recognized as a masterpiece that gave full range to his imagination and creative talent. But that was only a part.

He was also losing his family's land in which he had a claim but no more than his sister's and brothers' children. He had roots there; he had hunted its fields, fished its creek, as did I. The first fish I ever caught was a six-inch sun perch from Seven Mile Creek, which folds through the property. He had had the barns built where the colts and mares thrived running in the paddocks on the steep hillsides.

Then there were the people who lived there all their lives like Home Boy, and Fields, whose only chore was to keep cut a swath about a hundred yards square behind the house where lunch was served in fair weather. Uncle came home one summer day and that had not been done; he was furious and told Fields he was fired. Fields looked him in the eye and said, "Mr. Rogers, you can't fire me. This place owes me a living." After a pause, Uncle said, "Fields, you are right." And that was that.

It was long the custom for all the Caldwell boys to start to work in the summer at the age of nine, when they were water boys to the field hands. This consisted of riding their pony down Franklin Road from Longview to Elysian Fields with lunch in their pocket. There they strapped the water barrels to the saddle, which were filled and refilled in the nearest creek and taken to the fields. This all day job paid twenty-five cents a day. My brother Meredith Caldwell, Jr. was so flush with cash that I applied for a job several times, but nothing came of it.

Growing up this way developed a special affection and obligation for these people who remained, and Uncle never forgot that.

under the laws of the State of Tennessee. He had his house in there and his horses; he owned 100% of it so that was all right. But when he started taking somebody else's bonds for half of his business, I told him he ought to take his personal things out, which he did. It was not illegal to have them in there as long as the bank was solvent. It just wasn't a good idea.

I don't know why he originally put them in there, but he owned 100% of the shares.

Did you know his lawyer, Mack Fuqua? What was he like?

Yes, I knew Mack, He was a good lawyer, trial lawyer, but he didn't have an outgoing personality. He was smart; I think he did a good job on Roger's case.

Was there a pretty good chance of Mr. Caldwell's going to jail?

I don't know. Of course, they tried to put him in jail; they tried real hard. Will Norvell was our lawyer, but he didn't want to get into the case. He was not a criminal lawyer, so he recommended Fuqua who was.

Norvell committed suicide, didn't he? That's a strange coincidence. When did Mr. Norvell die?

That was a couple of years afterward. He didn't have any money invested in Caldwell & Company. He lost a good client, but he didn't lose any money in it.

Do you know how Mr. Caldwell felt about losing other people's money? There were a lot who went broke.

I think he was more concerned about losing his own empire—it went on for a couple of years. I think it was remarkable the way he stood up under the pressure he endured. I worked with him for a short time after all that, He had a company called Rogers Caldwell & Company, but that never got off the ground. He started again to get in the investment business, but he didn't have the capital. Without availability of credit, it was an uphill struggle.

Did he ever show any concern about that to you?

No, no. He never looked back, always to the future. He was always a very good friend of mine, which was unusual because I was so much younger. I went with him on all those BancoKentucky deals.[8] We'd leave here on

[8] In a Hail Mary attempt to keep Caldwell & Co. afloat, Rogers tried to make a deal

the train to Louisville—left here about five o'clock, get up there about eight. Jim Brown's chauffeur would pick us up, and we talked business there until two or three o'clock in the morning. Then we would get back on the sleeper, and get back to Nashville the next morning.

It made it sound like it was a very strange deal reading the book.
Well, I'd say it was. Jim Brown was a very domineering individual; he controlled things up there just as ironclad as Rogers controlled Caldwell & Company, although Brown didn't own the stock. But when he signed the deal, his board approved it. It hardly took him overnight to get his board to approve it.

The tape breaks off here.

---

with BancoKentucky. It didn't work. —Ed.

Frank Burkholder

Frank Burkholder went to Caldwell & Company right out of high school on April 1, 1920, and after its collapse went with Equitable Securities.

I was there because my brother worked there. He was in the tire business, and Mr. Caldwell was one of his customers. In those days most everybody had chauffeurs who took the cars into the tire stations to buy gasoline, get the tires checked, the cars washed and so on. One day when he was selling Mr. Caldwell tires, he said, "Burkholder, if you ever want to change jobs, come see me." That was a pretty good job in those days, but when there was some trouble in the tire company, he went up to see him. He didn't even know what kind of business it was. He was a good salesman even if he didn't know much about securities, and he did very well. Back then they gave you a book or two to read, and you trained yourself. He did so well that, when they opened the Louisville office, they asked him to be the manager.

I never went to college. My father failed in the lumber business, and then there were no such things as student loans. So, when I finished high school, I had to go to work. I came down from Princeton, Ky., and talked to my brother who introduced me to Col. Harvey Alexander. In those days, they thought everybody ought to have some training in a bank. So he went with me down to the Commerce Union, then a little bank down on Third Avenue with Ed Potter as president. I worked there for about a year when Dewitt Carter called me. There was an opening in the accounting department. When he asked what salary I was making, I told him $75 a month and he said that was fine. When I went up there, I had no idea what I was going to do.

Before I went they had sold some drainage bonds in west Tennessee. These were assessment bonds, meaning that farmers would pay an assessment to have their land drained. Some of them wouldn't pay their taxes and defaulted on the bonds. But they would still send the coupons to us for payment. So the ones we knew we could get our money out of we would pay, and the ones we knew we wouldn't, we wouldn't pay.

By that time I had become cashier of Caldwell & Company and a bank there called the Bank of Tennessee. We had two cash drawers.9

The front cash drawer was Caldwell & Company; the other was the Bank of Tennessee. To pay these coupons, I had to get them okayed by either Colonel Alexander, the manager of the municipal bond department or Ronald Voss, his assistant.

One day Colonel asked me how I would like to work for him, and I said that I had learned just about all that I could in what I was doing, and that I wanted to learn this business. I had to go back to Dewitt Carter; who was a vice-president, sales manager and most everything else, who had come over from the Forth and First Bank. He was the one who had called me to begin with. He objected to a remark he had heard that I had made and put me on six-month probation in my same position. But at the end of the six months, he let me go on up to the Colonel's office.

We had no records of outstanding bonds at that time. I had bought me a Ford car so Alexander wanted me to go all over Tennessee and make a record of the counties' and towns' callable bonds. It took me about two months of riding all over this state. These little towns had no hotels, just boarding houses. The roads were bad, and there were little ferries instead of bridges where you had to pull yourself across by overhead pullies.

When I got through with that, I was sent to Greensboro. This was 1927, and we were riding pretty high, had about twenty offices. We had two municipal buyers—one in New Orleans and the other in Birmingham. We could buy bonds privately back in those days and make a commission. They would come up here once a year to settle their accounts.

Then Colonel sent me to the Texas office, but he called me one day and wanted me to go to Florida. He said that there had been some defaults and he wanted me to see if I could get some of the coupons paid. He told me to go to Orlando and find some office space. I stayed down there all winter.

---

9 It is hard to understand now how usual it was then to deal in cash. When I was Treasurer of the Nashville Stock Yards around 1960, I made payroll every Friday in cash although there was a branch of the American National Bank right there in the building. I did it this way because that's the way it had always been done. One day Dan VanSant, our accountant, happened to be there and saw what I was doing, said, "My God, why you haven't been looking down the business end of a pistol yet, I don't know." After that, I paid with checks which the men cashed for themselves. Incidentally, Dan was a young thing at that time, but he went on to become head of the Nashville office of Ernst & Ernst which eventually became Deloitte and Touche.

That was after the crash had already come?
Yeah, that had already happened. Caldwell & Company closed on November 30, 1930. I was back here when that happened. Lots of people didn't know it was in bad shape. I didn't, my brother didn't; even the new sales manager didn't. Carter was trying to run the company; they were getting short of money.

Let me tell you what Rogers Caldwell did: it was pretty smart at the time. He owned the whole company and the Bank of Tennessee. The only way he raised money, which was pretty good, was to go out into these communities and sell them these bonds. Then he'd convince them to deposit the money in this bank and be paid an interest. We paid the money as work was done in building the road or school or whatever, whenever they needed it. So that's the way he made his money, and he bought a lot of stuff all around, built a big home out here on his father's land. He was quite a wheel.

It never dawned on me that the company could fail, but we weren't getting as many deposits.

How did you find out?
A fellow in the clearing department told me about it, the one in charge of looking after the money. I asked him what he meant and he told me that we had had a hard time making the last payroll. But they sure kept that thing quiet. I called my brother to tell him, so he came in and talked with Mr. Heitzberg who was smart as a whip, and easier to talk to than Dewitt Carter.

How long was it before the receivers came in?
Within a few days. They retained seven people who could give them information—Col. Alexander, Tommy Goodloe, and Heitzberg; there weren't many.

What did Mr. Caldwell do after they closed?
After a while he went back into business again as Rogers Caldwell & Company. He sold stock around town. Some of the people who had been with him went with him again like Tom Goodloe. I didn't and his nephew, Went Caldwell, didn't. He went with his father-in-law in the H.G. Hill

grocery company. You know he married Frances Hill. He stayed there a while, and then went into the wholesale grocery business himself.

What was Rogers like?

Oh, he was about the nicest fellow you ever saw. The best dresser. He had his suits made in New York, and his tailor just sent them whenever he needed them. He wore a Derby hat in the wintertime. I mean he was the classiest man. He always had Packards and I never saw him drive himself. Had one of those, I don't know what you call them, but had a glass between the driver and the passenger. When I saw him get out of that with that Derby hat on, I thought that was really classy.

Tommy Goodloe bought one of those cars that he wasn't using. Tom came from Big Stone Gap up in Virginia, and he and another fellow from up there wanted to go and show off. Took their golf clubs and everything. Those people had never seen anything like this before, it was real fancy. It's a real joy to me to even think about it.

Somebody used to come into the office selling apples and Rogers saw us buying them. Well then, he had them buy apples by the crate and pass them around every morning at ten thirty. You'd see a lot of customers begin to congregate about that time to get an apple. The porter in his white coat on would pass these apples to everybody on the first floor. That went on for quite a while.

I like that, I like that a lot.

Yeah, little things like that. That's got some class to it. The head porter there was Uncle Billy who thought he owned the damned company. I never will forget the morning I went up there to report for duty from the Commerce Union Bank; he wouldn't let me in. I told him I was coming to work in the accounting department. See, you had to come in through a locked door. Uncle Billy was there as long as I can remember and he just loved to pass those apples.

Rogers Caldwell was well liked, but he didn't mix a lot with his employees. He was kinda bashful as a matter of fact. He didn't like to make speeches. When he came to the sales meetings, he wouldn't say anything.10 The last time I saw him was at a party out at Tommy Goodloe's. I was with Equitable Securities Co. then and we talked.

---

10 This reminds me of one of the few pieces of advice Papa ever handed me, "Daughter, always tell the truth, but mighty little of it."

You know he continued to live in that big house out there on Franklin Road, and everybody thought he had a lot of money put away. I don't believe he did. I went out there when they had the auction sale of his racehorses just to see it. I didn't stay long, just went out of curiosity, I didn't see him there.

John Seigenthaler

Pulitzer-Prize-winning reporter for the Nashville Tennessean, *later its editor, publisher and CEO, founding editor of* USA Today, *founder and Director of the First Amendment Center at Vanderbilt University. Above all, a man of books and stalwart of the Civil Rights Movement.*

What were yours feeling about Rogers Caldwell?

He was a genius. There's no doubt in my view that he was a genius. He had a vision of conglomerates long before they were fashionable. The concept was ingenious but dangerous, in that it merged corporate America with the political and press establishments. It was not healthy for the political or press establishments but very healthy for the corporate. It provided you immediate support for your candidate and your corporate enterprise.

Were elections more important to businessmen then than they are now?

I wouldn't say so. But the opportunity to control a governor was there. Crump[11] was already an influence in Memphis, and the idea was that if you could wrest control from those who have it, you would then have it.

The alliance with Luke Lea some would say was a marriage made in heaven, some in hell. They were two personalities who, by themselves, probably would have survived and done well which may have been the poison for which there was no antidote.

Why was that?

I am a generation away from this and rely primarily on my uncle who was Luke Lea's office boy and others too close to the Caldwells to mention. If you talked with lawyers, they would tell you that Luke Lea was the power and, had they never met, Rogers Caldwell would have survived and his

---

11 Edward H. "Boss" Crump was a Memphis politician who dominated Memphis politics from 1915 to 1954 and Tennessee politics from the 1920s to the 1940s. —Ed.

genius would have worked.

Lea was a swashbuckling hero of World War I who bought the *Tennessean* shortly after the turn of the century simply because that was the only press available. It was the third-poorest paper in town behind the Nashville *American* and the Nashville *Banner*. But he hired Edward Ward Carmack, and his murder by Col. Duncan Cooper so outraged not just the readers in Nashville but all over the country that, overnight, the *Tennessean* was catapulted into a number one paper.12 In a relatively short time he took over the *American*, which had defended the governor, and, sometimes by inference and sometime by direction, the Coopers.13

Major James G. Stahlman, conservative publisher of the Nashville *Banner*, played that very adroitly. He maintained his position by not getting deeply involved with the governor or the Coopers. The *Banner* survived as a result of that. Aside from a relatively small political cadre14 the Coopers were pretty well alienated. It was magnified because immediately after the Supreme Court upheld Colonel Cooper's conviction and sent Robin Cooper's conviction back to the lower court for retrial, the governor signed a pardon for the Colonel. The story was that it was delivered to him on the steps of the Supreme Court, but I'm not at all sure that's so, but it fed the fires of outrage again and put Luke in the driver's seat.

He was one of those rare personalities, large in stature, big boy, very assertive, very moralistic about everything he said, everything he did, big

12 In 1908, Civil War veteran Duncan Cooper was 64. He had been a Democratic congressman and senator. He was publisher of the Nashville *American,* a conservative Democratic newspaper. Edward Ward Carmack was 50, and publisher of the Nashville *Tennessean.* He wrote scathing, front page editorials about Cooper. Cooper had threatened that if Carmack ever did it again, he would kill him. Carmack published another editorial. On November 9, Carmack encountered Duncan Cooper and his son Robin at 7th and Union, near the site of the Hermitage Hotel, then under construction. A Union saber had cut off three fingers of Cooper's hand, so when he pointed at Carmack, Carmack felt Cooper was aiming a pistol. Carmack fired twice. To protect his father, Robin Cooper shot at Carmack. Robin was wounded twice and Carmack was dead. Duncan Cooper and his son were sentenced to 20 years in prison, but Robin's sentence was overturned and Duncan was pardoned by Governor Patterson. In 1919, Robin Cooper was murdered. The crime was never solved, but, for years Nashvillians believed that Carmack's allies took their revenge. —Ed.
13 Duncan Cooper's sister Sarah married Dr. Lucius Burch, a Dean of the Vanderbilt University School of Medicine. Their son, Lucius E. Burch, Jr., who grew up at Riverwood, the family home in Nashville, was his nephew. Lucius Burch, Jr. later moved to Memphis to practice law.
14 And personal friends — my grandfather and grandmother Caldwell attended every day of the trial and sat behind the family as a gesture of support.

spender, big giver. Never apparently put much away, but always acted as if he were the wealthiest man in America—a Jay Gould or a John D. Rockefeller.

When we get into World War I, he has a regiment that he takes to Germany, and, as the officer, tries to capture the Kaiser with this group of Tennesseans. Then he comes back to town. By this time, you can imagine, he is the apple of everybody's eye. He serves a term in the United States Senate. I think he was appointed, not elected. But he's there, you see.

Rogers comes out of Vanderbilt—drops out because he knows he's too damned smart for any teacher he's got, and he also knows he's as smart as his father who is a parsimonious skinflint. That may be unfair to James E. Caldwell, but that's what I've read and I think that's what Rogers thought. He loved his father, admired his father. His father has a little book called *Recollections of a Lifetime* or something. Very moralistic in tone, very straitlaced, and Rogers, I think, was not straitlaced at all. Rogers' view of the world was so positive, he was such an optimist, so upbeat. He could not ever envision anything bad happening to himself. That makes for great drama right there.

Well, he comes out of Vanderbilt at the end of two years and goes to work for his father in the insurance business where he specializes in surety bonds. He gets enough business knowledge to know that there is one hell of a lot of money to be made if he has the guts to do what his father wouldn't have the guts to do. And so he starts Caldwell & Company with the slogan, "We Bank on the South," and starts wheeling and dealing. And as you know, he brought to Nashville ahead of the national trend the sort of exploitation that was popping, and it just popped here a year of two before it did anywhere else, but it did explode. Caldwell & Company didn't close until 1930, but it collapsed a couple of years before.

Stahlman was by this time very hostile to them because it was clear that they could own every newspaper in the world and every business in the world. He had taken the other side politically. He doesn't have an open alliance with Crump, but he is silently the beneficiary of almost everything that Crump's got going at the other end of the state.

Once they get into the local and state government and the Bank of Tennessee starts, it becomes the depository of state funds. When things go bad they've got such a hold on the government with the assets deposited in the Bank of Tennessee, they damned near bankrupted the state.

I really loved him, but I think I looked at him realistically, and I think he was pretty sharp. There's no other way to explain the liens on the house which was built on his father's property. He borrowed on that. When the collapse came, his father said, "That's on my property, you can't take that." So he worked out this deal whereby he lived in the house, I guess, until the fifties. Another thing about him is that there were honorable men who worked with him that were left in the lurch.

Dewitt Carter, have you run across that name?
Yes, in totally different lights. He was either the nicest man in the world or the man who stabbed Rogers Caldwell in the back. I think both of those are true. He worked out the same arrangement on his own home as Rogers worked on his.

But it's fascinating to me that those two men—Rogers living in that place that looked like the Hermitage and Carter living less than a mile away on Franklin Road for all those years, I don't know where they met or when, but it's inevitable that they must have. At any rate, when the end came, Carter expressed righteous indignation. You know, it's hard to argue that you would build that house on land that was not yours.15

I talked to Lucius Burch who said, "Here's the tragedy of the whole thing: the reason Rogers never made it back was that he loved that house too much to let it go. If he had done that, it sounded like people would have left him alone and he might have been able to make it again."
When John Jay Hooker was running for governor, Rogers used to talk to him about changing the name of the place from Ellington Agricultural Center. It was a real offense to him that that marvelous home place became an agricultural center and named for a governor. It just blasted his mind.

Let's go back again for a minute to the two men—if there had been a third partner, if it had been Caldwell, Lea and Dewitt Carter in that order. He needed Carter's technical knowledge of the time. If there had been a third party to protect them against themselves, manage well, not let them get overextended to that point where they were flirting with disaster.

---

15 I would argue it because our house behind Longview was built on such land, and I was an heir to the generation-skipping trust which Daddy could legally invade for family support just as Uncle could, although he had no children who would have been the eventual heirs.

Did Rogers know they were getting this close to disaster?
Oh, yes. Sure. You gotta know what you're doing to the Bank of Tennessee. I think the idea was if they could keep the front up, that the tide would turn. No one could envision the sort of total collapse that would come. I was born in 1927 and as I grew up it was not unusual for me to hear guests in my parents' home to speak disparagingly about Rogers Caldwell and Lea, one or both, the relationship was so interwoven.

Between Lea and Caldwell?
Yeah. Many people had trusted Lea's investment in the enterprises because he put up such a great front that it just couldn't go wrong, that it was a good thing for everybody.

Mr. Caldwell told me that they pleaded with Luke not to go to North Carolina to be tried, to fight extradition, which is what he did in Kentucky. He was a wonderful man. When you could get him talking about those times; he had a chuckle in his voice. "Hell, I wasn't going up there to Kentucky. I had no wish to go to prison. You knew those people were angry, it was white heat. If I had gone I would have been lynched. It wouldn't have been a trial; it would have been a kangaroo court. And I told Luke." But he said that Luke Lea was a man of absolute confidence in his own power to persuade.

The other thing was, I think, he thought he engaged in some sharp practices, but he certainly had no sense of guilt. He didn't consider himself as a victim of anything except bad times. He didn't think that anything he had done was criminal. He told me one time, talking about the book, about McFerrin coming up here to see him, but said he didn't come to see him but once. Said he had a delightful dinner with the guy, and then he said, "He wrote that book, and he made me look like a second-story man. I thought that was marvelous." That says what I just said, that he had no sense of guilt or shame. He thought that he and Luke were the chief victims, the big losers in the crash that came.

Were he and Lea still friends after that?
They maintained a friendly relationship. My sense of it is that in situations like that, everybody is looking for a scapegoat and each looked at one another. You know it's like with a president and vice-president; you're always looking over your shoulder and wondering.

What did he say about Dewitt Carter?
Very little. It was clear that he thought Carter had done what he did to save himself, but he was reluctant to talk about him. It would come up to me this way. He would say, "I read in the paper this morning a story written by Jane Carter. How is that young woman? She seems to be a fine writer." And that would give me an opportunity to mention her father. He would get that wise smile, but he would not blame him,

I talked to one man who said, "How in the world could any man who had gotten his bread and butter for his entire life have turned around and stabbed him in his back?" Then he said, "For the rest of his life Carter was shunned. No one in Nashville would speak to him for years."
I think there's a lot to that. But the same thing was true of Rogers Caldwell. He was a pariah. I have a feeling that all of them—Luke, Rogers, Dewitt and a couple of others—really became an embarrassment to the Nashville business community. When we were going down to lunch each Saturday, there was always reluctance on the part of the banking people. Most of them found something else to do. Sam Fleming went a couple of times.

Sam said he felt like Rogers was a victim of the times, that he just got the shaft.
I think that is a legitimate conclusion. On the other hand, when things really got bad, they didn't do anything about it, they let it get worse—perhaps because they couldn't correct it. They were both total optimists, I don't think that either man could envision that this wasn't going to come out just fine.

When things had been so great and then just shattered, what was he like afterwards?
Well, of course, a great deal of healing had taken place before I began to take part. So far as you could tell, it was pretty well complete. There was a great deal of scar tissue there you know, but I would have to tell you that he was… I only never heard him say anything bad about Dewitt Carter. I never heard anything bad about anybody. And he would not countenance

hostile conversation about anybody, certainly not at table, and, beyond that, his life was not influenced insofar as anyone could tell. There was no bitterness.

> While in this house please do not say anything unkind about anyone, bearing in mind that what you think of others is nothing like as important as what others might think of you.
>
> Rogers Caldwell

This hung in Rogers Caldwell's library.

That's what Cissy says—that he was not bitter, never talked about any of it, never looked back at what might have been.

You almost had to ask him. That was the only way I could ever get anything out of him. I would throw out a question, and he would come back. He seemed to know what the McFerrin book was going to be, but he had a feeling that he could bring the young graduate student to dinner and talk to him as a raconteur and a sportsman, that he would move in the right direction.

McFerrin said that he didn't answer any of his questions.

Sure. But you must remember that his idea of talk was about current affairs, trends in politics, business, government, books.

The Saturday luncheon was an all-male affair. It was a place of conviviality of sometimes twelve, sometimes ten, which is about what the table could accommodate. He would call me in the middle of the week to make sure that I knew that the people who were coming were people who were compatible.

That's interesting because I was under the impression that he would put people at the table who were not going to get along.
No. No. He really wanted them to get along. He would put people of totally different personalities together, but people in the mainstream of whatever was going on. For example, during a political campaign, he would have Pat Wilson who was raising money for Tip Taylor and me who was supporting Kefauver. He was not anxious to have conflict or controversy.

He would frequently call me and ask, "How are you getting along with the Mayor?" [Beverly Briley] went down there one Saturday absolutely drunk as a skunk, and made an ass of himself. I don't think he was invited back for a year.

That was an interesting visit because he had been associated with Dick Atkinson.16 I remember going down with the Mayor that day. Rufus Fort, Bill Weaver and, I think, Slaughter Brown were on the back seat; John Jay, the driver and I were in the front. There was some concern about making the Mayor feel comfortable because, while I had supported him for mayor, there had been some disagreement. So we wanted to make him feel at home. I don't know whether Rogers remembered, or that it had occurred to him—I don't think that he had—that he had been associated with Atkinson and it didn't dawn on me.

But, at any rate, Hooker called me and said, "Mr. Caldwell wants me to bring the Mayor. Why don't we stop by and pick you up?" I later found out that when the Mayor walked in Hooker's office, he had a big glass of Bloody Mary and said, "Guess what happened when wife and I got up this morning?"

Hooker said, "What's that, Mr. Mayor?"

"Well, we decided just to drink our breakfast, and we've been having Bloody Marys ever since."

To go out the Mayor suggest that they go in his car, so everybody piles in, and he says, "Hooker, you drive." So we go out Hillsboro Road and the traffic is a little crowded so he reaches under the dash and turns on a siren. I look over at John Jay, and he looks up at the ceiling. Well, we get down there and he is sitting in the middle of the front seat. Hooker and I get up on the porch and I say, "What the hell do you mean getting him drunk before he comes down here?" And he tells me about what happened.

16 A Nashville attorney and U.S. Congressman.

We then walk in, and there are already several people at table. Well, he squats down beside Mr. Caldwell's chair and shakes hands with him. The rest of us went on by because most of us had been there before, and there had been brief handshakes as we went in. John Jay said, "You know our Honorable Mayor," who is squatting there on his knees rubbing Mr. Rogers' hand, grabbing at his sleeve, and starts in on this confession about his relationship with Dick Atkinson when he was a young lawyer. We are all sitting there and I looked at Rogers and he looks at me as if to say, "What have you unleashed on me?" and says "Well, yes, yes" and the mayor went on and on.

Well, what was there to feel bad about? I thought Atkinson was good for Caldwell, wasn't he? He was the one who elected not to prosecute.
There was a big, big controversy leading up to that in those years and the investigation must have been devastating. I think the Mayor must have thought so, and he was just pouring out his soul saying that there was nothing he could do, that we had to do what we did. I wasn't entirely sure that Rogers knew anything except that the man was snockered. I'd say this went on for at least three minutes and there were eleven people sitting at that table shocked. I remember that Asa Jewel, mayor of Franklin, who came regularly, was in total shock that the model mayor had come in and started this confession.

It went on to the point that finally Hooker says, "Oh, hell. Come on, man, cut the crap. Come over here, and sit down." And Mr. Rogers says, "Oh, yes, yes, Mr. Mayor just sit right over there." Well, at that minute he spills a bowl of gravy all over his suit. Of course we mopped him off, the woman in the kitchen rushed out with a towel. It wasn't the first time anybody had ever spilled anything, but it didn't stop him from devouring the food. Time went on, and by the end of lunch he was in very good shape, and, of course, the meals were gorgeous, wonderful.

Tell me what you had.
Well, it was seasonal. It would be mostly chicken or turkey, and a good bit of wild game. When Harry would tell him that one of his huntsmen had arrived, he would excuse himself and head for the pantry. There you could hear loud greeting and congratulations, frequent laughter. The voices

would quiet while they spoke of dove, quail, rabbits, squirrels, coons, no possums which were thought too greasy, then rise again with thanks and he would hurry back. On Wednesday, ladies' day, when asked what the delicious dish was, he would smile and reply, "pheasant." You knew when the strawberries were ripe because you had strawberry shortcake then peach cobbler with terrific homemade ice cream. If there were two choices of meat, you would be expected to take both of them. Turnip greens, corn on the cob, whipped potatoes and gravy, green beans, butterbeans, sliced tomatoes, things of a summer garden, and the best cornbread in the world.17

Always magnificent desserts cooked right there in that kitchen by I guess the black guy,18 think his name was Harry. Rogers would go shopping frequently with him not only in Franklin, but at the Farmers Market in Nashville.

The people who would come were a cross section. Some of them who stand out in my mind were B.F. [Byrd], John Jay [Hooker], Amon [Evans], John Hooker, Sr., who began to bring his new wife. Rogers was complaining about that during the week. They came so regularly that they didn't wait for an invitation, just showed up. He would have liked for John to come, but he didn't particularly appreciate his wife who committed the unpardonable sin of giving him a television set for Christmas which made him indebted. And my impression was, and I'm right about it I'm sure although some of those around the table would be kinder about it, that he was very uncomfortable about her from the beginning. He said that when a man and his wife were together they are totally different people from what they are alone.

He used to talk to me about it, "What in the hell am I going to do? I don't know how to handle that." And he didn't handle it, it handled him. He was such a charmer, so hospitable that from the time she began to come it was a relief when Hooker was out of town.

---

17 If you want to know how, try this: Two cups of PLAIN white cornmeal, lard the size of a goose egg, big pinch of salt and enough BOILING water straight from the kettle to wet all the meal at once, stir immediately. Add a cold splash of real buttermilk, shape into palm size pones—be sure to dip your hands in cold water first, it's hot. Bake on greased cookie sheet in oven preheated to 425 degrees for about 25 minutes or until it is golden brown. Enough to serve the usual number of guests would double or triple the recipe. Serve very hot.

18 The cook was Emma.

Then B.F. and David Patterson occasionally. He invited me several times during the week, but I steadfastly refused because I knew he had those days set aside. Hugh Walker would go, Stanley Horn. Ross Bass when he was U.S. Senator, Albert Gore, Sr., Frank Murray—old Princeton All-American who was in business in Franklin. I'll tell you, although he didn't invite women,19 more than once he invited Lillian Stuart who was once Mayor of Franklin. You ought to talk with her because she was a neighbor and went over to call on him quite frequently. Henry Hooker came frequently, Pat Wilson, Andrew Benedict, William Miller who was a federal district judge—a Republican appointee, Judge Frank Gray all were regulars.

You'd get there at 12:15 and never get away before three. In summer after you had lunch you'd go out on the porch. B.F. did a wonderful thing after his death; he bought all those chairs at the auction and gave them to the regulars. He must have gotten ten or twelve of them—Captains' chairs—and put brass markers on the backs. Mine is at my office at home now. It was a thoughtful thing to do.

Shirley Patterson was there too, but I don't remember what the circumstances were there on Saturday. I think when you call someone to invite him and he'd say I can't come because of my wife, he'd say sure. That might have been it or Lillian might have said she wanted to come.

I'll tell you someone else, a lawyer named Lon McFarlan from Lascassas, a great storyteller, slightly crazy, on the Federal Trade Commission. He would tell stories which required him to get up on his feet, gesture, limp or something. Mr. Caldwell just couldn't stop laughing. He had a marvelous sense of humor.

His face was a sort of cross between a wise old owl and a Cheshire cat. At times he looked like an absolute lion. You read it most often in his eyes and mouth. He would much prefer to go to table immediately after the first guests arrived so he would not be seen coming in leaning on a cane.

He read a lot. You'd come in to his library, and a book would be open. There was a wonderful portrait on the wall of a Confederate soldier coming home after the war. I would give a lot of money to get that painting, if I had known when the auction was going to be, I would have tried to get it.20

19 On Saturdays. During the rest of the week there were many women.
20 There was no auction. There was just the distribution of the trust (I was the Trustee) under which he held the property. We all sat around the dining room table with a new deck of cards. One person shuffled, the next cut and the next dealt one card each except for Went. He got two, one for his nephew, Nichols Caldwell, who lived in Mas-

Straight ahead were the double doors into the dining room which were never closed. Beyond that was the pantry and kitchen. The porch was L-shaped, away from the street. He had a stationary bike back there which his doctor had encouraged him to ride. He never did in front of any of us, but it helped his legs.

Did he hurt himself falling off a horse?

Yes. Speaking of horseback riding, I think he and Silliman Evans used to ride together a great deal. As a matter of fact, Silliman Evans told me that he signed a check for the Knoxville *Journal* for a million dollars—on horseback. The deal had gone through and Silliman described it this way—he signed the check on the side of a saddle.

We were talking about guests he had for lunch. My wife and I always thought that there was almost a sense of awe about his wife. I asked him once about her and he said she was beautiful and had all the graces. She never once appeared at those lunches.

Lucius Burch came, as I recall, maybe once. Anybody of interest who was visiting in town came. Jim Neal came, not often, but a couple of times. Thomas Wardlaw Steele, Gil Merritt, Walter Robinson and Bill Weaver. Walter came because Bill brought him. Rufus Fort would be a good person to talk with. Dudley Fort—have you talked with him?

I did call Uncle Dudley, and he wouldn't talk to me. He said he went, but, "I just don't have anything to tell you."

Uncle Dudley? He did go. He is such a... I hate to call him a scholar, but I must say he does love Shakespeare. And at the drop of a hat will recite.

---

sachusetts. Every item had been appraised and given a dollar value. The diamond ace went to Nick who had written to Went that the painting was all he really wanted. He had known it when he was in Nashville for several weeks at the Induction Center here in World War II. So off it went to Yankee-land. I'm sure it would have been everyone's first choice.

The painting was never hung but propped on a cabinet under the bookshelves in the library. He wanted it close by, and that was done by leaving it unframed and easily moveable when he wanted to get to a book behind it. Incidentally, when he renovated the Franklin house, it was done by a master carpenter and his assistants. The cabinets and book shelves were identical to the ones at Brentwood House, a labor of much putting in and taking out until they were just right. That was not all. The lovely old house had been used as low rental property when he bought it; the only bathroom was where the library was later. He added the back porch, the kitchen, pantry, *porte-cochère*, the little guesthouse and the white picket fence.

He will give you a dose of Shakespeare and did so occasionally at lunch. But it was pretty much in context. He was, I hate to say this, but he was Arthur Godfrey Fort.

There was nobody who was not welcome at that table. There is no telling who his guests had been. It could easily have been the president or vice-president of the United States. But there were all kinds of dignitaries—everybody, everybody. Everybody who came to town—governors, senators, members of Congress, banking leaders from all over the country came, and they were entertained in an atmosphere of hospitality and familiarity that was not matched any place.

And Caldwell didn't lose all of his money.
Well, I think he probably did lose all of his. I just think he was a genius. I always thought he must have found some way to rat-hole some. 21

Every Christmas, he sent me a case of Champagne. I told him the first time he did it, "I have a policy against accepting gifts." The first year I came back to the paper as editor, we went away for vacation at Thanksgiving, and got back about a week before Christmas, I couldn't believe all the gifts I had received—cases of whiskey, sports jackets, even shoes that fit. I thought I had to do something about this. There were at least a hundred gifts all over the house; I said to myself, "This is outrageous. I haven't done anything to deserve all this; people are trying to buy good will." I couldn't send back a pair of shoes, a case of whiskey, so I called all the staff and we had a drawing—a case of whiskey one bottle at a time and all the rest.

So next years here came the case of Champagne, and I said again, "As you know, I have a policy not to accept gifts, but I appreciate it. I want you to know I had to give it away." He said, "A gift is meant to give joy.

---

21 That may be true if you call "rat-holing" the fact that the state allowed him a percentage of the proceeds from the sale of his racing stable. They also let Aunt Margaret retain proceeds from the sale of some furniture, and there was farm income. The house was paid for, the staff reduced to two; heat in winter was coal in the fireplaces of three rooms. As to his being able to stay in the house, the land was under a generation-skipping trust to the heirs—Ma May and Papa's grandchildren—of whom I was one. The state could get no clear title then nor, I believe, does it have one now. This is the reason that it was never sold but retained for state use.

I, for one, am grateful these years later that the state does retain Brentwood House and the land as a whole. Had we inherited it, it would have been divided and sold long ago. Regardless of its name, it is still there, and when I see it, as I do frequently when attending meetings at Ellington Center, I grin to myself and think, "'Mine,' said the cat as he looked at the moon."

And the gift is not necessarily meant to be a joy just to the recipient. It can be a joy to the giver. If you decide that it gives you joy to give it away, that's fine. But don't deprive me of the joy of giving it." So every Christmas, which had dwindled to a bag of peanuts or a jar of jelly from someone who hadn't gotten the word, there was the case of Piper. Everybody else has gotten the message, and Rogers had too, but it made absolutely no difference. It was the joy of giving.

I would always give him a book on Christmas, and by the time I got down there after Christmas; he would have read it. I said to him, "I'm shocked that you have already read that book. Do you like the author?" He said, "I read the book not because I'm interested in the author, but because I'm interested in you. I want to know what you are reading, and I think I know a little bit more about you because of what you have read and what you have given away as a gift." It was that sort of thing that made him a unique human being.

Colonel McCormick? Do you know about Colonel McCormick from the Chicago paper? He was a giant, a giant. He was absolutely the dominant figure of his time in American journalism. Ultraconservative, press-bound, Sissy Patterson's cousin, Joe Madill Patterson's. They are all in there and they all hated each other. But he was a great force.

It's that sort of thing—Sissy and McCormick and all, all of them were there at one time or another.

Who was Sissy Patterson?

She was also a press lord. There is a book out called *Sissy*. She owned papers in New York and Washington.

It wouldn't surprise me at all if she were there.

It was hard to travel to Nashville in those days, and yet people seemed to do it.

Well, you took the train. It took some time, but when you came, you stayed a few days. And when you visited in people's homes, it was a charming thing to do.

You know someone stayed in his house for a year. Colonel somebody, an English guy who helped him with his horses, and supposedly poisoned his horse named Hourless. He was so mad

that he told him to leave. But the guy didn't have any money, and Margaret told him to "go to that room up there." He stayed for another year, and he and Rogers never spoke to each other. He never admitted that the guy was in his house.

That's typical. That says something about why he never... he was not capable of knocking Dewitt Carter. My own view of it was that he knew that if he just dwelled on what he thought was betrayal, it would have destroyed him.

At the time of the disaster, the conversation had to dwell, seems to me, on economic problems, legal. There had to have been financial experts there, lawyers, politicians. He must have spent a wad of dough.

Have you asked anybody how he lived? When you get together with Wentworth, you might ask him, put it to him this way, "I understand that Luke Lea was broke, but Rogers was not?"

I've heard people say that he absolutely had no money, but some say he had some squirreled away.

He had to continue to live. I know he had some money; I've seen him go into his pocket and give Harry some to go buy something. It's possible he had something worked out with relatives. But how do you put on that sort of meal five or six times a week?

He bought that house in Franklin, too. That had to come from somewhere.

Again that came from the abovementioned trust for providing a homeplace for the succeeding generation. The corpus could be invaded for that purpose.

Mr. Creighton said there were huge vaults built in the bottom of that big house. That it looked like Fort Knox down in the basement. And he always heard the story that he would pay debts with old money coming out of the vaults in the basement.[22]

---

[22] There is no law against paying bills in cash. One afternoon when Uncle was getting ready to move to Franklin, I went out to pick up young David and Sheppard who were visiting. There was great excitement. Uncle had gotten the sheriff to bring two bank robbers out from jail to open the vaults. The dials were rusty and no one had the combination, so they had had to blow the locks. The children were running around in a huge cobwebbed wine cellar that would have charmed Edgar Allan Poe. There were row after row after row of cradled wine bottles. A treasure except that age had rotted

That's one of the great mysteries. He had an estate when he died—I don't know what it was, but they divided it up among the family. Some got money and some got furniture.

I wonder if he left a will.

I think he did. Cissy thought he didn't, but Mrs. Hill said he had an estate, and that she and Shirley were the executors.
You can check probate court.23

My sense of it was that Carter was a social climber as much as anything else. He had married well, and my guess is that Rogers kept him around the periphery of his own social life because he was useful. If you've got that many people in town, you need somebody else in the company to help hold hands.

What do you mean by that?
Well, you know, a ranking officer of the company who has the social graces and can sit at dinner below the salt and hold up that end of the conversation down there. I'm not sure, but I think Dewitt was one of the three or four people who were close to him.

---

the corks, the bottles half empty, and the few that looked hopeful tasted like cheap Sherry.
23 Again, Uncle did not have a will or an estate. The distribution was to the second generation as provided for in the Trust established by Ma May and Papa. I was executor at both Aunt Margaret's and his deaths with David Keeble, a family friend and retained lawyer, who tended to all legalities. Such generation-skipping trusts where the corpus can be invaded by parents or potential parents for the benefit of heirs were commonplace at that time and, I am told, still are much used. The distribution was apparently considered fair in that there was no word of complaint.

All of the furniture, paintings, books—everything— had been assigned a price which was
attached to each item, a master list kept, and the total dollar amount computed. This was done by an appraiser from Brownsville, a longtime friend of my family who also had conducted the furniture sale at Brentwood House, and helped Uncle and Aunt Margaret when they moved.

As an aside, I consider the way he hung the huge portraits from a very large house to a smaller was a stroke of genius—and they were all there, hung over the doors and every possible spot, but looked like they had been there forever.

Back to the process: Every participant in turn bid. The choice was for an article or cash. Round it went in order until everything was covered. In the meantime, Uncle's Secretary noted the name of each bid, and at the end of the process, each bidder had a list of what he had obtained and his total investment. What he had spent was subtracted from the total proceeds, and the balance was received in money.

McFerrin's book unfortunately is very dry, but the one thing in it is the letter that Carter wrote that makes the whole thing come alive.
Yeah, but it's a cover-your-ass letter, too.

You get a sense that it was chaotic, just wild.
That's right; that's right. John Jay knows all that. Or Henry Hooker might be even better. Or Guilford Dudley. Guilford came to lunch quite often without any slight feeling of... well, some of the financiers came, but they sort of shriveled and looked both ways before they went in.

I would say that there has to be a lesson in this world for a man who stared all sorts of adversity in the face, looked into the jaws of going to prison, looked in the jaws of hell, and who looked upon it, every day, with great fascination, great interest, and with a great joy of life.

Sam Fleming

Born in 1908, Fleming was a financial and civic leader in Nashville for many years, and the President of the Third National Bank.

Why do you think people are still interested in Rogers Caldwell?
Well, it all depends on what your relationship is with him. As a very young man, he was extremely successful. His motto, "We Bank on the South," meant something. He sold municipal bonds on counties and cities to people in the North where other people, investment bankers in particular, had not been able to. New York just didn't have confidence in municipal bonds in the South. They had no record behind them and the South was still very poor from the Civil War. You just can't visualize what it was like; there was no money, all the laws, the freight rates, everything was weighed against the South. That's when Rogers brought in the northern capital which helped tremendously to revitalize the towns, cities and most of industry.

Where did he find the money to do all that?
Well, he just found the contacts. He had a wonderful personality, and he knew the people who had money. For instance, he was the one who started the steeplechase up around Gallatin, "Grasslands"—ten thousand dollars to join. He got some of the richest people in the country to come down here, came in their private railroad cars, had lavish parties, great times. I think that the trophy for the chase was called King of Spain Cup. I don't know what that meant, but I suspect it was the real thing.[24]

It only lasted a couple of years, then the Depression hit. He had the personal contacts just by his own personality—a tremendously attractive individual.[25]

He built quite a successful company, made some wonderful purchases like the newspaper in Memphis, life insurance company in Missouri,

[24] It was a gold cup from King Alfonso XIII of Spain.
[25] Let me add the fact that, while my father was still wearing short britches, his father traveled frequently in developing and later selling his Cumberland Telephone Co. to AT&T — went to New York, Boston, Chicago, etc. He frequently took his three youngest sons, Rogers, Meredith and Dandridge, with him. On one occasion in New York, they watched as Papa accepted from J.P. Morgan, the chairman of the George Peabody Fund, the $1,000,000 to found the Peabody College for Teachers here in Nashville.

banks in Kentucky, the Nashville *Tennessean*, all kinds of things. The properties he bought were good properties, but he just made the mistake of financing them with short-term capital.

That's similar to what's being done by these entrepreneurs today, but they are financing it on long-term capital. Then he was unlucky enough to run right into the worst depression this country has ever known. Therefore, he was not able to hold his properties. He lost them because his creditors called in his notes like they were doing to everybody else.

I have a lot of sympathy for him. The fact is that he was a victim of the economic conditions of those days, and he did some things wrong after he was pushed to the wall. But people who lost some money on buying things that he had underwritten didn't like him. People never like anybody, of course, when they lose money. He took the whole brunt of that. But the people who did not have the unfortunate experience of losing money in his widespread activities considered him a very warm, understanding and resourceful individual.

I think one of the best indications of that is when he moved to Franklin, he had a Saturday lunch. Everyone came, there was stimulating conversation, and he was really a very warm person, but victim of a time when a lot of money was lost on the kind of things he had sold.

What did he do to save himself when things went down the drain?

He didn't do anything as far as I know. He started a couple of years before to take protective steps of selling off things to get himself out of debt. He'd have been all right, but I don't think he ever realized until it was too late just how bad this Depression thing was building up.

Where were you when Caldwell & Company closed?

I was in New York working for the New York Trust Co., but it was a national situation. I moved back down here in 1930, which was the immediate aftermath. The whole economy suffered on account of the failure of Caldwell & Company. There's no question about that, and he received the blame.

Was there hysteria in the streets?

Well, there was, but you must realize that right after that all the banks in the United States were closed. There was hysteria throughout the whole United States. The market went down and there was no way to sell anything to anybody regardless of how good it was.

I met with Mr. Ewing Bradford yesterday, and he said that it was difficult for Mr. Caldwell to get a lawyer in Nashville at the time, that no one would represent him.
Well, I don't know that that was exactly true.

As I say, lots of people lost lots of money on things that he had sold, and when you lose money you don't have much love for the fellow you bought it from. I think economic conditions were responsible more than Rogers Caldwell. A lot of the things he sold them had good value, but there was just no market for them. Take the New York Stock Exchange, the whole bottom just dropped out. I don't care how good your investment was, it was a money panic. All the banks were closing and nobody could borrow any money for anything.

Did you know Mr. Caldwell?
Oh, yes, quite well. I've known the Caldwell family forever. Mr. James E. Caldwell, his father, lived in Franklin where I was raised. He was raised by a kinsman of mine named Rossier out there. His mother had moved to Franklin from Memphis to get away from the yellow fever right after the Civil War. Mr. Caldwell got a job at the courthouse. He gave my grandfather, Newton Cannon, credit for getting him that job.

Were you surprised that he never tried a comeback?
I don't think he had the money to. The Depression lasted up until World War II and everything was in the war. After the war conditions weren't very good. Conditions didn't begin getting better until Eisenhower was elected president in '52. Rogers was then too old to make a comeback. He didn't have much capital. His father had left him some land and so forth, but he had to live pretty frugally.

What about his association with Luke Lea?
Luke Lea was a victim too. The *Tennessean* was all tied up in litigation. Now don't get me wrong, there were things that were done that you see when you read *Caldwell & Company*, which you have, when they were pressed to the wall, they did things they should not have done primarily

through the Bank of Tennessee which was not regulated. What they would do was use the bank to finance some of their ventures which were having trouble. They would go out and sell bonds—say Williamson County. They were required to put that money into the Bank of Tennessee, and yet they used the money in the Bank of Tennessee for their personal involvements.

They did pretty much the same thing as the Butchers did.[26] They had a private bank like that, and they put a lot of a lot of their stuff in there which they then used for their own actions.

The Butcher failure was not, in terms of numbers of banks, as large, was it?

Oh, no, but it was pretty large. With Rogers Caldwell in those days, ten million dollars was an awful lot of money, and his, I would imagine, was a forty or fifty million dollar figure. But the Butchers pretty much copied what Rogers was doing with the Bank of Tennessee.

Why do you suppose that Mr. Lea went to jail and Mr. Caldwell did not?

Well, I think that Lea got caught over in North Carolina. They indicted him, tried him over there. And Rogers, they never got him out of this state. The governor of Tennessee was very friendly with Rogers.

Was that difficult for him, Governor Horton, later?

I don't know but he was very friendly with Rogers, and also the Attorney General. Both Mr. Caldwell and Lea had a lot to do with electing Governor Horton. If Lea hadn't got caught over there in North Carolina, he probably wouldn't have gone to jail either.

That's interesting because Mr. Caldwell was convicted of six things, and then went up to the Supreme Court of Tennessee where it was overturned. It was said he hadn't gotten a fair trial because of publicity, and should be retried. The Attorney General, Dick Atkinson, never got

---

26 Jake Butcher and his brother, C.H. Butcher, Jr. were Knoxville bankers. In 1978, Jake ran for governor and was defeated by Lamar Alexander. In 1982, the Butchers and other Knoxville business leaders brought the World's Fair to Knoxville. In November of 1982, suspecting fraudulent banking practices, Federal bank regulators raided the Butcher brothers' 29 bank branches. When the United American Bank collapsed, it was the fourth-largest bank failure in U.S. history. In 1985, Jake and C.H. were convicted of Federal charges of bank fraud and went to prison. Jake was paroled in 1992, and C.H. in 1993. C.H. Butcher, Jr. died in 2002, Jake in 2017. —Ed.

around to retrying him. There's no doubt that favoritism was played.

That just irritated a bunch of people?
I'm sure it did. Don't misunderstand me. Rogers received the blame for a lot that would probably have happened anyway around here. But they put the blame on him and some of it was justified and some of it was not.

But isn't it also true that a lot of what Nashville is now is because of that money he brought in originally?
Not just Nashville but all Tennessee and the whole South. A lot of the public works wouldn't have been done in those days except for Rogers being able to sell the bonds. But on the other hand, there was speculation—the life insurance company over in Missouri, the *Commercial Appeal* newspaper over in Memphis and the *Tennessean* here and a lot else. They sold the stock in them and the stock went down to nothing, but they were good properties. If they had kept them, Lord knows what they would be worth today. If Rogers Caldwell had operated in the economy of today, he would have been worth more money than you could count.

I know from reading in the book that he sold Spur Oil to Mr. Mason Houghland.
No. He didn't sell Spur to Mason Houghland, the Germans owned it. Mason Houghland just worked for the Germans. After World War II he bought it out of whatever the War Alien Committee in Washington decided it was worth. He had a little slip of paper that gave him option to buy it. He got Senator McKellar to help him buy it for a song. But Rogers had owned that beforehand.

What do you think about the book?
Oh, I haven't read it in a long, long time. Factually it's true, but a little bit more emphasis on the negative side. I don't think he gave him much credit for the positive side of it.

Well, I'm trying to get hold of him. He's a retired teacher living in Florida. What do you think I should ask him if I can get him?
I don't remember that much about the book. I'd ask him where he got hold of his facts.

One thing Mr. Caldwell did just before it all fell apart was he merged Caldwell & Company with a bank called BancoKentucky. Do you know anything about that? It sounded very strange. It was a man called Brown, and, according to the book, he never saw Caldwell & Company's books.

Well, I think Brown was in just as difficult situation as Caldwell was. It was a matter of merging two negatives to make a positive. Instead of that, they made a worse negative.

Brown was a very peculiar person. He worked at night. He wouldn't come to work until about six o'clock at night and work until three or four o'clock in the morning—that kind of fellow. He had a lot of banks around Kentucky. He was a speculative sort. You've got to understand that anybody that owed money in those days and couldn't pay it, they just lost everything they had. There wasn't any way to go out and sell bonds or get anybody to invest with you; there just wasn't any money.

The size of the Fourth & First, the biggest bank in Tennessee, was only about twenty-five or thirty million dollars. The First American bought assets from them at a big discount. The Fourth & First stock sold at more than par even after they sold off big assets at the discount. As to the Fourth & First, there was nothing wrong with it; it was a good bank. And Mr. James E. Caldwell was an excellent banker, but he was a victim of being associated, or so it was thought, with Caldwell & Company. If he had run a full-page ad saying that Caldwell & Company owed them nothing or practically nothing and charged it off, they finally would have been a survivor. But it was a panic situation. The fact that Rogers Caldwell was the son of James E. Caldwell, they thought the Fourth & First was all tied up with them, but it wasn't. They went into receivership. They were not insolvent but they were not liquid. Depositors in those days could take all the money out of a bank in one day. So many banks went down not because they were insolvent but that they were not liquid. If you didn't have other resources to liquidate all your assets, you had to close your doors. They didn't have a guarantee of deposits by the government in those days.

I know that Mr. Stahlman of the *Banner* didn't like Mr. Caldwell. Were there other people in town who were after him from the beginning?
Oh, I don't know. You have factions in a town like this. My guess is that Major Stahlman didn't get along with Mr. Caldwell because of the power of the *Tennessean*. The *Banner* and the *Tennessean* were competitors. Caldwell was tied up with Luke Lea, and Stahlman didn't like Lea because they were competitors.

How did Mr. Caldwell behave when all this was going on?
Splendidly. Like a gentleman in every respect, and he was a gentleman. He didn't try to hide anywhere. He showed himself in all sorts of places although all those who had lost money, who blamed him for the panic, despised him. But he held his head up.

Tell me something about the way Caldwell & Company was run and the ways securities business is run today.
Well, the big difference with them was the Bank of Tennessee. Caldwell & Company was an investment banking house just like any other. It underwrote stock, sold stock and got a commission on it very much like it is today. It was not as much regulated as it would be today. There was no FDIC or any of that kind of deal; they pretty much operated the way they wanted to. The Bank of Tennessee had no regulation at all. Today the SEC is the big thing. They are constantly monitoring what the securities businesses are doing. In those days you didn't have any such thing as that.

A lot of people felt like the less government we had, the better. They didn't want the government interfering in anything.

Do you know what it was like to work for Mr. Caldwell?
It was one of the most sought-after jobs you could have when you got out of college—to work for Caldwell & Company.

That's very interesting, because the book makes it sound like he was very difficult to work for as a boss.
I never heard any of that, but I don't honestly know. I would imagine that he was demanding that people produce, but there's nothing wrong with that.

One last question, what were some of the rumors about what he did do with his money?

He didn't have any money. He didn't hide any money. Mr. James E. Caldwell had some very fine property out on Franklin Road, had a big tobacco operation on it. He had an insurance business which survived. As I believe Rogers had practically no money. He wasn't one to hide anything.

Jack Norman

A Nashville legal icon, a criminal defense lawyer who, when he was just beginning his career, defended Uncle Rogers as a consultant to Mack Fuqua.

This tape was fragmented, but this is what could be saved.

What [unintelligible] from affluence?

In this case, the introduction of politics. Fate scheduled Rogers at the wrong time. His power was just beginning when the Depression came on, and like many other people of intelligence, ability, aggressive personalities, they were cut down by it. All of his business ventures at the time they were conceived were solid. Kyrock27 was certainly standing at the door of opportunity. Colonel Lea was still at the *Tennessean* and wielding a tremendous influence. His other ally, Governor Horton, while he was not a strong man, he believed in the advice of Rogers Caldwell and Lea.

They were all caught up in the throes of the Depression, and at that time—it is hard for a young person to understand the politics of the time—there was a razor-edged blade that ran between the two factions. The McAlister, McConnico faction which was dominant and the opposition to that political and financial organization began with Governor Austin Peay who died and was succeeded by a much weaker man, Henry Horton. It was the Horton, Lea and Caldwell political alliance, along with the Depression, that brought their downfall. Had it not have been for the Depression, there's no telling what Caldwell & Company would be in the nation today. He had surrounded himself with able, ambitious, recognized young men, including one traitor, and he had a tremendous financial movement going which was all blown away by the winds of the Depression, aided and assisted by the bitter opposition of the opposing political faction in this state.

---

28   Lea and Caldwell owned Kentucky Rock Asphalt Co., a.k.a. Kyrock. "Kid Kyrock" was a nickname coined by Caldwell's political enemies for a scandal involving no-bid contracts the Kyrock company was awarded to build highways in Tennessee. —Ed.

Could you say that the two sides of the politics were the two Nashville newspapers and the people behind them?
Oh, the newspapers were just an adjunct to the movement.

Were they the most visible sign of it?
You mean the two Nashville papers? No, there were others that were divided just the same—Knoxville, Chattanooga—in each city there was an opposing press; one took one side and the other the other. Politics were bitter. You think this last presidential campaign rhetoric belongs in the closet or the basement? Man it was bitter, it was tough, it was mean, it was devastating back then.

But to get back to Rogers Caldwell, I would have to say that it really wrecked the financial empire that he was building, but his downfall was pressed hard politically. I always thought that the political influence invaded the courts where he would later be tried. It was mean; they were out to get Caldwell and Luke Lea.

Why were they out to get them? How would you describe the two sides?
Well, one was the Crump organization and the other was opposed. It was a power struggle. It wasn't a philosophical difference at all; it was a power struggle.

How was power measured then?
About the same as always. it was the governments who controlled them—statewide, local, seats in Congress.

But to get back to Mr. Caldwell: He was a misfit in that time of knockdown, drag-out struggle. I don't think in his younger days that he ever dreamed that he would be caught up in such a contest. Don't think he ever wanted any part of these bloodlettings. He was simply a man who wanted to succeed in his profession. He was an innovator in his bond business. Had it not been for the Depression, I think perhaps he would have survived the political part. But that just cut his throat.

Was the company already on thin ground?
I don't think so. You must remember that we didn't have the banking safeguards in those days. They came with Roosevelt.

Everybody had been buying on margins, and when the thing in 1929 and 1930 hit, it just exploded. The margin accounts were called in; they couldn't pay, with the inevitable result.

You told me that there was more prejudice against Rogers Caldwell than any other courtroom you had ever been in.
Well, Nashville and Davidson County were still in the Crump column despite the fact that Horton was governor. None of the political leadership in Nashville had any time for Henry Horton whatsoever. They didn't like him, fought him. You can't imagine how bitter the gubernatorial struggles were. It those days the governor ran the state; he would write a note to the Speaker on what he wanted and that was it. It wasn't until the '40s that the legislature began to exercise its own strength.

So Davidson County was pretty much all Crump?
Aw, yeah. It even trickled down to the populace; the people were involved in the meanness of it.

By the time he got to court, a lot of people had lost a lot of money?
Oh, yeah. I try to tell my children about the Depression. You young people can't believe how it is when the bottom drops out from under the national economy.
But we had all kinds of prejudices in the courtroom except for the judge. I think he got a fair trial. The jury... any jury responds to an influence that is as strong as the political influence was back in those days. They are part and parcel of the general political atmosphere; you could not find a jury which was not prejudiced. However, the reason we lost the trial before the jury... and by the way, you should not formulate any ideas about this until you go and read the Tennessee Report.

Does that have what was said at the trial?
No. It just has excerpts, the questions that we appealed on. You can get that in any law office; I should have brought you a copy. But you should read that because people forget things.
We lost the jury trial, and then took it to the Appellate Court and had it reversed because of errors of the court and sent back for retrial. But they decided not to retry. He never was acquitted and he never was convicted.

We would have won the jury trial had not one of his chief confidants not turned state's evidence and testified against him.

That was Dewitt Carter? Why, who got him to do that?

Oh, I don't know. I think it was because he was a first class… He's got a nice family, but I saw him sit up there and try to cut the throat of the man who gave him everything he had. His testimony crucified Caldwell.

Dewitt Carter died a broken man, shunned by his associates. Few people spoke to him, even the people who didn't like Caldwell. Ninety-nine people in a hundred don't like to see a man accept bread from a man then turn around and stick a knife in him. Dewitt Carter spent the rest of his life in…

But I would advise you, you can never understand unless you go and read the summaries.

Did anybody ever talk about why Carter did that?

Ah, everybody did, but it was all speculation. He was given immunity, but he was guilty of what happened himself. You couldn't need more reason than that.

What kind of things were they accused of doing?

That they had accepted accounts on margin in excess of what the banking laws required, they had switched funds to cover up a multitude of things. I can't recall; that's why you need to read the record. The indictment was a long one, multiple…

How long did the trial last?

About thirty days, which I think was the longest that any criminal trial had lasted up until its time. There were so many specificities.

How did Mr. Caldwell react to the trial?

He was the perfect gentleman as he always was, a courtly gentleman. As I say, you need to read the descriptions in the newspapers. It was all reported from the view of each side. You can't appreciate how keen, vicious and mean the attitudes of the one toward the other. The *Tennessean* was Colonel Lea's and the *Banner* was strictly in the Crump column. All of the political clout of Nashville was Crump against Caldwell.

I differed from most people in one respect. I don't think he knew as much about it as people thought he did. It was such a big thing and he was removed from so much detail.

Was he out there selling?
Oh, no. He was the front man; I would sit there and watch him. He seemed as uninformed about it as I would have been.

Was he a good businessman?
No doubt, but he was a top executive. This thing had grown big, and he was far removed from the details. His underlings handled all that. That was the reason Carter could do him so much damage by contending that he knew all about everything. I never could make up my mind whether Caldwell was a party to the shenanigans, and that there were some shenanigans was absolutely true, or that he even had knowledge of them. It was so large and he was traveling all the time. He was on a plane so much higher than where the machinations were going on.

I don't think he could have escaped the general knowledge, but don't think he ever knew. You must remember that he was surrounded by this coterie of ambitious young men. Ambitious, and, remember, they were rooting in the pot too. They became awfully sophisticated. A lot of them came off the Vanderbilt campus mighty sophisticated.

What was the public reaction to the collapse?
According to which side of the political fence you were on, except for those who had lost money. They were vicious; it was a matter of politics. It was, "He got my money." Not the company got it, he got it.

There were a lot of them weren't there? Did that bother Mr. Caldwell?
He was never the same man. He died a very saddened man. He used to have a breakfast at his home out in Franklin years later. Everybody could see it way down under... Here was a very respected young man; the public never did love his daddy too much either. Mr. Jim Caldwell was the brains of the early banking business here, but he was ruthless sort of fellow, and Rogers, who was not that at all, had to bear some of that with the older people of the community. We had to contend with that among

the older element. No, he died a sad man. I don't think he ever thought he deserved... he tried to... See, after that they went into civil courts and took his home away from him.

Why do you think he was never able to make it back again in the business world?

I don't think he ever had the will to. Once you have had that stigma... He lost his sense of initiative; he felt he had been disgraced before his people and was just resigned. From then on he kept a close coteries around him that was narrowed. A lot of the affluent families who had worshipped at his feet and his table before this and were ready to crown him king of the social world deserted him as they usually do. That, regardless of who you are, whittles you down. A sad man, a victim of the time.

You must remember, son, the higher you get, the more successful, the more unknown enemies it creates who come to dislike you even if they don't know you. A sad chapter in the business and political life of this community. Had it not been for the Depression, they would have weathered the political storm because they were no babes in the woods. But once you are defeated and knocked down, they run from you like rats leaving the ship. I'm talking about the blue bloods, the so-called blue bloods for whom I've got no time. He was a victim of his so-called friends. They just ignored him. There were a few who supported him, but very few. It surprises you in times like that how they run and who runs.

Luke Lea, Jr.

Luke Lea, Jr. was the son of Col. Luke Lea and, with him, was convicted in North Carolina in the early 1930s. His father went to prison, but he was pardoned. He never worked with Caldwell & Company, but they were friends (as he was mine) and lunched with Uncle frequently.

Tell me about Rogers Caldwell. What did he enjoy?
He enjoyed his friends, his family. He was a reader. He enjoyed sports; he owned the Nashville baseball team at one time. He was a foxhunter. He enjoyed racing his horses in Kentucky, Chicago, New York and New Orleans He had a mare that he liked very much, Lady Broadcast. She won a lot of important races.

When he worked, he was out of town a lot, wasn't he?
No, I'd say fifty/fifty. Naturally he had conferences with bankers and business people in New York and Chicago, and then in Louisville when the Bank of Tennessee and the First National Bank of Louisville entered into a merger.

As I understand it was done to keep Caldwell & Company from going under.
At the time the merger was made, there was no question about Caldwell & Company or the Bank of Tennessee failing. It is my recollection, and we can look this up, it was made in March or April and the Bank of Tennessee wasn't in trouble until late summer of that year.

I know considerable because my father and I went to see Mr. Brown in Louisville, and told him that he would have to put four million dollars into the Bank of Tennessee or it was going to fail. Mr. Brown replied that blood was thicker than water, and that Mr. James E. Caldwell's Fourth and First Bank should put up the four million. My father told him that it was impossible for Mr. Caldwell to do that for his son, to show that type of favoritism. So Mr. Brown promised to have it down by the next day, but it was not down the next day, or the day after and then it was too late. I don't remember the exact date, but it was early November.

What sort of a person was Brown?
Tough. A hard customer. And peculiar in his working habits, didn't come in until about five o'clock, then worked until 11 or 12 at night. He had a director who told him he didn't like the hours he kept. Mr. Brown asked him how many shares he owned and how much did he want for them. He wrote him a check for them right there. Didn't like anyone giving him any lip.

What was Mr. James E. like?
One of the finest men you could ever know. He was president of the Fourth & First and of the telephone company at one time. He left the bank promptly every day at twelve o'clock and went home to Longview, took a nap on the living room floor, had dinner at two, got on his horse and rode to Elysian Fields, his other farm further out Franklin Pike. Rain, snow, sleet or hot weather made no difference to him. On Sunday he and his family went downtown to the First Presbyterian Church. A distinguished gentleman, in my opinion, and the same applies to Rogers.

What did Rogers do in his spare time?
He rode horseback, hunted—with a horse, not a rifle. Never heard of him shooting anything. Quiet, determined, I would say, boundless energy hidden under a cloak of calm.

What did he enjoy most about business?
Entertaining, being with people, transacting business for people whom, I think, he thought he was helping. One example is the bonds he handled to clear land in west Tennessee. An earthquake, as you know, created Reelfoot Lake and the land is so low that the water backs up. The drainage ditches let the water back into a river, and open up that land for cultivation.

There no were roads in Mississippi nor levees to amount to anything. Mr. John Oman made his living by building levees by using mules and scoops. About the time he made the bid with the Corps of Engineers, tractors came into existence. A tractor outfit in Dallas loaned him tractors to demonstrate that they could move this dirt much cheaper and quicker. Rogers financed some of these and the building of roads in Mississippi, Arkansas, Louisiana, Alabama and Tennessee.

What was Dewitt Carter like?

Carter was an enigma to me. Very affable, sociable person. He completely turned on Rogers, and destroyed himself in this community when he did that.

Why did he do that?

He was afraid he was going to be prosecuted. He took immunity to testify against Rogers Caldwell. Just like these people today take immunity against Fate Thomas.[28] He took immunity to testify against Rogers Caldwell. Didn't anyone tell you that?

Tell me about Ed Heitzberg.

Very decent, clean-cut person, nice wife, Lillian, and he was just as smart as he could be. He owned a shirt company later on, and did very well.

What happened to Dewitt Carter later?

I haven't the slightest idea. He fell from sight as far as I was concerned.

What do you know about Rogers' involvement in the 1928 governor's race?

It was a very, very unpleasant race. Local people here were divided between two factions. One was my father, Rogers Caldwell, and various other political people. It would take me some time to think of who they were. The other people would be the mayor, Hillary Howse, Jimmy Stahlman—publisher of the *Banner*, Hill McAlister. I'd have to stop and think about the difference between the 1928 and 1930 elections.

I understand the 1930 was not nearly as bitter.

The way I remember 1928 was that Governor Peay died about October,1927 and Horton, the Lieutenant Governor and the Speaker of the Senate, automatically became governor.

Lewis Pope, who was head of one of the departments, wanted to run for governor. Hill McAlister wanted to run, and another man, I think, named Gwinn in west Tennessee. It was a very bitter and personal fight.

---

28   Davidson County's High Sheriff for 18 years, Fate Thomas was a political power until his death in 2000. Beloved for taking care of his constituents, he served four years in federal custody for using his office for personal gain. —Ed.

And what did they say bad? Was it mostly Horton and Pope?
McAlister was very vindictive. But his chances were ruined when some country man asked him how many hams did a hog have and he answered four. Crump was very anti-Horton; he was with Hill McAlister. The country people ruined McAlister. My recollection is that they ran: Horton first, McAlister second, Pope third, and Gwinn fourth.

What did Rogers do?
He didn't do anything that I know of. He may have contributed some money. I know he voted for Horton and his people were for Horton.

I heard he was his finance or campaign manager.
No, he wasn't. I think Gordon Browning, and a man named Grover Keaton and one named Charley Love ran that campaign. Rogers may have contributed in brainpower, and contacting people.

In 1930 Horton was elected again. The reason was that in 1929 the legislature changed the election commission laws and took the power away from Crump who then had to support Horton. That's why it was easier.

How did they take the power away from Crump?
By putting the power where it belonged, with the state taking control of the election commission instead of the local counties. The Crump people could give out any kind of majority they wanted two weeks ahead of time.

Do you agree that Rogers was very happy when he lived out in Franklin?
Very happy. There's no question in my mind about that.

How did Rogers feel about Dewitt Carter?
He was very much hurt about that. He had made Dewitt Carter, paid him a very good salary, saw that he was well received in the community. When he turned on him, he was hurt just as anybody would be whose friend turns on you. That's human nature.

Why do you think Rogers never ran for office?

I think he never had that desire. He was occupied with his family, his friends, his business. He never had any children of his own but always had them close around. He was close to his mother and father, and especially to his brother, Meredith. And he wanted to help his brother, Charles, who had problems of his own.

What did Meredith do?
For a long time he was head of the Nashville Union Stock Yards. He came up and was head of the Fourth & First Bank's bond company. He was much smarter than he was given credit for, and really came into his own when he came up from the stockyards. He brought in Brownlee Currey and started him.

When Caldwell & Company failed, they had all sorts of businesses, and some of those have gone on to be major successes. A lot of good came out of the ashes. Do you have any idea what some of those were?
I can name you the following: Ed Heitzberg was a success, Lee Davis became head of the RFC in due time, Tommy Goodloe went to Equitable Investment Co., Brownlee Currey, Peck Owen and George Bullard organized Equitable. He financed Spur Oil Co. and brought in Mason Houghland, and out of that, young Calvin Houghland owns about 39% of the Nashville Trust Co. In Louisville, he had the insurance company that the Lampton family has now. He had another insurance company in St. Louis run by another man who turned against him, Hillsman Taylor.

Tell me about Hillsman Taylor.
He was with of the Missouri State Life Insurance Co. in St. Louis. Caldwell & Company acquired that, and Rogers put him in as president. He didn't do anything to help Rogers, and whoever bought Missouri State kicked him out. He's got a son still alive living in Memphis.[29]

What did Rogers do between the thirties and the time he moved to Franklin?
He stayed out in his old house and he had friends out regularly. He looked after the farm and led the life of a retired gentleman. He was very quiet, very calm, and always a fine host.

---

29 The novelist Peter Taylor. See p. 198 —Ed.

Do you think it was difficult for him to not be a part of the action?
I guess it's human nature that, if you have once been a part of the action, you want to continue. But I think he enjoyed being an observer.

Someone said he became a semi-recluse.
He certainly wasn't any recluse. He had people out to Brentwood House and then down in Franklin every Saturday and Sunday for long, lingering breakfasts, and luncheons for a wide variety of people most of the rest of the week.

How did the Caldwell & Company failure affect James E.?
Broke him. He lost the Fourth & First National Bank because of it. He didn't have any notes or liability so he still had his home and his farm, Elysian Fields. That is what Rogers and Meredith and some of the sisters inherited.30

An attorney, named J.C. Stevenson did a very smart thing. He convinced a judge that Elysian Fields was held in trust and that they could sell it and keep the money in the trust. If they could have kept the property longer, it would have been a great fortune.

Didn't you know that Rogers Caldwell didn't have anything except his interest in the provisions of that trust? I think very few people did.

When did the farm have to be sold?
It didn't have to be sold; it was voluntarily sold. Elysian Fields was in a trust, but it could be sold off gradually and the proceeds put into the trust. It wasn't being farmed.31

I was told that Will Norvell was his corporate lawyer, but when he got in trouble, Norvell would not represent him. Is that true?
Yes, that was true because Will was not a criminal lawyer. That's the reason he hired Mack Fuqua. Another thing was that Fuqua had as adviser in

30 This is not correct. It was a generation-skipping trust for Papa's grandchildren or potential grandchildren, my generation, who were the heirs, but Daddy and Uncle, as successor trustees for us, could invade the trust for our benefit. I had a copy of the instrument until recently, and am told that this was a much-used practice at the time, and still is.
31 Again, I believe Luke was mistaken. As stated earlier, I remember the bumper 76 acre tobacco crop in 1937. Cattle were grazed for quite a few more years. My father drove out to check on them almost every afternoon and took me with my small son (born in 1943) with him. Son David could call cattle before he could talk. Papa died in 1944, so it was farmed well after his death.

the background the best criminal lawyer there ever was in Nashville, Jack Norman, who was very young at the time and never appeared on the scene. But he had the knowledge, knew what to look for, all things pertaining to criminal law. Mack was just a good research lawyer.

Do you think it was a bad policy to have James E. and his friends sit with him in court?
No. I think it was a good idea. It showed that he had a lot of support.

Is it true that the merger of the Fourth & First with American National Bank saved Nashville?
I think yes because the American Bank was not very strong. If it hadn't have been for the Reconstruction Finance Corporation putting $4,000,000 into the capital stock of their Corporation, I don't think the American Bank would have survived either. I think the management broke the American Trust and the American National Co. I don't know about the Nashville Trust Co. I think the American National was insolvent, and I remember on the December 31, 1932, the statement that was published in the Nashville paper and which they gave to the Comptroller of the Currency that they had kited $600,000 worth of checks. They had six officers and/or directors who gave a check for $100,000 each on the American Trust Co. which was deposited in the American National Bank, and they gave the American Trust Co. checks on the American National Bank for the same amount. So they inflated their statement by $600,000. So I assume they were insolvent.

Do you know why Rogers never gave a piece of Caldwell & Company to Dewitt Carter?
I don't know. I think there just wasn't enough time, that had it lasted longer, he would have given a piece to Carter and Tommy Goodloe and Ed Heitzberg. I just don't know.

Caldwell & Company was doing [. . .], but never got in trouble for it. They were really surprised. Would you say that was a legitimate feeling? I talked with a man who knew people in New York City who knew Rogers. They were horrified at what went on down here, and what they were doing to him. Said that there were things

going on in New York that were much, much worse than anything.
I'd say yes. I think where he got in trouble was with the deposits in the Bank of Tennessee. He made a trade with Mr. Brown and Brown did nothing.

Wentworth Caldwell

Wentworth Caldwell was the son of James E. Caldwell, Jr., who died young. His widow, Anne Nichols, from Colorado Springs, lived at Longview for many years. It was she of the little electric car with the cut glass bud vase at her shoulder who taught Elsie and me to play three-handed bridge, and tried to keep me in line. One day as I was eating crackers in Ma May's sitting room she said, "Shirley, you are making a terrible mess with all those crumbs. I bet you don't do that at home."

"No, ma'am, that's why I come down here."

Rogers became like a father to me after my father died. We lived in a house on Caldwell Lane right back of Longview where I was born in 1904 and my brother in 1900. When my father died, we moved into an apartment in town about 1918. Soon after we moved, my brother Nichols was killed in an automobile accident.

Rogers was interested in helping, and gave me afternoon work. I ran errands and drove the older people. I felt a part of it, and, although I was not an employee, he personally paid me a small sum.

When I went to Vanderbilt in 1923 I lasted about six months. I was doing so well at Caldwell & Company that I just dropped out and went to work full time in the municipal bond department. At that postwar era, the Company was starting to boom. Municipal bonds were very good to finance the building of post offices, court houses, streets, schools and so on.

You said he paid for your honeymoon?

Yes. When my father was dead, he sort of filled the bill. There couldn't have been any better guardian. He liked people, very outgoing. He had friends all over the country, and he entertained constantly.

About how often?

Oh, my heavens, There was somebody always in the house for dinner and houseguests from everywhere. All sorts of people. He would take a liking to somebody, say a horse trainer or something, invite him to stay for a weekend and he would stay two or three months. You can't imagine it.

What happened when Caldwell & Company closed?

Well, they appointed a receiver who came in and took charge. He just fired everyone on the payroll, including me. My father-in-law gave me a job at his H.G. Hill Company. If it hadn't have been for him, I don't know what I would have done.

What happened on that day? Did he know it was going to happen or was it a surprise?

Well, it certainly was a surprise to me. I didn't think anything like that could happen. That was the first week in November, and up to January I was unemployed for about a month until I went to work for the Hill Company; so I was only out of work for that one month.

Did you not realize what was happening?

I was young—twenty-five years old. A young fellow of that age can't know what can happen. Now after all the years that I have lived, I know that all kinds of things can happen.

Was it an exciting place to work?

Oh, absolutely. Rogers was very generous and paid a wage you couldn't get anywhere else. It was a top job during that period.

How much better wage than others were they paying?

Oh, I couldn't even guess, but it was much better. When young fellows came out of school, the first place they went was to Caldwell & Company. When I was there, there was Dan Brooks who later was president of National Life, Guilford Dudley who became head of Life and Casualty, Tom Goodloe, people like that. It not only offered experience in the investment banking business, but it also had all these connections. Like Mason Houghland, Rogers brought him to Nashville and he took over this Spur Oil Co. that Rogers owned. He would take a young fellow who he liked and looked like a good prospect and give him a job if he wanted it. Most of them did.

  The failure of Caldwell & Company in 1930 was a great shock to a lot of people, not only me. It cost them their jobs. But it was inevitable because the Depression had come on. They did a lot of banking and a lot was done on borrowed money. When the crash came on in 1930, all the banks wanted their money, and he just couldn't pay off. That was the truth of the matter.

The stock market crash came in 1929. Did no one realize that it was coming on?
I don't think so. He survived one year after the crash of 1929. One of his principal partners, named Brown, owned the National Bank of Kentucky in Louisville. Rogers was hanging on a limb trying desperately to save his company. He explored every route, but those people were having troubles of their own, and they were not able to raise enough money to pull him out.

That's what happened, and so when the receivers came in, they fired everybody and liquidated all that they could. That was hard going because the market was breaking. When the Roosevelt administration came in, the first thing done was to shut down all the banks in the country. It was just a very difficult time.

What was Brown like?
He owned the Kentucky Hotel in Louisville and his offices were there. He was a peculiar fellow, only worked at night, started about eight o'clock and worked on through to morning. He was very wealthy, well connected, and had lots of resources.

The last trip I took with Rogers, we drove to Louisville and stayed for three or four days at the hotel, shared a room. He was trying to bail his company out working through Brown who was at the same time trying to save his own bank. We would meet at night and discussed the things they were going to try to do, but they never could get them together. I think the National Bank of Kentucky went under at about the same time as Caldwell & Company.

What I understand is that National Bank of Kentucky bought half of Caldwell & Company, but it wasn't enough. The deal was unusual in that the Bank of Kentucky never saw the books of Caldwell & Company. He was just dealing with Rogers Caldwell.
That's correct. That's right.

How did he feel when he was on that trip? Was he excited?
He was anything but excited; he was desperately trying to save his company. That was in October 1930 and he went under in November—that was the last gasp. I didn't realize how important it was until I got thrown out along with the others, and I realized what it means to be on a payroll you can depend on.

What was his mood? You say he was desperate; how could you tell?
When we shared a room at the hotel for three or four nights, he was up and down all night. I was awfully young and didn't understand what was going on. But Rogers didn't complain to amount to anything. He didn't want to carry his burdens to other people.

Did he talk with anybody about how he felt, to his wife? I know he was always very positive, but I wonder if there was anybody he unburdened himself to.
It would have been his father if anybody.

He had just moved into that big house, only there for about two years before this thing took place. Prior to that he had owned Oak Hill and that's where he did most of his entertaining. My wife and I went to several pre-marital parties they gave for us there.

Rogers loved people, loved to entertain. He always had somebody living with him for no reason that anybody else could understand. Take old Porter Lewis, he just moved in at Oak Hill, had everybody looking after him. He was just an old codger, but Rogers liked him.

He had a horse trainer who came from England who had been a Colonel in the British army and shot up at Gallipoli; Rogers liked him, thought him interesting and funny, so he just moved him in and took care of him. Didn't make any difference if they were the richest people in the world or the poorest, he just loved them. He was the most outgoing of all the Caldwells, most of them were very reserved.

Tell me a little bit about James E.
Well, he was one of my patron saints. He's the one who made the money to start this thing and got to know all these people. He was an avid reader

and worked like a dog to get things going. He deserves a tremendous amount of credit in my book because he's the one who put the Caldwell family on the map, so to speak. If it hadn't been for him, Rogers would never have gotten off first base.

What did Rogers do after his crash?
He tried to get back into the swing of things. He went back to Fourth and Union and opened an office there trying to get back into investment banking business. But it had gone so far that he couldn't.

Then he tried other things. He had a cheese factory in Columbia, and that didn't work out. Then he had a patent medicine business, and that didn't work. All these things that Rogers tried just didn't quite make it. People had lost confidence in him, were afraid of him. Times were hard, and it just didn't work.

Didn't he have a soft drink business?
Yes, he had that too. And he had political connections like with the RFC, which was helping out people who wanted to do things like that. He got some money from them. But the awful truth of the matter was he just never could get going again.

He offered me a job after I went into the Hill Company, but I want stability in life; I want to know that my paycheck is going to be cashed. I had to pass him up. He was trying to open a securities business, but he couldn't get anyone to go along with him. He finally just threw in the sponge.

But Rogers never lost his sense of humor, nor his liking for people, never burdened people with his troubles. He'd have a group of men out for a delicious lunch and they'd all sit around and have a bull session. Everyone wanted to go because you would meet interesting, important people.

Was James E. as friendly as Rogers or was he more reserved?
He was very reserved. He didn't care about friends; he had plenty of them at home. He had his own business and he looked after it. He loved to farm, accumulated a lot of land out on the Franklin Pike. Farming was just in his blood. He had his business interest in town, but he came home every day and rode all over that farm on his horse.

There were seven family farms that he owned that adjoined each other. The one where Rogers built his house was called the Smith Place—beautiful land. He just went out there and built on it because it belonged to his father, and nobody questioned it. When the State took it over, it was a long, ugly trial.

It took a long time, didn't it?
It did. It took several years because my grandfather fought it all the way to the last ditch because he felt like he was right, and he didn't want to lose his land which was sort of sacred to him.

And then Rogers moved to Franklin?
Yes. He went to Franklin and bought an old, run-down house. He redid it, with a couple of carpenters, into a charming town house. It was a two-story, handmade brick, right on the street, beautifully furnished with the furniture from the big house.

When Rogers was in big money, he would buy anything that he liked. He had good taste, wore the best clothes, shoes made in Scotland. I know, because I used to break them in for him. I had big feet and he didn't, so he'd give me these brand new shoes to wear for a while to break them in. He had his clothes made by the best tailors in the country. He was just the last word in his prime.

Tell me something about his wife. I haven't covered that much.
She was a Trousdale, lived here in Nashville, and grew up with Rogers and that tribe. When Rogers began to boom, Margaret was the last word—had more beautiful clothes, an automobile with a body made in Paris and that sort of stuff. I mean they were living high on the hog. But Margaret was a charmer, very generous and a beauty. A lot of times when Rogers was out of town, I used to go out there and stay with her almost every weekend. I loved it.

What did she do to entertain herself when he was gone?
Oh, that was no problem. She had more friends that you can think of. She played bridge. She rode. Rogers had a beautiful stable of show horses for her, and she went to horse shows and showed her own horses. She was very active.

Rogers bought Oak Hill—a huge, old, Victorian place from the Van Leer Kirkman family to live in while he was building Brentwood House. They were a prominent family but its people died out or moved away. When Rogers moved to Brentwood House, it was sold to John Cheek and the house was torn down. It is now First Presbyterian Church property.

When we were kids we loved to go out there, it was the only house in town that had a swimming pool, tennis court and a private racetrack known as the Hermitage Stud. Old man Kirkman raised racehorses, trained them on that track.

If you went to dinner at Brentwood House in its heyday, what would you have had?

Oh, lord, I don't know. I wasn't so food-conscious at that time. But it was multiple courses, beautiful china and crystal, flowers, beautifully served and all that.

Did they have live-in servants?

Had a house full of them. All of the rooms in that arched section to the left end of the house, off the kitchen, were servants' quarters, and there are several cottages behind the house.

Tell me about the building of Brentwood House.

Andrew Smith had a farm out there facing the Edmondson Pike, an old homeplace on beautiful land. My grandfather bought it after Smith died. Rogers loved it, hunted on it a lot. When things were going good, and he wanted to build a place of his own, he told his father that he'd like to build a house there. His father said that was all right, that it was all in the family, and to go ahead. So Rogers tore down the old house, and built a new one that faced the Franklin Pike on Hogan Road. It was a pretty two-story frame house. When things began to really get really good and he got into big money, he moved that first house down on the Franklin Pike at Thompson Lane and rented it to Ed Heitzberg who lived there for years with his family.

He got his architects and started laying these plans. It took about two or three years in the building because it is made of oversize brick, handmade in Virginia. He didn't spare any expense, but built exactly what he wanted. He supervised every move that was made. The two years he lived there before the troubles began were very eventful. He entertained people from all over the world; they were constantly coming and going.

Did it affect him greatly when his horse, Hourless, died?

It did. Hourless was star of his racing stable. One of his foals was a filly named Lady Broadcast which won several important races. He was so generous in letting friends use him as a stud that many of the best steeplechasers still around carry his blood line.

He kept an apartment in Miami and his horses were down there during the racing season. He would move them around according to the time of year. I don't think he ran anything in the Kentucky Derby, but he won some important races. He loved horses, liked to see them run, took a lot of personal interest.

He did keep a box at the Kentucky Derby, invited his New York friends to come down. Then he'd bring them to Nashville and have big parties at home. They were the cherished parties of the year to be invited to.

Uncle and Colonel Joe Dickinson

Ross Evans

How did you come to Caldwell and Company?
I went to work for Caldwell & Company in 1926. I got tired of selling cement and living out of a suitcase, and wanted to work in one place. So I applied as a bond salesman and went to work for them. I didn't have any experience in bonds, had to have some training. Primarily they gave me some books to read, and then they gave me a few customers to call on after I had been there three or four months.

Did you know Rogers well? Was he liked by the employees?
He was a friendly person, but reserved. Yes, they all liked him.

What about his father, was he around much?
He wasn't around for business. Mr. James E. Caldwell had the Fourth and First National Bank which was across the street down at Fourth and Union where the Commerce Union was and the Radisson Hotel is now.

What was the relationship? Did Caldwell & Company borrow much money from the Fourth and First?
I imagine they borrowed all they could. They borrowed a lot of money from a lot of sources. They had to; they were doing a considerable business. They had a limited capital, not enough for what they were doing. Therefore, they had to borrow.

Why were they under-capitalized?
Well, no particular reason. When things were going good, they could borrow the money. But when the Depression came on, that was another story. They had to sell everything they could get their hands on to pay the debts.

Is that the reason they failed finally?
Well, let's put it this way. If you had a hundred million dollars worth of capital and two hundred million dollars worth of loans, the chances

are you would have survived. But if you had six million dollars worth of capital and two hundred thousand dollars worth of loans and business was shot, in terrible shape, you didn't have enough cushion.32 Then you go broke. That's a pretty good description of what happened.

What was Ed Heitzberg like?
He was a non-communicative person, real smart, but not a mixer and a mingler.

And Dewitt Carter?
I would say that he was more affable of anybody, of Caldwell or Heitzberg. I think he was as smart as either.

Who was really pushing the Company to be bigger? Who was the real brains?
I don't think Rogers was a brilliant financier. I don't know how to put it. He was good on finding deals, but somebody else worked them out, like Heitzberg and others.

What job did Heitzberg perform? What did Carter?
When I first went to work for them, Carter principally had to do with the sales. Heitzberg worked out deals. And all three were raising money. I think they got along with each other for a long time, but there was bitterness at the end between Rogers and Carter because the company had failed. I suspect that each thought that the other one was going to blame him for the failure.

Didn't Carter testify against Caldwell in the end?
I would put it this way: he testified for the record, and the record was against Caldwell. You see Rogers Caldwell was a free and easy kind of a fellow. He could get people together for a deal, but I wouldn't think he was smart enough to work them all out, to work the details out. If you were buying a company, you would be interested in knowing everything about it—what its finances were, what was the chance to improve sales, improve everything. I don't think Rogers was capable of analyzing things to that extent. So he had Heitzberg in there, a corporate setup, Tom Goodloe was one of them. There were several people in there, and they would analyze things.

---

32 That doesn't sound accurate to me, but that's what he said.

What was the relationship between Rogers and Luke Lea?
I don't know exactly. Luke Lea was a wheeler and a dealer, and I'm sure he brought several situations to Rogers. He got interested in the *Atlanta Constitution*, I believe, and the paper over in Memphis, the Press Scimitar. He probably said, "Now, Rogers, let's go down there in Atlanta and buy that newspaper," and Rogers would say, "Well, that sounds all right." Then he would call corporate in to look it over, to see what it was worth, that sort of thing. Everything was so blown up, so out of proportion to what it should have been. Everything, stocks, manufacturing companies, real estate was on the high level of activity.

Was that the reason the company failed?
If you buy a company say for a million dollars that is absolutely solid, with good rock bottom assets of a million dollars, the chances are that that company in a depression would have gone down, from the market standpoint, to twenty-five cents on the dollar. I don't think Caldwell & Company bought many companies at exactly what they were worth. Paid too much, say a million and a half. Then they'd go out and borrow a million and a quarter, or a million and a half. They didn't have any cushion to play on when things got tight.

When were you aware that the company was in trouble?
Ah, I'd say about six months, a year after the market crashed in 1929, and a year after 1929, they went broke—in 1930. I knew they were under a strain before the crash.

So you must have been mighty concerned when the market did crash.
Oh, Lord, listen, I was just like Caldwell & Company except on a smaller scale. I had money borrowed on stocks and things like that. At that time, you only put up 10% margin. I'd buy a stock on ninety cents on the dollar of what it cost. So when the crash came, it was worth only twenty cents on the dollar. I was broke, just a small example of what they were as a big example.

Was it obvious to everybody that they were in trouble?
It wasn't obvious for three or four months.

Were you there on the day it closed? What was it like?

Yeah. All the conversation was about what would happen next. You didn't have a job, no chance to make any money. No one was going to buy anything from you under the circumstances, not knowing what was going on. We just loafed around in the office because we didn't have anything else to do. Then a receiver was appointed, and they kept a good many of the employees on hand to find out what it was all about. They had to have Donovan because he handled all of the books, the finances and all. So several continued on some sort of a salary. All the officers were out. I don't remember Rogers being around.

What was the mood in Nashville toward him after the company failed?

Well, he had his friends, and he had his enemies, just like anybody else. I think it was kindly for the most part. I know that it was with me.

Did the company stay in business to the end, did they just slow up?

Well, they were in bad financial shape; the banks were trying to collect money and they were liquidating things as fast as they could. But when they just came to the stopping point, when there was nothing else to do, they just had to give up.

Did you know anything about the BancoKentucky deal?

Just what I heard. I really can't tell you much about that. Talk with Mr. Goodloe, he can tell you all about it. That was one of the last maneuverings to save the company. It was a merger of some kind, but I don't think it ever went through. That was the last straw.

What happened to Carter, Heitzberg and Donovan after the company failed?

Donovan was kept on by the receivers. The rest just went home.

Did Heitzberg leave town,

No, he couldn't for a while. He had a home out here on Franklin Road. He was a very aloof person

Somebody told me he was the one who hid all Rogers' money for him.
I never heard anything about that. Nobody hid any money for Rogers; he didn't have any money. He was broke.

Where did Dewitt Carter go?
He went into a securities business, called the Nashville Securities Company, I believe. I had heard that Carter had tried to get Rogers to pull in his horns. He had worked for the Fourth and First Bank at one time, and he knew more about finances than Rogers did. He could see that it was unsound.

It seems to say in the book that both Rogers and Carter were in on the start of the company together, and that Carter always wanted a piece of it. Were you aware of that?
I heard something about it, but don't know anything. I wasn't privy to that much of the company.

How many salesmen were there in the Nashville office?
In the Nashville office I'd say about six or eight, maybe ten. When it went bust, I was handling the banks and individuals in Middle Tennessee and in the Chattanooga area in securities.

I assume that all those people who had invested lost their money when the company went flat.
No, not a lot. For instance, I sold to the banks, mainly municipal bonds, and I don't think anybody lost money on a municipal bond. I sold some stocks that Caldwell was interested in like the Kentucky Rock Asphalt Co., the Missouri State Life and so on. Most of them went broke like everybody else during that time. It was a matter of working out of the organization. You couldn't sell anything to anybody. If you were in something, you were just hooked. You just stayed in until it went under completely or improved some.

Did the state of Tennessee lose money when it collapsed?
Yeah. They had that big lawsuit trying to recover.

Did they get any of it back?
Well, they got his home out there.

Do you think he should have gone to jail?
You couldn't possibly know about the situation back then. You are too young. But everything was inflated. Everybody from the shoeshine boys on up were buying stocks, things were rolling so easy. You could buy anything and make money on it—if you got out of it right away. Take myself; I was young and inexperienced, and I bought a lot of things on hunches, because Caldwell was interested and I had confidence in them being all right. But they weren't right for a depression. They were all right when things were going for several years. Everything was up. Nothing today was less tomorrow than it was today. That's the reason Caldwell could buy a deal and the banks would loan him the money.

Somebody told me that one of the reasons Caldwell and Company failed was that they had too easy credit.
Well it wasn't any easier than anybody else's credit at that time. They had no trouble with their credit.

Who were the other companies who were doing the same thing as Caldwell and Company?
There weren't any others in Nashville. You had some brokers in Nashville. J.C. Bradford was formed in about 1927 or '28. It went broke during the Depression, but was able to buy a seat on the New York Stock Exchange by borrowing the money from the American National Bank. He was a very close friend of Mr. Paul Davis over there, and Mr. Davis worked out a deal that let him stay in business. I think he compromised his debts, that the American Bank rolled off the debt and didn't throw him into bankruptcy. I don't know that, but that's what I think.

And nobody would do that for Caldwell and Company?
No, they were too big and owed too much money.

Did you know Mack Fuqua? What was he like?
Yeah. He was a nice person, I knew him well. Took his own life.

Some have told me that Mr. Carter was never the same after he testified against Rogers, that people turned against him. Is that true and if so, why?

I think that's true, a lot of people did. If you're a friend and have a lawsuit, and you testify against him, then his friends are going to turn against you. I knew Carter better than I knew Rogers because I was with him more. I felt a little funny about it. I liked both people, but Carter had to tell what he knew. And when he told that, it hurt Caldwell. I don't think that anybody ever felt that Rogers Caldwell was a crook. I think that he was a wheeler and a dealer, and that he got caught with too much debt and went broke.

I don't remember the details now, but I don't think Dewitt was trying to be malicious, that he was just trying to tell the truth. When I was working for them, I was a young boy and didn't question anything. But, if I knew then what I know now, I probably wouldn't approve of anything that was done.

Rogers Caldwell started out in the municipal bond business. If he had stayed in the bond business, he never would have gone broke. But he got into Tennessee products, the Kentucky Rock Asphalt Co., the Missouri State Life Insurance Co., mortgage loan companies. All of those things were different from municipal bonds. You can buy $10M worth of municipal bonds on a competitive bid and if you have a legal opinion that they are legitimate bonds, you can go to any bank anywhere and borrow at least ninety-five cents on the dollar because they are marketable, first-grade security. He could have handled $200M worth of bonds with a capital of no more than $5M, and he wouldn't have lost anything.

Why do you think he didn't do that, just ambition?

He was just in the securities business. If somebody had something to sell, they would go to some securities house to handle it.

Why do you think he never made it back?

He tried to make it back, but he tried to start too high instead of getting back down to earth. If he had moved out of his house out there and moved into an apartment, rented his house and worked like the devil, he would have had the sympathy of everybody.

A lot of people say that he had saved a lot of money.
I don't believe that he saved a dime. His father had set his house up in trust. I don't think he should have lost the house. Even if he sold the house, he should have returned the value of it to the trust. If he had done like everybody else had to do, he probably would have made it back in a small way. I think it was just the times and conditions that made him as big as he was, not ability. He was a generous person to those who worked for him; he hired good people right out of college. Most of the salesmen were college graduates. I wasn't. I was trained in sales. Everybody who was with Caldwell & Company did right well for themselves in a year or two after the crash. Everybody was just broke. I was.

What did you live on? What did you eat?
Well, I was just married, and I really didn't have enough money to feed myself. There wasn't any business; everybody was broke.

When Caldwell & Company busted, I had a customer who had plenty of money and she wanted to get it out of the bank because the banks were all failing. She wanted to buy some municipal bonds. I wasn't doing anything, just walking around in a daze and thinking about what I was going to do. I told her that there were some bonds in New York, in the Chase Bank, that belonged to Caldwell & Company as collateral and that Chase wanted to liquidate them, and I could buy them. I got those bonds, and I think I made about $750.

This is hard for you to believe, but you could go to the grocery and get your car filled with groceries for $5. It is just unbelievable. I picked up a few more little deals like that, but as time ran on, I ran out of money. I had a grocer that I had traded with for years, I told him that I was broke, had no money and needed groceries. I had a charge account with him—that's when you had charge accounts—and he told me to get what I had to have and that he would carry me. He said that his wholesale grocer, Robert Orr, was carrying him so we would just work it through somehow or other. I wanted to do something; I was trading out of my hip pocket. I decided to set me up an office, but I didn't have any money to do that. Then I got myself a hundred dollars or so, so that I could get myself some furniture, but I didn't buy any. I rented some office space for $15 a month that included the use of their telephone and their secretary. So I went into business. I went to my friends and customers and told them what I was doing and asked that they do some business with me if they had any to do. They were kind to me, but most were broke like I was. But I rocked along and gradually got a start, made a living anyway. You got to remember, you didn't have to have much.

When did they start to have an income tax?
I think that was 1914, so they already had that. A corporate tax was only about 12%. Your personal income tax was hardly anything.

What do you suppose Rogers lived on? He was only about forty when it blew up.
I don't know. I don't believe that he deliberately fed money to his wife, but I would assume, since he was so prosperous, that she had money too from his business. We're not talking about big money, not then, we're talking about just a little money. I would have contracted with somebody for $150 a month because I couldn't get a job. I just had to start my own job. Later on, I went with Cumberland Securities Co., which was made up of three employees from Caldwell & Company, Mitchell, Voss and Payne.

Do you think Rogers had a weakness?
If he did, I don't know what it was. For years around here his name was magic.

Robert Lee Davis, Jr.

Born in 1901, Davis was the son of a Methodist preacher in North Carolina.

I started full time at Caldwell & Company in 1926 and stayed until it closed on November 13, 1930. I kept the records for the trust called Shares in the South, Inc. that Caldwell had organized to sell common stock. When they closed, the trust was still active, still had money in the bank. We didn't owe anybody so we didn't go into receivership. I was the assistant secretary/treasurer and later secretary/treasurer until the Reconstruction Finance Corp. reorganized the Nashville office in March 1932.

Tell me about Shares in the South.
It was a common stock trust which Caldwell had, and he was way ahead of his time. It was a stock holding company, an investment company which sold stock to the public. Caldwell had divisions in about twenty-three states including a New York office.

Was that in Shares in the South?
No, that was Caldwell & Company, but Shares in the South operated through their offices. It was just another set of books, and I was a Caldwell employee.

I graduated from old Trinity College in 1923 before it became Duke University. Then I started at Vanderbilt in 1924 to get a master's degree, but I had worked my way through two schools and was in debt.

Caldwell & Company, organized in about '23 or '24, was booming and they needed people. I went to see Mr. Dewitt Carter, a vice-president, fine gentleman. I gave him my resume but told him I had no experience in securities except what I got from books. Mr. Carter said, "Well, Lee, we can put you somewhere in the mortgage loans or in real estate, in the advertising department, in bond buying, accounting. Where do you think you would like to go? The accounting department is where everything flows. You ought to understand the organization and we are reorganizing the accounting department right now."

How old was Carter?

I'd say he was between thirty-five and forty. Rogers, the boss, was just ten years older than I was. We were all young men, and the beauty of the organization was that he was a far-looker, much ahead of his time. We didn't know what an entrepreneur was in those days, but he was a speculator, I suppose.

He took too many chances, but he was doing what I thought was needed at the time—underwriting municipal bonds... The problem was then, and still is, that underwriters don't want to fool with small issues. If you want five or ten million dollars, they'll look at you. But the small towns and counties didn't have any such need. Mr. Caldwell was doing business with houses mostly in Chicago. He would visit the small towns which needed half a million to put in a sewer plant or whatever. Keep in mind, there was no Securities and Exchange Commission in those days, no regulations. He wasn't violating any law...

Incidentally, in about 1925 he went on the radio, WSM, which was just getting organized as the first radio station in Nashville. The theme song was "Come On Down South" and the slogan for all of the advertising was "We bank on the South."

He was advertising on WSM?

Yeah, he was one of their first customers.

He was primarily in industrial bonds, and that led him to industrial development. A good example was the old Andrew Jackson Hotel, which is now gone. He issued about $350,000 worth of 7% first mortgage bonds to build the hotel. If I remember right, his commission on that underwriting was 10%. They sold the bonds; they didn't have to go to Chicago or New York. I remember that he sold some Alabama Mills textile bonds, that type of small denomination bonds. Then a stock issue would come along. It was the same thing they are doing nowadays but without any rules or regulations.

What he was doing was unusual for the time?

Yes. He was a pioneer in financing small businesses. As a matter of fact, the bankers still haven't learned how to do that today. All they want is big businesses, and are getting bigger with these mergers. The people in these merging companies are getting scared about losing their jobs when there's no need for two sets of lawyers, accountants and so on. They are leery and Congress is getting concerned.

I've always been an advocate for small businesses ever since my experience with Caldwell & Company.

So, he was making money backing small businesses?
Yeah, he had salesmen who could go out and sell the bonds. In addition, he organized a bank holding company which got control of several banks in Knoxville and Memphis. Then he organized an insurance holding company.

He was doing the same things that are now being done with the approval of the SEC. The only thing is that the SEC doesn't ever approve anything. They just say that this is full disclosure, we think. But they always say we haven't approved anything; you read it at your own risk. That's the fallacy of SEC: anybody who gets a prospectus from a broker usually says, "Oh, well, that has passed the SEC." Well, it doesn't have the approval of the SEC—they just say that this may be true. I'm a critic of SEC on that score; they don't take any responsibility for anything.

So then Caldwell got into the insurance holding company business?
Yeah, bank and insurance holding companies; I forget what all else. After I had been in the accounting department with Mr. Donavan for about a year, they were organizing the Shares in the South and asked me to handle the paperwork. Tom Goodloe was a main person in that. I prepared the notes for the in-house Committee. I wasn't on the committee; I was just a clerk. They would discuss the notes and decide to buy this, buy that; then I would issue the order through the wire broker, Mr. Philips. He sat in the front lobby in a little bitty office da-da-ditting in Morse code to Kidder-Peabody in New York.

[Rogers] was pioneering in all kinds of businesses that were needed to enable the South to grow. The student who came over here from Chapel Hill and wrote the book came too late. He came to see me and interviewed anybody around here who had any connection. But mostly he was reading the newspapers, and everybody was down on Rogers and his daddy, Mr. Jimmy, at the Fourth and First because all the banks had closed. With the banks closed, you didn't have a dime. You can't understand the Depression unless you were there. When the banks closed, everybody thought that the Rock of Gibraltar had sunk, and that there was bound to be something crooked.

What was the atmosphere in Nashville at the time?

Ah, put 'em in jail. Put 'em all in jail. Everybody was bringing lawsuits; only ones making money were the lawyers. But nobody could pay them, so they were having trouble too.

They were trying to get Rogers up in Kentucky because he had organized the bank holding company, the BancoKentucky. Tried to get him extradited but Governor Horton wouldn't approve. Hindsight is good but I'm a long way from all that now. But I've thought about it, and talked about it, after my twenty-one years with the Reconstruction Finance Corp. (RFC)33 when we were doing exactly the same thing.

Later on the RFC started making loans to small businesses because the banks wouldn't do it. I organized Lee Davis & Associates to make small loans if they are set up on an amortized base. Before that time, the banks didn't know anything about amortizing loans. Even on home mortgages, they set them up on a two - or five year basis, and you only paid the interest and then renew it for another period of time. Caldwell never did get into the home loan business.

Did he have a reason for staying out of it?

I don't know. I think he had everything he could say grace over with the commercial and industrials.

He had a wholesale oil company, Apex Oil, which Jimmy Perkins, a previous bond salesman, took over after the failure. He changed the name to Red Ace and later sold it for some millions. What the smart boys are

---

33 I could find no one familiar with exactly what the RFC was, but I read that it was a U.S. government corporation initiated in 1932 during the Hoover administration to help reduce bank and other failures. It succeeded in a number of cases but bogged down when the bureaucracy failed to disburse much of the funds. The publication of the names of recipients at the demand of Congress significantly reduced its effectiveness because it appeared that political and racial considerations had motivated certain loans. Under the Roosevelt administration it was merged with the Federal Deposit Insurance Corp. (FDIC).

doing now, there's nothing new about any of it.

Here's the other factor. The banks were selling stocks and bonds and securities, any kind of paper they wanted to. They called it the bond department, but sold anything. That's what they're trying to get into now; they want to open the door. But that was the reason for the Glass-Steagall bill which said either to stay in the commercial banking business or go into the securities business. That kept them separated, and it's still on the books.

Is that when the SEC got started?
Yeah. See that was under Roosevelt; he came in '33 and immediately closed all the banks. They had been closing state-by-state, city-by-city, but he just closed them all.

Why do you think that Caldwell & Company failed?
Because he owed too much money and didn't have enough collateral.

And why do you think that he, himself, never made another fortune?
I guess he figured it was just too much. He had been condemned so much, and time had passed when they got through with all the lawsuits. One suit that took so many years[34] was about his home place. That was on the books at Caldwell & Company. Caldwell had advanced the money to build the house but built on his dad's property. So the state couldn't get a deed to it.

Mr. Caldwell finally moved down to Franklin. I used to see him occasionally, and he was always pleasant. He was a very congenial fellow. He was a good salesman to start with and they had good salesmen. But it was a terrible time during the Depression; nobody had any money.

Tell me about the atmosphere in Nashville at the time. Did you know that Caldwell & Company was going to close?
Oh, no.

I did one thing that I was proud of but at the time didn't realize the significance. Shares in the South, for which I was the bookkeeper,

---

34 The suit took twenty five years. See George Barker's "The Rogers Caldwell Story."

had money in the bank in New York—several million dollars, which was real money in those days. They were in government bonds while we were hunting other investments, but we also had an account with the Bank of Tennessee. That was the private bank that Caldwell organized, and it was another set of books in Caldwell & Company. The Bank of Tennessee kept asking us to transfer some money in the New York Shares of the South into the Bank of Tennessee's account. We would transfer $25,000 or $50,000 until, as I recall, the account got up to something like $300,000. It just dawned on me that the Bank of Tennessee's total capital was $100,000, and here we were as another corporation as a customer had a deposit in their account for $300,000 with no collateral, no security, no guaranty.

So, at the first opportunity, I asked Mr. Carter, "It occurs to me that Shares of the South stock holders are at risk for $300,000 unsecured deposits and the capital stock of the bank is only $100,000. Shouldn't we get the money transferred back to New York or put that balance down?"

He said, "Lee, you are right. Let's see if we can't find some collateral to give to Shares in the South to secure that deposit. Go downstairs to the Trust Department, and see Eddie Goodloe and Ernest Smith and see what they can find."

I went down and Eddie said, "Well, if Mr. Carter said so, we'll see what we've got." He began to go through the trust ledger. "Here's the discounted bond issue, $500,000, that are all pledged to the Fourth and First Bank. Turn to the next sheet. This bond issue is all pledged to the St. Louis bank." He went through the whole book; they were all assigned. Finally he got to the Shares in the South, and says, "Well, here are 23,000 shares of this stock, we've been making the market buying and selling, we've got that much here. No one wants that for collateral."

I said, "Whoa, why won't that be good for us?"

He said," Well, that's all right if you want that."

I said, "If that's all you've got, we'll take it."

How much was a share worth at the time?

There was no market for it at that time.

But the 23,000 shares were not worth $300,000?

Not on the market after the crash. But it was a credit anyway. I got the stock delivered to me for Shares in the South as a pledge to secure that deposit. Mr. Carter had to have the committee to okay all that. I didn't have the authority to do anything except ask the question. Later on when the trust liquidated it was worth $10 a share. That was $230,000 against $300,000, so we didn't lose all of it.

Did Mr. Caldwell own anything in the Shares in the South?
I don't know, but a lot of the banks did.

It held together after the company went bust?
Yeah. But there was nothing we could do; there was no market for the securities. I was sitting in an office about this size with a secretary. She was getting a hundred dollars a month and I was getting two hundred, and we were paying forty dollars a month for rent. I prepared the statement, and sent it to the stockholders, about what was going on, what securities we owned, and what the financial condition. I always included a letter saying that if anybody could think of a better way to conserve the assets, please let us know. Of course, there were a lot of mad people because Caldwell had sold them some stock, but there was never any lawsuit or anything brought.

Later on the lawyers for the receivers for Caldwell & Company tried to get those 23,000 shares of stock but I said I had no authority to do that, they had no rights to it and that we were going to retire that stock when the time come.

Didn't Mr. Caldwell own most of the Caldwell & Company himself?
I never did know how that worked. You see, there were only Dewitt Carter and Ed Heitzberg, who was the other principal officer. Now whether anybody else owned any stock, I don't know.

Did you go to the trial?
No. I saw all the ugly things in the newspapers. That's where that fellow over in North Carolina got most of his ugly information about Caldwell & Company about what people were saying because they were hurt.

What were people saying?
They were saying that it was the bankers who brought it on, and Caldwell was instrumental because his daddy owned a bank. Of course, when the two banks merged, Mr. Jimmy, his daddy, had to step out, and Paul Davis and his group took over. A few of the officers stayed with the merged bank, but that was a rough deal.

The sad thing about the Depression and Caldwell was that he got in politics with Luke Lea.

What was Luke Lea like?
Not much, in my opinion, but that's hindsight.

Incidentally, you know what sent them to prison? The Liberty Bank here on Union Street was a state bank, and because of his influence with Governor Horton and so on, he went to Mr. Donnell, a principal officer in the bank, and got him to issue a certified check for $25,000, as I recall, on Liberty Bank. Colonel Lea made the mistake of putting that in a bank over in Asheville. When everything popped, the cashier's check bounced, and Mr. Donnell, who had issued the check fraudulently, committed suicide...

That wasn't the only suicide we had in the banking business. Most of the bankers had a pretty big stake in the banks themselves. When everything went so black, they said to themselves, "Well, I've lost everything I've got, what's the use?" They'd go out the window. When RFC came along two or three year later to finance things, the jumping had pretty well quit.

Tell me more about politics and Mr. Caldwell.
Well, he was playing footsie with Colonel Lea because Colonel Lea had all this influence over state politics. I say that was Roger's biggest mistake. He was taking enough gamble just on reasonable securities business without gambling on politicians, especially one like Colonel Lea. He was a hero because he went after the Kaiser; there was plenty of talk about that. But they didn't talk about what he did to the people in Tennessee.

Which was what?
Well, he went broke in the newspaper business, the *Tennessean*. He wouldn't pay anybody. He owed everybody. It wouldn't do any good to file a lawsuit against him to try to collect anything; everybody knew that

because he advertised that in the newspaper. He had the last word in the newspaper and he put it right on the front page, that he was being sued. He never owed me anything, so I don't know anything about that. But that's the reputation he had.

How did he and Caldwell get together?

I don't know. I expect the Colonel saw a blooming possibility and went to see Caldwell. I expect that was the approach, and Caldwell listened to him. Maybe he thought that would help him sell some Kentucky rock asphalt from this plant we had, get the state to buy it. That's just one angle.

Caldwell got political influence?

Yeah. Yeah. Caldwell might have had that on his own if he had wanted to. But you get an ex-senator, or a temporary senator—Lea was a fill-in appointed by the governor, then you get the newspaper that got you in that position.

That's how Lea got to be a senator? He was elected?

No. No. I don't think he could have been elected.

Why do you think Carter testified at the trial the way he did?

He was trying to tell the truth, but he didn't want to hurt Mr. Caldwell.

He wound up getting him convicted, didn't he? Isn't that what happened?

I don't think so. I didn't know he was ever convicted.

He was convicted.

I had forgotten. I was sympathetic to Carter's position because hardly anybody associated with him. If there are any shady dealings anywhere, and you are trying to be honest, and you're before the jury, sworn to tell the whole truth. I felt like he was trying to tell the truth and still not hurt Caldwell. They had been friends; he had brought him in, relied on him. The vice-presidents were the key people who had the authority along with Caldwell.

What was Heitzberg like?
I didn't know him too well. I was just a boy, a youngster, one of the clerks. I don't know how to describe him. I thought he was shrewd and smart. He didn't have the personality that Carter had; he was strictly business. But, bear in mind, I'm talking about over sixty years ago. I'm a walking history book, but I'd have to document a lot of this.

But Mr. Carter was a nice fellow?
He certainly was, and very well thought of here in Nashville. When this was over, his character wasn't defamed in any way that I know of. As a matter of fact, he was a member of the West End Methodist church and very active out there.

That's interesting; I talked with a fellow a few days ago who said that everybody shunned him after he testified.
Well, everybody was afraid, I think. I don't know why anybody would take that position. I ought to go back and read the testimony and newspaper stuff. But I felt like he was trying to be honest, and there might have been some shady transactions.

Did people in Nashville know that Caldwell & Company was in trouble before it failed or did it come as a big surprise?
I think it was a surprise. In '29 everybody was surprised.

Then Caldwell & Company didn't fail until a year later?
Yeah. They managed to stall it off for a while, but it didn't take long. I think everybody knew when the banks were popping all around, it was bound to go.

The big New York banks tried to do some financing themselves by organizing the National Credit Association where the banks were supposed to put in a pool of money. They tried to save this bank and that bank by taking the collateral notes. Hoover and the Congress decided to let the government do this because it was too big for anybody else. So the RFC took over some of those loans and let the other banks off the hook.

Were you aware of anything they were trying to do to keep Caldwell & Company going?

No. I think the closest I ever came to seeing they were in trouble was when we went to the trust department to see what kind of collateral was available and everything was pledged. They didn't have any free assets, didn't have any working capital. They were asking us to transfer those 23,000 shares because that was a subsidiary of Caldwell & Company. That indicated a shortage of cash flow.

So dealing with credit was one main problem?

When cash stops flowing, that's when you are in trouble. I suppose if I had been a little smarter, but there wasn't anything I could do about it. As I said I was just a clerk at two hundred dollars a month. In those days, if you were on anybody's payroll for anything, you were one of the lucky ones.

Incidentally, all the fellows who were at the RFC sales department organized security companies. Carter organized one called Nashville Securities. J.C. Bradford organized in 1927 but he didn't have any connection with Caldwell & Company. Carl Payne and Case Mitchell who were principals with Caldwell organized Cumberland Securities. Guilford Dudley was president of Life & Casualty, and, when the RFC made the loans to the banks, all of his Life & Casualty stock was pledged to the bank for a note of $100,000 or more. Of course Life & Casualty stock wasn't saleable either—maybe $1 a share. So he was stretched out.

Everybody was in the same place; the cash flow just stopped. That is why Roosevelt started setting up corporations like the WPA, Works Progress Administration. Get out, and dig a hole, and then fill it up. But some of the holes were worthwhile—planting trees or building drains were good. They would give a fellow some dignity; we didn't have welfare system then.

I'm a conservative, and the reason they set up the RFC as an independent corporation was to keep the bureaucrats from spending the money—wanted it to be known as a lending organization, not as a giveaway.

Ewing "Commodore" Bradford

Mr. Bradford's father was in the coal-mining business, raised the $125 tuition to put himself through Montgomery Bell Academy with a paper route, and worked for his $325 yearly tuition to graduate from Vanderbilt in 1929. He got a job paying $100 a month with a Chicago securities firm which sent him back to Nashville as a salesman with Caldwell & Company. Later he was with Equitable Securities Corp.

Mr. Bradford was a determined storyteller and his interview went so far afield that heavy editing was called for. When he got focused on the subject, he had the commendable practice of making clear the difference between what "they said" and what "I know."

How this business rolled out is that as a young man, Rogers bought a security house from a fellow named Goulding Marr and renamed it Caldwell & Company. It was a very fine company, a good operation, very profitable and dealt most in municipal bonds. By the time everything got so wild that there was an awful lot of money looking for a place to light. Everybody thought that stocks were going up, property was going up. The Fourth and First Bank stock was selling at about $100 a share, and everybody thought it would go to $140. People were just speculating.

In the meanwhile, Mr. Caldwell hooked himself with Governor Horton and Luke Lea who owned the *Tennessean* and involved in politics. He was getting into things that were wild; they ran out of really good things to sell like municipal bonds. For instance, they went to Birmingham and were building a hotel, issuing bonds. They were taking those bonds and building more; they were pyramiding.

Was that legal?
Yeah. It's legal now.

He had set up the Bank of Tennessee which was a depository, a private bank—didn't have checking accounts or things like that. They bid on bonds at one price if the municipality wanted all the money immediately, and another bid if they wanted to deposit the money in the

Bank of Tennessee. Where they were getting double use on the money—a commission for buying the bonds, and interest if it were deposited. I can't give you the details because I don't know them. Those things got so big that they lost the ability to handle such things.

Some people hated him and some loved him. Why is that?

In any set up, if a man has some influence on your life, and particularly on your financial life, and it doesn't work out, you say the old scoundrel cheated me. If it goes up, you say, well I was sure smart picking this out and buying it. You know what I mean?

Mr. James E. Caldwell was a great factor in the growth of Nashville. He had a bank, and the function of a bank, since the beginning of time, is simply to act as a depository for money. Second, it is to lend money to people in the community to promote business. The third thing is to make money for the stockholders. That's all.

There were many people in town who said that had it not been for Mr. Caldwell, I would never have been successful. When I went to him for a loan when I organized my business, he was most helpful. He advised me and gave me a line of credit, and here I am today a rich man.

There were few people in Nashville who had enough money to start a business. If you wanted to do that, you had to go to the people who had it. That's historical experience. Most every man who has ever been in business goes to seek a line of credit.

Rogers Caldwell, according to the information I have, didn't drink, he entertained people in his home and he would pour it to them. He followed the hounds, and he had such people as the presidents of these banks in place like Bowling Green and such. He would have them come in for the hunt, and things like that.

If Rogers Caldwell had not gone broke, there's no doubt in my mind, Equitable Securities would never have been formed.35

Did those men work for Caldwell & Company?

Some of them did. But the ones that actually did were the people who worked for the bond department at the Fourth & First Bank. Mr. Meredith Caldwell, Mr. Rogers' brother, was manager of that bond department. He

---

35 After the fall of Caldwell & Co., Equitable Securities, an investment bank offering credit cards, travel and banking services, was founded in 1930. In 1968, it merged with American Express. —Ed.

had a limited knowledge of the securities business. It was said around town that he didn't want to manage the bond department, so he hired Brownlee Currey to run it for him. Brownlee graduated from Vanderbilt in 1923 and went to work for the bank out at the West End branch. He did such a good job that they brought him downtown and put him in the bond department under Mr. Meredith Caldwell.

In December 1930, Brownlee and Peck Owen [Ralph Owen] and Laird Smith raised $45,000 and organized Equitable Securities which grew to $120 million by 1978. We stepped in to do the securities business when Caldwell & Company fell.

What was the feeling like when it all collapsed?
Well, I have a theory that you will never have a revolution in this country; everybody is always so concerned with his or her own problems that they don't know what the other fellows are up to. Mr. Caldwell continued to walk up the streets, speak to you, and was just normal as the day was long. But everybody knew that the Caldwells were busted, that Mr. Rogers had a lot of lawsuits and that they were trying to get his home away from him and that sort of thing. But everything went on very normally. If you were making $100 a month to spend, you were working like the devil to make more, and weren't paying any attention. You saw people making shifts, you saw prominent people in the financial world that owed half a million dollars, trying to pay it off, sometimes ten cents on the dollar when they really didn't have to. They were just looking after themselves.

What did Mr. Caldwell live on the rest of his life?
Nobody knows that. He was a farmer. His father had had the controlling interest in the old Cumberland Bell Telephone Co. when the telephone business was in its infancy. They wanted to buy it from him and he agreed as long as they paid him $500 a month for the rest of his life, so we know he had that.36

I do know a little bit because I knew his lawyer, Mack Fuqua. He was a country boy from out here in Madison. I bet the Caldwells had a hard time hiring somebody to defend them. There were too many people

---

36 I cannot believe this was anywhere near right. In Papa's book he says that he took the proceeds and bought the bank. I do know that he was given free long-distance service for life because my brother and cousin Dan were courting girls in Louisville. They had loud discussions as to who got first shot at calling on Sundays when we gathered for dinner. When Papa got word of that, courting slowed considerably.

intertwined in this thing. Mack defended them every way they turned, by golly.

I used to say that in the heyday, there were people around who had two houses, two wives, two automobiles, and they ended up with no house, no wife, and some were selling their Cadillacs to Negro businessmen and buying Fords.37

---

37 I know this is true. Mama had a Cadillac Town Car—one of those things with an open driver's seat and a roll-down window between the chauffeur and back seats. Communication was via a small telephone. When things got tough, Momma would fill the back with seven or eight neighborhood children, roll up the window, and off we would go to the picture show. It was a jolt when it was sold to Zima Hill, the town's most successful black funeral director.
And things got worse. Mr. and Mrs. Weinberger had a dress shop that carried designer clothes straight from Paris. Mama paid her back account with my gorgeous, shiny black patent leather show pony cart; their daughter had equestrian ambitions. It didn't matter except that I loved it; I had outgrown my hand-tailored riding habits and ponies.

Overton Ward

Miss Ward was a pioneering young businesswoman who broke through the limited secretarial roles of her time to become a part of Caldwell & Company from its early stages until its collapse.

After I had been with them for about two years, some of my friends decided to go to Europe and wanted me to go. I didn't want to lose my job, which I was crazy about, just loved it. I went to see Mr. Heitzberg, head of the department, and told him I had this opportunity, but if it meant losing my job, I didn't want to go. Mr. Rogers said that there were some big things coming up, but that he didn't want to stand in my way. So they let me go, and when I got back they put me in the new corporate underwriting department. Before they had just been in the municipal bonds business which was what the company was founded on.

They wanted to put someone up there who had been there for a while, so they put me there. I was flattered. Mr. Prescott was head of the department and Mr. Tommy Goodloe. There were just four of us in that office, and that's where I stayed. I was full of energy and I did love it and worked hard. I got a raise every six months as long as I was there—a small one, ten dollars. But ten dollars back in the twenties was a good bit.

What was the pay, do you remember?

I started at $60 a month. I ate lunch at Kleeman's almost every day. It was a fine restaurant; some of its recipes are still used here in Nashville. I alternated between two things that were delicious and each cost fifteen cents, coffee was a nickel, and I left the girl a nickel—so my lunch was twenty-five cents. My $10 raise was a lot of money.

I'll show you how green I was: when I first went to work, I was supposed to get $30 every two weeks. My first check was for $32.50. I went down to Mr. Heitzberg and told him there was an error in the accounting department, and that I had been overpaid. He told me that I had caught on faster than they had expected, and the extra was just to show their appreciation. Wasn't that nice of them?

When Caldwell & Company failed in 1930, I was one of the lucky ones who were retained by the receivers, Major Smith and General Douglas, who came in to complete the process. I was very grateful. By then I wrote up all the depository agreements.

What were they like?
General Lee Douglas was a courtly man, and I liked him very much. Major Smith was a nice man, I found out later, but he was a big gruff, rough-talking person. He took Mr. Caldwell's office, and I just couldn't stand the thought that we were being taken over and seeing these people moving in. I was in my early twenties at that time, and... This is very personal, and I don't know if you want to hear… and I hope you won't pass it on because I'm not proud of it. But I took some papers up to the office, and he was sitting there with his feet on Mr. Caldwell's beautiful desk. That whole top floor was where Mr. Caldwell, Mr. Heitzberg and Mr. Carter had their handsome offices. They had their own dining room where they entertained people from out of town.

When I saw him there with his feet on the desk and when he didn't rise when I came in, that annoyed me. When I came out seething at his rudeness, he followed me and said, "Jane." Then I said, "My name is not Jane, I am Miss Ward." I was boiling, as young and redheaded as I was in those days. Then he looked at me and said, "Well, you're all Janes to me." It made me so mad that I slapped him—the only person I ever slapped in my whole life but I gave him a good one. It startled him so that I got on the elevator and made my getaway.

I told my superior, Mr. Voss, what I had done, and said I might as well pack my things now. But it did me a lot of good; he was so crude, and I had been used to gentlemanly treatment. I have been so fortunate for my whole working life in that. So Tubby (Voss) said we'd have to wait and see. Along about five o'clock a call came for me that Major Smith wanted to see me. I thought, "Well, this is it." and I went back up to the office where he was reading his mail. He asked me to close the door, so I did and sat in the chair opposite him.

He started talking about where I lived and what kind of movies I like. I couldn't believe it. He went on to say that he had a daughter named Molly and that she was older than me and so on. I decided to be polite too. Of course, I had no choice, but I had cooled off by then and was concerned about losing my job. They weren't easy to find at that time. He talked on, and then finished reading his mail and dismissed me. I went back down stairs, and told Mr. Voss that I just couldn't figure it out, that I had certainly thought I would lose my job.

So the next day went by and then he called me back upstairs, but it was just for talk. Of course, what had happened went all over the office. On that third day when I was in his office, Mr. Goodloe walked in. He didn't knock or anything—just walked in and said, "Major Smith, I just want you to realize that we think a lot of this little girl, want you to know how we prize her." Major Smith just said, "Well, I can understand why you would." He was a perfect gentleman from then on. I think it startled him so much that it made him realize that there were some nice girls who worked.

What was Mr. Heitzberg like?

Oh, he was such a grand person! He was a very smart man, trained in the law before he came over into that business. I'm sure you know that the real brains of a securities business is in the buyers. A lot of people can sell, but don't know what to buy.

Why is that?

Well, when a new issue comes out, you need to be able to delve into the background, know how to study a prospectus, and make the decision as to whether it will be a profitable. The salesmen then take that information to sell. Of course, everybody can't sell either, but with the proper information they can. But they might not be able to see the possibilities; that's where the know-how comes in. Mr. Heitzberg was the head of the buying department.

When I first went there it was mostly municipal bonds which Mr. Caldwell had started with, but they added a mortgage loan department which consisted of Mr. Clark Hutton and Mr. Lem Stevens. Mr. Stevens was a distinguished engineer who was the Founders' Medalist at Vanderbilt. That department became greatly enlarged as time went on. We took that whole building eventually.

What did Mr. Caldwell do?

He was out of town a great deal visiting New York and our other offices. We had big ones in Chicago, in New Orleans, Birmingham—all around.

I kinda forgot what all we did have, but there was a long list on our letterhead.

When we finally collapsed, I cried buckets. I was in on the last hours more than the other girls because of what I was doing. I knew how desperate our situation was. Mr. Caldwell was trying so valiantly to work this deal in Louisville, and I think that if he had just had two or three days more, he would have made it.

Was that the insurance deal or the bank deal?

It was BancoKentucky. I think he was crucified in the press later and people thought that he… Well he did do something that he shouldn't have done—he used other people's money, in a sense, to gamble on. But I'll always believe that he thought he could do it—pay everything back. In other words, he didn't do it willfully; that's my feeling. If it had worked, he would have been the greatest hero in this part of the country. He was trying so hard, and it was by such a narrow margin that it didn't work. He lost millions in '29 when the stock market went down, but had enough left to carry on for a whole year. They pared down some; they let all the married girls go because they had husbands who could take care of them. Those were the days of apple selling. There's hardly any way for people nowadays to comprehend what the situation in the whole country was.

How did they do that?

Well, they had to lay off people and combined departments. Our people would go out in the country all over the South and see what the different communities needed—new schoolhouses, roads, courthouses and so on. They would show the local people how they could get the money to do these things by selling bonds. One of our salesmen went up to Tracy City where the roads were so bad that their slogan was, "Pull poor Grundy [county] out of the mud." It went over big. So they sold the bonds and built some roads.

There were no roads at all in Mississippi until we helped them sell highway bonds. Then we would get the deposit of the money. That was the problem later, of course, but that was just a part of the business. They had the Bank of Tennessee there to handle it. When a contract was let, say for a highway, they don't need all the money at once. The bond money was turned over to the town or whatever, but they only needed it in dribbles as the work progressed. We had the deposit of their funds money in escrow, paid them interest on it. That's what the depository agreements were—they guaranteed the money. Then I would take them over to the Fourth and First which was where we banked because Mr. James E. Caldwell, Mr. Roger's father, was head of that. It's an interesting business, I'll tell you that. I love the investment business.

How would you describe Mr. James E.?

He was very dignified gentleman. I never got to know him, very few people did. I would see him almost every day on the street. He wore striped trousers, a frock coat and top hat. He had a white beard, was always immaculately dressed—pearl studs and all. He wasn't a very tall man but very trim. He would walk down Union Street and looked neither left nor right—straight ahead. He was a great family man. Every Saturday he and Miss May had a big family lunch of vegetable soup, cornbread and apple pie. They never knew how many were coming. In those days we worked until one o'clock on Saturdays. Wentworth always left a little early because he said somebody might get his place at the table. He was my immediate superior in the bond department. At the end he went to work for his father-in-law. Mr. Hill. So he was not there after they closed the doors.

How long before it failed was it known by the public?

Well, I knew it because of my job but didn't talk about it. A lot of the people in the company did not know, I'm sure, but there was no reason for them to know. But as time went on it was rumored and then became almost public news.

Why did Mr. Carter turn state's evidence?

I don't know because it made me so mad that I never discussed it with him. I guess he thought Mr. Caldwell should not have tried to make this last deal, but should have closed up much sooner, but I don't know. He had been taking this great big salary of $37,500 which was a lot at the time, and riding the gravy train. But when there was something he could do, he wouldn't do it. If things were going as wrong as he testified, he could have quit at any time. But he didn't.

His wife and daughters were so nice that I finally forgave him.

Did you go to the trial?
No, I didn't. I was working for the receivers, but I wasn't called to testify. I was fearful of being called; I'm sure I would have lost my head on the witness stands if they had said something ugly about Mr. Caldwell. I wouldn't have gone.

When the company failed, I wrote Mr. Caldwell a letter and told him how much I had loved working there. Later I was told that Mrs. Caldwell read the letters to him and some of them were not very nice. A lot of people were mad at him, you know. She said, "I don't remember this young man." I had signed it Overton Ward and when he explained who I was, she said, "Well, it's the nicest letter you have gotten." This pleased me very much because I was so fond of him.

Do you think Mr. Caldwell ever forgave Mr. Carter?
I have no idea. I don't think he dwelt on the matter and I never heard that he had anything to say. But it was very bitter at the time. But then Mr. Caldwell built a nice life for himself in that lovely old house down in Franklin. Some people thought of Mr. Carter as a hero, but I never did.

Some people say procedures were very loosely run.
We were very efficient as far as I knew. Of course, I was not in a position to judge because I was not in the accounting department, but I had no reason to think they were. I think that was what made me mad when I read the book. I need to go back and read it again. Mr. Tim Donovan was head of the accounting, and Frank Burkholder was in the Bank of Tennessee before he came up in our buying department. When the company failed he got a job at Equitable, became a vice-president.

So much money was made out of the Caldwell & Company failure. For instance, Mr. Lem Stevens got the Bankhead Hotel in Birmingham for a song and the Seventh Avenue Garage sold by the receivers and these were the foundation of his fortune. He was such a nice guy that this didn't make me mad. Jimmy Perkins who worked for Caldwell & Company made a lot of money with Red Ace Oil Co. That was bought for a song. The thing was that nobody had any money. And those who did have some to invest just made a killing.

Sidney McAlister

The crash of the stock market was in 1929, Caldwell & Company failed in 1930, and after that all hell broke loose in Nashville. Some people say that Caldwell & Company did it. That's what is so interesting, some people say absolutely yes, and somebody else will say something totally different, both seem to know, to be certain, and neither one agrees with the other. Did you read the book?

Yes, I did, and spent a long time speaking with the author. He said if he were writing the book now, he would be much harsher on Rogers Caldwell than he was the first time.

My father thought that James E. Caldwell was the brains of the whole outfit, and when James E. died (in 1944) that the wheels came off. The wheels were coming off anyway. He was a really smart man.

I remember, as a child, seeing him drive his horse and buggy up Franklin Road and Elysian Fields Road every afternoon. They owned all this land. His farm and Rogers' farm met here at Elysian Fields Road. They raised, at the time that I was a child, thousands and thousands of pounds of tobacco. They must have raised three hundred acres of it by themselves.[38]

We moved out here on Hogan Road next door to Rogers in about 1934, and had a great relationship with Mr. and Mrs. Caldwell. She

---

[38] The tobacco crop in 1937 was impressive—69 acres—all well above a man's head. I remember the year and the crop well—it was the year I graduated from high school. I had invited three classmates from my boarding school to visit, and my father took us out to see it. We walked among the rows and were soon out of sight of one another. Sidney's guess of three hundred acres is overblown but understandable from the point of view of a boy. Elysian Fields was a large farm, but not of the magnitude he suggested. It was surrounded by farms of similar size which were still intact before the rash of subdividing after World War II. It was composed of seven contiguous farms including the one of about seven hundred acres where Uncle's house is. Each had its original home cottage where the farmhands lived, and only at harvest time were extra hands hired. Each also had its tobacco allotment of about the usual ten acres which collectively made the large acreage possible. This is after the time when they said they were broke. They had a staff and maintained these two farms in glorious style. This overlooks the fact that this land was more than self-sustaining; farming was a substantial source of income.

would pick us children up and take us to Belle Meade Club to swim. I had neither been to, nor even heard of, Belle Meade.

What really blows my mind is this: he ran an eight-inch main from city water line from the corner of Franklin Road, up Hogan Road to his place, which must have been five or six miles. Can you imagine what that must have cost? Our farm had ninety acres; lord knows what he had.39

Mr. Hacker was his caretaker; he had forty to fifty hands who worked in his tobacco every day. He rode a white horse down Hogan Road in front of the forty or fifty black people all singing spirituals as they came in front of our house. They paid me fifty cents a day to carry water on my pony in wooden kegs. I would ride to the spring, fill the kegs up, came back and watered all the hands in the fields, then ride back and fill up again to do the same thing, all summer long.40

That sounds like a lot of help if you were broke.
Let me tell you some more. There were racehorses, trainers, and jockeys. All the jockos were named Wilburn, there were four or five of those boys and most are living today. They were exercise boys.

There was a stallion up there that no grown man could get around. They paid me a quarter or fifty cents to walk this horse every day. I'd go in his stall, hook him up and walk him around the barn until my father found out about it. There are a lot of horses that have been abused that will only let themselves be handled by children.

Now here's where we come to the end of our Rogers romance. When we bought this place on Hogan Road, there were all these gateposts, about eight of them that went to our house. There were two huge gateposts that went to Rogers' house. Our property line ran right down the middle of the road so we owned half of the property going to his house and one of the huge posts was on our property. Every day somebody would drive into our yard and ask if we were caretakers. My father was raised with Rogers, and one day he went to see Mr. Rogers and said he was going to make a deal. I'm going to give you my big gatepost, and you leave your great

---

39 There are about 700 acres where his house was built, which was a part of the about 3,000 acres of Papa's Elysian Fields farm.

40 This was a sort of rite-of-passage for about twelve-years-old boys. Cousin Went tells of it in his youth, my brother, Meredith, spent several summer at this. I even tried to apply but nobody listened. The pay was always fifty cents—surely a spur for these hopeful entrepreneurs.

big gatepost right where it is and move mine to make two entrances, so I'll have one and you'll have one. Then people won't come into my house wanting to know if I'm your caretaker.

Mr. Caldwell didn't agree to that. Some time earlier he had run a one-inch water line from his eight-inch into our house where some old maid aunts lived. So when Daddy started to dig up the gatepost, Rogers Caldwell dug up the waterline and put a deputy sheriff on the pile of dirt and told him if anyone from our place came to replace the line, to shoot him. Daddy got hold of Mr. Cecil Sims and they got an injunction against each other. This was in court for twenty years. Every time it came to court, Rogers won and the Clerk wrote the opinion that Rogers ought to have his way because he was a personal friend of his. Finally they took it all the way to the state Supreme Court, and we won it.

In about 1955 my father was very sick and died within a few months. When I went in to tell him we had won the case and were going to take the gatepost down. He said, "Son, forget it. I've got no fight left in me." But I got Dad and put him out in the yard, got a big bulldozer and knocked those gateposts down. On top of that post was a 750-pound lead eagle. That night when the gatepost was lying on the ground, his hands stole the eagle. It was so heavy they couldn't pick it up and they hooked it up to something and drug it down Hogan Road until the car blew up. The next morning we followed the trail down and found the eagle in a ditch covered with leaves. It was ruined and I expect we sold it for scrap.

A bunch of people wanted to buy the farm, but everybody was scared of the title, couldn't get a clear title. I don't think the state has a clear title to it today. The state doesn't worry about titles; we worry about titles.

In 1955 there was the big freeze. Everything was frozen—not electricity, no water, no anything. We lived in one room upstairs where there was the only fireplace. All the trees had fallen on Hogan Road. After two or three days, I decided we were going to have to start digging out but we were not going to dig out… Now we hadn't spoken the Caldwells in quite a few years, but that morning I walked up to his house at seven thirty in the morning. A butler opened the door in full tuxedo. He was still living that good years after he was supposed to be broke.41

41 I can speak from first hand knowledge: in 1955 I was there at least twice a week putting and fetching my own two children who spent almost every weekend with Uncleand Aunt Margaret from the time they were each about six months old in 1944 and '47. The "butler" would have been John Chamberlain—the description of a "tuxedo" is absurd. A white coat yes, he would have put that on when he walked in the house that morning

He had hands; he had farm equipment. I tell you who you really need to interview is the black guy, I think he his name is John, who worked for him.

John Chamberlain?

Yeah, John Chamberlain, that's the right one. You need to see him because he was the bagman. At the first of the month John went around and paid all Rogers' debts—hay bills, feed bills, all the stuff for the horses. He used to take money in a satchel. The reason I know this is that because where I parked every morning, I used to stop in and have coffee with Mr. C. C. Liggett who had a Purina distributorship. One morning I went in, and he said," Come in here, Sidney. I want to show you what I got. He had a great big bundle of bills, the old ones bigger that they are now. He said that every month Rogers' foreman came in and paid with these big bills. He didn't know we had been having all this trouble with Rogers.

Ed Steele who lived down on Hogan Road was an FBI agent. I picked him up every day coming into work. I told him about it, and he called his buddies at the secret service. They confiscated the bills and asked Rogers where he got them. He said he didn't know that they were just lying around the house. And that was the end of that. I don't understand it.42

The fellow, who built the house, Wilbur Creighton, said he put bank vaults in the basement.

I've never been in the basement, and I don't know. But he did have some unusual things. He had a Rolls Royce in the garage out there. I guess it was about a 1926 model, and it was hand painted all over like a checker

---

as usual. John and his wife, May, with their two children, lived in one of the white cottages right behind the house which is now the little museum at Ellington Center.

By then they were quite used to wintering quite comfortably with the furnace just warm enough to prevent the pipes from freezing. Three rooms were warmed by coal burning in the fireplaces- for you youngsters, coal burning grates are much more efficient and easily tended than wood.

42 It is not easy for one generation to understand the habits of an earlier one. At a time that I well remember, and I am only five years older than Sidney, there was always cash kept at home to pay for many expenses. There were no credit cards, few branch banks, and many people had no bank accounts to handle checks. The large bills were supplanted by the smaller some years before 1955 but they were still legal tender and were still decreasingly in circulation.

board.43 It was magnificent. We used to try to figure out how we could buy it and all that. We didn't know anything about cars, but Neil Cargile, Jr. bought that car from him, took a new battery and a little gasoline up there, and damned if he didn't drive that thing out in about an hour. We all stood there and watched; couldn't believe it.

---

43   It was a German Duesenberg and the body was wicker. It was Aunt Margaret's car, and since she became chaufferless, she gave it to Neil Cargile when he was about fourteen years old. He traded it for an airplane of sorts which he flew around our neighborhood from a grass strip in his front yard across Harding Pike from "Belle Meade." He finally misjudged a takeoff and ran it through a fence. He walked away, but that was the end of that.

Ed Nelson

Ed Nelson is the grandson of Charles Nelson of the First American National Bank which, under difficult circumstance, took over Papa Caldwell's Fourth and First Bank in the melee of the 1930s.

He was the President of the Commerce Union Bank, and now has his own Nelson Capital Corp.

To start off, tell me what you think went on after the collapse of Caldwell & Company.
The Rogers Caldwell that I knew was a gentleman who invited friends from various walks of life to his house for lunch on Saturdays. You would know the principals, but there would always be three or four who had not been there before, people you would not see again for a year. There was always a variety. Mr. Rogers was always interested in the current news—whether it was elections in Williamson County or the world.

He certainly had no appearance of what you would think of as a raider or a man who would willingly inflict pain on anyone, including animals—just a thoroughly sensitive person. He never, to my knowledge, discussed the past nor was it frequently mentioned in his presence. He was an interlocutor, a moderator, a questioner rather than a reporter, a facilitator. Yet about him was appropriate grit. He had something of a baiting sense of humor—not in the sense to take advantage of you but enough to put you off guard as you talked.

He had great affection for his servants—the cook, the houseman who served the table of twelve or fourteen people. How you could sit there and observe his gentle action and fit that personality to a robber baron or cause a Depression seemed impossible. The bad side was exaggerated, and most things that were said about him were said in a negative way. If people lost money or jobs during the Depression, in uneducated circles, that's where people believed that that's the fellow who caused all this. That plus the state's continuing effort to get his personal property which went on for a long time and kept him alive in the news world.

He probably, it's all guesswork for me because I was very young in the '30s, built his substantial empire on his optimism, his courage, his desire to make things happen, his initiative. Once you succeed, no matter how kind, how well-motivated you might be, external events surround you and you become a victim of the times. And, if you are involved in as many things as he was, you are a bigger victim. I take great pride in having known him, having associated with him, because of his kindness and his character which didn't just develop in late life. His interest in life and his kindness to others was just as ingrained in him as a young man as an elderly one. His own success, as I said before, determined his kind of fall and the ripple in the waters, the waves that he made that hurt his reputation. His intelligence, his desire to be a part of the community, was to make things happen. He had the tradition of the agrarian South, was a part of that. He liked the trappings of the old South—the horse racing, the literature. His portrait of the soldier coming home was one that no one who ever saw it would ever forget.

Where did it hang?

In the small library. Went Caldwell told me that it was so covered by the grime of the ages that when it was cleaned there was the body of a dead soldier laying across the saddle of the horse he was leading—a ghost of the past.44

Those trappings—the pictures of Lady Broadcast and his other horses—they seemed to me to be more a part of his spirit, his soul than anything that reflected his financial career.

---

44 I think Went was mistaken. Brockhurst, the artist, was an early 1900s illustrator at the time when fine magazines were the internet of today. There was not time for the ages to conceal anything. My guess is that, if there was a dead soldier, he had simplified the image by painting over the body to avoid excessive sentimentality and leave the viewer to his own interpretation.

The painting is now long gone to Massachusetts with cousin Nick Caldwell (Went's nephew and only son of Nichols, the oldest grandson). [The painting is at Wentworth Caldwell Jr.'s house. The dead soldier is clearly visible. -Ed.] So let me tell you what I remember: the canvas, about 3x5, was never framed, and rightly so because it sat on a shelf in front of the books in the most lived-in room both in Franklin and Brentwood House, the library. When you were looking for something you could just pick it up and move it further down, but it was ever present and handled with care. The picture showed a spring green mist engulfing woods cut briefly by a mud road. Facing away is the back of a water-soaked figure with a grey/brown slouch hat. He is moving on, with probably that same loping stride of Brother, about to disappear into woods at the turn of the road — to what? That is it, but it conjures, wordlessly, our not-so-distant forebears.

You are not the only person who has said that.

It gave any guest the feeling that he was a part of something important, part of history, part of what was happening or had happened. It made you respect some other people whom you might not have otherwise known or thought much of.

When did John Jay Hooker run for governor? Mr. Caldwell was a big supporter of his, wasn't he?

About 1970. Of course he was for him, but John Jay had a very tumultuous relationship with his father, and I don't think they were ever invited at the same time. John Jay might have been a little too vocal; took to the stump too easily and became angry. You remember the sign Mr. Rogers had on the wall asking that nothing ill be said of anybody at his table. But certainly that was a part of the political scene then. This was particularly Democratic politics because there weren't any Republicans.45

Rogers was pretty liberal, wasn't he?

He was liberal in spirit, but conservative by tradition. He wanted to get things done, to build, to acquire, and I don't think he objected to making some money along the way. He liked sports, liked the competition, enjoyed the fights even if he was not a part, the constant effort to build something. If he seemed to find it good to sit back and enjoy watching others struggle, you never had the feeling that Rogers Caldwell was out to get anybody.

The dreams and memories that I have expressed is what I am left with—a gentle man who enjoyed the action of life, enjoyed the debate between forces and chuckled at the outcome.

---

45 This wasn't altogether accurate. Pat Wilson, Mr. Republican himself, was a frequent visitor.

Peter Taylor

Mr. Taylor had had a stroke at the time of this recording, and his mind pivoted to such things as the lost State of Franklin, the writing habits of Henry James, and his aunt who was "the worst social climber in the world."

Hillsman Taylor, his father, had been head of the Missouri Life Insurance Company in St. Louis, which had become a property of Caldwell & Company. After that, for what reason I don't know, he had to move to Memphis. He was bitter, and thought that Uncle had betrayed him when they had been such great friends. Peter's Pulitzer Prize winning novel, A Summons to Memphis, *is based on this. The last scene in the book is of their accidental meeting at Clara's restaurant in Sewanee.*

Someone tapped Uncle on the shoulder and said that an old acquaintance of his was there and mentioned the name. Uncle got up immediately and walked across the dining room. I could watch them in front of the entrance where the bright light cast them in silhouette. After a face-to-face pause, they flung their arms around each other, then turned and walked outside to talk.

The rest of us were through with lunch when they came back in and parted. Uncle had his lunch, but the expression on his face called for silence. After that meeting they corresponded regularly for their remaining years.

Peter was ever the storyteller even as his mind wandered, and there were flashes of clarity with these nuggets:

Everybody went broke, and said Rogers Caldwell did it, but nobody got broker than we did. People said they were broke, but my mother still had a chauffeur. But we were so hard up she couldn't buy him a chauffeur's hat. So she gave him one of my father's old hats which was much too big, so it had paper stuffed in it riding around town. There was always a cook in the kitchen and maids.

An interesting thing about all this is that everybody did the right thing. Yet, when Dewitt Carter testified against him you could say that was the right thing, and you can also say that that was not the right thing.

At the commemoration of the opening of Grasslands, I have pictures of my mother and father and Rogers. She had a drink in her hand; she always said that she didn't take a second because "it makes me see double and feel single." They didn't have much in common. She couldn't stand to get on a horse, but she did sometimes because that was what everybody was doing, but she really didn't like to ride. And Mrs. Caldwell didn't either. It's probably what they had in common.

Do you have any opinion as to why Dewitt Carter testified the way he did?

I don't know. I remember him as a name because my father was bitter about his testimony. Rogers had been a great friend of his; he had come up in his organization. My father seemed to think it was saving his own skin at any price.

It's interesting because people have told me about Rogers' house, that over the years it got run-down, not that it fell apart, but they weren't painting it, weren't keeping it up, but that the public perception was that he had all the money in the world because he was living in that big house. I remember someone saying that Margaret said she was so glad that she had had arguments with Rogers when they were building the house about putting showers in the bathrooms instead of tubs because it was so much easier to wash out showers than tubs.46

---

46   If they argued, Aunt Margaret lost. There are tubs.

Wilbur Creighton, Jr.

Wilbur Creighton, Jr. of Foster & Creighton Construction Company, the general contractor which built Brentwood House and its barns.

He really loved that house. Tell me about your involvement.
Yes, I know that he did. It's an exact replica of the Hermitage. The only difference is the four upstairs bathrooms. They are semicircular additions to the wings adjoining the core of the house. There were no bathrooms at the Hermitage. Even the bath on the first floor was a closet.

You were the general contractor. Who was the architect?
Marr & Holman was the local firm and there was another northern one. Jerry Holmes was the man who was in charge of the work for the other architect. Bill Wright was superintendent for us, and, incidentally, also the superintendent for the restoration of the Parthenon at the same time.

What man on the job would Mr. Caldwell have dealt with the most?
Bill Wright. He was a construction genius, but he couldn't read or write. His wife read the specifications to him at night for him to memorize. But he was a natural builder, could do anything with his hands.

When they laid the job out and put up the batter boards, Bill told Mr. Caldwell, "The house is being built in a low place on the top of the hill. You won't be able to see all of the porch as you come up the drive." I was there when they were talking about it and he persuaded him to have it raised a few feet. He just had a natural instinct for building.

One of my experiences while I was still a senior at Vanderbilt was when I had a crew of men finishing the roads. Mrs. Caldwell called me to the house and said, "I want to move this tree down to the drive; I'll show you." The tree was maybe twenty feet high, not too big. So we dug it up, balled it and dug a hole where she said, and planted it. We were finishing when Roger drove in and saw that tree; he slammed on his brakes and said, "Who put that tree there?" I said that I had because his wife had told me to right after he left. Then he said, "I don't give a damn what she said, you take that tree back and put it right where you found it." He sure knew what he wanted; it's one of the biggest trees you see out there today.

I'll never forget that; he was in all those financial troubles but had his mind on his trees!

Did he have any trouble paying his bills?
No, he paid us right on time. I guess you read that he was building on his father's land so he really didn't have to pay us at all. The state had to do a lot of legal maneuvering before they got any of Mr. Jimmy's land.

But getting back to the house. There were a lot of things that were exactly like the Hermitage. The most distinguishing was the circular stair which, like the Hermitage, is put together with wooden pegs and glued, not nailed.

From what I understand the house is beautifully built. Was it a higher standard of construction for homes than was usually done around here?
Well, I think so because we had the best subs we could get. We weren't really in the house-building business, but we did this one because he wanted us to and we were also building his Caldwell & Company office on Union Street. It's too bad that it was torn down; it was a fine building.

I remember a lot of things. One thing was that the brick in the back of the fireplaces was laid in herringbone. When the architect got ready to draw the plans for them, Bill Wright pointed out to Mr. Caldwell that his fireplaces were built for coal grates which needed a different pattern. The Hermitage had wood fires. The plans were changed.

Then he had in that basement concrete vaults that would make Fort Knox look small. There were places under there for anything he wanted to store. I'm sure he stored a lot of money back in there because when it came time to pay off, he paid a lot of it in old bills.

When was that?
I'm not sure about the dates on these things because it took the state ten years or more[47] to get that property. He paid us. When things kinda blew up, we were finishing up out there—finishing the grounds and the stables. Just different things, we built everything there. That stable, as

---
47 It was twenty five years.

you can see even now, was a real show place. He had an English colonel come; his name was Shropshire, a British colonel from World War I, as his horse manager. He had some famous horses out there. One was named Hourless.

I heard he got poisoned.
He did? I didn't know that.

Who was Shropshire?
He was a colonel in the British army in the cavalry. He was a real old, hard-ankle colonel with a lot of stories to tell. He was quite famous.

Why would Mr. Caldwell want to build that place like the Hermitage?
Well, I don't know. It was the most famous building around here, and he just wanted to reproduce it. I guess he thought of himself as another Andrew Jackson. I never knew of a financial Andrew Jackson.

But anyway, he did. The brickwork and everything you see on that building today is just top quality. They had some chandeliers in there that were taken out. I think one of them may have been burnt up in the barn over at Oak Hill where the church is now. I don't know where the other one went—Franklin or somewhere. Hugh Walker or someone wrote an article about them that you may run into somewhere.

What were other features in the house that made it unique?
Well, in any house that is a copy of an old house, you have to make a lot of changes. You have to put ducts in where they didn't have ducts before. They were concealed so you don't know where they are. You could do a lot of things in there because the walls were so thick, maybe eighteen inches. We just took the plans and did it exactly like the Hermitage, the same dimensions and everything. Same type brick, I'm not sure where they came from, but they came from out of town. They matched the slave-made hand-pressed brick in the Hermitage. They were made for that house to match it in color and everything, hand-pressed, not just the usual wire-cut brick. Every detail was followed by the architect, and they did a lot of research on the paint color.

I keep reading that the house cost about $350,000 to build. That was a lot of money for a house.
That's probably right. But that didn't include the barns and all that. I'm not sure about that, I didn't make a record. There weren't any barns in the South that would compare with those at that time.

Tell me about the main barn.
All I remember is that it was very unusual to spend that much money on a barn. It was common conversation that more money had been spent on a barn than most people would spend on a mansion.

One thing was that it was so large. They made those horses just as comfortable as you would be if you lived there yourself.

How much would other big houses cost at this time?
Well, we built some that cost more than that. At that time, we built the Guilford Dudley house called Hunters Hill. Guilford Dudley was my uncle; he was my grandfather's brother. We built Runcie Clement's, the John Cheek house, all those Cheeks built big houses, the Tom Tyne's, Dick Martin's. Those houses were different amounts, but they were pretty close. The Guilford Dudley house, it was all stone, but it didn't have all the barns.

So three hundred thousand wasn't outrageous?
Well, it was. I built a house in 1931 for myself for $7,000, and I'm still living in it. It's appraised at $200,000. But it's all relative; you can't go by those kinds of things. I've added to it.

He had a little building out to the side that was used as an office. That's what people did in those days; had a pretty little building that they used for an office or library. I don't know whether he used it as an office or not.[48]

To understand Rogers Caldwell, you have to understand his father. He's one of most interesting characters whom I know. There is a book on his life which he gave my father in about 1920. He was obsessed with buying land, and bought every piece he could out of the Franklin Pike where he lived.

---

[48] Small out buildings were commonplace in those days and earlier. Taken from a French tradition, they were called "*garçonnière*" since they were used by sons when they came of age to be given private space removed from the family. Brother had one in the back yard at our house on Caldwell Lane. Uncle used his as a guesthouse.

I remember him very well; we built the Fourth and First Bank for him. He came in one day and saw that the plans were designed with columns all over the lobby. The architects in New York were designing it like any other bank on Wall Street. But Mr. Caldwell told my father, "I don't want anything like that, the bandits will get behind those columns and shoot at the tellers. I want an open space because my desk will be there so I can see and talk with anyone who comes in." Well, my dad and the chief engineer designed concrete trusses. They were the biggest beams ever put in a building in the South—fifty feet long, four feet wide and six feet deep—something like that. They were bridge beams and spanned that lobby.

Why do you say that I need to understand Mr. James E. before I could understand Mr. Rogers?
I don't think Mr. Rogers would have been as successful as he was without his father's backing, experience, reputation. I'm sure that had a lot to do with the people who would trust him on these big deals. He did some things in the South that had never been done in the world in putting things together.

Was Mr. Caldwell's reputation hurt when Rogers went out of business?
I don't know that it was hurt. He was retired by then. I don't think anything could change Mr. Caldwell's reputation.

I used to see Mr. James E. A friend of mine, Sam Porter, rented a house from him when we were building on Franklin Road. I'd go up there from time to time, and we would hunt all over the property. One day we stopped at the spring which had a sign saying QUARANTINED.

Mr. Caldwell came by on his horse, had a beard hanging down on him, you know, always dressed real nattily. He pulled up, didn't get off his horse. He had a dipper where he could reach over and get a drink of water. I said, "Mr. Caldwell, this spring's contaminated." He said. "I've been drinking out of this spring for forty years, and I'm going to keep on drinking out of it,"

They closed all the springs in Davidson County because they'd all been contaminated. You can't drink out of a spring in Davidson County due to septic tank contamination. Just closed them all instead of saying this one is all right. Of course, there wasn't anything wrong with that spring.

Then Mr. Caldwell came in our office one day. They were building the road through Melrose and we had the plans getting ready to get started on the road leading up to Franklin Road. Mr. Caldwell said, "How wide is that? Let me see the plans." So I rolled them out and he just blew up. He said, "Get me a set of those plans." I sent up, and paid fifty cents for another set for him. He went up there and doubled that thing. So what you see in Melrose is twice as wide as it was at first. We widened the whole thing.

Do you think Rogers was a good businessman, or was he just lucky?
I think he was a good businessman. He had a lot of good people working for him, all these boys at Vanderbilt with me, all of whom made fortunes. One of them, Peck Owen, bought American Express.

Why do you think he never made it back?
I don't know. Of course, everybody lost their shirts in that Depression.

Libby Zerfoss Fryer

Libby Zerfoss Fryer was of the class of '41 at Vanderbilt, as was I. She knew everything about everything without being pedantic. I'm sure she was Phi Beta Kappa. We didn't have classes together; she studied political science and economics while I was into languages and history. Her parents, Dr. Tom and Dr. Kate Zerfoss, one of Nashville's earliest woman doctors, had been friends with Uncle in their youth.

Believe me, whatever Libby said was not only true but right.

Who taught Rogers the business?
It was his father who taught him. James E. took him and his two younger brothers[49] with him when he traveled to the centers of finance when he started the Cumberland Telephone Company. They even went with him to New York City to get the George Peabody $1,000,000 grant from J.P. Morgan, who was the head of the trust that handled it. He wasn't a little boy, but still a boy. That was where he got his learning. He told me about that—what I'm telling you is not secondhand.

I first met him in Franklin when he moved here. Somebody told me that Mr. Caldwell wanted to know what I was doing because he wanted somebody to catalogue his books. I was fooling around in politics at the time and working as the town librarian.

I went to see him one Saturday morning, and after we had talked a while, he invited me to stay for lunch. I'm one of the few women who were there for lunch on Saturdays since that was when he saw his political buddies.

Who were they?
Mr. Frank Murray, they had been friends for years, and Jack Whitfield, who knew what was really happening in the Democratic Party. Mr. John Hooker, he came a lot and brought his new wife. People said she wouldn't let him come unless she came. He often had Asa Jewell, then mayor of

---

[49] Meredith and Dandridge.

Franklin. Russell Brothers, Pat Wilson50 came some, Mr. John Sloan quite often, John Seigenthaler some but not a lot. An invitation to his lunches was vied for; it was the hottest ticket in town.

He thought that husbands and wives limited each other, that they never were the same when they were together. So he saw to it that people came separately, which was a lot more interesting. He went way back with that notion.

He treated me differently; he was nicer to me than to all the rest of them put together. He really liked me; we had good conversations—politics and books. That was the thing; he told me that I had made his library come alive. I thought I was going to catalog it in the sense of a librarian, because that's what I am. But it ended up that wasn't what he wanted at all. What Mr. Caldwell wanted was for the ones he was most interested in to be on the bottom two shelves in clusters by subject matter so that he could find them.

Joseph Dickinson, an artist and friend of mine from Brownsville, conducted the sale of the furniture left at Brentwood House after Uncle and Aunt decided what to take to Franklin or give to Belle Meade which had recently become a state historic property. Next, he moved them, decided what went where. His genius showed in hanging the portraits, all of them, including the two Earles and the Catlin paintings of Andrew Jackson and the huge General Gideon Pillow. They looked as much at home as if they had always been there. On moving day Uncle went off to his office as usual, but when he went home for lunch it was in Franklin. His bedroom was furnished as he had left it that morning, his clothes hung in the closet the way Harry knew they belonged, friends were on hand and lunch was served on the same china and white linen. BUT his books were arranged the way they had been at Brentwood House, not in accordance with his changing interest.

Do you have any idea where his personal correspondence was?

I have no idea. I was sick about it; I was right in the middle of all this and I knew about all the problems, but I respected him to the point I did not write things down. I felt that would invade his privacy and changed the whole basis of our friendship.

To shed light on this: May Buntin Hill and I were co-executors of the trust, but we handled only the household property. David Keeble, a

---

50 Also in our class of '41.

longtime family friend and his lawyer, did whatever is needed at someone's death. His personal correspondence was never seen by us.

What was the library like?

The library was a small room next to the dining room with bookshelves that went all the way to the ceiling on all sides. He had magnificent books. He told me that he had gotten them from all over the world, particularly through New York dealers. It meant more to me than anything when he said I made his library come alive. We talked about them at length but what he really wanted was to have the ones he liked best within his reach. He sat in a wingback chair with the light coming in over his shoulder and I had a little ladder so that I could take each book down and hand it to him. Whichever book he wanted near, I would put it there, but I'd try to put the books on hunting, horses and such together.

A lot of the books were gifts and I was reading "To Rogers Caldwell" from all sorts of people, and I asked who that was. He would tell me about all these people he knew who had given him these books. They were his friends, interesting people. He would tell me about them and their relationship. That's what he wanted—the books that meant something to him where he could find them. We talked about them, and I learned a lot.

My mother had known him and Miss Margaret, with whom she and my aunt had gone to Europe with when they were young. Our families had known each other forever. My great-uncle was president of a small bank in Kentucky which had failed, caught up in some way with the Fourth and First, and when he came down here and sat in Mr. Caldwell's office, he did not leave until they gave him the money for his bank. So I had more contact, knowledge and association with them than most people had.

But he loved those books, and the association that he had with them.

On Saturday Bob Crichton, whom he liked a lot, sometimes came early, and we would sit out there on that porch... His men friends never understood why I was there. I think it bothered them, but that was a long time ago. I remember little John Jay Hooker telling him about Kentucky Fried Chicken and Minnie Pearl and what they were going to do.

But let me tell you one story I thought was hysterical. Mr. Caldwell always sat at the head of the table with his back to the library, and I always sat at his left. Well, little John Jay unexpectedly brought the Nashville mayor, who was high. There wasn't a place for him at the table, so Mr. Rogers moved over to make room for an extra chair. Well, come time for the dessert, Harry was passing chocolate sauce for the ice cream. The mayor was waving his arms around and hit the dish; chocolate sauce went all over Mr. Caldwell's white linen coat.

Mr. Caldwell said he told John Jay never to bring that man again.

One day, some people came from the Smithsonian to look at his portraits. He said, "They want all my pictures. What do you think I ought to do?"

So I said, "Well, Mr. Caldwell, how do you feel about your portraits? Do you like them, enjoy them?"

This is exactly what he said, "I like possessing them. I can just go from room to room. I get so much pleasure out of seeing them."

So I said, "Well, that's that."

I bet they could kill me at the Smithsonian.

On Tuesdays he had his newspaper friends and writers. F. M. Williams, the sports writer from the *Tennessean*, and Hugh Walker, who wrote the historical books column. Stanley Horn, Dr. Leland Crabb and Campbell Brown went back to his early days. There were always fourteen places at the table and they were always filled. Thirteen men and me. He was protective of me. You know there is a difference between assumed manners that can turn on and off. His was a natural manner, what he had grown up with. He was courtly and naturally very kind.

The bad times in his life were terrible for everybody, and yet his friends were still his friends in the later part of his life. He also became friends with a lot of people in Franklin. Part of it all was the drama. He had been a superstar, super rich. Anybody who had had a house like he had in Brentwood, my Lord in Heaven, it was the most beautiful thing that ever was.

I remember we had a spring dance and a breakfast afterwards out at Brentwood House on account of Keith and Jim, his nephews. I've never seen anything as magnificent in my life. The thing I remember most is that there were real candles burning in the chandelier in the dining room. I saw it that night and it's a picture I'll never forget.

What do you think happened to that? Is it still there?

I don't know. Those gorgeous marble mantelpieces are still there. But he had a super lifestyle—the horses, Grasslands, travel. It was a gracious type of living that he was brought up in with his father and mother at Longview. It was just a rare time, a rare time.

I did a paper one time at Vanderbilt when I read the McFerrin book. Mr. Carter, the father of my good friend, Frances, showed me the letter he had written to Mr. Caldwell to stop certain things that they were doing. I remember that he sat me down at a table and just handed me the book opened to the letter.

When I was in school, my two best friends were Frances Carter and Margaret Heitzberg. I never did understand why they never spoke to one another or go to each other's house.

Did he ever talk about Carter?

No. And I would not intrude. I felt like in those last years that I was very privileged. I knew they were interesting times.

Certainly everybody in Nashville has a copy of that book.

Well now, let me tell you about that book. Have you seen the first part of the old, the first book? It said that 250 copies of this book were printed. I worked at the Nashville Public Library reference room. They had a rare books section that could not be circulated or given to people except under very strict circumstances. And that was one of them. They said that the reason that book was there was that it was a limited copy, and that the Caldwell family and friends wanted it out of circulation.51

51 I questioned exactly who the "family and friends" were who made such a request, and so for the first time at this late date, it was time for me to read what was said. I borrowed my son David's copy, Uncle's original copy which he had given him, and THERE IT WAS, the letter Mr. Carter had shown Libby alerting Mr. Caldwell "to stop certain things that they were doing."

There was the letter Libby mentioned—nine single space pages of size ten font — dated May 20, 1930. Daunted by the length, print size, tone of the letter and that it was one man's opinion, I browsed the table of contents and index. This copy was from the University of North Carolina Press, 1939, and states "This edition is limited to 1,000 copies."

In the preface McFerrin thanks Timothy Donovan, former secretary of Caldwell & Company and in charge of the office of the receivers, for his help. He then thanks "for access to essential material and leads to other valuable sources, Messrs. J. Dewitt Carter and Frank D. Marr for graciously furnishing information in interviews." He spoke of no other effort to talk with anyone else connected with Caldwell & Company.

Then I read: Chapter XVIII, "Criminal Prosecutions." "The trial of Rogers Caldwell involving the Hardeman County trust was set by Judge Chester Hart of the Davidson County Criminal Court. Caldwell's efforts for change of venue, on the grounds that public feeling in Nashville against him was so great that a fair trial was impossible, was denied by Judge Hart, who said that his own private investigations and observations convinced him that undue prejudice did not exist.

"When the State began presenting evidence on June 10, 1930, its principal witnesses were three former officials of Caldwell & Company: E.B. Smith, E. A. (Tommy) Goodloe, and J.D. Carter, who had been called before the Legislative Investigating Committee earlier in the year. Timothy Donovan had also testified but he was not called as a witness because of his reluctance to tell anything that would harm his former employer and it was established in the trial that he had nothing to do with trusts.

"These introductions as state witnesses added bitterness to the trial. Smith and Goodloe could hardly be classed as effective witnesses for the state since their testimony tended to show that Caldwell was not familiar with the condition of the trusts because he did not supervise the internal operations of the company, and that Carter was the official responsible for the trusts.

"When Carter came to the stand it was an entirely different story. On direct examination he repeated the testimony he had given before the Legislative Committee earlier, going into every detail which painted Caldwell in as bad a light as possible.

"On cross examination, he testified that he had received a salary of $37,700 a year, that he had not spoken to Caldwell nor offered help since the crash of the company and that he furnished the State all the letters by himself and Goodloe as exhibits. The cross-examination tried unsuccessfully to draw out of Carter that he, rather than Caldwell, was responsible for the conditions of the trusts. He maintained that he was merely an employee and was not responsible.

"Caldwell was the only witness for the defense. On direct examination he testified concerning the early operations of the business, the hiring of Carter as bookkeeper at $175 a month and his advancement to vice-president, the placing of Carter as head of sales and then adding the accounting department of which the trust department was a section, and the reorganizing of the accounting department at the suggestion of Carter. He stated that Carter had the supervision of the trust department and that he relied upon him to manage it properly for he had every confidence in him. He testified that he had later assumed responsibility for getting the trusts straightened out because he felt that Carter had failed to make the proper efforts, and, that after he took charge, he received very little cooperation from Carter. He denied that he had read Carter's letter because he was so busy with BancoKentucky that he had not had time, and that there was no need for Carter to write him letters since their offices adjoined each other.

"On cross-examination the State attempted to get Caldwell to admit that, as a president of the company, he was in charge of all of its operations, and hence responsible for the trusts. He maintained that the company was departmentalized, and that he paid Carter to do things which were necessary in his department. Caldwell based his defense largely on the fact that the company had grown so fast and had such wide and diversified interests that he, as president, had to supervise that he had no time to look after the detail of the internal operation which had been largely left to Carter.

"The case brought in a verdict of guilty on the one of three counts of fraudulent breach of trust, and set the punishment of three years imprisonment. Caldwell was released on $10,000 bail. Later, a motion for a new trial was denied by Judge Hart, and notice was given for an appeal to the Tennessee Supreme Court. The Supreme Court remitted him for retrial to the lower court largely because the trial court had denied change of venue based on evidence obtained from private investigation by the trial judge, and the verdict of the jury necessitated its giving full credence to Carter's testimony and rejecting that of Goodloe and Smith. The inference was that the jury was affected by the prejudice against Caldwell at the time of the trial.

"Judge Hart stated that the new trial would be set immediately, but Attorney General Atkins took no action to do so. His inaction may well have been due partly to the fact that his chief witness, Carter, had been somewhat discredited by the Supreme Court's decision. In any event, a date was never set for retrial and the court's decision had the effect of acquitting Caldwell of the charges."

This is what the McFerrin book says.

May Buntin Murray

May Buntin Murray, then Hill, was the second child of Aunt Elsie (Mrs. Daniel Carter Buntin), who was the only surviving daughter of Ma May and Papa. May's first husband, Shade Murray, was father of her children, Shade, Jr., Daniel, Leticia and Adelia. After his untimely death, she married Horace Hill, Jr. who was then widower of her cousin Edith.

Everyone says that he was a complete gentleman, very nice, pleasant to be around.

He sure displayed that around his table. You know he used to have these luncheons every day. He had these gamblers on Monday, literary friends on Tuesday, Wednesdays was ladies day, Thursdays the servants had the day off, Fridays he picked up those he had missed earlier in the week, Saturdays were for political friends.52

---

52 Uncle did gamble on politics and sporting events. At the Stock Yards, where he had an office during his later years, to lay a bet was no problem. Almost everybody there had a bookie. His office, adjacent to mine, was visited from time to time by some of Nashville's known gamblers such as Al Alesio who ran a casino and nightspot in what is now Metro Center and was a frequent caller near election times. But for lunch guests—no. His pattern of lunch guests was more flexible than described. True, Saturdays were for business and political friends. Wednesday was for ladies. The older regulars such as Aunt Elsie, Miss Sadie Burch and Miss Milbrey Allen arrived together chauffeured in a large black something, in fashionable hats, white kid gloves, wafting Chanel, full of smiles and the latest goings-on; he loved it. Sunday breakfast was for family. Monday, Tuesday and Friday were for regulars from Franklin and Nashville such as Larry Howard, Frank Murray, Hugh Walker, Campbell Brown, Stanley Horn, Leland Crabb, Dudley Fort, Bill Ormes, Emmy Caldwell, Libby Fryer, Alyne Armistead, Lillian and Beau Boardman—all involved people. These were the best days. You never know who was coming or what interesting out-of-town guests would be with them.

One who came when she was in town was May's cousin Rachel [Rachel Adelia Craighead Buntin Wilmot Armstrong]. To me she was the best looking lady ever to come out of Nashville—by far. Tall, perfect figure and features, pale porcelain skin, dark, long, straight hair worn in a bun at the nape of her neck, she was kind, thoughtful, talented, a compulsive talker, exhausting and daft. In the late '40s, between husbands two and three, she lived in Nashville with her mother at Tulip Grove—the great house across the pike from Andrew Jackson's Hermitage. It was then at the end of its 100-year lease from the Ladies Hermitage Association and is now part of the Hermitage complex.

Do you think that was planned?
No, it was just natural with him. He was a great listener, and he would say the right words to urge you on.

I spent a great deal of time as a girl out there with Aunt Margaret. Mamma went to the country in the summertime and I stayed in town out there. You know how young people want to stay in town.

What would you do?
Oh, I would have dates and such; Aunt Margaret was one of the best friends I ever had.

She and Mama took me to attend the Masters School right outside

---

She was named for Rachel Jackson, but in Palm Beach where she wintered, she saw to it that she was known as Diana.

Being settled in Nashville for a while, she wanted to stir things up as she did anywhere she was. She couldn't have done it in a better way—she gave French cooking lessons which certainly changed my life for the better. A culinary wizard, her classes were held in the houses of Belle Meade matrons. My most vivid memory is of her standing in Margaret Ann Robinson's formal living room dressed in off-white linen, wide brimmed black straw hat, and black stiletto-heel shoes. By her side on a small table was a platter with about a 22-inch trout, guts and head gone. She picked up a dagger-shaped knife, carved a ring around the base of its tail, then down the spine, peeled back a small triangule of skin, punched a thumb-hold. Then she faced us neophytes, took that fish by the tail in her upraised left hand, and with her right snatched the skin off in one swoop. Houdini himself would have been impressed.

I won't leave you there. Into a large poaching pan in the kitchen she poured a great splash of good white wine and a bit of water and brought it to a rolling boil. In went sprigs of tarragon from a bottle of vinegar (this was before Nashville grocers were herb-minded) with a bunch of trimmed spring onions chopped with a cleaver—barely missing her perfectly manicured fingers at each whack, turned the heat to medium and in slid that fish. All the time she talked—telling us that you can always invite the Prince of Wales to stay for lunch if you keep on hand fresh eggs for an omelet, salad greens, unsalted butter, a loaf of good French bread, and a decent bottle of white wine.

She removed the lid, prodded the fish with her finger, nodded her hat, slid the fish to a serving platter, turned the heat up, reduced the liquid, took it off the heat, gave a final stir to a mixture of warm melted butter and whole beaten eggs, gradually whisked the mixture into the hot liquid. Slowly it thickened, emitting a smell straight from heaven. She lavished the sauce over that white, white fish, added a decorative hand-full of parsley. Voilà, Trout Royal Albert!

More of Cousin Rachel: a mighty letter writer she was and, as such, of concern to Uncle. He did his rights and propers by responding to all of his mail within 48 hours—Mrs. Cook, his secretary, was a whiz at this. The problem was that Rachel did the same, so there was a constant stream of diminishing interest. At the same time, he had a dear British friend who followed the same pattern. As Uncle put it to me *Voilà*—he had to try to get the two of them together. It worked—I heard no more about it.

of New York City. Uncle Rogers had an apartment on Park Avenue near Grand Central Station with a Filipino who did everything. It was 1929 and I was fifteen, didn't know a soul, and was so home sick. Well, I cried and Aunt Margaret cried; we cried so hard we couldn't even go out to dinner the last night. Mama didn't cry.

I remember the morning when Shirley found her in the bed; she had died during the night. Uncle Rogers called me, and I called Miss Milbrey Allen, one of her greatest friends, and we went out to do what was needed.

She was just a typical southern belle when Uncle married her—from Nashville, a Trousdale, to the manor born, knew how to run a great house, and had all the social graces.

It must have been very upsetting when they lost the house.
Oh, he really loved it, and his family. He was Ma May's favorite—Uncle Meredith was Papa's favorite. Uncle Rogers, Meredith and Dan were the three youngest children born after the two little girls died. Ma May said that when the other children were talking about what they wanted to be when they grew up—firemen, policemen and so on—Uncle Rogers would say he wanted to be a daddy, but he never had any children of his own

Was that a problem in later years?
No. Miss Marie Ransom, Aunt Margaret's lifelong friend, allowed her youngest child, Mimi, to live with them for several years. They really wanted to adopt her. And, of course, young Rogers, after Aunt Margaret died, stayed out there with Uncle Rogers so much. David Patterson and my Dan were there, too.

Tell me something more about how Rogers was complex.
Well, you know, he was a business genius, and had real magnetism. People loved him; he had so many friends. I remember that Mr. Porter Lewis, a bachelor, kind of a Dickens character, stayed out there a lot. Uncle liked to have him around, kept his horse for him. He was referred to as the Keeper of the Wine Cellar.

He had another houseguest, a Colonel somebody.
Oh, yes, he came to see about the horses; Uncle Rogers felt like he overdid

what he told him to do, and killed Hourless, his stallion. He ordered Colonel Dickinson to leave. But it was during the Depression and Aunt Margaret felt so sorry for him that she put him upstairs in the Red Room. Uncle knew he was there but they never met. It went on for a year or two after the horse died. Someone else may know more of the details, but I've always heard that Aunt Margaret just took pity on him. He had been a colonel in the British cavalry.

What did the fellow do that killed the horse?
What I heard was that the horse was sick and Uncle Rogers had made some suggestions, and he thought that Colonel Dickinson just overdid it. They started out with show horses. Aunt Margaret was a beautiful rider. And they had the two Shropshire brothers who lived in the cottage behind the big house. One of them showed the horses and the other saw to their training.

Aunt Margaret, Mamma and I took a grand tour when I was about twelve years old, and met Uncle and Mr. John Branham in Saratoga. We stayed in the old United States Hotel. I think it burned, but it was very famous in 1926. That was when he was going into racehorses and established Grasslands which opened in 1929 at a big party at "Fairvue," its clubhouse. Mrs. Branham put on a great show for all these out-of-town people. She lived at "Foxland Hall," which is close by.

When his company blew up, did his friends stay with him or did some of them run?
I think most of them stayed. Tom Goodloe was one who stayed. He worked for Uncle, and he used to go out and ride with him every Sunday. I think most of his intimate friends stayed—Paul Rye, Fay Murray, Went, Tommy. Mr. Carter was the one who really did him in.

I don't know... there is one thing about our family, they never complained or talked about it. I was really just as free as could be to make any friends. Of course, everything was swept out from under the Caldwells, but there was no bitterness as far as the younger generation was concerned. At least, there wasn't in my part of the family.53

---

53 I can say this: I never felt any bitterness towards anyone. That sort of carries down, you know. If your family feels that way, then you catch it. I think that was a great deal due to Uncle Rogers.

What was Luke Lea like?
Well, he was very, very attractive. The same type of magnetism, and very well born.

Was he a good guy or a bad guy?
No, I don't think he was a bad guy. He was a great friend of mine. He died in his mid-fifties. He was in prison for two or three years.

Did he and Rogers remain friends in later years?
Yes. Uncle Rogers didn't have an enemy.

What about the political enemies? The McAlisters?
Laura, the daughter, was a great friend of mine. The family never said, "Well, you can't do this or do that."

Was it harder on Uncle Rogers than on Aunt Margaret when they were unable to adopt that little girl?
Of course not, he loved Mimi, but I don't think he ever wanted to adopt any children. She lived with them a long time, but I don't think when it came to adopting, he did not.

He just loved his enormous family and took us all in. David and Sheppard were there a lot and Rogers and Goldyn Trousdale, Aunt Margaret's nephew. He just liked having children around and always did.

When did he build Brentwood House?
About 1927. I remember all that. They lived at Oak Hill, the old Kirkman place after the Kirkmans had all died. I don't know whether he bought or rented it to live there while they built the new house. He was so excited about it, and Aunt Margaret was too.

I remember when I was working on Cheekwood the man who came from Thomasville, Georgia, to work on the Capitol back in the '50s. He said it was the most beautifully built house he had ever seen—construction-wise. Marr & Holman did that. Mr. Holman was a great friend of Uncle's.

I'm going to see Mr. Creighton, Jr. tomorrow. I believe he was the contractor.

Well, you tell him that Mr. Dinkle from Thomasville said it was an absolutely magnificent house.

At that time, I think there were just 25 millionaires in this country, and Uncle was one of them. So everything that could be was put in. Nothing was spared. In the *Illustrated London News* there was a picture of the Queen's dollhouse, which Aunt Margaret loved, especially the dining room furniture. So Uncle Rogers had it copied for her. I have all the papers on that. The whole dining room was designed around that. It was just a difference of scale from the dollhouse. There were 26 chairs, the table and the sidepieces.

Edith bought this furniture when it was sold in preparation for their moving to Franklin. So this dining room is designed for it. Unfortunately, the leaves to the table were not stored in the right temperature, so they have gotten a little warped. They're a little on the bumpy side, but I like that. 54

Margaret was still living when the sale took place?

Yes, she was. All the furniture was Aunt Margaret's, so it didn't come into the reckoning with the state. They took the things that they liked best that suited the house in Franklin and a little house across the street that was bought. She put a little furniture there.

In his will, he left all the furniture to his nieces and nephews.55

Did any of the other family lose money in the failure of Caldwell & Company?

I think we all did.

---

54 At the time this was taped at May's house, Edith had died and May had married Horace, so "this dining room" which she mentions is the same one.
55 I think May is confused about this. As co-executor, I remember it like this: When Aunt Margaret died, she left her real property to the Brentwood House Trust for Uncle Roger's use for his lifetime. At his death, everything remaining went to the heirs as provided by the Trust (these were his nieces and nephews since he had no children of his own.) He had no will; the dispersal was just according to the terms of the Trust.

As to Aunt Margaret's nephew, Goldyn Trousdale, he, not being an heir in the Trust, was excluded. It was the family's decision that he should have the things that had belonged to Aunt Margaret's family. The main item was a large portrait of General Gideon Pillow, an ancestor, but there were other things that were important to his family. I was told that soon after he got the things, his wife divorced him and off they all went with her to California.

Some people say that a number of people who had worked for him went on to make fortunes. Do you know anybody who was able to do that?

I think a lot of younger men like Brownlee Currey, Guilford Dudley, Wentworth, Tommy Goodloe; they all worked for Uncle Rogers, and all later made fortunes. They had gotten that experience and the contacts.

What do you think caused the company to collapse?

I can't really answer that. It's just so spread out into so many facets. It was like a house of cards, once the ripple started. Nashville thought that Uncle Rogers was responsible for the whole Depression.

Why did people think that?

Well, when people lose money, it bites deep, and they have to find somebody to blame. I think a lot of people blamed him. But he was ahead, and when things got bad, somebody had to take the blame, so they just blamed him.

Did his getting into politics contribute to people's feelings?

I think it did. I don't know, but that was Kyrock.

I don't understand about Kyrock.

Well, I don't either. All I remember was a lot of cartoons about Kid Kyrock.56

I have never gone into the kind of gruesome things in our family, and there sure were gruesome things. I couldn't do anything about it. I really inherited from my family to think good things about most people. I don't hold grudges or things like that. I have never been told other things about my family.

---

56 At this time paved roads were made of a material which froze and developed potholes in winter and had to be redone every spring. "Kyrock" stands for Kentucky Rock Asphalt, which was sold to the state as an improved material to reduce this extensive maintenance. Uncle had an interest in the company, and was accused—rightly or wrongly, I don't know—of political malfeasance in selling it to the state.

Shirley Caldwell-Patterson

Interview done in 1989

How do you think the failure of Caldwell & Company changed Mr. Caldwell?

I don't know. Sunday dinners were almost the only times I saw him, and then there were so many people that I knew him as just another uncle, didn't see any change at all, but then I was only eleven years old.

Only after Son David's birth in 1943 did that change, and we became very close. At six months the child was still riding in a lined laundry basket when Uncle invited him to spend the night. The two of them had become friends at Sunday dinners without my noticing.

I was amazed that Uncle and Aunt Margaret would want to undertake such a thing. But they did and I was delighted. Whatever he needed went off in a tote bag, and he slept in his basket. They never asked for instructions, I never gave any and we all thrived. Gradually one night turned into two, and then regularly into weekends and longer. When Daughter Sheppard, named for her stalwart great, great grandmother, came along three years later, it wasn't long before they had them both.

In winter the library and downstairs bedroom were heated by coal-burning fireplaces.57 The big downstairs bedroom had an electrically-heated dressing room big enough for a small bed where Aunt Margaret slept; Sheppard, when she graduated from her basket, had the little bed at the foot of the big canopied one which David and Uncle shared. Meals were served on a card table in the library with the usual white linen, Royal Doulton and George II silver—sort of perpetual camping in a grand manner.

It must have taken much energy as well as ingenuity. But it was a happy place.

To maintain it or just keep it?

Both. To have to argue with the state and all that. Legally, the land didn't belong to Uncle, just the house. The property was in a generation-skipping

---

57 And the kitchen by the coal stove.

trust from Ma May to the grandchildren as heirs, one of which I was. The reason the state never sold the property but developed Ellington Center instead is that they never had a clear title. And still don't, that I know of, but probably statutes of limitations have kicked in long since.

In attending monthly meetings of my Cumberland River Compact which are held there, I am a constant visitor at Ellington Center. When I look out over the little-changed grounds, there is gratitude for it being still in one piece which it would not be had we heirs have gotten hold of it.

We meet where the two-stall stud barn once stood and Hourless and Fields held court. He had his own cabin but, come dark, he bedded in the straw with his friend. Here, too, is the spot of my earliest horse memory—being set on the back of that great dark and gentle stallion. I was so young that all I remember is seeing my feet sticking straight out in front and rubbing his sleek hide with my thumbs. Facing my bed still is his life-size sepia photograph by Underwood & Underwood, the New York photographers who specialized in horses. It is just the head and powerful neck so dark that the lopsided quarter moon in his forehead stands out just like the reflected light in his eyes.

Why do you think he held on to the house so long?

It was his home, his creation. He cared deeply about how he lived, was responsible for the design, furnishing, and its management. In his *Age of Jackson*, Arthur Schlesinger describes the ideal "life of a Tennessee gentleman living on a fine plantation near Nashville, entertaining his friends, racing his horses and heatedly talking politics." Perhaps he had illusions.

It is a replica of the Hermitage adapted to modern living. The added curved arched wing that swings back from the service side of the house for the laundry and servants' quarters is a structure of rare beauty. It was an institution, and he just didn't want to leave it. He thought he was right, and then, certainly, his machismo was involved as well as the already-expressed feeling of responsibility to those who had always been there and had no place else to go—not just those alive but those dead and buried along with Hourless and Fields.

His ultimate reason was that to leave meant that he had lost the land that belonged to his family, not to him. Already the failure of his business had meant grave financial loss for his father, mother and the rest of us, but losing a part Elysian Fields must have been devastating.

Was there any specific thing that caused him finally to leave?

A number of things—Ma May died, then Papa; Longview went to Aunt Elsie who moved there for a while but, with the lack of domestic help which followed World War II, it was just too much. She moved back to town and Edith with Uncle Charley moved to an apartment across the street from her. The land was being broken up and sold. There was no seeming end to the legal wrangling. The state had forced the quick auctioning of his racing stable with enormous loss of value. Everything had changed and, of course, everything must end at some point.

When he finally faced reality and moved to Franklin, his creative urge was rekindled. That was potent stuff for him. He took about two years and a couple of master carpenters to redo that derelict to a charming house—as charming, on a smaller scale, as the one he left. He just had a touch.

Why do you think he was different when he got to Franklin?

He had lightened his load, had a house that he liked, could afford and was easily maintained. Papa had come from Franklin, so he was no stranger. A clutch of new friends joined the ones he already had. He was not as isolated as he had been on Hogan Road. Uncle was curious about everything that had happened, was apt to happen or was happening as it happened. He had my two children a good part of the time and, a bit later, his nephew and namesake, Rogers. This was a closeness that lasted until he died. We all suited one another.

He had given up on trying to make a financial comeback, welcomed the constant stream of people who came to see him and continued to carry on correspondence with friends all over the world. It was easily accessible for people to come, and they did. Libby Fryer said it was "the hottest ticket in town."

How big a staff would he have had in the '40s?

There was a cook/maid and houseman who lived with their two children in a pleasant cottage behind the great house where Dan and Sarah Joyce had once lived after they were married.

Uncle at home in Franklin

They deserve a biography of their own: John Chamberlain came as a young man from Westmoreland, Sumner County to work tobacco at fifty cents a day, the going wage. To come from Sumner County was a leg up—it and its neighbor Maury are the two most beautifully fertile of Tennessee where graciousness put down roots earliest on the frontier, but Nashville in Davidson County was more generous.58

Anyway, John was a natural gentleman who caught Uncle's eye. He with his family were soon nearby and, under this experienced teacher, they both became not just good cooks but knew exactly how to run a polished household.

When Uncle moved to Franklin, they came to Belle Meade to live in the cottage there in the side yard and John became custodian at the Stock Yards. Their third child was born and named Benjamin Franklin Byrd Chamberlain for Sister Allison's reliable doctor-husband who was so helpful to us all. As time passed, John became an integral part of the group of waiters who were much in demand by the town's carriage trade to assure that their parties were *just right*.

When the Stock Yards was sold to Bobby Mathews, he swore that it was not the thirteen acres in downtown Nashville that attracted him nearly so much as the presence of John Chamberlain.

All of Elysian Fields was run as one piece, some three thousand acres. When Papa died, farming was greatly curtailed. Brother and David ran cattle out there, but that was about it. Another thing was that, after the war, the interstate highway system started coming through the property and the land had a value well beyond farming.

I think you have to look at Uncle as an example of a number of people of his time. I can do that easily because of my own father. Their *modus vivendi* were similar; they did not expect to do manual labor much beyond chunking up the fire or throwing on an occasional log. It would simply have never occurred to them.

Once I flipped through the mail that contained a postcard summoning Daddy to do roadwork for the county. I was horror-stricken with the

---

58 This bit will probably be taken for hokum, but David Love, Wyoming's geology icon and protagonist of John McPhee's *Rising From the Plains,* summered in Dubois when I was there, taught me how to pan for gold and convinced me that there are places on earth that emanate creative forces. For Uncle, this was such a place.

vision of him out digging ditches in his white buckskin shoes. When I took the news to Mama, she explained, to my utter relief, that that was just a device to collect road taxes and that he really didn't have to do that.

It was a formal life for all of them. I never saw my father, until he was bedridden with tuberculosis, in anything but a three-piece suit. The same was true of Uncle. And as to Papa, he was even more formal; even when he rode to the farm, he was described in the press as "natty."

The word formal is not exact because they were relaxed people who could banter with anybody about anything.59 Certainly, in comparison with the way people live now, they were formal. Mama dressed every evening for dinner in what Brother called a "long-tailed dress" and she was gorgeous. We three girls were not told to do the same, but there were lovely things hanging in the closet that were hard to ignore, and, when we did, we were told how nice we looked. But above all, it was absolute that we were on time, minded our table manners, and were considerate of the servants.

After Caldwell & Company failed, did he keep the same friends or did some people desert him?

I don't know; don't even know who they all were. But of the ones I knew, I don't think he lost any, even those who had done considerable business with him. But whoever they were, he sure was long on friends, interesting ones.

What about going to church?

Aunt Margaret went to church and took whatever children were on hand to Sunday school. Ma May and Papa went regularly. But as to Uncle, that is an interesting question. A friend whom I still see, Damaris Steele, wrote a history of the First Presbyterian Church, which was our church if we had one. She tells me that, Uncle was much involved as an Elder and such until the Depression. After that he never went except for a few weddings and funerals. That says a lot, but I don't know exactly what.

Who owed the house in Franklin? Did he own it?

No. It was in a generation-skipping trust but could be invaded to maintain a homeplace for his children. He never had any but could have on his own or by adoption, so all residues came to the children of his siblings.

---

59 Banter is a nice word meaning talking with whimsy to servants, friends and children—particularly children.

What did he live on if he owed it all to the state?

I don't know what he lived on; that was none of my business. But I don't think it was all owed to the state. When it had his racing stable auctioned, he got part of the proceeds. I'd guess he continued to invade the Trust, which he could legally do. The land was being gradually sold off at Elysian Fields at a good price that would have added to his share of the corpus.

One man tells me that John Chamberlain would come by to pay Rogers' bills from a roll of old big bills.

It is hard to understand now that it hasn't been long since cash was used much more than it is today. I'm sure Uncle had cash on hand, and the old bills were gradually being phased out instead of being called all at once. This took several years.

Some people said he lived under reduced circumstances; other said he lived like a king.

In comparison with how he had lived, he did live under reduced circumstances. But if you have a small, beautiful house with two servants and constant guests that is living like a king to a lot of people, including me.

He had a facility... he could take the greenest hand out of any tobacco field and within weeks show him how things should be done and it was done. Then there were beautiful things that belonged to Aunt Margaret. That wasn't unusual; in the households that I knew, furnishings were always considered as to belonging to the wives as a matter of course. In its much smaller way, his life was as elegant as always because he knew how to get things done properly with what was at hand.

Do you think that extended to business?

I believe that this ability is what enabled him, at such a young age, to lead a group of even younger men with little or no business experience to create, in just a few years, the premier financial house of the South, which Caldwell & Company was.

However, I am surer that without the contacts with the moneyed people of the East and Midwest which started when he was still in knee pants traveling with Papa on telephone business, it would not have been the same.

What did he do at his office at the Stock Yards?
Well, he came in every morning. His secretary, Mrs. Cook, who was devoted to him, looked after him as he took care of his correspondence and whatever needed doing in regards to what was left of the farm and the selling of the land. By then Papa was dead, and it was left to my father and Uncle to handle all that.

And all of that land was no small thing. A good bit was bought by the federal government for the interstate system interchanges. They were in a hurry, and the drill seemed to be that they would take it by eminent domain for a certain fee, then you took it to court to sue for the real value, which you got. Also, after the war ended, with the $10,000 GI allotments to the servicemen coming home caused the rash of subdivisions to appear, which was extremely lucrative.

There was a constant stream of people who came just to talk. He was intensely interested to know what all was going on in politics, sports, business—everything. He sort of held court is what he really did at that office.

The Stock Yards was a pleasant place where livestock was bought and sold—a handsome building that smelled like a barn. If you were raised in the country, as I was, that smell is beguiling. That is if you don't object to the overtones of manure which, being a horse person, I don't. The reason it had a bad name for smell was because of the nearby Neuhoff packing house and the city incinerator.

When did he start having the luncheons?
When he moved they became almost every-day affairs. Tuesdays were the best—the literary and history bunch. There was Hugh Walker, who wrote the Tennessee History column for the *Tennessean,* Stanley Horn, who was one of our best-recognized Civil War writers; Campbell Brown, a retired Marine Colonel, was a China buff and in charge of placing the historic markers that are still all over Nashville; Dr. Leland Crabb, author of *Belmont*; and Professor Windrow, who taught at Peabody; Dudley Fort, who was well-read on most any subject, as was Libby Fryer, who was so helpful in arranging Uncle's books to his liking.[60]

---

[60] One of the most interesting days of my life was when we all went after lunch to the old City Cemetery. I saw the tomb of my great grandmother, Ann Rogers, the aforementioned aunt of William Clark who, with Meriwether Lewis, made the first trek across the United States in 1808 and was later Superintendent of Indian Affairs

Was his wish to be at home at night left over from the time when he traveled so much?

I expect so. He laughed and say that he would go anyplace in the world as long as he was home in his own bed every night. He had trouble with his legs, and the older he got, the worse it became. For several years he had a feeling of instability and walked with a cane. Of course, at that time, every man carried a cane as a part of their dress.

What did you think of *A Summons to Memphis*?

I like it a lot, am an admirer of Peter Taylor. I witnessed the last scene where the two adversaries meet after many years of separation. I don't remember whether Peter specified that the scene was in Sewanee, but that's where it was.

When David was up there in school, we drove up almost every Sunday to take him and some of his cronies to lunch at Clara's. I remember the day the scene took place—suddenly Uncle got up from the table, and went to speak to some man whom I didn't know. They walked outside, sat on a bench at the doorway out of my view. They were gone for such a long time that David went to see if he were all right. Just then, they came back inside, shook hands and Uncle introduced David. When he came back to the table and had lunch, all he said was, "That is an old friend." It was Hillsman Taylor, Peter's father and protagonist of his book.

On the way home, he said nothing of the incident. I didn't ask, and it was not until I read the book that I recognized what had happened.

What was the relationship later between him and Dewitt Carter? Do you know anything about that?

No, I don't. All I know was that Frances, his older daughter, and I were the same age, in the same class at Vanderbilt. There certainly had been ill will, but my family was adamant that no such things be projected into the next generation. She and I were never close because we saw different people and never had classes together, but there was no animosity that I was aware of. She was very attractive and cut a wide swath through Vanderbilt.

---

and Governor of the Missouri Territory. After that, we walked up Shy's Hill to see the remaining breastworks of the Battle of Nashville in a small park, then over to Peach Orchard Hill, another battle site. History fascinates most from authorities talking among themselves.

I think that Mr. Carter died at a fairly early age, but I don't know. I don't remember ever laying eyes on him, nor would I have had any reason to.

Tell me why he was so happy when he moved to Franklin?
The strain was off. They had a house full of children. He was pleased with this house, knew he had done a good job. Aunt Margaret liked it. They were a funny couple. One of my favorite stories was: Uncle totally ran the house, he hired, trained the servants, shopped—everything. One day, Aunt Margaret mentioned that she didn't think they had a very good cook. He looked at her and said quietly, "Margaret, my dear, new wives are not difficult to come by, but new cooks are impossible." It wasn't mentioned again.

Why was it easier for him to have people in Franklin than in Brentwood?
It just was easy for many to just walk down the street. Much is said about his Saturday lunches, but the rest of the week was filled with Franklin people, some of whom came every day, and brought interesting visitors.

Bill Ormes, who had the radio station, lived right across the street, Larry Howard, who had the electric service, Judge Gray, Libby Fryer, Beau and Lillian Boardman—she was mayor of Franklin at one time and he was with Merrill Lynch—Ruth Kinnard, who became a judge. I can't name them all, but Franklin was, and is, full of interesting people.

One day Jimmy Driftwood came… do you know who he was? The fiddle player, singer, composer from Mountain View, Arkansas, who is credited with saving Arkansas fiddle music from oblivion. Even after he became a star with his songs, "Battle of New Orleans," "Tennessee Stud," he went collecting the old music in the hills and hollows of his state. I think the archiving of that may have been why he was in Nashville. He looked the part: jet black hair parted in the middle, plastered down on each side, dressed all in black with fringed sleeves, thin as the rail of a snake fence.

He was beguiling the assembled when Jesse Stuart appeared. Who knows how much Jesse is read now, but he was then a literary lion. He wrote stunning novels about Kentucky mountain folk and was an interesting but unfortunately loud and compulsive talker. Poor Jimmy never had a chance.

Nat Caldwell,[61] the repeated Pulitzer Prize-winning investigative reporter for the *Tennessean*, was the greatest dash of salt to the soup. He

---

61 No kin.

would show up regularly, sometimes a couple of times a week. But he frequently came uninvited because he seldom knew where he would be at any given time. On one of the ladies' days, there came a loud knock on the front door. Harry went to answer it and hurried back. He told Uncle that some tramp was at the door demanding lunch, said his name was Nat Caldwell and to tell Mr. Rogers.

Sure enough, there was Nat with a week's growth of whiskers, dressed in last-century cast-offs, grinning. In the process of writing his prizewinning series on homeless people, he lived with them under the Woodland Street Bridge, but he had come for lunch. Uncle got up and went to the door, which he almost never did; you could hear them coming back, loud and laughing. A chair was pulled up, and, after a few rufflings from the feather-hatted ladies, Nat worked his charm. Sounds of gaiety rang.

What I'm trying to do is to scotch the notion that these gatherings were stolid or repetitive. The frequent flashes of theater keep them alive these many decades later. It was as close to a French *salon* as Tennessee is apt to have.

Uncle was a good listener, rather than trying to impart his experience. I think that was one of the reasons he got along with ladies and with children to whom he spoke to as fellow adults and listened without interruption to their opinion.

Was he always that way?

He was when I knew him well, and I believe that people don't change much. They can lay down one thing, pick up another, make all sorts of changes but, it seems to me, basic personality doesn't change a lot. And more than that, I believe that the older people get, the more like themselves they become.

What was the relationship with Luke Lea?

They were neighbors, knew each other forever, and were the two "glamour boys" of Nashville—one a sort of Croesus, the other a Mad Anthony Wayne. Nashville was small; it was the tail end of an era when everybody knew everybody else, especially if your farms were south of town. There was a good bit of intermarrying. For example, your wife Cissy and I are not only Caldwells, but are also kin of Luke Lea through the Warners on Mama's side.

The book *Caldwell and Company* blames a lot of the troubles and particularly the anti-Rogers feeling on Lea.

I just don't know. Uncle was loyal and not a gossip. I never heard one word derogatory of anybody, although sometimes you could pick up vibrations when he was disapproving.

What was your grandfather like?

A patriarch. He was just something else, the armature of this enormous family until the day he died at ninety in 1940.

First off, he was magnificent, with his perfectly trimmed white beard, erect carriage of a born horseman, immaculately dressed—always. One Saturday night after Ma May died, David, my then-husband, and I went to Longview to see him. No doors were ever locked, so we walked into the back sitting room and there he was seated at a card table playing solitaire with a little radio beside him tuned to the Grand Ole Opry. All the lights were on, although the rest of that great house was dark; he may have been the only person there. He was dressed in his usual Prince Albert coat, black tie and white shirt with the high starched collar. I was suddenly overcome and said for the first time ever, "Papa, you look absolutely gorgeous." He smiled and said, "Thank you, daughter. My creditors demand it."

When he rode to the farm at Elysian Fields every day in winter, he wore a nutria greatcoat and Russian-style hat. Mama persuaded him, against his sense of the proper, to let Underwood & Underwood take his picture in this the next time they came from New York.62 Later, they reported that it had caused a stir when displayed in their window on Fifth Avenue; several people had come in to inquire if it were Leo Tolstoy.

My son David was born in June of 1943, and I took a picture of him lying in Papa's lap.63 While I was taking it, he said, "Look at that poor little baby. It makes me want to weep to think of the troubles he may see." Of course, he was reflecting on his own life which had been of highest peaks and lowest valleys. His entire youth had been one of loss—his father, his home, his land—of dire poverty, hunger, fragile health.

---

62 See photograph on p. 75.—Ed.

63 See photograph on p. 77 —Ed.

So he was around when all this was going on. I just wonder what effect he had on Rogers.

My own father and Papa were much closer. Uncle was more attached to Ma May. We lived so close. Daddy walked down every night after supper and sat with him for a couple of hours. Mama and Kay, Ellen's nurse, and I sat on the floor and played Russian Bank, a vigorous two-handed card game.

Was he in any way changed after his father died? Some children are liberated when their parents die, and do whatever they had wanted to do.

I don't think there was any of that—no familial psychosis that you read about in Faulkner. When you have all that number of boys, with problems of their own, you are wise to let them go their own way. He was wise.

Did James E. spend a lot of money keeping Rogers out of jail?

I don't think so. He did spend a lot to keep hands off his land and he mainly succeeded.

There was a family joke about what he said as we filed in to tell him we were getting married. It was discovered that he had stock responses. First, he asked who it was, which was a shock since we had been hauling whoever it was to Sunday dinner for what seemed forever. Next, to the girls, he advised: "If he is marrying you for your money, you would do well to straighten that misconception out immediately." May Buntin said when he said that to her, she cried. To the boys he merely warned, "Don't hit a pace you can't hold." Unlike today, when you married, you were on your own until your inheritance came due.

What happened to the land?

It was gradually sold. As one of the heirs, it is the reason, along with what I got from my mother's parents, that I could travel the world and not have to work for a living. And as I am ever his grandchild, there is still something left from him to leave to my own children, grandchildren and, now, great-grandchildren.

Aunt Margaret

Thus far these remembrances of Uncle seem to be of men's words and Saturday opinions. Aunt Margaret seldom appears. But, if she is seldom seen, it is not because she was secluded in her boudoir or the attic. She heard Uncle's opinion that couples are more interesting when not together and probably agreed... Except on Sundays when she was present at the other head of the table, adding to the conversation with usually very funny tales of her own comings and goings.

She came as close to being a blithe spirit as I ever knew. Pretty she of the dark blonde—later white—hair, waved and curled—was out and about doing lady things with the like-minded. Quietly, as far as Uncle's Saturday friends were concerned, she was lunching and playing bridge at friends' houses, doing whatever it was that ladies did, and playing with the omnipresent children.

My earliest memory of her was at their turn for Sunday dinners: Fields would stand with a watchful eye as she drove the young around the greensward behind the house in her little square willow basket-shaped pony cart at a fast trot, four or five of us at a time. Dressed in her floating flowered linen, she chatted without a lot of notice of where she was going, but the pony already knew.

She drove her car in about the same way to the point that Uncle got Son David, at thirteen, a limited license as designated driver to such as Sunday school and other unmentioned destinations. Both he and Sheppard learned to drive in Uncle's car on the dirt roads and fields around the house.

Their library in Franklin was so small that it housed only one serious reading chair. So she did take to the *chaise longue* in her light and cheerful upstairs bedroom where she passed her time in reading and talking on the telephone—both of which she did a lot. When you went up the stairs, she was welcoming, her conversation cheerful and full of the latest goings-on.

Wednesdays, ladies' day lunches, included her Nashville friends. I don't remember her making many new ones in Franklin except Uncle's—she already had enough to keep up with.

One of her closest was Miss Marie Ransom. Her child, Mimi, lived almost full-time with them when she was very young. Another of her children, John B., became Director of Admissions at the University of the South at Sewanee, where they built a classic little French house on the brim of the mountain overlooking the green, green Collins River valley. In the living room parked a real one-horse sleigh in front of a bay window where groups or singles could muse or pontificate by the hours.

Margaret Trousdale Caldwell.

In the woods secluded behind the house was a one-room log cabin that just fitted petite Miss Marie and Aunt Margaret. Instead of mortar between the logs, it was sheathed in glass so you could see out. It held just a stone fireplace and bunk beds which would only fit two of their size; I could stand in the middle with outstretched arms and almost reach any of the four walls. In back, a lean-to supplied a basin, shower and commode. In front, a fire-ring steadied a large iron cauldron hanging from its tripod where they swore they cooked their meals. It seemed more suited to Macbeth's witches:

> *Double, double toil and trouble,*
> *Fire burn and caldron bubble.*
> *Fillet of a fenny snake.*
> *In the caldron boil and bake*
> *Eye of newt, and toe of frog,*
> *Wool of bat and tongue of dog,*
> *Adder's fork and blind-worm's sting,*
> *Lizard's leg and howlet's wing,*
> *For a charm of powerful trouble*
>   —WILLIAM SHAKESPEARE.

I thought of Miss Marie as slightly daft, and hoped to be just like her at her age.

In winter, Aunt would visit in one of the ancient cottages in Beersheba where she roughed it gaily with the rest, and frequently went to Keeneland for the races with a funny friend whose face and tales I remember but not her name.

As to her loss of the great fortune in the 30s, she seemed to take it in good stride without, heaven forbid, whining. Except for the psychic shock for both herself and Uncle, which must have been severe, her life did not change much. She continued to be well-housed, kept her own lovely things, had closets full of fine clothes that never went out of style, many friends doing the same things. Missing were the extravagancies which in hard times would have been unseemly, just as they are today in the depression of 2009. As to living in two uncentrally heated rooms of a huge house, that was made the best of. There was hot water, coal-burning fireplaces plus an electric heater in the bathroom, which was adequate, a good cook in the kitchen, someone to fetch and carry and help tend the small children running around. They just appeared to relax and enjoy it.

Aunt Margaret Caldwell in younger days

JOHN WILSON THOMAS, JR.

Born: 1856 in Murfreesboro, Tennessee
Graduated: Vanderbilt University, 1877
Married:1878
Died: 1913 in Nashville, Tennessee

Occupation: Railroad Engineer, Conductor, Operator, Train Dispatcher, Trainmaster, Roadmaster, Secretary to the President, Purchasing Agent, Assistant General Manager, General Manager, and, with the death of his father, President in 1906.

Plus all that, he taught my Mama to run Engine One of the Nashville, Chattanooga & St. Louis Railway, the TENNESSEE with the headlight marker 101C. It was a very special engine from the Rogers Locomotive Works, Paterson, NJ, a plant built in 1832 which also turned out the Civil War GENERAL, which for many years has been on view in Kennesaw, Georgia.

Others say that it was built by Harkness & Son of Cincinnati. Either way, she was shipped by steamboat down the Ohio then up the Cumberland to Nashville to arrive on Christmas Day, 1850, to be greeted by about everybody in town. This gleaming new 20-ton eight-wheeler was unloaded on the riverbank at the foot of Broad and pulled by mules to the new frame station on South Cherry Street (now 4th Avenue) accompanied by the myriads.

Those were the days when executives used company property as their own. My favorite story is of Mama running her with Grandfather's private car, with the cook and service car on the spur that paralleled Trace Creek near Waverly. There she shut down the boiler and everybody went fishing for a few days.

He died six years before my birth, but Mama (whose favorite I was) regaled me with him (whose favorite she was) to the point that he was very much a grandfather. Her memory of his red hair made her wish for a red-headed child, then grandchild. Alas, at each of the nineteen arrivals there were only mouse-browns and a few blonds. However, at our last family funeral, there was Blue, her great-grandchild playing hopscotch on the headstones with her bouncing hair just the right flame color.

Following in his father's railroading footsteps of railroading, my grandfather Caldwell once remarked, "He never was the man that his father was," but possibly that was inaccurate. John, Jr. was a railroader's railroader who designed and patented a Pneumatic Switch and Interlocking System which was still in use in 1945 and probably still is. He sold the system, with restrictive rights, for $30,000, which, using the accepted formula of increase of dollars over time, would amount to many millions.

But there was much more to it than that. He was indeed a railroader's railroader and knew well the hazards of crashes and dead men when there was no control from a central switching system, and this he had the mechanical genius to provide.

John W. Thomas, Jr.

III

AND ME, SHIRLEY

O World, I cannot hold thee close enough!
Thy winds, thy wide grey skies!
Thy mists, that roll and rise!
Thy woods, this autumn day, that aches and sag
And all but cry with colour!

EDNA ST. VINCENT MILLAY

AND ME, SHIRLEY... who thinks of myself as a lightweight scholar, product of a first-rate education by teachers patient and skilled enough to build intellectual curiosity into an indifferent mind, a compulsive conservationist with long, long love of land and the running waters of the earth, and a nine foot, 6/7 weight rod, barbless hook, upstream fisher who could cast a fly the size of my little fingernail lightly enough to catch many great trout.

This I know and know full well that the adage that at the end of life what is most regretted are the things left undone for me *ain't necessarily so.* In this my ninety-fifth year, I know I have waded great rivers of the world and explored its mountains—Milford Glacier, the Andes, Alps, Apennines, Cuillins, Pyrenees, Smokies, Rockies, the seat of the gods themselves, Olympus, and others of unknown names. For many a summer, on foot or horseback, I followed the footsteps of cousin Will Clark where he crossed the country with Meriwether Lewis more than two centuries ago up the Yellowstone, into the Bitterroot, over Lolo Pass and beyond the beyond.

Best of all, this was done with one who loved me and welcomed to be loved to the height of my desiring. Thanks to Rudyard Kipling for "But weep that they bin too small to sin to the height of their desire" The world that knows not Kipling is a lesser place.

Us Chillun

On November 6, 1919, I was born early on a frosty morn in the South where William Faulkner rightly says, "The past is never dead. It's not even past." The bond from birth with the land and the goodness of people for miles around was all within fingertips of my origin. I have strived with some success to placate the evils of slavery and take a productive place in the fate of our South, as Papa says we must, and of our earth, as I say we can.

Brother and Me

Meredith, Jr., called Brother, then Uncle Brother by the next generation, the firstborn in 1916, was handed over to our father and to himself to grow up as befits one who, by Presbyterian faith in predestination, was expected to be exceptional on his own. He was. But first he was my brother.

In the beginning, we shared a bedroom with Lula, our nurse. An earliest memory is of whining with an earache cradled in her lap by the open fire and watching. She with a silver teaspoon poured Argyrol from a tiny bottle, warmed it over a candle, tested the heat on the underside of her wrist and poured in my ear—instant peace. I quieted as she screwed in the glass stopper and put it into my grasping hand. There the miracle of cobalt blue gleamed in the firelight—a first awareness of that seductive color.

Bonding with Brother evolved from usefulness. He and I consistently beat the neighborhood—mostly small girls, but a lot of them—at football. He showed me how to snap the ball between my legs, run beyond the goal line and turn around. He then tossed the ball underhanded slowly enough for me to catch with both hands and the help of my skirt. Six points!

Later Mr. Oscar Noel, father to grave Oscar, brave Hayes and Catherine, on the next farm rigged his basement with a mat to teach the nearby boys to wrestle. I was Brother's sparring partner at home and became myself rather adept at full and half nelsons. This talent may have been genetic—my first granddaughter, Meredith Speer, held down the 120 pound slot on her boarding school wrestling team in Vermont where not many boys of that weight wanted to fight until she began winning her rounds. How embarrassing for those macho boys!

As Brother was growing up and space for the coming girls was needed, he was blessed with his own *garçonnière* in the back yard which he allowed me to share even though there was a problem. When some other child was left for the night, Brother was adamant that he not be crowded, so I shared the other single bed with the guest. No telling where Mama was. The bottom line was that he was the one I bonded with rather than my younger sisters.

To read of his life in *Merrill's Marauders*, which tells of the military expedition in the jungles of Burma in World War II, it is amazing that he survived those four years to return to his expected life without complaint or bravado. The only thing I remember his saying was in response to a question about food rations, which had to be air-dropped: "We were always short. In a pinch one day somebody wounded a monkey with a rock. When we started to kill it for a meal, it cried—real tears. I didn't eat any."

There were lumps in his early road which he took in stride. Schooling was a minor irritant but he quoted poetry by the ream such as Sir Walter Scott's:

The stag at eve had drunk his fill,
Where danced the moon on Monan's rill,
And deep his midnight lair had made
In lone Glenartney's hazel shade;
But, when the sun his beacon red
Had kindled on Benvoirlich's head,
The deep-mouthed bloodhound's heavy bay
Resounded up the rocky way,
And faint, from farther distance borne,
Were heard the clanging hoof and horn.

If this has not broken you out in goose bumps, poor you.

He also read history and finance to keep updated in trading cotton futures which he did at a very young age with some skill. But Latin was taught by the application of the textbook to the seat of his pants to the point that almost his every afternoon was thus occupied.

Because of the uncertainty of his schedule, he was given a Model A Ford at thirteen in the days when driver's licenses were not required. This broadened his horizons, as he learned to apply mud to the license plate to escape detection while he shot duck and trapped muskrat, coons and mink at Radnor Lake, then owned by the L&N Railroad for the pleasure of its executives. One day he returned with a dead mink which he presented to me. I was confused because I figured it must take a lot to make a coat and I knew not what to do with it.

At age nine, he was employed in summer as water boy for the field hands at Elysian Fields at 25¢ a day, which I considered a great opportunity. It just consisted of riding your pony down the pike to where the work took place, strapping water jugs to your saddle and riding back and forth to the creek for drinking water. This was my first inkling of inferior opportunities for women to earn real money; no one said anything when I applied for the job. But at age six, I rode without a saddle, which may have been a factor.

He was friends with these farmers who knew the hills and hollows where foxes ran, and Saturday nights with them were given over to hill toppin', which meant building a great fire on a high rise, casting their hounds and tracking them by their baying. Since everyone knew the voice of all the dogs and foxes run in circles, progress was followed and bets placed. Naturally there was enough good red whiskey to last until dawn when all came straggling in. This is what he told me, but I was never invited in spite of begging.

He saved his pay to buy a Walker hound named Rock who had his 15 minutes of fame when Uncle Rogers arranged for him to enter, as a single, the field trials at the festivities of the King of Spain's Cup steeplechase at Grasslands Club in Gallatin. Blue-blooded hounds came by train from afar to suck the dust of our beloved Rock, just as we expected.

Rock's home life was one of luxury, since we had no kennel, and he lived on the back seat of Brother's Model A, in which I was fragrantly delivered to Ward-Belmont and Brother went off to his daily fray with the Latin book.

Parlor at Belle Meade. My sisters Allison, Ellen, and Me.

In 1924, Allison arrived and was named Ann for family icon Cousin Annie Allison, who summered at Longview and wintered in her apartment near Ward-Belmont, where she was the Day School Principal who got to tell everyone to stand up straight and mind their manners. She was the bane of my second-grade existence. Every morning she brought a bottle of milk to me, her skinny kinsman, and watched as I drank it down. Although she did have the tact to do this in the hall outside the classroom, I was so mortified that it was swigged down with great gulping sounds.

Back to sister Allison. When another newborn cousin was named Anne for her paternal grandmother, Mama changed Ann to Allison and so it stayed. I hardly knew her. She had a series of hovering nurses, most of whom I liked but little heeded as Mama and I traveled with my ponies to faraway horse shows.

Ellen appeared five years later, in 1929. I was even further afield by then, and she had a nurse until she was twelve. I didn't and don't know much what they did, but she was pretty, cheerful and funny-spirited, and Kay, her last nurse, was a real sport. She led the summer night after-dinner games of Red Rover and Kick the Can for the neighborhood and was a wicked hand at tetherball.

Once upon a time, she took me with her to visit her widowed father down in Lincoln County on the Alabama border, which was about as far in the country as you could go. His unpainted crossroads store had its Nehi cooler and one gas pump on the front porch and cracker barrel next to the cheese case inside. The only other building was their house next door, similar in design and vintage, where I slept in my first and only feather bed. Paradise!

There was a strawberry-blond farmer hankering to marry her who took us to fish for sun perch in Elk River and mustered baseball games in his pasture where we used cow pats for bases and dodged others as we ran. On Sunday night we rattled his Model T truck into the real outback where the Holy Rollers shouted in tongues and rolled around on the floor of their bush arbor lit only by a fire and a few oil lanterns.

That I was closer to my young sisters than remembered is seen in that I am still an authority on nursery rhymes, which are again being honed for my just-born great grandchildren, Caldwell and Griffin Gardner. But I was Mama's spoiled pet. Who else was not turned over to nurses, traveled the country to horse shows from age eight, shared with her the double bedrooms at Belle Meade, got the new automobiles starting at twelve, a blond Pontiac coupe with crimson soul and lining, sent to boarding school in New York when our house on Caldwell Lane burned?

My Mother, Ellen Thomas Caldwell

At my first Christmas home from school, Belle Meade was in the offing. Mama and I crossed the iron bridge over Richland Creek, drove up the rutted drive through tangled vines, dried grasses and downed limbs left from twelve years of being left empty, cold and bleak except for dust, bird droppings, cobwebs and a pair of brass chandeliers of naked cupids in the parlor. Upstairs there was a great stuffed owl, an ancient reducing machine and, in my father's to-be room, the huge canopied bed left from the long-ago visit of super-obese President Taft. Defiant on its elephantine legs, immovable, its tattered silken fabric breathed slowly with the wind through the cracked window panes.

We didn't stay long nor say much. I underestimated the talent of that dear lady in rescuing this landmark from twelve years of neglect with painting, papering and crimson rugs for double parlors and great halls. The kindness of firemen and strangers who rescued the furniture from my burning house and additions from Grandmother Thomas made this house a home. By the fall, we were ready to move in when the farmer across the road trimmed the trees, mowed the grass, replanted the boxwood and vegetable garden.

Margaret (Dillie) Duncan
Born: 1859
Place: Nashville, Tennessee
Died: 1939
Place: Nashville, Tennessee
Children: John III, Elizabeth (Lizzie),
Martha, Ellen (my mother)

Grandmother Thomas seems a bit eccentric as I start this, but she probably wasn't for her time and place. First, she was rather small, as were many Southerners who grew up during the Civil War, due to limited diet and general hardship. But later she made up for all that in living as she chose within the limits of her times.

When the horn of her box-shaped Packard sounded coming through the gates at Belle Meade, sisters Allison and Ellen and I knew to be on hand to greet her. Under the *porte-cochère* Julius, distinguished in his chauffeur's cap, and she, warmed by a forest-green velvet lap rug of those pre-automobile heater days, were grinning as she lifted her fists in the air. There she was, fully armed with two ice cream cones in each hand dripping on her white gloves. He handed her out, but not before we had relieved her of her burden.

There we would stand leaning over, licking the meltings and dripping on the pavement. Then the procedure was reversed and off they went back down the driveway, beating the same tattoo with the horn.

Aunt Lizzie and Grandmother Thomas

But not then for me. In September, Mama and I set out for school on the three-day train trip to New York, waved off at Union Station by kith and kin. Housed at the new Waldorf Astoria, we had a hat made to fit over my long mouse-brown hair when it was done in a psyche knot at Lilly Daché—very French—crossed Park Avenue for tea with an ancient friend of grandfather and great grandfather Thomas—very elegantly tedious—went to the theater and heard Ethel Merman sing—very nasal.

Then it was time. "Shirley, you are going to be homesick—something you have never been. I'll stay three days so you will know where I am, but I won't call. Don't call me unless you really must, for let me tell you this—your grandfather was utterly opposed to your coming east to school, told me I was making a grave mistake. I think he's wrong. My time up here in school was good; I wouldn't trade it for anything."

With a hug, kiss and grin she was gone. Back upstairs in my single room were two gardenia bushes in full fragrance. They had come since we unpacked my clothes.

I didn't call and she wrote me every day I was there.

Spence School

Spence School was a precise operation. Dressing was quick—a wash basin in each room, tweed skirt with a choice of color of Brooks Bros. pullovers and cardigans. NO jewelry! Breakfast at 7:30 gave little time for the *Times* and *Herald Tribune* outside the dining room door. 8:15 found us coated and hatted, lined in twos behind Mrs. Siedler the swift, and across Fifth Avenue into the trees of Central Park. Back home by nine when classes began, no bells were rung but at the moment doors were closed, brave was the girl who dared to loiter.

Every College Prep student studied algebra, English, French, history and biology every school day. The Finishers substituted history of art, music, aesthetics and whatever for the math and science, I know not. Except for math, classes were seated in a circle in small classrooms for never more than ten. Discussion was the objective as much as instruction and everybody, including me, was expected to speak.

The rest of the days, from seven until 10, were as closely knit—weekly visits to the nearby museums—the Met, the Guggenheim, the Frick—

basketball or volleyball in the gym. (As an example of attention given to the psyche, backward me was named captain of the Gold Team and mighty was the competition with the Blacks.) Two and a half hours of study hall six days a week, a seemly time for afternoon tea with the best of thin-sliced bread and butter, sewing lessons on Friday evenings cheered by ridiculous skits, bathe and dress for dinner in long dresses. Saturday evenings were for closely chaperoned movies or the theater. On top of that, there was Koussevitzky and the Philharmonic every Tuesday evening at Carnegie Hall and the opera in Mrs. Andrew Carnegie's box at the Met every Friday evening during the season.

I almost forgot Daily Assembly. Once Steven Vincent Benét, author of the epic poem *John Brown's Body*, which we were then studying, jarred the hall by casually remarking that a woman takes her hair down for only one of two reasons, to much behind-hand tittering. That was by far the most daring thing of my whole two years.

Assembly was the bane of my early days. When there was no speaker, students were alphabetically assigned to speak from the stage on a current event. My Cald, to my horror, put me high on the list. As we would have said at home, I was a lost ball in the high weeds until some kindly soul tipped off Mrs. Siedler, she the fast walker and keeper of the peace in study hall. Together we chose the simplest, shortest item available and outlined the key points that I could remember without reading, but Fate had other plans.

Two days before my appointment with hell, Miss Spence, our elderly Headmistress, died. Mourned with pomp by all except me who said nothing—hypocrisy would have been blatant and my hope too high that no one would remember that I was even there. But that was not to be; a couple of weeks later, there I was—giving the second-worst speech that I or anyone else ever gave. But it was done.

I write this not for pity but as an example of how good teaching can impart intellectual curiosity and enthusiasm in a relatively short time—in my case, two high school years.

In my first class, algebra, great letters over the blackboard inscribed, "WRITE DOWN WHAT YOU KNOW," a mantra staring you in the face and constantly repeated. This Socratic reasoning—if you know that A = B and B = C, then A must = C—still holds after a couple of thousand years. To this teacher, not to write down what you knew was as serious as flubbing the equation itself.

Miss Eaton, the British biology guru, also had Socrates to thank when she never directly answered a question. She asked a series of small questions which you could answer easily, or with a bit of help, until you had the joy of answering the original question yourself. It took time and infinite patience—which we had. I spent seven hours with her every week either being tutored or in class.

In French class, no English was spoken except by me—*in extremis*. Having already spent two fruitless years of effort at home, my only advantage was in having an inkling of the grammar which was lacking in some of the others who spoke fluently.

French teachers have a reputation for short tempers, but this dear woman with the beautiful voice to repeat, repeat, repeat, turned me loose at the end of those two years to opt for my degree in French at Vanderbilt and a Francophile to boot. I am grateful.

Monday morning found Mama gone and me ensconced for a couple of days in a squishy armchair with proper reading light in the silent library looking at page one of Hilaire Belloc's life of Napoleon. My elders were closeted somewhere, planning what to do with me. Mama's only demand was that I not be put back a year. The asked-for list of summer reading containing only a couple of Zane Greys received no comment. After a perusal of the stacks with Mrs. Siedler, here I was and off I went.

Actually, it was pretty interesting, and lunch was served sooner than expected. The grand surprise was that on Wednesday, when assigned a European history class where Napoleon was being discussed, I had something to say. Glory be!

What Spence School offered was immersion learning, which was recognized by the armed forces as we entered World War II to be by far the most successful way to teach raw recruits much-needed foreign languages, and that success breeds success. I was being schooled for fifteen hours every day in a way that was met with approval and enthusiasm at my age, not yet rampant with hormones.

In the block between 90th and 91st streets of Fifth Avenue, facing the Park, a great house surrounded by green, green grass is now a museum, or so I heard from a young man at a dinner party in Dubois, Wyoming, years later. He had just been named assistant curator and love was in his voice.

It dawned on me what had become of the Carnegie house. Sure enough, it is our only national Museum of Industrial Design, a part of the Smithsonian complex. This was the view from my sixth-floor bedroom—tennis court, lavish garden and 64 rooms lived in by one elderly lady, Deedee Miller's grandmother.

She invited our graduating class to a luncheon straight out of Edith Wharton. The dining hall with its lofty ceiling held the immaculately set table with 30 armchairs, behind which stood some equally immaculate footmen in white satin knee pants and silver shoe buckles. On our being seated, Helen Rudd Owen said in a low but audible voice, "If there were a few more, we could dance after lunch."

Mrs. Carnegie did not join us until we were finishing. A small woman (dare I say mousy?) dressed in gray, she circled the table to smile, shake hands and exchange a few words with each standing girl. When she got to me and I thanked her for having shared with us her box at the opera, she asked where I lived.

"On a farm in Tennessee," I said.

"What do you raise?"

"Tobacco and cattle."

"Angus?"

"No, Mrs. Carnegie. Polled Herefords."

She patted my hand and moved on. I did not realize at the time that she summered at Skibo Castle in Scotland, where she had plenty of Angus of her own.

Her granddaughter Deedee's life did not go well. She was in the finishing school and I in college preparatory, so we had no classes together, but in a class of 32, everybody knew everybody. She went to Scotland right after graduation and married a friend of her father and near his age, but she died young.

Her wedding invitation was a period piece—thick, heaviest bond, slightly off-white with gorgeous stamps, it included not just the invitation to my mother and me to the wedding, but a railway ticket from the nearest seaport and a welcome to stay at Skibo—all engraved in gold. We didn't go; I was studying to take the college entry exams at the time.

Back to bold Helen Rudd who spoke of dancing. She was the big, dark straight-haired granddaughter of William Jennings Bryan who proved by a jury of his peers in the hinterlands of Dayton, Tennessee, at the "Monkey Trial," that Christians are not descended from apes. He was and did many things, including being a perennial Democratic candidate for president on the anti-gold standard currency platform.

On Saturdays when we had unsupervised study hall in a classroom, Helen would stand on top of a desk and orate his most famous and often-repeated "Cross of Gold" speech with all familial bombast.

Early summer after graduation was given over to visiting in Maine.

At Marjory Snare's family cabin near the Quebec border, there were canoes tied at the dock on its quiet lake. But it rained and it rained. I learned to play bridge considerably different from the three-handed game played with Aunt Anne and Elsie. My being the only possible fourth, they were patient and there was warm fudge cake from the kitchen and a fire glowed on the hearth.

The only other people we ever saw, except for the cook, were on our sole venture out to a night spot of sorts in the village across the border in Canada. At the one other occupied table were three boys who talked loud and laughed a lot. A juke box was fed. Finally, one came over and asked the prettiest of us to dance. She was not only the prettiest but the tallest. When she uncoiled and looked down from a good six inches, he only said "Mon Dieu." They left to muffled hoots.

It was not a late night.

Kennebunkport was calendar art of a New England seaport with abandoned tall ships decaying into the bay. Loulie Rice's handsome father was waiting for us in the fog aboard his schooner. (For us inlanders—a schooner is a two-masted sailing ship with the tall mast at the back.) We pushed out to sea but no further—visibility was zero. The cabins were pleasantly lighted and the steward, trim in his white jacket, served something for dinner which this picky eater didn't recognize. There was no threat of seasickness in the dead calm. Next day was the same with a whisper of rain. Day three opened with no sun, but swimming was in order. I disdained the steps and platform lowered to the water and dived instead from the deck.

There is a joke somewhere with the punch line: "Kiwi! What a sensation!" I didn't manage my entry at the right angle—too far out—and the water must have been right at thirty-two degrees because it wasn't frozen. Oxygen and bravado sucked out and only panic led me back to the steps.

In the afternoon when we could sail up the rugged coast, the Adonis of the crew with shoulders as wide as an axe handle stood on the bowsprit. Armed with a handheld harpoon, he struck and brought in a 60-some-odd-pound tuna. Once again, "What a sensation!"

A fish of that size is tricky to land and was done with a Rube Goldberg mixture of lines tied to a smallish wooden keg that acted as a bobber until it wore itself out and then was hauled aboard with the brute force of two husky lads.

Hilda Wheelwright had a fast-maturing, slightly older brother who made Bangor a fine place. Her father was heavy into harness horses; we went to the races every day. To drive a two-wheeled sulky hitched to fast trotting horses in hot competition is no minor sport. Wagering on his entries, they were good and father an expert, was a sure thing.

Later in the summer, Marjory, Loulie and Hilda arrived in Nashville. We Sunday dinnered at Longview, Daddy drove us to Muscle Shoals to explore the recently completed TVA dam and power plant and to Elysian Fields to see the record Burley tobacco crop—67 acres and all over seven feet tall—and the herd of Herefords, not Angus.

The moving van came for most of the furniture and rugs from the front hall and double parlors to park overnight in the barn. Mama put on the most gorgeous ball that Belle Meade had seen in many a year and probably ever since. I had a white silk jersey dress that did all the right things and my best friend's older brother, for whom I had hankered for seemingly forever, was surprisingly attentive.

We all four cried at Union Station, where they started their long trips home. I have never seen them again. It dawned on me the difference between the life of the young in the South and that of New England. I preferred my own.

Belle Meade

In 1941, Mama gave me a copy of *White Pillars: Early Life and Architecture of the Lower Mississippi Valley Country*, by J. Frazer Smith. On the flyleaf, she wrote:

> *To Shirley "Belle Meade" Thanksgiving, 1941*
> A welcome portal! Worn by passing feet
> is the threshold which, for a century or more,
> behind its shelter has offered a retreat
> for youth and age alike—the friendly door.
> A silent sentinel it stands holding the place
> it held through all the years, and o'er
> it clings to quiet dignity and grace—
> but still a friendly door.

My recollections of Belle Meade differ from Smith's, which is of much interest, but a mite overblown, so I have somewhat abridged: "In 1853 John Harding built Belle Meade, the third house erected on his estate just west of Nashville. Since 1896, there were 5,000 acres under stone wall. It became the outstanding stock farm in America with a reputation as the cradle of thoroughbred horses in the United States.

"As you stop to read the marker on the pike, notice the stillness of running water under an iron bridge from which one glimpses the grey mansion scarcely visible through the avenue of cedars. About half way up, the drive is divided by a heart shaped pool outlined with a formal bed of small leaf periwinkle and star of Bethlehem. A large circle starting at the pool connects at the upper end with the stone paved walk flanked by two stone posts. Here, leading from the posts are enormous boxwoods. A wide bed of English ivy ties the front of the house to the ground and, like sentinels on guard, there stand two old holly trees.

"The veranda is graced by six square limestone pillars of two stones, each supporting an entablature of simple design. I strongly suspect William Strickland, who was building the State Capitol at the time, was the architect. He had with him a copy of Stewart and Revett's *Antiquities of Athens* with a drawing of the monument which was the inspiration for John Harding's house. Here we have Nashville's contribution to the Greek Revival tradition which was the favored influence of the day.

"To preserve the spirit of the South, it is most desirable that her old mansions fall into appreciative hands. Otherwise some of the most admirable examples will be lost. Belle Meade is fortunate in the hands of Mr. and Mrs. Caldwell. Their contribution to the house is most noticed in the interior." Upon entering one sees first the circular stairway that winds three stories from the great hall. A warm color is supplied by the Bohemian glass transom over the entrance and upstairs door leading to a small balcony. The color scheme on the main floor, as well as the circular stairway and second-story hall is keyed to this glass—the floors are covered with the rich crimson in the manner of the 18th and early 19th centuries. The wallpaper, a Creole pattern of white background with medallions of urns of roses in grey and ivory was originally found in Louisiana, and the woodwork in the entire house is white. Between the doors leading to the double parlor is a Chippendale sofa in French blue silk damask and flanked by a pair of rosewood commodes holding etched glass Hurricane Shades with white candles which are lighted every evening.

"On the other side of the hall is a Duncan Phyfe sofa, in striped crimson and gold, over which hangs, as she says, Mrs. Caldwell's most prized possession—the life size portrait of her father and Aunt Ellen as children. Under the curve of the stairs a Duncan Phyfe table holds the lamp given long ago to the family by Aunt Kate, a slave.

"The parlor runs the depth of the house with two pair of French doors at each end to tie the indoors with the outside. The side of the parlor broken by two doors opening into the hall had a French pier mirror with gold leaf base filling the space between."

That mirror may have an interesting history. It originally came from Belmont, and Mama bought it for me some years before with money I won at horse shows between about 1925 to 1932. When most of us chillun with chillun of our own moved away, leaving only my mother, father and sister Ellen at Belle Meade, and it was sold, that mirror at 10 feet square was too big for any wall space and so was professionally crated and locked in a closet at the Stock Yards. Not too much later it disappeared and was never found. Just recently, some 70 years later, there have been articles about a Belmont mirror having been returned and rehung in its very own place. I can only hope they are the same. But if they are, think of the story it would have to tell!

"On the opposite wall are two fireplaces with Adams mantels. Here the wallpaper is French Colonial of medallions of deep pink and yellow roses, mauve tulips and a small trailing vine of blue flowers. The cornices are gold leaf and a pleasing glow is diffused by crimson silk damask curtains matching the carpet.

"A baby grand piano, the only modern note, is draped with an ancient vestment brought from Mexico a half-century ago. Another piano is more at home in its Victorian setting between the two mantels. This is of carved rosewood, made by Samuel Gilbert of Boston. The drawing room furniture of carved rosewood, made by Belter, is upholstered in crimson. This room is Victorian par-excellence with none of the usually stuffiness but all of the brightness and charm."

In about 1940, one of those slick magazines like *House & Garden* published a special edition called something like "Ten of America's Greatest Rooms" in which this room was featured.

The sitting room looked like the one we had on Caldwell Lane with the same familial brown velvet sofa that Sister Alison naps on today and the portrait of our Welsh great grandfather whose eyes follow whereever you go or do.

The dining room, which almost glowed in the dark, had chalk-white walls with crimson medallions and the same red rugs had the same oval table and chairs that I had squirmed around forever trying to avoid anything that was set before me. Certainly one of the memorable meals was when we celebrated the silver anniversary with 25 dimes, quarters, half-dollar pieces and my father sat down from carving. He shook his head slowly and sighed, "I sure would have never thought I'd spend this evening surrounded by six women and not a man in sight."

"Next to the dining room is Mr. Caldwell's study containing the only one of the original massive Belle Meade mantels, a livable, masculine room of red leather chairs and bookcases.

"Upstairs an Austrian pattern of wallpaper in pale French blue gives an air of tranquility to double bedrooms connected by wide sliding doors. These two rooms are so similar that the impression is of the opening between must be an enormous mirror reflecting the first room.

"The exigencies of diplomatic entertaining for which the builder of Belle Meade was obliged to offer required ample space, hence the substantial old kitchen of generous proportions. This kitchen is connected to the main house by a large enclosed porch paved with immense stones, six feet by four and two feet thick."

Frazer Smith may have missed something here. The kitchen was built well before the big house or the demands of entertaining. It is my understanding that this structure was the next built after the original log cabin overlooking Richland Creek because of the remaining hostility of Indians called for greater protection. The generous proportions of the rooms of about 20 feet square—two upstairs and down, each with its own fireplace—and solid brick construction would have been far safer and more livable. There is also reason to believe from its location and similarity of design that the rare three-story smokehouse was built nearby for the same reason.

It is obvious that major additions were attached to the original Strickland design, but considerably later: the bathrooms, *porte-cochère* with its upstairs porch, the porch off the study, the enclosure between the house and kitchen, the change of mantels and the vapid cupids playing tag on the parlor chandeliers. These changes from frontier exuberance to somewhat dowdy Victorian were made without much harm and certainly more convenience.

The heartbeat of Belle Meade started early in the kitchen. Six-foot plus, 270-pound Tom Hall, strong as an ox with laugh to match, rekindled the kitchen stove, lit the wood fire in the study and stoked the furnace. A couple of pounds each of bacon and sausage sizzled in big iron skillets, trays of biscuits browned in the oven. Two pitchers of orange juice fresh from squeezing waited. For a while after the war, when Brother and David were again home and our houses were being built, there were seventeen people—nine adults, three infants and five servants—enjoying three meals a day except for Thursday and Sunday after breakfast! And there was my Lena, immaculate in her pale grey uniform, starched white apron and ever-present black cloche of straw in summer and felt in winter. (For you young 'uns who don't know what that is—it's a bell-shaped hat that pulls down over your ears.)

My blessed Lena ruled the kitchen with ease and good humor—daughter of a slave, a listener and a storyteller of plantation life on the lower Mississippi where she was born: "Christmastime was the best. Crops were in, and right after Thanksgiving the hunt began for the biggest of logs. When it was cut, a pair of oxen hauled it into the creek to soak until Christmas Eve when it went into the kitchen fire place. Next day after dinner everybody came to see it lighted. There was much smoke from the wet wood but it didn't matter. As long as a single ember glowed, nobody did any work."

Miss Proudy, the chatelaine, taught her to play the piano, to read, to write with a calligrapher's hand, to master the art of French and Creole cooking, then saw her off in marriage to Nashville where she became the joy of Uncle Rogers' kitchen and later ours. Her brother was a Pullman porter, a high status job at the time, and an actor who came to Nashville in the role of Moses in *Green Pastures* at the Ryman Auditorium.

Having no children of their own, she with her husband, Joe, raised Rebecca, orphan daughter of her dead sister. Rebecca married in Chicago and produced a musical child to graduate from the Juilliard School of Music in New York, top of the heap in that world. That is what I call Progress.

Brother, her real favorite, teased her with dubious tales: "Lena, you should'a seen me last night. I went out to this place in Brentwood where the dancing ladies took off all their clothes." "Oh, Mr. Meredith, why don't you escort some nice young ladies like Miss Henrietta Hickman?"

"But Lena, that's who was with me."

With such exchanges he walked slowly back and forth at the back of the kitchen throwing the ice pick with easy accuracy into the back of the pantry door—first with his right then the left hand—probably his most useful skill in the Burmese jungles. I practiced to some avail when no one was around but it was tough to follow a master.

The day that she died, I had sat holding her hand and listening. "Miss Shirley, all I want is a little peace. I am so tired and feel so bad." I had to go home to tend the two children she helped me raise, but on the way, I pulled into the Hill's Grocery parking lot and wept overlong.

There is a painting in a coffee table book of American art of a barely lighted cabin in dark woods with smoke coming from the chimney and, above, a gleaming golden chariot descends "coming for to carry me home." If anyone ever deserved such a ride, it was she.

White Pillars' section on Belle Meade contains a toast to its benefactors: "May they enjoy its gracious shelter for many more generations. The rest of us may rejoice for something fine in American life is preserved here."

That was not to be. The climate did not change, but the race did. After World War II, so much changed that Belle Meade is now a museum for wandering strangers. When all of us young moved on with our children and the farmer across the pike who mowed the grass disappeared, the Association for the Preservation of Tennessee Antiquities (APTA) was formed to do what it does so well.

A vestige of instant history was Miss Ann, Mrs. Guilford Dudley, as she stood in the balcony of the House Chamber of the State Capitol in all her ninety-pound glory, smiling beneath a wide brimmed hat swathed with a pale pink tulle veil that hid every sign of her aging. As she spoke to those boys down there on the floor, they would not have dared not to give her anything she asked for which, in this case, was the money to buy "Belle Meade and its beautiful acres for the people of the great state of Tennessee."

The longer ago it is, the less strange that I should have ever called that great house "home." I grew up at Longview but saw sisters Allison and Ellen grow up at Belle Meade. It is the casual happenings, unplanned, unexpected, that bind.

Through its door Brother returned after his four-year Army hitch, including five months of combat in Burma with Merrill's Marauders. One morning early I was downstairs with Son David when a taxi pulled under the *porte-cochère* . Brother hauled out and strolled up the back steps, nothing in his hands. We looked long at each other, then hugged, laughing. He pointed his thumb at my four-year-old, and asked, "Is that mine or yours?"

"Mine. Yours is upstairs."

Brother before Burma

"Well, I guess I'll go on up."

Up the winding stairs he went, thin in his uniform, but then he always was. I stood there stunned. He was home.

When Allison and B.F. Byrd were married, plans were simple. Hope Hardy from Little Rock as maid-of-honor, then Ellen and I circled down the stairway and stood watching as Daddy and Allison, at her loveliest, followed. Candles burned and fires in the drawing rooms warmed the winter guests. At the bottom of the stairs my six-year-old Sheppard in velvet dress and lace collar held my hand, but when Allison arrived, she, uninvited, traded my hand for the bride's and held it during the ceremony, smiling upward.

There were Christmas Eves and its trees. In the morning, a 12-foot-tall pine tree was hauled into the middle of the parlors, erected, strung with lights which were left burning and the doors closed. Gradually the Christmas smell of cedar was everywhere as it warmed. Dinner was a feast as Daddy stood at the head to carve the turkey and serve the thin-thin-sliced aged country ham. Mama was as glamorous as a star ruby, as was he in formal dress. Aunt Lizzie, Mama's oldest sister, was frequently on hand being her most charming. The rest of us looked pretty good, with even Brother in his dinner jacket, and Lena had done her Louisiana best.

Momma served the Charlotte Russe from her end of the table but then coffee was in the sitting room in the fragile small cups of Great Grandmother Thomas. (They are too old to be for after-dinner coffee—a late comer in the porcelain world—but may be tea cups from the age when tea was a treasure. Sheppard now has them and uses them for the rest of us on Thanksgiving and Christmas.)

The King James Version of the Christmas story was read—"There were, in the same country, shepherds abiding in the fields keeping watch over their flocks at night,'" and *The Night Before Christmas*—"With Ma in her kerchief and I in my cap…"

Warnings against being caught awake by Santa Claus were repeated, and, after putting the buttered beaten biscuits and milk on the hearth for him, the small ones went only half-reluctantly to bed. The rest of us went into action to hang the aging boxes of ornaments, the icicles and angel hair to the dictates of Cognac or Benedictine that carried on until near getting up time well before light.

The few hours in-between had wrought miracles when wide-eyed children and sleepy adults caught their first glimpse. Still dark outdoors, the room shimmered with lights glistening on the familiar baubles, fires burning in the fireplaces and candles. The awe didn't last long when it was overtaken by a blizzard of scattered paper and ribbons and the sound of ohs, ahs and look! Soon after light, the troops came in from the kitchen and the rattling of paper resumed as their presents were opened. Lena sat at the piano and played for caroling. Finally, Brother appeared palming a cup of coffee, and the miracle breakfast was served.

As time moved on and we with our young had scattered to our houses out back, the trees become more works of art. Morris, who succeeded Tom Hall, had a deft touch with feathered doves, satin bows and silk roses—each had a charm of its own but not quite the same exuberance. It was all beautiful and spacious, but life was no better or worse there than elsewhere. At my now 94 years, I might just opt for a cabin I know or a waterproof tent in infinite space with the critters that hoot and howl in the night.

Vanderbilt

In the fall of 1937, life changed. For most of the summer, tutoring to take college entrance exams took precedence and I was headed back east to one of its women's prestigious colleges. That didn't happen. When September came, there was not enough money and I was home for good. Mama was apologetic; I was relieved. Confidence in my being able to do well at one of the nation's best was shaky. And so, I went to Vanderbilt.

As an example of her dreaming up things that I would like to do unbeknownst to me, she suggested a bed be put on the upstairs back porch so that I could sleep outdoors all winter. She was absolutely right—it was downright splendid!

Staying home turned out to be disconcerting. I had seen the lights, heard the great music, wandered the museums, most exciting, evolved a thirsty mind. It was astonishing how many of my now fellow students took what a reputedly fine university had to offer as secondary to horsing around. The concentration of effort and evidence of results that was Spence School had become a much valued pleasure.

Having never been to school with boys and not acquainted with many males but cousins, it was dazzling. An early lesson should have been a forewarning: First class—Botany 101—this eager eye lit on the most gorgeous and succeeded to will that we be seated side by each. Sure enough, his last name began Bu and mine Ca—alphabetical seating. Things began well—he was a beautiful football player with short dark curls, marble blue eyes, no textbook, and my assigned lab partner. For a time he showed up, gazed over my shoulder at the text, asked odd questions and that I answer "here" to his name at roll call should he be absent which was most of the time. Lab was three hours once a week when the first two weeks he appeared, sat on the high stool and cleaned his fingernails with a pocket knife. That was it; he receded to wherever it was that such heroes recede.

I joined a sorority, became someone I had never been, majored in French because no one else did until Charles Darwin from Cookeville showed up—fresh from Paris and the Sorbonne. Needless to say, the two of us were welcomed by the French Department, especially by dear Dr. Rochedieu who tried to persuade me to go to the University of Geneva, his Alma Mater, for graduate study. That was not then on my list of priorities. Years later in that glorious city, surrounded by snow-covered mountains while blue and purple pansies bloomed by the lake in February, it was obvious why he had been so persistent and disappointed.

For the first two years, the leftover drive from Spence was strong enough for a clear road to Phi Beta Kappa, but, as hormones took over, it weakened, and I missed it by .008 of a point. At nineteen years old, I thought, in the natural course of events, that you married the first person with whom you were intimate, and so it was. But there was more to it than that.

When my father attended my graduation ceremony, it came as a surprise. It hadn't occurred to me that that was something in which men involved themselves. Cousin Jim and I were the first two of the family to graduate from college since before the Civil War when Ma May's father graduated from medical school and Papa's mother from the Female Seminary in Nashville.

There was I in black robe and mortarboard accepting the diploma with Magna Cum Laude writ large and gleaming. On the way home, he quietly mentioned it might be time for secretarial school—which I did—for three days of introduction to dictation in short hand. Good grief! That I knew well and could discuss at length the how, why and when the French conquered England in 1066 meant little or nothing then as now.

I was given a job at Red Ace Oil Co., a jobber for cut-rate filling stations, and so was cousin Jim. I don't know who was the more useless. Finally, we were asked to call on Mason Houghland at Spur Oil as a potential customer. Mason was the father of my best friend, Nancy. I had known him well for years and he was the first adult I ever called by his first name.

I made an appointment and off Jim and I went to his office in the handsome old Bradford house on Franklin Road. (It was soon after torn down to be replaced by an automobile sales room—such is progress.) He greeted us, gave me a hug, and led to a beautiful library looking into the trees. Tea service was laid and poured. We chatted pleasantly for a while, and, as we left, I asked him if he needed some gasoline. He chuckled and said no thanks, that he had plenty.

Poor Jim was naturally quiet and I don't remember that he said anything. He had to make a living; I could opt out and soon did.

Wedding at Belle Meade

Weddings at Belle Meade were beautiful for their simplicity. In May 1942, the day was late-spring warm and bright and the rain gods complied. Because of some old saw that the bride does not see the groom on their wedding day, Brother and I played golf and lunched with a British RAF pilot here for R&R whom we had befriended.

Soon afterward, Mama and I took turns soaking up to our chins in the huge porcelain bathtub sturdy on its lion's claws. I sat on the laundry hamper in front of the window as usual and we talked. Hesitantly she apologized for waiting so long to tell me about matrimony, but had felt it unneeded before. I assured her that maybe it was a bit late but that it didn't matter, we'd let that slide.

When it was my turn, she dressed and went to sit at her dressing table to sweep her now graying hair into its immaculate French twist. Then she came back to sit on my perch; she looked gorgeous in her two tones of light brown organza over a silk slip. There was a problem.

"Momma, you have put your slip on backwards." The décolletage was extreme.

She and I had a longstanding ability to read each other's minds with a bit of body language. When things were tedious in the extreme, as now, she would look straight at me and cross her eyes. She had to dress all over again while I looked out the front window at the guests gathering down by the pool with its tall urn of pink and red peonies.

When she and Eloise helped me into May Buntin's heavy silk wedding dress with its bertha of antique lace which just covered my shoulders, there on my pale arms were red lines of sunburn from the morning golf. So be it.

At the bottom of the stairs was Daddy in his cutaway, twelve-year-old Ellen, and seventeen-year-old Allison looking solemn and beautiful, kinsmen John Sloan, Jr. and Sarah Polk Burch at about nine and six were shown how to carry the long train of the gown and veil. Out we went in proper order through the great double doors flung open to the glorious sound of the Jubilee Singers.

We navigated the front steps and a few feet down the stone walkway when suddenly I couldn't move. The trailing skirt had hit a snag. There was no one there with the young ones to help, but with only a pause they picked the whole thing up and tucked it under their arms. Off we went across the grass to a smattering of applause. When we got to the right place, they arranged all into its lovely sweep without hesitation, help or chatter.

David was there waiting, exotically handsome with high cheekbones, a splendid dancer learned in his few months as a plebe at West Point, and infinitely sure. The deed was as smooth as always. Mama knew how to do such things. The supper was just right, I expect, but not for me, whose appetite was long gone. I don't remember much except the rollicking glee of an old friend not seen in many a year. In the kitchen, when I went to thank the servants, there was Slim, the farrier who had traveled with Charley Hatcher and the ponies in their boxcar. Champagne flowed freely and Slim was up to it. His laughing and hollering rolled from the kitchen all the way across the pike.

David and I left early for our drive to Gatlinburg—out the back gate, up Leake Avenue and on to Belle Meade Boulevard with me sobbing without a handkerchief to blow my nose. It must have been a depressing sight. He kindly said, "If you want to go home, let's do it now." Horrors! I blubbered and shook my head no. "Well, you drive. I am going to get on the back seat and take a nap." And sure enough, he was still there in the grey of dawn when I pulled under the *porte-cochère* of our hotel in the mountains.

Gatlinburg was a small, different place 67 years ago; the Smokies are eternally glorious. We walked the nearest trails, crossed path with a mama bear and two cubs by getting well off the trail; they ambled past with only a few backward glares. The Rhododendron Dance Hall, before it became the Gatlinburg Recreation Center, was stomping good fun with the fiddlers from up in the hollows, and the caller's nasal twang left no doubt what we were supposed to do.

In our wanderings, we found the Buck Horn Inn off on a gravel road and moved in. Designed by a student of Frank Lloyd Wright named Goff, no electricity, good provisions, few other guests and so quiet that just to be was enough. The rest of the week was idyllic. My sense of confusion cleared, and I looked forward to trying my hand in Abingdon, Virginia.

Domesticity

I had supposed that the main object of marriage was to create a home—a place of joy of just being with someone for whom you care enough to swear to commit the rest of your life. This was not to be.

David was sort of an only child of an only child of an only child. His much-loved mother divorced his father early when he took to teaching the babe to ride by holding him in front of his saddle while jumping the farm's wooden fences. Then she went to Louisville to make a living as a medical technician while she left him in nearby Hodgenville in the care of his grandparents. Here he moved back and forth between them according to his whim of the moment. As for me, I was totally unprepared for domesticity by inclination or training. The two of us together knew less than nothing of home building.

Abingdon is a small Revolutionary War town in southwest Virginia where he had lived for several months after leaving Vanderbilt and from which he commuted sixty miles to Damascus, Virginia, to teach in an airplane construction trade school. Its claim to fame was the early Martha Washington College for Women, which had been transformed to an inn, and the Barter Theater, training ground of young actors for the New York stage. This had been formed during the Great Depression and lived up to its name by trading a dozen eggs for an evening of *Waiting for Godot*. It still thrives now by taking only hard cash, and these young exotics wandering about town added a dash to the mix.

Come Monday morning, I walked, carless for the first time in half of my life, with ten dollars in my pocket for groceries. The only familiar note was Mike, David's great Irish setter with a red plumed tail who knew where the grocery was for good reason. When we got to the meat counter, the butcher tossed him balls of raw meat to catch on the fly. Having never cooked a meal, decisions took a while. There was no hurry, David had left way before breakfast time and would be back sometime after seven.

Keeping in mind what I had learned by watching Lena in the kitchen, the whole day was occupied. Shell the butter beans, shuck the corn, get acquainted with the kitchen—a converted stairwell with stove, refrigerator, sink, and one overhead light three steps down from the living room.

The car had been packed with dinner service and flat silver for six, including the goblets I had won in horse shows, silver serving dishes, lace table mats with matching linen napkins, and one pair of bronze lamps. Our apartment was the second floor of an elderly and absently kind lady's town house. She had left a welcome gift of beefsteak tomatoes on the dining-for-two kitchen table under the eaves with a note of welcome and asking that we make her garden our own. The rest was pretty basic: a double bed, chest, straight chair and ceiling light in the bedroom; one sofa with small side tables which the lamps totally occupied and made a futile effort to humanize the lighting—a ceiling light and two white painted "dinette" straight chairs and table. With flowers from the offered garden arranged in a mixing bowl, the table looked all right if more than a bit incongruous. The beans with plenty of butter and heavy cream, fresh corn on the cob, tomatoes and ice tea with garden mint were a success. The whole baked chicken (it was not sold cut into pieces in those ancient days) refused to brown and, with its legs sticking straight up, looked pitiful and almost criminal to eat.

That evening David said he had switched work from Damascus to Bristol's airplane factory which was a closer (but still over an hour) and paid better, and that he would be on the night shift. So we breakfasted together at the all night café, slept, and did something about early afternoon supper. The rest of the time he seemed to either be asleep or gone. It was a mess. We soon moved back into his ground-floor room where he had lived before at the Martha Washington Inn.

Except for Karen Hall, she of the free spirit and raucous humor, I would have been at a total loss. She lived with her mother and younger sisters in the big square red brick house atop their hill on the edge of town, and had besieged David (along with one or two others in this eligible male-starved small town) before I arrived.

She was in the habit of driving into town every morning in the huge black family car and did I don't know exactly what, but one thing was to feed Mike and take him for a run. A small, agile, independent young thing had the nerve to say what she thought, and her canted view of human nature was especially funny in this slightly pompous Virginia town. What we did, I don't remember, but she was never boring, and her being there leaves a certain regret that I didn't try harder to make this town a home even for a while.

To belabor the transmigration of this soul, I mention these:

We were invited for dinner and cards by friends of David at a jewel of an 18th-century farm house. When we sat down at the bridge table, there laid a full deck of antique hand-painted cards; the kings were the image of George III, the queens of the Queen Royal and the jacks of the Heir Apparent. If that lovely old house has been paved over, as it probably has, with all my heart I hope that deck made it, at the very least, to the Smithsonian.

David volunteered me to teach Sunday school without my knowing or his having the least idea of my inclination toward my grandfather's skepticism of Christian dogma. I had attended Sunday school long before, but this was a farce. I had no idea of what to do, and was given no instructions, much less a curriculum. But a savior appeared in the form of a driven fourteen-year-old girl with a loud voice who was headed for the ministry. She took over *con brio*.

Then there was the church service for which I joined him. When he was always twenty minutes late, I asked why and was informed that his grandmother had always been twenty minutes late so that she could enter alone.

The bottom line was that when my father offered me plane tickets to come for visits, I repeatedly took up his offer. By October, I was pregnant, the draft sent David to flight training, and I was home. There I, then we, stayed for quite a while after the war until the government sent the $10,000 Victory Bonus to all GIs. That bonus did miracles for the multitude of the returning young to restart their education or to house the coming baby boom.

It is comforting that behaviorists agree that maternity and domesticity are not wildly acceptable to all women equally. In post-World War II days, the push to get women out of the workplace and into idyllic homes shook even me to feel abnormal. My concept of childbirth was the evening that Mama excused herself from the dinner table. Before my ten-year-old bed time of eight thirty, Dr. Bailey came out of the bedroom smiling and followed by the trained nurse who appeared when anybody ran a fever. Immaculate in her white uniform and starched cap perched like a cupcake atop her round face, she carried Sister Ellen, a squalling red wrinkled face wrapped in a white blanket. Surprise, surprise! It was just what mamas do without a lot of conversation.

When my turn came, there was more to it than that. I don't know where David was, but Daddy, Mama, Allison, Ellen and I piled to St. Thomas Hospital where I wished they would all disappear. When I came out of the daze, it was midnight, and they were all gone when somebody handed over the most miraculous of creatures for his first meal and then took him away. These all-too-short visits went on for a couple of weeks in the hospital and another two when we got home with a nurse.

With Libba and Bobby Chalfant

Then he was all mine—sort of. Having been almost constantly in bed for all that time was debilitating. The nurse told me a lot of something and departed. I hardly knew this miracle child, but, bless nature's soul, she who cannot be denied, for the next decades he has been equally miraculous. Three years later, my blessed Sheppard arrived in much the same way. She, the now psychoanalyst, tells me that ideal for a self-reliant child is a "good enough" mother. That I think and hope that I was. They have both created self-reliant, healthy, productive, generous and civil lives for themselves, and we are friends.

Just looking at the finished products, possibly that could be said, but on pondering the subject, what rears its head is the afternoon that I was some minutes late getting home. Sheppard, age four or five, was sitting on top of our Springer Spaniel, solemnly petting its head as he lay on the front step. There was not another soul in that house.

The eleven acres across the fence from Belle Meade, which had been a truck garden during the war, were divided and lots given for a Stork Hollow of cousins which produced Brother's five, Dan's two, Keith's three, Jim's one and my two to grow up together. Being off a through street, they were relatively safe except for the usual falling from trees, off roofs, bicycle wrecks, and broken glass on bare feet. All of which was provided with instant succor when Allison married Dr. Byrd. He was ever-ready to be Vanderbilt University emergency with a calm voice, needle and suture in hand. Parmer School was within a block walking distance. The barn at Belle Meade had spooky charm and provided a home for Dixiecrat, a sorrel horse for any number of young at once without saddle or bridle. And, of course, Richland Creek out front was a challenge in fair and stormy weather.

There were the raw materials—a pleasant house and two healthy children with playmates at hand, all cousins. David and I went out to dinner every Saturday night with friends from Vanderbilt, but I felt trapped. Things were just not going right. I joined the Junior League and did its expected volunteer work but, to me, they were dead ends with no bottom line. I read—Moon's Drug Store was a blessing. Dr. Moon, a reader himself, had a first rate lending collection with the works of the up-coming authors such as William Faulkner with his graphic mirror of the South, Thomas Wolfe of *Look Homeward Angel*, not *Barbarians at the*

Gate, and others without number who traced the progress of the writing world. And I knitted while frustration clicked through those needles.

It seemed that the kitchen was my destiny. Convinced from early days that the dinner table was the seedbed of civility and pleasant living, I took French cooking lessons, the table was properly set and candles lighted at six thirty so that my twosome could get to bed. The chair at the head of the table was frequently empty and David's dinner in the warmer. For various reasons he returned at eight thirty or nine and the process was repeated. Then he read the paper until bedtime. It soon occurred to me that I hardly saw him face-to-face except on Saturday night. It was like one hand clapping.

As my twosome grew, there was the prospect of Sheppard's going to preschool and things looked up. I took a correspondence course in bookkeeping. In passing, let me tell you that it was one of the, if not the, best courses I ever took. Even for those cash-rare days, the price was right for what you got—a great loose-leaf notebook of four-page lessons. They were so simple that four or five could easily be done in a sitting and mailed back for correction. If there was something you didn't understand or failed to get an A, there would have been a call from the headquarters and help be at hand.

Come fall they were both off to school and I went to ply my new trade—keeping books at David's office which he had established at Stock Yards. It was good fun and we lunched every day at the White Cottage, a pleasant Mom-but-no-Pop restaurant nearby. A number of problems were soothed, but not all.

Nashville Union Stock Yards

In 1914, the beginning of World War I, my grandfather, Papa Caldwell, looked around the chaos and followed his formula to "recognize a need, provide a dependable solution at a price the largest number could afford, and make money at the same time." He bought the several small livestock dealerships, some surviving from before the Civil War, in North Nashville. Soon the Nashville Union Stock Yards became the second-largest in the country—just shy of Kansas City. Almost all drayage of military matériel was by mules, and Tennessee mules were among the best. His favorite son, Meredith, my father, at heart and experience an agrarian in an agrarian age (just like Papa), was in charge.

After the war, in 1921, the brick Exchange Building was built and became the center of the noisy, smelly agribusiness serving livestock farmers of Middle Tennessee and southern Kentucky in the heart of Nashville—thirteen acres of board fences and tin roofs a few blocks from the Capitol. From here, the national livestock market was broadcast every day at noon over the pioneering WSM radio by the U.S. Department of Agriculture. A record number of 7,535 head came in a single day. By then, many were cattle but most were hogs. The mule market had dried up with the advent of motorized farm machinery, as had the use of flatboats on the river and the railroads.

Nashville Union Stock Yards building

By 1974, when it closed because of traffic jams and increasing cost of water and taxes, it was obviously obsolete and sold for redevelopment. Again, Papa was right: "The only thing that you can be absolutely sure to leave your children is in land." In the meanwhile, the Stock Yards had a value well beyond the monetary. Like Longview, it was another sort of family enclave useful for all sorts of things.

The handsome red brick building dominated its setting. Built at a time of rising prosperity, the main floor was raised above the flood line—a must when this low-lying part of Nashville flooded almost every spring prior to the TVA dams. The entry, a quarter circle of cut stone steps leading to three large glass-paneled double doors, faced the corner of Second Avenue and Adams Street. The stone architrave is carved with heads of bull, boar and ram. The oval marble foyer, containing the cashier window of an American National Bank branch and the cigar stand (which sold almost everything), led straight through to the large administrative office with doors at both ends leading to private offices. To the right was my father's and Brother's and to the left Uncle Roger's and Cousin Dan's. In the center was the administrative office, the vault (now that the building is a restaurant, wine is stored there) and Cousin Winston's insurance office, the one Papa started in his early career for any kinsman who might need or want work.

My Father, Meredith Caldwell

Dear Cousin Winston, shellshocked in World War I, was totally deaf but read lips so well it was not noticeable. He and Cousin Mary lived, with their three children, across Caldwell Lane from Longview. She and Ma May were both born gardeners and between the two, I thought, raised all the buttercups (daffodils) in the whole world.

He was also a family archivist, for who can imagine what. Once I was shown the Imperial Russian bonds—parchment with great double eagle seals of gold leaf, gorgeous calligraphy, signed by the Tsar himself—true museum pieces—all carefully rolled in his safe. Years later when the Soviets called them at an infinitely reduced price, Cousin Winston was long dead and no one had any idea of where they were.

The Yards was successor to the former position of water boy at Elysian Fields. It put the boys to work, useful and tough, to learn the meaning of making a living, and to get acquainted with people they might otherwise have not known. The family joke about "shirttail to shirttail in three generations" was avoided by three whom I remember working there—Allison's Barney, Brother's Rogers and my David.

As to the girls, all three of us girls—Allison, Ellen and I, plus my daughter Sheppard, did our stint. We didn't drive beasts or muck out stalls, but we learned something of tracking money and knowing fine people outside of home base.

Mr. Tidwell was one of the two superintendents who was there for his whole working life from 1914 to 1974. His quiet voice and good manners helped set an example for all who entered. The women were called ladies and addressed as Miss plus their first names, and the older men as Mr. with their first names, except that Daddy was Mr. Caldwell and Brother was Mr. Meredith.

However, outside it was different. Brother said the greatest compliment he ever had, he overheard from a couple farmers sitting on the top of the fence of a cattle pen.

"That Mr. Meredith?"

"Yep, that's him."

"Mean looking son of a bitch, ain't he?"

Certainly Mr. Tidwell was a hero to me. During later years, most business took place on the first three days of the week. Thursdays and Fridays were so quiet that his daughter Elizabeth, the mainstay of daily transactions and my good friend, and I alternated coming to work—Friday was mine as the traditional payday. Because it was the way it had been done, payment was made in cash. One day our auditor, Dan VanSant from Ernst & Ernst (who later became its honcho when it became Ernst & Touche,) saw what I was doing. He smacked his head with the heel of his hand and shouted, "Don't do that! You don't know how lucky you are not to have been knocked in the head and robbed! There's a bank right there; they can get their own checks cashed." So that saved me from that, but not something similar.

Son David, in school at Sewanee, bought a German shepherd known for being not too concerned with discipline. Soon afterwards, the dean called him in and announced that either one or both had to leave campus. So Karl Rudolph, Herr von Rumstead, became my darling. We traveled together, including to the Stock Yards where I threw his leash over the radiator and he slept most of the time right behind me—except when Mr. Tidwell came in every day bearing a carton of chocolate milk to much tail-wagging.

One quiet Friday we were there alone when a well-dressed young black man came in the office asking directions. Karl Rudolph slipped his leash and bolted around the corner of my desk; the man ran back into the hall toward the front door with the dog gaining and me right behind. He turned, pulled a pistol from his pocket and, for the first and I hope last time, I was looking down the wrong end of an exploding revolver. When he shot, the noise ricocheting through the building was all but drowned out by the screeching of a dog shot in the eye. There was no one in the building or they had ducked out of sight. The man was gone and I was in a panic chasing Karl Rudolf, trying to catch him, when Mr. Tidwell came in from outside and went immediately to the cigar stand for chocolate milk. He stopped me by catching my shoulder as I passed. When the dog rushed back, he stepped out and extended the carton. They eyed each other for a second then a nose sniffed the carton which had, as usual, been completely opened so he could get to it.

"Hold this and I'll get Ernest [his son], then you bring your car out front; we'll get to the vet." An x-ray showed the slug lodged in a bone, so he was given antibiotics, a few days at the vet's (with chocolate milk), then home. The eye looked all right but its sight was gone; the shot had gone in the right corner and, except that he occasionally bumped into things when making a right turn, he lived out his normal life.

Remembering Mr. Tidwell, I think again of the words of Loren Eiseley in "The Star Thrower" where he tells of Homer speaking of Odysseus returning home after years of war on the plains of Troy and only being recognized by his dog: "The magic that gleams an instant between Argos and Odysseus is the need for affection across the illusion of form. One does not meet himself until one catches the reflection from an eye other than human."

I did not think the young man meant me harm, but Karl Rudolph did.

Only after I had been keeping David's books for three or four years and was thoroughly vetted by VanSant, did Daddy offer me the position of Treasurer and Vice President. It was the first time in my advancing years that I generated money of my own that only partially went to household expenses. The fact that my father was sure that I was competent was no small thing.

Mr. Earhart, my 75-year-old predecessor, was straight out of Charles Dickens—pure Victorian. He was not the obsequious Uriah Heep of *David Copperfield* but the format was the same. Indeed, he was master of all he surveyed (he was nearsighted and didn't survey far) and his procedures were 75% art form. He said almost nothing while I followed him around for several days to learn the drill.

No desk for him, but two ten-foot slanting shelves with drawers beneath covered in hunters' green leather. The height was convenient to stand at or sit on the high stool on rollers that he could scoot around on the polished concrete floor in his three-piece suit. Each move was deliberate as he turned the dials of the great vault and pulled the twelve-inch door of solid steel open, turned on the light and disappeared inside. Some minutes later he began to reappear to set out his books, one at a time: the large grey cloth-covered journal, then the ledger, the file for invoices and, most splendid of all, the double folio book of dark green ribbed velvet cornered with bright red leather imprinted with scrolls of gold. Then he set out two heavy glass inkwells and a collection of straight pens. With great precision he opened the books to the proper place, aligned them and started to process the various papers that lay in the wire in-basket. Voila, he was ready for a busy day.

Each piece he studied over the top of his glasses, and then chose a pen, dipped it in the inkpot and, with a flourish, slowly made the entry in the perfect script of his ancestors. When time came to total a column of figures, he addressed the adding machine with its loud clicking handle. Then he tore off the tape and laid it aside while he took his eraserless cedar pencil and re-added to make sure the machine was right. Only at the end of the day, when all was finished, did he open that huge, gorgeous book and rewrite every transaction.

On Mr. Earhart's last day, with some pomp and a watch, he departed. Then blessed Elizabeth Gilliam, Mr. Tidwell's daughter, showed me how to work the vault combination and where the necessities were kept. In this inner sanctum were shelves galore—some empty and some with boxes that looked like they hadn't been disturbed in years. And there stood the whole series of green velvet-backed folios with dates inscribed on the spines going back to 1914.

There was also a small safe in the vault whose door was left ajar. It contained the book of canceled stock certificates, tax stamps attached and all pertinent information inscribed. It also housed the great seal of the Nashville Union Stock Yards, Inc. used to impress the gold discs on all new issues. In one of the many otherwise empty drawers, there were the loose handful of military medals that Brother had brought from Burma, and a small red velvet jewelry box of some Tennessee River pearls and a slip of paper with my name.

From then on the adding machine whirred, equipment use was reduced to essentials, the romance of days past was gone, and a brash minimalism had arrived. But I was jolted back to recognizing the value of this exaggerated past when we were in the process of transferring ownership. There was a railroad spur through the property from the early days when much stock arrived and departed by rail. The serious question arose as to who owned that right-of-way, a question of big dollars. I was panicked, had no idea of how to find out. Within minutes, Elizabeth opened one of the never-opened file drawers and pulled out a document, dated, signed and witnessed, showing that the Yards retained ownership.

The highlight of the year was the Fat Cattle Show sponsored by the 4-H Club—a private group founded early in the 20th century to connect public schooling with rural life and to introduce new agricultural technologies through the children. On the second Saturday in December, broadly announced by both newspapers, 2nd Avenue resounded to the mooing of fattened steers slowly parading fresh-washed and tails curled, and the excited voices of children leading them.

Inside was less sedate. Mr. Cates, THE Nashville caterer, transformed Daddy's office into a white tableclothed feasting board for some fifty merchant chiefs and politicians. Twelve o'clock lunch featured two-year-old country ham (rare to find then, impossible now). The bar opened at eleven and most everybody came early. The sound level rose as John Chamberlain and helpers poured generously.

John should have been declared a National Treasure. He could and would do everything from cleaning the administration building every night to making any post dinner or cocktail party a complete success.

When the auctioneer called out, the now-jolly buyers were generous to their country customers. I remember the day when the champion brought $9 a pound. For a 1,000 pound plus steer, that was almost $10,000. When the checks were paid out, they cheered many a doleful child's face.

So there were usually five or six kinsmen in that friendly, lucrative, no-nonsense place, doing useful things and staying within talking distance of each other. When time came to close and the newspaper noted its passing, I was interviewed by the *Tennessean* reporter Marsha Vande Berg. With her first question about how I felt, I dissolved to the point of having to blow my nose and couldn't speak. We became instant friends for the while she stayed here—she is still missed.

Something Else I

Meanwhile at home, time passed faster than imagined possible. Son David was still in school at Sewanee. Sheppard, who had been away at school for three years—a last year of high school in Switzerland and two years at Stephens College—had a dead-end job and was engaged to John White, a Vanderbilt Law graduate she met through Big John Hooker.

At her engagement party, Bill Eason spoke of his and Susan's going again to Greece. They told how they had enjoyed it the year before and encouraged us to go. David laughed and said it was last place on his list of things to do. When Bill asked why I didn't come on my own and David wandered off, it struck me that the time was now.

Increasingly I had been puzzling the rest of my life. The only solutions that had surfaced thus far were to become a proper alcoholic matron or to do Something Else.

Traveling alone for the first time was not comfortable, but it happened at a good time. The trip was sponsored by Washington University in St. Louis where Nashvillians had close connections; I would be among friends.

Application and check sent, investment was made in the oxymoron of all times, *Greek Made Easy*. The alphabet challenged any, much less this forty-seven-year-old's, brain. Sentences to memorize, bits of poetry and a few pleasantries are all I remember. The best was the first, *"ma resi poli na ka limbo meta phengari."* "I like to go bathing by moonlight." You can't go too far wrong with that!

With the arrival of a reading list, it dawned on me what a unique opportunity I had stumbled into. Knowing almost nothing of Classical Archaeology, I was to be under the tutelage, *in situ*, of an icon of that world, Dr. George Mylonas, prime excavator at Mycenae, the center of an early pre-Hellenistic age and setting for plays of Euripides.

If he were willing to devote his time, I would do no less than the homework—read the list and plow along with the Easy Greek. Come the day in November, I was ready. I thought.

The night flight from JFK to Athens brought us into dawn sun over the "wine dark sea" of the eastern Mediterranean to Piraeus, port town of Athens, then over the utterly magnificent Temple to Poseidon on its rock jutting into the sea at Cape Sunion.

Piraeus was as dingy as Kazantzakis describes in *Zorba*. The first sighting of the Parthenon through the littered industrial section was unreal. To remember it first on its crag embracing the morning sun brings shivers. This could be no place but Greece and no place in the whole world can rival it.

The heart of Athens is Syndogma (Constitution) Square with its monument to the Unknown Soldier guarded by Zouaves marching slowly back and forth, stiff legged, in their white knee-length tightly pleated skirts, crimson sashes, billowing sleeves and tasseled shoes.

Slightly downhill, a swarm of small tables were tended by fast-moving waiters in universal black pants and short white jackets. Indeed these figures could be symbols of the country—anywhere you go and sit at a table of any description, one appears, fully prepared.

The Grand Bretagne hotel, internationally lauded and seat of intrigue beyond measure, smiled over its balconies with flowers at the northwest corner. The main street led to our hotel and, slightly further, to the National Museum.

We lunched at a taverna with a glass cooler out front where you order by pointing this and this and this. The hors d'oeuvres are all SO good. Tzatziki—cold, cold yogurt with lots of chopped fresh cucumber and garlic with a big chunk of warm bread—don't miss it. Choose one of the little flat fish to be fried with thin potato chips and served with sliced tomatoes and sweet onions dressed only in cold-pressed native olive oil. Pick a table, sweep the cats from the chairs, sit down—all will come in order.

Nearby is the walkway of polygonal stones up to the Parthenon. Pay attention, you climb an artistic and engineering miracle often ignored under the horde of worry beads and pistachio hawkers. People moved, at a comfortable pace, up and down the steep rise through the Propylaea, monumental gateway to the sanctuary, which is itself of interest beyond its handsome proportions. Here lies a section of thousands-year-old Mycenaean defense wall and the later small Treasury to Athena Nike with a depiction of her tying her sandal. A small thing in itself, but a first view of a goddess performing a human task and the transition of hundreds of years to the realistic Classical Period and on to the Decadent of writhing snakes and warriors much copied by the Romans.

The contrast between the hilltop of eroded soil, stones and scattered architectural residue with the harmony of the Parthenon itself is silencing. When Dr. Mylonas spoke, it was slowly. By the end we were filled with details of the wonder of man's work which I cannot possibly describe.

On the first evening we dined, wined and danced at our hotel roof garden within easy reach of the temple floating in the light of its *son et Lumière*. Another Something Else was developing a taste for the local libations. *Retsina,* white wine aged in pine barrels to produce a strong resin flavor, is an easily acquired taste. Word has it that this developed during a period of Turkish occupation—they wouldn't touch it.

Breakfast was at a sunny table with friends, most of whom had been here before and made fun of my Christmas morning excitement. We walked down the street gaping into the windows of one of the world's greatest custom fashioners of gold.

Then, there it was, the National Museum, so small compared to our Met. Inside, the displays were crowded with less sense of order, but with the arrival of Dr. Mylonas, the magic began. He welcomed us with otherworldly elegance then wove the magic web of ancient history, including that of the golden death mask of Agamemnon, whose indomitable fortress we entered next day.

Last, he took us to the great room where stood alone the huge bronze naked god from Artemisia, in warrior pose at the moment of heaving a trident or is it a lightning bolt? Is it Poseidon or Zeus? No one really knows, but I opt for Poseidon since it was hauled from the sea all in one piece after it had fouled the net of a fisherman.

Southern Greece is cone-shaped with waves of mountains weaving into one another, then sliced perpendicularly by the Corinth Canal, a natural fault between Attica and the Peloponnese with a short connection at Corinth which was widened in Roman times. West from Athens, across the canal, the twisting roads made the trip seem long, but we were in Nauplia, sea port of Mycenae, by late afternoon, and I worked up my nerve.

When our bus stopped at the wharf, people collected to watch— including a number of young men, one leaning on a bicycle. I walked into the crowd to him, stuck out my hand, grinned and said *"Ya sas! Nauplia ma resi poli."* ("Hail! Nauplia pleases me much") with which we shook hands to scattered cheers. He stepped away from his bicycle and, with a Shakespearean sweep of hand, offered it to me. I wobbled down the rocky road along the beach with him running beside, chattering English phrases, turned around and came back. We grinned, shook hands again and waved as I followed my fellow travelers into the hotel.

It was done, I had at least one Greek friend and his name was Pericles.

The Lion Gate with its cantilevered arch and facing crouching lions in bas-relief is certainly one of the most recognizable of archaeological sites. There Dr. Mylonas stood in the morning sun chatting with us wonder-seekers to the click of cameras. I don't remember how many we were but, with the guides, it was always possible to hear everything and ask questions. Which was just as well. With the exception of the defense wall of huge polygonal stones so laid without mortar that a playing card could not be inserted, and the tops of the famous shaft graves which Mylonas had discovered, there was not a lot to see across the plateau of what had been the seat of power for centuries. Only a few years later when I worked as a field archaeologist could I understand that when a site is excavated, it is gone, only to remain in pictures, reports and the minds of its excavators. But here there were two exceptions:

The tholos (tomb) is separate from the main site. A wide, downward-slanting dromos (road) enters the bottom of a dome. Only the underside of the exposed cantilever stone roof, dirt floor with a center marker and door-shaped openings on the sides are visible. Here the bodies of the powerful were placed in ceremonial fashion at the center until all flesh was gone, and bones were then put unceremoniously with the rest in the side room.

A water source is indispensable for such citadels, and this one was long a puzzle. Only recently it had been found and excavated separately by a downward tunnel of some 30 feet to where water visibly bubbled. The still-rawness of the spadework held the excitement of the discovery without which this most important question may never have been answered.

Next morning was for exploring other sites of the area:

Tiryns, a similar monumental hilltop citadel of slightly later date, revealed its own sophisticated underground water and sewage system, including metal pipes.

An extensive medical center of several structures included one having to do with snakes which I don't understand. However, such centers making this connection are numerous at other sites, and the *Caduceus* (the symbol of the staff with entwined serpents) is still with us on things medical.

Most dramatic was the stone amphitheater at nearby Epidaurus seating 15,000, which still attracted full-houses in the summer season. Dr. Mylonas stood at stage center and, in a normal voice, spoke words of Euripides—easily heard, if not comprehended, on the top row.

The terrain changed going north to seem a stage set—irregular roll after roll of wave-like hills of almond orchards (a frenzy of pale pink in the spring, I am told) and olives mounting upward to Delphi and its temple to Apollo on a side plateau of Mount Parnassus. Here the Oracle attracted the rich and mighty seeking answers to ominous problems. In darkest hallucinogenic secrecy, questions were posed and answered in such mysterious words that they could be interpreted to always prove true.

The Sacred Way from the village to the sanctuary is lined with treasuries where gold from the grateful was stored. Their design is similar to the temples except that there are columns only across the front, the backs and sides squared off without decoration. We can easily recognize the design in old banks, major buildings in Washington and thousands of others.

Up a rise are scattered ruins of the theater and stadium where the sacred games were played and the chariots raced. Dedicated to Apollo, the sun god, who daily drove the heavens in a golden chariot, the races were of grave importance. Certainly the world-famous and most complete bronze statue of the Charioteer in the small museum testifies to that. He stands slightly larger than life-sized, perfectly balanced; only the left arm is missing. The right hand holds the remnants of reins, sweat runs down his neck. Unlike the Poseidon in Athens, his original tinted glass eyes in place focus on the seminal moment. You wonder which moment this is—of victory or of challenge.

Leaving Delphi, the cross-country trip was briefly interrupted only twice:

At a crossroads, it was explained that here Oedipus killed his unknown father. The story goes that the father, warned by an oracle that he would be slain by his firstborn, followed a custom of the day, and left the babe exposed on a rock for the ravens. Oedipus was found and raised by a wandering shepherd whose king, over the years, discovered the youth's exceptional qualities and took him for son and heir. When the unknown father and son met, they were rivals and bound to fight to the death. Then, according to custom, Oedipus was married to the dead king's wife, namely his mother, and tragedy followed. Down through ages this has called forth psychological significance and given a boost by Sigmund Freud.

It occurred to me how little people change over thousands of years. Here we were at what looked like any country crossroads hearing a tale not much different from our own Hatfields and McCoys of song. "Oh, the Hatfields and the 'Coys, they wuz reckless mountain boys and you know'd there'd be some killin' when they'd meet."

We paused in the mythic kingdom of Croesus, he of lust for gold. When given one wish by a grateful god, he asked that everything he touched would turn to gold. It was granted. His beloved daughter turned to a statue and he starved to death.

"THALLASSA! THALLASSA !"—"THE SEA! THE SEA!" shouted the remnant of the "Ten Thousand Greek Warriors" according to Xenophon in *Anabasis*. They knew they were home from their unsuccessful war in Persia against its king, Ataxerxes.

Piraeus was still dingy, but there was our small sleek ship with a wisp of bouzouki music from below as we boarded. The trip changed—we were closer together and became better acquainted with each other and the Greeks at regular evening libations and dinner at ever-changing tables. Being by myself and not wanting to make social arrangements every night, I staked out the table where young Sammy Howell, a few other early teenagers and the ship's doctor sat. Their enthusiasm for what they were seeing was gratifying, and I made my second Greek friend—the doctor.

Rousing bouzouki music and dancing (men only) was followed by Dr. Mylonas' talks on what we would do on the morrow. The first evening he spoke of the two fixed stars of Classical Archaeology:

Heinrich Schliemann, a German wholesale grocer by profession and a lucky romantic at heart, waited until middle age when his fortune was secure to prove his boyhood conviction that Homer's *Iliad* was history, not fantasy. He used it as a guide, and everywhere a spade was sunk, treasures sprang from the ground. He literally dug up the reality of Troy.

Having set the thinking of ancient history upside down, he pushed his luck further by deciding to have a Greek wife. He held a lottery to marry the girl who could recite most flawlessly the entire poem. Although middle aged, he was considered a great catch, and mightily did the Athenian girls practice. His luck held; the most beautiful and best-educated won and it is said that they had a splendid time. She loved wearing the golden jewelry of antiquity, which may help account for the museum in Berlin having such a superb collection.

Sir Arthur Evans, close behind, dreamed too, but with more care and less flash. He had already been to Knossos on Crete and, because of premonition and surface finds, bought the whole site before he started. Everything lay at hand as it had for Schliemann, but his technique and recordings were more careful. Particularly his dating process, which took Egypt as the touchstone, remains remarkably accurate in placing the Minoan era centered at Knossos from the Neolithic period—4,000 to 3,000 BC. This proved that here was the first center of high civilization in the Aegean world, with great cities, lavish palaces, fine art, writing, codified laws, all peaceful enough to leave no evidence of defensive walls. It controlled trade north from Egypt to the Greek mainland and east to Asia Minor by strength and diplomacy.

A night sail took us far south and morning found me looking out of the porthole, "with what gratitude, what joy" at Heraklion, the main port of Crete, the most Greek of the islands. We headed for its museum, which superbly displays the island's artifacts. The samplings of frescoes are lighthearted paintings of the natural world in fresh, clear colors. The most endearing artifact to me was a skull-size bowl of one piece of milky green rock crystal carved as the head of a duck facing backward over its shoulder—as they do—to form the handle.

The afternoon trip to Knossos was filled with the fruity smell of grapes drying on canvases in the arbors to become raisins in the sun. The ruins themselves were interesting to one seeing ruins for the first time. Sir Arthur's main purpose was to lay it out in proper positions, but the details of the restored frescos, particularly in the resurrected Throne Room, were jarring. The intense dark reds, orange and yellows were hot and heavy in comparison with subtle tints of originals in the museum.

With supper under an arbor, the jukebox blared American jazz. By midnight our ship again plied the Aegean northeast to the Turkish coast and the plains of Troy.

As famous as Troy is from Homer, it is a poor place to the archaeologically eager but ignorant without Dr. Mylonas to draw the word picture. There was simply not much to see—a huge flat, treeless, semi-desert expanse with an unbelievable small hump of dirt with slit trenches and a bit of stone wall.

It did reveal how the contours of the earth change over a relatively short time. The coast of Turkey is so silted that the site of the harbor where the Greeks would have landed has receded out of sight

Samothrace lacks a harbor, and its rugged coast leaves it the most mysterious of the northern islands. To go ashore calls for fair weather, small boats and a willingness to walk—our number was limited.

Originally settled by the Phoenicians, the far-ranging seafarers of the ancient world, it established a reputation of secrecy and barbaric rites, including ritual prostitution and human sacrifice. King Philip of Macedon and Olympias, the parents of Alexander the Great, were both initiates.

The French discovered the Winged Victory which graces its grand staircase of the main entrance of the Louvre. In a stone niche of the ravine overlooking the sea still stand five fluted columns with Doric capitals from whence this Nike is thought to have come. In those days, or even today, how was it possible to move that huge piece of marble from this rugged island to Paris? How many more such treasures do the Greek seas hold?

Below is what I thought:

WINGED VICTORY OF SAMOTHRACE

I have done it
        as I swore,
                that Paris morning grey with rain.

Breast to thigh
    strain the tender marble folds
        ready moving pulse of flight
            mobile wings aquiver.

Forbidding mountains leap from sea
    cut by morning's rising sun
        driving forward geometric wedges
            fog whitened.

Ancient jetty bearing lightly
    dark haired child with almond eyes
        offering wordless cyclamen and vasiliko
            aphrodisian herbs.

Are we home now, you and I,
    Is this the time, is this the place,
        neolythic amulet wrought by human
            sprung from earth?

We shall go, as once we must,
    up the path, four thousand years
        grove of almonds, scent of pines feel the
            chilling Balkan winds.

Axieros, Demeter, Elektra—the shining ones,
    Hekate, Cerythea—Mothers of the rocks
        three breasted goddess with Kadmos, underling
            Epiphallic god.

They were legends when you came,
    Altars covered by newer gods,
        Sanctuary astride crevasse of earth
            Speak the rape of Persephone.

Up the cavea, wild as goats,
    Clutching grasses, gasp for breath.
        Now I feel beneath my feet marble rippling under water.
        Now I gaze the endless sea,
            Now I hear Phengari sighing.

I have done it as I swore Paris morning gray with rain.
    But what know I of loneliness
        of fragmented hand
            that yearns for home?

Shirley Caldwell-Patterson
Samothrace, Greece, 1968

Something Else II

Homeward bound, I pondered what would take me back to Greece, but now was time for Sheppard's wedding. Surprise! When the cab pulled up at home on a Sunday afternoon, she was out by the trashcans, tearing stamps off a lot of envelopes.

"I just decided not to get married," she said, as we hugged and kissed, "and don't want to waste the stamps." I gave her a hand. She didn't continue the conversation, so neither did I. My nest was not empty.

My daughter Sheppard

Gaiety was afoot. Mamas had decided on a debutante season with a rash of luncheons, teas, balls and presentation at the Swan Ball for Cynthia Chandler and my Sheppard. The memorable moment was when they and two Austrian boys did a two-couple polka to rollicking music that makes Austria so endearing. There the four were, arms linked, going round and round, faster and faster. The girls' feet began to rise slowly until their legs swung parallel to the floor with their gowns clinging. When their feet slowly descended, the couples broke away and continued more sedately.

Time passed with my blessed two now-adult children and me, exploring for a satisfying life which, with a few lumps, we managed. David, in his last year at Sewanee, brought friends home to visit on weekends. Bruton Strange, who had gleaming eyes for Cynthia, came frequently. He told of his friend, Cathy, in Athens teaching English at the Hellenic American Union. There it was—except for a teaching certificate for working papers. Dr. Byrd tracked my transcripts at Vanderbilt for the 12 credits needed for a temporary teaching certificate. Voila! There my papers were—I could be legally employed in Athens.

While that evolved, another Greek contact cropped up. H.G. Hill grocery was a local treasure where you saw and chatted with almost everybody—including Hulda Cheek Sharp who came all the way from Brentwood. When she asked what I was doing and heard my scheme, "You must come for dinner Friday. Jean Demos will be there. Rafael is on his way back from Athens now. He has two sisters, Eugenia and Coralie, who is head librarian at the Gennadius. You must know them."

As I drove to Owl Hill, the smell of honeysuckle was an omen. The house, designed by Bob Street, is one of our really good contemporary houses, "full of the sounds of gaiety by night." Husband Walter, creator of the art department at Vanderbilt, had a broad range of friends, of which I was one since my Junior League work was spinning classical records with comment at his direction at the newly formed Nashville Public Radio. We were nine at an urbane, funny evening. There was amazement at my proposal and some envy. Jean Demos cheered me on and armed me with a letter of introduction plus a promise that one would be mailed.

When I told David, the elder, what I was up to, he said, "Well, hurry up because as soon as you're out the door, I'm throwing David out."

Which was just as well; it was time. Had I stayed at home I might still be hanging on his coattail and doing his laundry.

Cathy signed me on as a welcomed transient teacher and found a pleasant room in a pensione within walking distance of the school. Its tiny balcony overlooked a posh square for outdoor dining—perfect site to play fly on the wall. AND she met me at the airport, fed me supper and deposited me safely.

I didn't see much of her after that. She was engaged to marry a Greek, which seemed to take a lot of doing. We did have dinner a few times after classes, but it didn't work. They brought an extra man for me, I supposed, but not speaking, much less understanding Greek, I smiled a lot and wished I was home and people-watching from my perch. Our paths rarely crossed at school. I wrote her a letter of gratitude when I left and hope that was enough.

Classes were from 9 to 12 p.m. Circadian rhythm quickly adjusted and the school laid out a curriculum that was as interesting to me as it was to my students who spoke English. To speak fluently was/is a passport to good job, so attention was no problem. The powers-that-be had the sense to give the most experienced students the least experienced teachers like me. So I was off and running but left with what to do with the rest of my days.

Athens in 1967 was a perfect choice—every place I needed or wanted was within a few blocks, a fifteen or twenty minute walk. Even at midnight there were enough people around to feel safe walking home—the only time that city was quiet was during siesta in the afternoon.

The first morning, I loitered long over good coffee with lots of milk and even better bread as I eyed my fellow pensioners, none of whom spoke English but smiled. Marina, the resident manager, did speak English and told me the Gennadius was just up the hill, seven blocks, on our same street. "You can't miss it."

Everything was just up or down the hills since Athens consists of small plains among approaches to three mountains—Hymettus, Lykavitos, and Lycabettus. (I can't believe that I remember those three names.) She was right about not missing it—so beautiful.

Armed with the Jean Demos letter, I looked in the shop windows so as not to be too early to access Kyria Coralie Demos. When I did, she seemed to have been waiting for me and lavished a true Greek welcome—a kiss on each cheek. In her office, questions flowed—what had I seen, how had I decided to come, how was Jean, Vanderbilt, what did I want to do? "I want to know Greece—ancient and now." She stood up and led to the main reading room—"You will want a carrel, this one. Where do you want to start?"

I asked her to tell me.

Well, "Poetry first, then we'll see." She had her own grateful guinea pig and started by handing me a small paperback, *Five Greek Poets*. "Here, this is for you. Come when you want."

It never occurred to me to have a carrel; they are for real scholars. AND at the renowned Gennadius of the famous American School! For those of you who might not know, a carrel is a tiny room in a library stacks, and all your own so you can leave papers out and books open. Mine had a small, easily opened window with a sliver of sun, a straight-back chair sturdy enough to tilt against the wall and the smell of books. But on reading page one I knew it was no time to linger inside, for this again was a first day of the rest of my life and needed close attention.

Back down the blocks to Syndogma Square, the heart of my Athens-to-be, the big open plaza in the Greek sunlight was overlooked by the Parthenon and the beflowered Grand Bretagne Hotel. It was half full of people with noses in newspapers, talking or just sitting, and its kiosk provided the *International Herald Tribune*, one of the world's great papers. My table of choice in half sun/half shade from the trees was where I sat, reared back, opened the paper and brought forth a white-jacketed waiter. "*Ena cafe, parakalo.*" I said casually, and guess what? That's what he brought!

Little did he know that he was to be another Greek friend simply by my tipping in then-strong U.S. currency. Patterns in life are agreeable to me, so when I showed up each morning the table was free and coffee appeared without order. Hector began repeating English phrases and correcting my few Greek ones.

After the newspaper, my little book brought forth George Seferis, Nobel Prize winner as poet and diplomat, whom a critic once said "strove in both roles to affirm the dignity and humanity of his people at each stage of their bitter destiny—in defeat, dictatorship, occupation and the agony of civil war—he experienced the woundedness of being Greek."

In *Mythistorema*, Seferis wrote:

> "having known this fate of ours so well
> wandering among broken stones, three or six thousand years searching
> in collapsed buildings that might have been our homes
> trying to remember dates and heroic deeds will we be able?"

There was much to learn in this glorious sun, and I was feeling less alone in this other life. A couple of hours and three coffees (served in tiny cups, very strong and about a quarter inch of sludge at the bottom—good hot, warm or cold, so were for sipping), then later, I went home with two perfect peaches and a bag of pistachios from the green grocer on the way. Propped on my bed, I lunched, considered teaching, and napped. Supper inside the cafe outside my window consisted of whatever was the daily special. This too became a daily habit and the waiter expected me with the first course already in place. Then off I trotted the blocks to the Hellenic American Union, a project of the United States Information Service.

Teaching was not as difficult as expected—the objective was to get them to speak lots of English and, at the same time, expose them to some of its fine writing. To get them to talk was no problem as I stood up from my desk and walked toward them. "I am glad to be here and even gladder to have you all to speak English with. I am Shirley Patterson of the United States from Nashville, Tennessee." There was a cheer of sorts and repetition of "the Grand Old Opry." After some conversation about that, I asked them to stand in turn and tell who they were and something about themselves. It was almost electric; few knew whom they sat beside. Their names were like music as were those of their home villages, which most mentioned.

When they finished, I sat back at my desk watching. Sooner than expected, they quieted and looked back. "Who has read the assignment?" They glanced around, grinned and about four hands went up. "I am told that the reason most of you are here has to do with getting better-paying jobs. Is that true?" More hands went up. "You have spent some of your or someone else's money to be here. Is that true?" Hands popped up all around. "Well, together let's keep that in mind and see that you get your money's worth. We may even have a good time."

The first assignment was Robert Frost's, "The Road Not Taken." We read it in unison and talked about how it pertained to us and the road we were taking. This was largely repeated for the next two hours with the next classes with about the same reaction. Then off I went back down the quieter but not empty blocks to my very own home away from home. An all right day.

Next morning in my carrel, there was a note pad, pen and two books, Robert Graves' *Greek Myths* and Sir James Frazer's *The Golden Bough,* plus an invitation to lunch to meet sister. *The Golden Bough* is a dauntingly huge book (a condensation of ten original volumes), but I had asked her to choose. I tilted my chair against the wall and started again on the first day of my next years. Frazer covers European myths and their archaeological evidence from *Alpha* to *Omega*; Graves sticks to the Greek. Both are fascinating!

Days were repeated with some interesting variations:

Frequent lunches with the sisters were full of good conversation which, unrealized at the time, led to my next Something Else. The American School is home to US archaeologists when they are in Athens. They take their meals at one big table where work in progress all over Greece is about the only subject, as I discovered the following summer when accepted for its summer session.

Imagine, ordering your three-minute soft-boiled eggs while hearing that Iris Love has found the missing hand of a third century statue just unearthed at her excavation on Kea. She remembered a possible one in the store room for fragments just down the hill at the National Museum. There it was.

I traded English lessons for Greek with a fellow teacher and student, Theodoro Dalakas, who frequently invited me to the Sunday afternoon movies in the *Ethnicos Kipos* (National Gardens). They were almost always Westerners—John Wayne dubbed in French with Greek subtitles called for a lot of explanation.

He invited me to the wedding in the home village of a cousin where he was the equivalent of the best man. We drove a couple of hours north through the plains where Kalamata olives are grown, to "kidnap" the bride from her parents' house. (Think of the origins of that custom!) That proved easier than expected, her father escorted her, beruffled in trailing white, to the gate and off we went to the church.

Orthodox churches are not built for congregational comfort; there are no seats. You don't see much of the ritual; the ones of any size are divided by a screen behind which much goes on. There is no music but the chanter never flags. Sunday ceremonies go on all day and parishioners come and go at will. This was not a Sunday, but a wedding, and the village church was small without the partition; there was a difference—the bride and groom stood side by side joined by a single ribbon that formed circlets around each of their heads. When one moved, the other had to. And move in unison they did—for a long time while the chanter did his part and the priest admonished them. With many candles burning and guests breathing the oxygen, the exuded carbon dioxide built up a hallucinogenic brew that caused one old lady to faint. When the doors were flung open to send the united into the world accompanied by handfuls of symbolic thrown egg-shaped candied almonds, joy was indeed unbounded.

The wedding feast at the bride's family house was pure Zorba. The newly-married arrived early by Theo's car in time to greet the guests strolling from the church, some of the elders in their native dress. On the front porch under its arbor of still-green grapes, a long trestle table and benches were set for the about fifty guests. Layers of butcher paper, which could be removed when soiled, supplied plates, napkins and table cloth down the center of which were loaves of bread warm from the village bakery, smallish ripe, ripe tomatoes, baby onions and cucumbers, salt and molds of local cheeses awaiting the several lambs crackling on spits in the yard. Whole lambs at each end of the table were laid out with awesome dirks to be not carved, but cut to pieces by the two fathers and passed, fingers by fingers, down the table as it filled with guests. There were no forks but many glasses for the jugs of *retsina*. At the center of the side facing away from the house sat, in chairs, the priest in his gorgeous robes and tall black hat, bride and groom and the foreign guest—me, who alone was provided with a knife, fork and plate with a golden rim and hand-painted picture of Jesus! The sun filtered through the grape leaves on the musicians with strange instruments and the amazed me. I had thought of Mama, what she would have suggested, and took a silver wedding present (the only one I saw) and gave my best shot into this most joyful of afternoons. When it was my turn to give the toast, she would have been pleased with my "*iseihygia e poli cronia*" (health and many years, very phonically spelled).

The bride and groom in their town dress, Theo and I set out back to Athens about sundown, all speaking English with ease. Somewhere in the dark we turned off the road to a stone building sacred to Pan where there was music, slow dancing, a terrace overlooking a quiet pool emptied by a little waterfall, coffee, baklava and urbane conversation. Home by midnight, it was a day that I might never have seen.

The American Express office was the place to get mail (Aunt Lizzie wrote two or three times every week and Mama occasionally, she was bedridden.), cash my cashiers check in US currency, which was worth more than drachmas. And, they offered day trips to nearby islands, which filled most of my Saturdays and Sundays.

The best was to a small island refuge for wild peacocks. Usually there were family groups who took lone me under a wing, but this time there was one David Caldwell, an easily remembered name for me, a multilingual South African from Cape Town. We, with some ten others, sat in a little pavilion on top of a rise for lunch served by the waiters in white jackets, listening to the raucous birds screaming and occasionally flashing their vibrant blue. Only he and I spoke English, but across the table were two voluble French couples who included us in their conversation. He had no trouble, but it took a jolt of *vin ordinaire* for me to participate at all.

That evening we had martinis in the oak-paneled bar of the very British Grand Bretagne, which I had been curious to see. A truly fine dinner in the great dining room was as posh as expected and the wine was not *retsina*. We walked up my hill, had a second and third and fourth coffee outside on Kolonaki Square and parted at my dark door. Next morning he was homeward bound.

This was 1967, the year of the Six Day War in Israel which showed itself in Athens with the sudden influx of refugees. Our pensione overran with a band of English-speaking Welsh students who had been studying land use planning in Tel Aviv. Their leaders arranged to transfer their studies to the Athens center of Konstantinos Doxiadis and I was invited to go along.

It was as exciting as being invited to meet Frank Lloyd Wright, my hero. First, he was gorgeous—a big northern Macedonian Greek, the blondish Alexander the Great type, very fit, brown hair. His splendid voice resonated all the way to this interloper on the back row, telling us in no uncertain terms that in a successful city everyone lives within a twenty minute walk of everything needs—job, shopping, recreation and home. (I was certainly an example of that—I lived carless in Athens for six months and never more conveniently.)

His work is/was familiar to lucky tourists in the series of Xenia (meaning stranger or visitor) Hotels built at many historic sites by the Greek Tourist Office. Small, one story, they are a mixture of ancient charm and creature comfort using easily available, inexpensive local materials and handicrafts.

The school term ended in August and closed for a month; I had used up my means to stay without the added pay and recognized that I was no teacher nor wanted to be—too much repetition, with little recognizable end product. It was not enough with archaeology in the wing. So I was homeward bound.

Something Else III

My Sheppard and David were continuing to mature into civil, constructive and self-reliant adults thriving without their absent mother who, at a late date, was trying to do the same.

Home again, the first move was to find the boss of the language school at the Greek Orthodox Church and ask admission. The priest laughed and said that wasn't what I needed. If I wanted to speak Greek, he would help, but with private tutoring. So it was—three nights a week for a couple of hours. (FYI—Greece has three languages: Ancient, Biblical and spoken. I needed the spoken and wanted the Ancient.)

I hope he was a better priest than teacher; he made the mistake that many foreign language teachers make. We started off declining irregular verbs. (This was only useful in an unexpected way—several months later in the final exam for Dr. Lloyd Stowe's class in Ancient Greek he asked for the 37 forms of the verb *eime*, "to be." I nailed it.) We went on to memorizing 10 or 12 isolated words each session. That and reading the Lord's Prayer was far afield from what I needed: how to find the bus stop or a bathroom.

Next—find what Vanderbilt offered in Classical Archaeology—

insignificant, only two semesters. But what it lacked in size was made up in quality—Dr. Ned Nabers, Princeton numismatist (specialist in ancient coins), and top field photographer for his alma mater's prestigious excavation in Greece (only two permits per season were awarded to about five countries). Our numbers were small, some six or seven, so we met in his office. I don't remember any of the other students or why they were there. Textbooks were useless because data changes with every excavation. We used a pocket-size paperback, *The Greek Stones Speak,* with infinite pleasure. Fifty years later, I keep my copy at hand as a talisman—ragged as a text should be with almost every word underlined. I never pick it up without thinking of Dr. Nabers who, on his alma mater's field trip to Egypt, was photographing the group sitting several layers of stones up on the Great Pyramid. Seeking proper perspective, he backed too far, fell and killed himself.

We had become friends, and he did his best to provide me a way forward via the summer session of the American School in Athens, where I would not just learn but make connections to do fieldwork. This program was designed for Classics teachers, PhD candidates and VIPs, none of which I was, and so I was not surprised when I was not accepted. But misfortune for someone else opened my door—an accepted professor broke his leg at the last moment and I got his place.

Some ordinary days are never forgotten, such as one in September, 1967, when I walked into the great stone chemistry building, Garland Hall, at Vanderbilt. The warm sun poured in behind me to flash the dust motes from the carpeted stair. The smell, called the most accurate of all memories, was of age and books. Mine in my pocket, fresh from the bookstore, made for a happy soul.

The Ancient Greek class was attended by eleven pre-med boys (much medical jargon is Greek) and this 49-year-old prissy woman who had the gall to argue with the professor over the date of Homer's *Iliad*—480 or 490 BC? I had a drop on them by already knowing the alphabet and having unlimited time for homework. We progressed through Aesop's *Fables* and an abridged version of Xenophon's *Anabasis,* which I still harbor in my soul. .

Life was good enough. David and I exchanged words about what we had been doing; I was no more interested than he. When early classes started, I moved into ousted Son David's room and rigged the maid's room into a study. Except for the washing machine, it was quiet and all mine with wall maps and publications increasingly stacked on the floor.

Sunday dinners still rotated from Longview to Brentwood House to Belle Meade, but it was not the same since Papa died. Aunt Elsie, his only daughter, inherited Longview and moved from her home of many decades. One of Uncle Charley's daughters, Edith, inherited part of the remaining property and remained where she long had been the source of strength and more than competent management. Even she became more outspoken. Smoking came in from the cold of the garden and occasionally whiskey appeared. Manners were relaxed; things were said aloud that would not have been said earlier.

One Sunday at Uncle's there was a larger group than usual. Among them was Lucius Burch, my cousin Elsie's husband, up on an infrequent trip from Memphis. It was not mentioned, but I knew that she had ousted him from their house and sued for divorce—only to invite him back after a malignancy was diagnosed on her leg. He had, on the condition that a contract between them be signed permitting mutual freedom of action. Having visions of her own in Ireland, she signed it.

After dinner, most of the ladies left the library to the men and gathered in the double parlors. Edith, her chic self, holding a cigarette in perfectly manicured fingers, said in a raised voice, "Well, have you all noticed how Lucius looks at Shirley like he could eat her with a spoon?" No response. . .

Cousin Elsie and I had been constant companions until 1934 when our house burned and we moved west of town. I went off to boarding school. She and Lucius Burch eloped to great gnashing of familial teeth. The night Aunt Elsie called Daddy with the news, she was crying and urged him to come immediately and do something. In his quietest voice he said, "Elsie, you and Sadie Burch have been arranging this ever since they were born. If I did something it would be to congratulate all four of you. Get a hold of yourself, Sister," and hung up.

They moved to Memphis and Lucius to his uncle's law firm. (This was 1937, when the Great Depression of '29 still lingered. He was the only member of his graduating class who had a job, at the princely salary of $50 a month.) After that, I saw her almost not at all.

He was almost eight years older than I and our infrequent early meetings usually involved his getting me out of trouble, like when I was 12, jumping my fox-hunting mule over the stone wall, the ditch and to the paved road. As a socially backward 14-year-old, I joined a sorority and, come time for the spring dance, had no one to invite as an escort. Family rallied around with a dress from Edith and Elsie's 22-year-old beau, Lucius, for a date, which was embarrassing to this child who should have been at home asleep.

The next time I saw him was much later, during the war, when I took my first trip to Amarillo to see Husband David in flight training. Mama called to tell Elsie that I was taking the night train to Memphis and had an all-day layover, please do something about me. Elsie had other plans and turned me over to Lucius, who met me at the station, fed me breakfast at the Peabody, handed me the morning paper and a magazine at his office until time for the early picture show, said to see it twice, handed me a huge sack of popcorn and said he'd pick me up when it was over. (It was a Leslie Howard picture and I cried both times—lovely.) We supped with Marian and Buddy King on the Peabody Roof. They, having recently had a party, brought a big jug of left-over whiskey sours to set in the middle of the table—very gay even though those were my pre-drinking days. All worked smoothly until I was boarding the train. Lucius asked if I had my train ticket, and I found that I did not.

"Climb aboard," he said, "and I'll retrieve it."

He ran back to the counter and returned with the ticket just as the train was about to head for Texas.

For years after the war the only time I saw them was at the steeplechase in Nashville, and then only every two or three years. There were dinner dances at Belle Meade Club after the race and, when they were here, he and I would sit at a small table in the bar and talk about what we were doing, reading, thinking. He was a listener. His eyes didn't slide to the distance, nor did he shift in his chair. When Edith said he had been looking at me, I was surprised—it had simply not occurred to me. But I wanted to believe what she said, and so I did.

Several weeks later, an invitation came to the wedding at Riverwood (his mother's Nashville house) of Lucius' youngest daughter. I showed it to David but knew he would say no. After decades, I was on a quest to do the unthinkable: The late Indian summer sun was warming as I walked through the open door of that handsome Greek Revival house, looking the absolute best I could muster. Sheppard had lent me her black silk suit with a wide white collar that rose from the neck like a calla lily. He, in the front hall greeting the guests, came forward grinning. He took my hand, "Come on, let's speak to Miss Sadie, then I want to hear what you have been up to."

Plowing through the crowd, we found her in her usual blue damask chair by the fire place. "Well, I hear you have been teaching in Athens. You must tell Lucius all about it; he is charmed by everything Greek nowadays. But first we've got to get this wedding over with. Go on, Son. Do whatever needs doing. Shirley, you stay here with me."

All marriage ceremonies, black and white, at Riverwood took place in front of the fireplace in the front parlor. The Episcopal minister stood resplendent in his vestments, solemnly waiting beside grinning John Pritchard before the low-burning fire. The path opened in the quieted crowd when Lucia, lovely in a gown that looked like it had stood there many times before, entered with her father in a dove grey morning suit that fitted his shoulders like plaster. The ceremony was long and covered everything to make for an "until death do us part" marriage, but it was not to be. Elsie had been close by, but I did not see her after the ceremony.

Lucius came back, kissed his mother, took my elbow, blocked interference toward the dining room, backed me in the corner next to the stairs with "now, start." We talked of Greece, which was much in vogue due to the exuberant movies, *Zorba the Greek* and *Never on Sunday*, about my being back at Vanderbilt and having applied, thus far unsuccessfully, for the summer session of the American School in Athens. When I wound down he asked what I intended to do next.

"I intend to go back when school is out and haunt them until they let me come along in July." There was a long pause before I spoke again. "Come... Go with me in June."

A furor came between his brows as he stared back for another pause. "Yes," he said. "Of course." The oxygen sucked out of the suddenly noisy room.

"Lucius, I want to go home now and don't know where my car is."

"What is it?"

"A dingy red secondhand bug. There can't be but one."

It was there as I went down the front steps. "Apologize to Miss Sadie for my not telling her good bye," I said. "Tell her anything you want to."

My house was quiet and empty when I flopped into a chair—flopped and sat and nothing more for what seemed a long time. The telephone rang and that beautiful, resonant voice that I was to hear almost every day for the next 28 years, until death did us part, said, "I'm thinking that since we're going to Greece, we ought to get acquainted. I'm going to Destin Friday to do some diving. Come, go with me. I'll fetch you in Nashville."

"Yes. Of course. But I have a midterm exam that day, it will be one o'clock."

"I'll come early to visit with Miss Sadie. You come to the house as soon as you can. We'll lunch with her and leave your bug at Cornelia Fort Airport—no one would want to steal it." And so it was.

He flew a twin Comanche that looked like it was doing three hundred mph parked in the hangar. Mighty was the roar at takeoff. At 500 feet, he rolled over on the right wing. There I was, jammed against the door looking straight down into nothingness. Eons passed—probably thirty seconds—we leveled off. I looked at him and he looked at me. Nothing was said for quite a while.

Over the engines' drone he told me he went to Destin to dive frequently. He had a small spit of land overlooking the north bay, complete with an antique house trailer and maid service from a woman down the road. He used a dive boat belonging to Dick Rosen, whom he described as a lovable rogue. Dick and his wife Frau were, Lucius said, among his best friends.

"You will like them," he told me. "They are both so good at what they do."

Destin in 1967 was a fishing town, unlike the roaring resort it became. There were miles of white beaches along the calmly lapping Gulf. That's where we headed—me with my first flippers, goggles and snorkel.

"I assume you can swim," Lucius said, showing me how to gear up. Then he headed straight out to sea and disappeared. After considerable fumbling and wheezing, I managed to follow, but could see no one. The Gulf is very salty, very buoyant, and with just a slight motion of the flippers I was surprised to be comfortably bobbing along. But where was he? When a shout came from the beach, I nonchalantly crawled back to shore. It was obvious that he had been underwater most of the time.

"It's time for a toddy and supper," he said. "Frau is a real cook."

All of which was true but, among strangers, the enormity of what I was doing seeped through every pore. I could eat nothing nor think of anything to say. On the way home he asked what was the matter. I tried to explain pure misery.

"What do you want to do?"

"Again, I need to go home."

"Tonight? Or will tomorrow do?"

"Tomorrow will do."

He put me in my bug and stuck a piece of paper in my shirt pocket.

"I won't call," he said. "But here is my number at the office. You decide."

Nine o'clock Monday morning couldn't come soon enough.

Hie Thee to the Mountains

"I haven't been to the mountains recently," he said. "How about LeConte? Invite Dorothy Reid as chaperon; we'll leave her in Gatlinburg for one night while we go up."

Dorothy was delighted. I shopped at the Army Surplus Store—there were no outdoor suppliers then—for a backpack, Boy Scout boots, heavy socks and rain gear. The trailhead for LeConte (third-highest peak in the Smokies) is about halfway up the mountain, which leaves another 3,000-foot climb over about seven miles. Lucius adjusted my straps, pointed out the trail blazes, and said, "You can't get lost." He heaved on his pack, which I could hardly pick up, and was gone. In defense of his manners, it is as hard to walk too slowly as too fast. Everybody has their own stride, so you are almost always alone. A hundred feet up the trail it dawned on me just how ill-prepared I was. The pack pinched and swayed, so I stupidly loosened the straps when they should have been tightened. There were already hot spots on my feet from the unbroken-in boots. (Should have soaked them thoroughly in warm water, put on heavy wool socks, then the boots, and worn until dry. This molds them to your foot shape.) My toes hurt all the way to my knees.

By the time I got out of sight of the trailhead, I understood life's boldest lesson: there are situations to which the only solution is one foot in front of the other. Somewhere along the way he was sitting on a rock, waiting. When I hobbled in and was asked how it was going, I told him in graphic terms. "Take off your boot," he said. "Let's see." When I put my foot in his lap, he frowned at the lacquer of recently pedicured toes, then at me. "You've got a lot to learn." With his Swiss Army knife scissors he whacked off my big toenail. "They are hitting the front of your boots, no wonder they hurt. Take off the other." When that one was done, he set in with a roll of moleskin, medical science's greatest gift to hikers, a soft pad that sticks to the skin and stops blisters. "That will be better. Come on." Again he was gone.

Surprisingly, the sun was still up when the sound of metal striking something filtered through the trees. There he was straddling a log, swinging an adz—taking instruction from the Abe Lincoln-shaped workman of the closed-for-the-season lodge. I had never seen one; it looked dangerous—a heavy piece of sharp metal attached to a pick handle. Stand with one foot on each side of a good size log and swing it toward you—a moment of inattention and you'd have short legs.

Svea, a Swedish outfit, made a light kerosene stove with a top adequate to boil a couple of generous cups of water for tea. With a slosh of rum and lots of sugar, the world turned back into a lovely place and pitching camp became a snap. Supper was a goodly chunk of antelope salami, a round of brie warmed in its foil atop a second round of steeping tea, a small loaf of warmed peasant bread, apples and dark, dark semisweet Bakers chocolate.

The walk to a rock overhang led toward the setting sun. A black rain cloud came from the east slowly enough for a long time of bright raking shadows over the mountains and the green, green valley below. He sat back on a flat rock, patted it and "Come sit down." Nothing was or needed to be said—this was why I had come.

A Cavafy poem says it:

> "I did not tether myself.
> I let go entirely and went.
> I went into the luminous night
> to those pleasures that were half real
> and half reeling in my brain."

Later it rained, and suddenly women's voices were heard as a camp was pitched nearby. He got up but came back shortly.

"That is one of the most remarkable things I ever saw," he said. "They are two French women with eight or ten girls. When I asked if I could help, they smiled and said '*Mais non, merci. Ca va bien,*' and were just about ready to bed down for the night—in this rain."

Sun up the next morning, the French stalwarts were long gone. Breakfast was cowboy coffee, ginger cookies for dunking, remaining chunk of meat, and apples. Toes were fine, moleskin had held, it was all downhill—joy to the world!

I haven't seen a beech forest for decades, and I hope there are some still standing. There is an acid in these trees that prevents growth of other species so the grove was an open mass of tall trees of butternut yellow leaves still hanging and carpeting the ground. To add to that glory, when rounding a curve, there he sat like an oversize guardian of the bubbling spring near the trail. Tea was ready and, again, all was right with the world.

"It is a commonplace of all religious thought, even the most primitive, that the man seeking visions and insight must go apart from his fellows and live for a time in the wilderness." This opening of Loren Eiseley's "The Star Thrower" foretold our coming life together—I am ever grateful.

Coming down that last thirty yards of golden glow, I wondered who was that man grinning, this most unexpectedly excellent brewer of tea? Someone asked Melina Mercouri her definition of an attractive man. Melina's instant instant reply: "One who likes me.' I knew this one liked me—Edith had said so and I had found out. But what else? What would he be in five years? 10, 20? As it turned out, 28 years.

"Pride and ferocity are virtues as well as love.
    I call to mind the dark mountains along the south;
The rock-heads in the cloud and roaring cliffs,
    the redwoods cracking under the weight of wind;
These things wash clean the mind.
We even can face our lives, to bear them or change them. . ."
                          Robinson Jeffers
                          Not Man Apart

He was a writer of letters—short ones scrawled on a legal pad almost every late afternoon; a sender of books like the ones quoted above, marked with exclamation points, which arrived within the week. He used the telephone and tended to his business, which was his city of Memphis in the uproar of civil rights. I sent first my copy of *Five Poets*, then the travel guide from two years before, later the Kazantzakis' *Zorba, Stavros Michalis,* and *Last Temptation of Christ*.

It is hard today to comprehend the isolation of being born in 1912 on a big farm in east Nashville. His father, and later his older brother, was away from home for the four years of World War I with the Medical Corps in France while his mother, with almost no help, ran the farm and the large herd of Jersey cattle. (In the process she learned to drive the milk truck and, at the end, refused ever to drive again.) The two of them, with his elderly grandfather, Duncan Cooper, who had inherited Riverwood, were the only white people on the place. His nurse, whom he said he loved beyond anyone, had been born a slave. His playmates were the sons of the colored farm tenants and their playground Cooper Creek bottoms where, he said, they "roved like foxes." (It is now a part of our urban natural area, Shelby Bottoms.) They waved and hollered at the keelboats bringing timber and good corn whiskey from the hills and hollows upstream, and saw the steamboats, the H.G. Hill and the Joe Horton Fall, take on the load of their wheat crop for market.

This grandfather, who ran away from his school in Philadelphia at age 15 to ride with General Forrest during the Civil War, had a saying which, to Lucius and to me, was a mantra:

"He who would possess his soul
Must hold on tight and let her roll."

An intriguing quality was Lucius' capacity to be totally absorbed in whatever he was doing. When he walked, he could outwalk a horse for hours; when he hunted birds, he clod-hopped behind his dogs for six or seven hours at a time; when it was deer or turkeys, he sat in a blind without sound for the same; when he practiced law in Memphis, the political powers-that-be (Boss Crump's) got furious; when Memphis was almost burning, at the request of the ACLU, he was getting, *pro bono publico,* the injunction against Martin Luther King lifted in federal court; when he made tea, he had plenty of sugar in his pocket and for horses there was horse-cake; we would follow him anywhere.

Later, when we were gone for longer, exactitude with his mail was high-tech for the time: all was posted on Friday by Miss Moss, his secretary in Memphis, in a big brown envelope which also included fresh tapes and batteries for his *grabadora* (Spanish for "dictaphone.") Usually right outside the post office, he started reading at the top then lay in my lap as he dictated responses. When he'd finished, the tape went back into the self-addressed envelope and into the out-mail slot and off it went...

A portable radio for the morning news kept him posted on the world. New books came with the daily mail. His excitement with Jacob Bronowski's *Ascent of Man* caused him to offer a $500 prize to any of his children or grandchildren who read it and took a simple test. His copy is still on my coffee table for pickup reading—you can open it on any page and be hooked by the physics of musical harmony or the way that Pythagoras concocted his Theorem with square tiles laid in rotating positions.

The law, aversion to the Crump machine and belief that every man (later he would say every person from my hammering) deserves equal right to make the most of himself—these were the armature of his life.

Thanksgiving came and went, hunting season started and I learned what real walking meant over the sodden West Tennessee farmland, watching with exhausted fascination his two elegant white setters work the brush for quail.

I had given up shooting long before, at a social opening-day dove hunt when I was left alone, wounded one and watch it flop in agony. It had to be killed, but there was no way I was going to wring its neck or bite off its head. From about ten feet I atomized it with another shot and knew instantly that killing, especially to be socially hip, was not something I wanted to do. Never again, but I sure could eat them black-peppered, browned in butter, covered and steamed in a dash of black coffee.

Christmas afternoon, after dinner at Riverwood, was his usual time to take off for Cabo San Lucas at the tail end of Baja California for a couple or three weeks of diving. I didn't go; my classes restarted just after New Year's. When he got back, Memphis was in an uproar with civil unrest; the garbage collector strike and the march through town had taken place. One early April day, he succeeded in Federal Court in getting lifted the injunction against another march to be led by Martin Luther King. When he got home after court, he had the call telling of the shooting of Dr. King.

Ten days later, the wedding of May Buntin, a widow, to Horace Hill, widower of her cousin Edith, took place with Elsie, her sister, as Maid of Honor. Spring had come and the marriage was celebrated with familial pleasure. There was little talk of the shooting. He and I spoke of Greece—I had been accepted by the American School and was expected July 1.

Night Flight

The night flight from JFK to Athens landed in the early afternoon. Just to walk into the Grand Bretagne hotel was like finding yourself inside a Lawrence Durrell novel. The flowers on our balcony smelled like flowers; my Syndogma Square seen from the upside-down rather than the downside-up was different—my former table was occupied by a couple with their heads close together. The bowl of fruit, flowers and the quiet of the sixth floor were familiar—the peaches like my former lunches. The hushed paneled bar where I had been only once before for a pair of martinis was something usual. But as the light faded outside and dinner was in order, Lucius looked around and asked, "What and where is Plaka?"

"No telling, somewhere down there. We'll find it." I had never been there but visualized the warren of outdoor cafes in the old part of town close to the Acropolis entrance. The pale yellow street lights came on and I could only ask, *"Sas parakalo, pou eine e Plaka?"* to every stranger along the way. They answered with smiles, points and explanation, none of which I understood. The question became a joke, and I took on the nickname of Sas (which is the second-person formal form of "you"). We finally found something—but not what was expected—one cafe with lights on and one brazier fired.

"Let's settle for this," said Lucius. "We'll get the best table."

Standing in front of the cooler, he pointed at the tzatziki, then with thumb and little finger stretched wide and the rest tucked like holding a glass, he said "retsina" and measured with his hands a large carafe. By then the waiter was into the game and, when an octopus was selected, he was delighted. Indicating that we were in no hurry by tracing the slow orbit of the moon with his thumb and shaking his head back and forth, we were all laughing. A baby squid was also chosen, and a mullet for me. Lucius hissed—

the sound of frying—and *pommes frites* were added. Toward the tomatoes and onions he made slicing motions and poured oil from an invisible cruet. Last he flung out his arms and said in flawless kitchen Spanish, "*Mas tarde, muchas, muchas cafe y dulces!*" The waiter knew exactly what was wanted, led us to the brightest table, shooed the cats and went about his business. If this was not the Plaka we expected, it was a step ahead. Two hours later the Happening began around the corner in the dark.

The Two Nights that Bracketed the Full Moon

The two nights that bracketed the full moon were magical; we had chosen well the time. All lights were off on the Acropolis as we climbed the heights and people were noted only by the shadows they cast. Do not fail to pause at the monumental gateway (Propylaea) to see the Mycenaean wall, and the bas-relief of Athena tying her sandal at her Treasury. Further up was the much-pictured Erechtheum with its colonnade of strong women carrying the roof on their heads. All was awash in moonlight.

Circling the Parthenon was slow and silent until we settled on one of the first great steps and intermittently listened to our murmured streams of consciousness—things one knew and the other did not. I had the advantage of place and used it to monopolize the conversation:

"Look at the shadow of the piece of missing wall behind us," I said, pointing to the ground. "Now turn around and look at the one on the wall behind. They have been missing for a relatively short time. During the Turkish occupation this was used as an ammunition dump and someone lobbed a shell to blow it up. His name is even known—Herman Schwartz—a German mercenary. Some of my friends here were teenagers when their freedom came; it's that recent."

That Athens is dedicated to a goddess and the word itself ends in *ns*, a pre-Hellenic word ending, tells that this was a powerful female-dominated center before about 1,200 BC, when a new culture brought the Indo-European language and imposed male gods. They probably also brought the first domesticated horses—hence the legend of centaurs, creatures half horse and half man at first sight might easily be taken for one magical animal.

It was the habit of conquerors to build their symbols atop the old. The Parthenon itself is built on top of an earlier temple, and one of Christianity's most graphic examples is in Rome where a Renaissance church was built atop the Ara Pacis, the Altar of Peace of Augustus Caesar himself.

My students were fine and we got along well; they said they liked my slow speech, it was easier to understand. They had little trouble with the big words since most of those were originally theirs; it was the smaller ones and especially our inconsistent English pronunciation that was hard. When it came to exams, what we call cheating was rampant—they thought of it as just helping their friends. There was no way to stop it, so I rationalized that it was justifiable because well-spoken English is one of the few means of getting a well-paying job. There was a bit of the Benjamin Franklin attitude of hanging together or starving alone.

They liked best the Hemingway short story "A Clean Well-Lighted Place." The language is so simple, so direct. The story is of a wounded survivor of the Spanish Revolution whose only remaining pleasure was to have such a place for his daily meal. They were so close to the same sort of thing themselves.

The British sent Constantine, one of the Queen Victoria's many grandsons who were spread around to run Europe, to tell Greece what to do. He hasn't been gone long; guess he was better than the Turks. Then came the Colonels to be ousted by Karamanlis—my young friends were excited by him as being progressive and appointing Melina Mercouri, star of *Never on Sunday* and a member of the parliament, as the Secretary of Culture.

Don't trust my modern history. I'm sounder before the late fourth, BC, which reminds me of a course at Vanderbilt in Aesthetics. The professor taught that nothing decent had been done since the Renaissance, was heavy on the pre-fourth-century Greece, ignored the Romans as engineers but poor imitators of art, skipped to Italy and France. By then the term was over.

There was one exception: Frontier Day, when we wore costumes even to class, caught his eye. I was Daisy Mae in short blue-checked gingham, matching sunbonnet, fully armed with a long rifle that Mason Houghland lent me. Dr. Sandburn was charmed, and declared these rifles to be the exception to his rule. He passed it round the room for everybody to feel its heft, examine its delicate engraving.

"Yes, I knew him, great quail hunter. He had a farm across the road from the Harpeth Hills Hunt Club—lots of birds. What did he have to say about Daisy Mae?"

"Nothing, but he sure was impressed with that gun, gave it a forty minute lecture."

The moon was setting and it was cold as we found the way back, inevitably reminding me of the Sappho fragments that form a haiku: "*The moon is set and the Pleiades. The night is cold. I sleep alone.*" I was grateful that, for me, this was not the case.

"Shall I leave a call for in the morning or shall we 'not in the least hurry the journey?'"

Breakfast on the balcony was as good as Paris' best—sweet butter, delicious, lingering. Then, shod in walking shoes, we strode the main street on the shade side (you can tell the natives from the tourist by the side of the street they chose—sun side for the visitors) to the museum. Led to the great statue—Poseidon or Zeus?—he stopped. So slowly did he walk, examining each detail, backing off, coming close that I walked away to leave him alone for a time. When he finally came out, he said, "It's Poseidon. I used to want to be reborn as Verdi, now it's whoever did that."

Our plan for this month together was to not have one. You can always find a place to sleep if you travel light and, in Greece, all you need to do is sit down—someone will show up eager to feed you. We were both inoculated by Dr. Eddie Mims' English 101, compulsory for all Vanderbilt Freshmen. The young would memorize poetry—or else. Number one was "Ulysses"; if you could recite this, an A+ was a shoo-in. With the passage of years, we ex-Freshmen are a dead or dying breed, but here again is the last verse from Lucius gone and me at 94 years.

Come, my friends,
'Tis not too late to seek a newer world.
Push off, and sitting well in order smite
The sounding furrows; for my purpose holds

To sail beyond the sunset, and the baths
Of all the western stars, until I die.
It may be that the gulfs will wash us down:
It may be that we shall touch the Happy Isles,
And see the great Achilles, whom we knew.
Tho much is taken, much abides; and tho
We are not now of that strength which in the old days
Moved earth and heaven, that which we are, we are;
One equal temper of heroic hearts,
Made weak by time and fate, but strong in will
To strive, to seek, to find, and not to yield.

Alfred, Lord Tennyson

By late afternoon our load was lightened by rolling my clothes into the backpack where, carrying no tent or sleeping bags, there was plenty of room. Goggles, flippers and snorkels fitted into side pockets. My suitcase, with a quick visit, was stored at The School, for which he showed proper respect. When ready to push off on the night ferry to Crete, on the top deck, in the late sunshine, beer bottles in hand, tales of our parallel lives were traded.

Heraklion

After a night of being rocked in the cradle of the deepest Aegean, there again was the harbor—dingy as before—a place to get out of, but not yet.

Their museum is the world's greatest for Minoan art and, to me, the most beguiling. To come to Crete and first be introduced to Knossos as restored by Sir Arthur Evan's concept is a mistake. There is a difference of opinion as to whether the Minoans were heavy-handed bosses of the ancient world at the crossroads of Egypt, Greece and Asia Minor or the power that enabled peaceful interaction. My Dr. Nabers at VU opted for the latter, citing the absence of defense walls until centuries later during the Crusades when European Christians came to slaughter the natives of Jerusalem and were slaughtered in return. Start instead by seeing this collection of Minoan artifacts so well-displayed, reflecting interest in the natural world, particularly the sea, in colors of enthusiasm and energy.

The afternoon was different. I had read that the funeral of Nikos Kazantzakis brought the largest crowd ever to congregate here. He had been an active member of the church, even spent over a year at the silent Mt. Athos in meditation and prayer, but when his *Last Temptation of Christ* was published, he was excommunicated, which forbade burial within the city walls. When he died, his followers brought him to a tomb atop the wall overlooking the harbor.

We climbed rough stone steps to the slab of white marble (some twelve by fifteen feet) on a slightly larger base facing the sea. Square cut with no embellishment, the inscription is three short lines—*I HAVE NOTHING. I WANT NOTHING. I AM FREE.* Name, no dates, a flush container for an eternal flame.

On our right there sat on a low wall in perfect profile a bent woman swathed in blackest mourning, head bowed, silent, motionless. We walked to the left to examine the strikingly contemporary grave. Sitting on the opposite low wall, I told him what I would have had she not been there—that the island in the near distance was the birthplace of El Greco. For those of you who may not know, he was one, if not the, most famous of all of the Spanish Renaissance painters who, among other things, did a series of Saints all in a very recognizable elongated style. At Spence School we made regular rounds of the neighborhood museums, including the Frick, where a huge one hangs to be seen first as you came in the front door—I think of St. Jerome.

Very, very gradually the lady in black had straightened. When we left, she was sitting erect, head up. We nodded but did not speak.

Hagios Nikolaos

Hagios Nikolaos, one of the small harbors on the northern coast, was a village of some sophistication. Our inn was a pastel-colored reception and office with the dining room under an arbor at the back overlooking a boatless cove. The guest rooms sprinkled down to the shore were typically Cretan—thick walls, tile floors, furnished by a built-in chair-height solid step-like structure that encircled the entire room. With cushions they were chairs for many, with mattresses they were beds, the rest were tables or whatever you needed—ultra convenient, all whitewashed. Color was added by handmade rugs and coverings, fresh-cut flowers and the ever-present bowl of fruit—this time it was figs.

We supped early to watch the afterglow; there was lamb, so good! Then the snorkels, etc., came out for the first time. The mouth of the cove was a long haul, but this time Lucius swam close by. It was so easy, so beautiful, so altogether ours. Coming back, the moon changed it to liquid—what? Once upon a time, a broken medical thermometer spilled mercury (pure poison) on the sitting room rug at Longview. I lay on my stomach playing with it—watching how, unlike other liquids, it clings to itself in silver beads that could be pushed into smaller or bigger forms without ever losing its sensuous shape. The sea was such silver rolling effortlessly, changing shape and shadows.

Next morning early, I hied myself to the kitchen, where the cook had jumped ship and worked a while in New York and so spoke English. Over our chatter, he fixed a tray with coffee, warm bread, honey and figs with heavy cream. Lucius got up to shake hands with lavish thanks. Soon we were headed down the coast with much lunch in a basket.

That part of Crete was thinly populated; we didn't see another soul. Then a road sign with arrow pointed ahead: *Kato Zakros*.

"Good grief, I know about that," I said. "It was one of the great Minoan ports, and, equally important, it was here that the tablets were excavated which Michael Ventris used as a Rosetta Stone when he deciphered Linear B." (A primitive Mycenaean lingual forerunner of modern Indo-European Greek.)

As we went on, the road turned to gravel and ended on the magnificent beach of a cove with upright stones like pillars at the mouth—surely the birthplace of Titans. At the far end of the beach was a stone hut from which approached a magnificent man. His head was covered with short gray curls like the caracul sheep from which Russians make their hats. His left arm was missing from the shoulder down, an injury caused by dynamiting fish, as he made clear by noises and hand motions—he seemed very proud of it. There was no way to tell if he were a guard or had just built a house and moved in. It didn't look large enough, unless he slept catty-cornered.

The basket was fetched; the jug of *retsina* came first, then chunks of cold lamb with a mint condiment that was sweet, sour and hot, a still-warm loaf, tomatoes and onions to be eaten like apples, and a sweet that looked like shredded wheat soaked in honey with lemon and spices.

In some way I'll never quite understand, they carried on a conversation—one speaking Greek and the other kitchen Spanish and broken English. *"Pou eine o Kato Zakros?"* I interjected during a lull at which this Zorba creature looked at me as if I had risen from the sand. (Greece was so male-dominated that the only couples I knew who married quickly divorced.) He pointed to the low purplish hills behind us, but said there was little to see and that the small stone structures on the beach before us that continued out of sight underwater were superstructures to a wharf of unknown date, but probably very old since this extreme east end of Crete is known to have fallen four meters (12 feet) at some ancient time.

When there remained neither drop nor crumb, he rose with a deep bow to me, an abrazo for Himself, and retired, never to be seen again. We swam to the gates of the cove and settled on the rocks to gaze seaward to Asia Minor between naps and quiet talk.

Lucius told me about the chaos straining Memphis after the killing of Martin Luther King, expounded on the rare opportunities that catastrophe alone can bring if advantage is taken and how that works. Would that he were here now to tell me that again.

In the last few weeks I have read two things: The Yellow River in China now warns its two million people that their water is no longer safe. The great Ogallala Aquifer, largest in the US, which supplies irrigation water to eight western states of our so-called "bread basket," at the rate it is going will be depleted within twenty-five years. My great granddaughter less than six months old, what of her future?

Lucius wandered back to the first time he crossed swords with "Boss" Crump in his first case as a recent law graduate in 1937. One "Piggy" Moore, a known local gambler, was incensed by a notice from the Mayor to leave town for good and sued. Lucius got the case moved to Federal Court, where he got a judgment for the Plaintiff on the grounds that no specific crime was cited. Piggy was exonerated and indignantly moved to Las Vegas where he became a pillar of society. He still sent invitations to visit.

"We ought to go," Lucius said. "You'd be treated like the Queen of Sheba."

It was dark in the arbor, but a place was found for salty us. This life was habit-forming, so over dinner we allotted two additional days.

Then mounted two to one Moped, we headed south to the coastal mountains with the idea of exploring a Crusader castle, but there was no place to refuel. Being rescued opened a whole "new experience." (Himself held with the words of a French philosopher who declared a good life is summed up in the acronym SARNE which stands for Security, Affection, Recognition and New Experience.)

This new experience came on a very small white burro, ears flapping. He was a true Cretan, dressed to the teeth in highly polished knee-length boots, baggy black pants, balloon-sleeved white shirt and crimson sash. His black moustache was perfectly trimmed to flow well below his chin. There is such a thing as the "Cretan Strut," which was displayed even as he was seated on his mount's rump. Had he been on its back, his feet would have dragged and possibly all would have collapsed.

Lucius' greeting was pure pantomime. That Lucius was twice his size mattered not; it was a meeting of giants, with the smaller in the role of hero. They agreed that getting fuel was no problem and then an offer of a ride, which was accepted. Down the road with the same aplomb, Himself rode with back straight, knees bent to avoid foot dragging, switch lightly in hand. On his return there were compliments exchanged and we proceeded up the hill to the house where I was finally spoken to. With my best pronunciation, *"Kali mera, Sas."* he answered with a swoop, *"Kala, kala!"* and even held the door open for me.

The house was larger than ours at the inn but with the same structure around the room on which were seated about ten people. More continued to arrive until it filled. Our host made a speech while we were served on a tray two large glasses of water and small plates of very sweet preserved figs. The two stars retired somewhere and returned with a container of kerosene which the host, with the rest of us following, carried out the front door and refilled the scooter to overflowing. Everybody shook hands with everybody else and off we went with waves and fluttering handkerchiefs.

The ferry ride up the Aegean coast off Turkey brought its own new experience when the boat stopped and a caique came from shore of a small island. The harbor was too shallow for the ferry, which stopped twice a week for mail and passengers, if there were any.

"What about taking a look at it?" Lucius asked. "Let's get our stuff and stay until its next call."

The boatman told us that this was a strange place and we could go back to the ferry if we didn't like the looks. The look was a stage set of aquamarine water over white sand in a small bay blocked from view by a low breakwater, a few bobbing fishing boats with prows sporting great blue evil-eyes that repel unwanted spirits. Two or three more seaworthy boats had dashboards hinged to struts on the starboard side that could be lowered or raised as needed. Small but steep hills rose on each side—atop the left, the old village brooded, on the right rose an ancient white church. In the V between were three structures: the open lagoons of an abandoned desalination plant eroding back into the sea, a four story hotel of the same period but in better shape by not much (these remains were left by the Italians who occupied the area for some years until after World War II; front and off-center was the taverna/wharf where we tied off.

A man waited on the stone platform, which was also his front porch. He shook hands with Lucius and thanked him in English when he gave a hand to the work. I started to but he asked me to sit down. He was not only the proprietor of the taverna, but also the chief stevedore, which was just as well because there was no one else in sight. As the caique lightened, the load was stowed inside. Soon Himself put our backpack against a post and told me to ease inside and look at the man's bookcase.

There were about thirty volumes, new and old, carefully arranged according to language—French, English and Greek. All that I recognized were *The Rise and Fall of the Roman Empire* and Kazantzakis' *Freedom or Death*.

When the unloading was done, our host became the hotelier, warning us not to be surprised that some things worked and some didn't, including the elevator. We walked up three flights to a room facing the sea where the breeze fluttered sheer curtains and the only sound was the lapping of the sea. The plumbing worked but the water in the taps was part sand. Furnishings were sparse but adequate for a pair carrying one backpack; the bed was made with military precision.

Lunch was anytime, so we followed him back and accepted beer when he explained that drinking water was the rarest thing on the island but that he did have some stashed away. Fish, octopus or squid were the menu, which did we prefer? After starting a fire in the grill, he shed his trousers to his swimming trunks, reached for mask and net, dived for some five minutes, returned with the order and disappeared inside. There was someone else in the kitchen by the sound, but we never saw who. Almost immediately there appeared a bowl of hummus and, again, warm bread, which we three demolished. The small flat fish he rubbed with good green olive oil and local herbs from a folded newspaper. The cooking smell was of manna and with the usual tomatoes and sweet onions, there was no doubt.

After a long siesta in the breeze-filled room, our host offered to show us the best beach where there were a few trees for shade. He said he had notice our snorkeling gear and handed Himself a spear gun. It was a lovely place with a small pebble beach and the late afternoon sun sent forth raking shadows which turned to a pink/orange glow while they free dived for a larger fish that was later baked to perfection. Again, just the three of us sat late over tiny cups of Greek (Turkish) coffee while he told us about this island of Semi. Being so close to the Turkish coast had put it in the crossfire of warring factions for centuries; so small and lacking arable land left one occupation—smuggling.

Whether that was still an occupation was not discussed. There was evidence in the larger boats in the harbor; the dashboards on the left side traditionally shielded light from being seen on the coast during night travel. What sort of things would they smuggle—something light, in high demand, durable—like Elvis Presley tapes and contraceptives? Was wariness of strangers rational?

This was not our host's home island. He didn't mention where he was from, and we didn't ask—Lucius had stressed that this was an odd situation, and that I should resist my natural inclination to ask questions. He did say that he had spent several years in New York as a chef. That was easy to do, he said—you just sign on for a trip to New York and jump ship. Everybody needed a good cook. Then he tried Paris, but homesickness finally brought him here.

Exploring the island was easy—it was so small—but its people were impossible to find. We were obviously disturbing—we just never saw anyone except our fine host. The view of the sea from the hilltop church was worthy of Apollo, to whom it was originally dedicated. Its door stood open and in the cool inside there were four candelabra, about shoulder high, hand-wrought of unmatched iron rods supporting the arms of candle holders. The short parts that held the stubs of candles shone like gold—they were spent brass cartridge cases!

Days were dream-like, indolent with spotting schools of fish, perusing borrowed books, talking when there was something to say. But near sundown, things changed—the great octopus hunts were on. It went no further than the rocks right off the wharf, but they were sneaky critters, the smartest of their species. When danger is sensed, they squirt out a great blob of black ink with a repellant odor; by the time the ink disappears they are perfectly camouflaged in color and texture. And they can slither into crevasses so small you would never suspect. However, place a prod in front of their hiding place and they would attack it. That's when the work began. Loosen the octopus from the prod and beat it exactly 66 times, not 65, not 67, against a sea rock, then cook. Textured like a bicycle tire, it smelled of three-day-old fish. Host kindly presented me with a plate of freshly netted squid fried in olive oil to look like daylily blossoms, tasted of mild shrimp, and a rare lemon.

When the caique arrived from the next ferry, the men hugged and kissed each other on the cheeks. As we putted out to board, our host waved long from the taverna, Himself quietly recited the Kazantzakis inscription, "I have nothing. I want nothing, I am free."

The American School of Classical Studies
Americaniki Skoli ton Klassikon Sfouthon

The month passed. Himself went home and I to school, The School. As we waited for his flight, there was a martini each and nothing to say. Out on the street I started to cry so hard that it was too embarrassing to take a taxi. I walked some eight miles from the airport, blubbering me with a bundle of clothes rolled under my arm and blisters rising.

Aleta, my golden haired, porcelain skinned never-before-seen roommate late from the Dutch East Indies, frowned when she opened the door to our room and saw disheveled me. "Sometimes I hope you will tell me what is the matter," she said. "But sit down; dinner is not for a while. I'll get you a drink of water."

A small radio was playing country music—the Armed Forces broadcast of the Saturday night Grand Ole Opry from Nashville. Suddenly I laughed. Here I was, after all those months of struggling to get here, a total ass. *Straighten up, Shirley, look like something!*

I told her of opting to walk from the airport and that my feet hurt, but not that love had kicked me in the face. There we were—two instant friends from opposite sides of the earth chattering away in lilting British English and Southern drawl—at probably one, if not the, most prestigious schools on earth.

Drinks and—best of all—thin, warm fried circlets of eggplant were served at 8:15 in an elegant drawing room. There were the twenty of us, nineteen Classic scholars—PhD candidates, teachers, VIPs—and me, with a like number of pros. At the immaculately set table, my dinner partners were two very fit middle-aged men—one toasted brown, with a faint Texas twang, the other of a cloistered pallor sounding straight out Windsor Castle.

Conversation centered on progress at archaeology's dream site, the Athenian Agora. This cultural, commercial, political, religious town square, recognized birthplace of democracy, had been licensed to The American School in 1931 (still is) for a seemingly eternal work-in-progress. Its newish phase, largely funded by the Rockefeller family, was the Stoa of Attalos, the ancient multipurposed shopping mall. This very long, two-storied, covered portico with rooms attached used for merchants, offices, artists, religious groups—most anything—was our goal for the morrow.

It was so beautiful! Seen first from the end, it stretched longer than a football field but seemed to go on forever. It was like physically walking into a geometric theorem, which actually it was. Ancient Greeks used a mathematical equation known as the golden mean (or golden ratio) which I cannot possibly explain but it has appeared in architecture, painting or book design for at least 2,400 years as the perfect proportion to the human eye. Made of Pentelic marble and limestone with fluted white Doric columns on the front and Ionic at the back, the potent Greek sun threw such shadows as to tie it to the universe.

Having never been in a postgraduate setting before, my curiosity was fast satisfied. It was a do-it-yourself-by-doing exercise in living an urbane life, increasing knowledge in the field of your choice and imparting it to others in a way of your own way.

What impressed me most was the number of women treated on par with the men. How is it that the archaeological world accepts them so easily? The only answer that occurs to me is that, although the profession is interesting and prestigious, the pay is relatively poor.

When I was an undergraduate at Vanderbilt, there were no women professors and the first who was finally recognized as head of a department was in Classics.

To say that our learning was do-it-yourself-by-doing was no exaggeration. The campus was a cluster of handsome houses just across the street from the Gennadius Library where I had had my own carrel the previous year.

From somewhere my assignment for the session arrived with instructions to introduce myself to the librarian at the British School and seek her help in researching a written report on a subject of my choosing; prepare to deliver a forty minute talk, *in situ,* at the Temple to Apollo in Corinth on the statuary of the east pediment; be familiar enough with the Battle of Marathon to assist the student presenter when we followed its progress on the battlefield itself. Hmm. . .

Being a country girl, I chose to write a paper on bull leaping, a daring feat performed by fragile boys and girls that I had seen depicted on so many friezes and pottery, especially in Crete. The brows of the librarian rose but she threw herself into the subject—together we found almost nothing. The feat has never been replicated, even by Spanish bullfighters who came for that purpose. It was surmised, but not proven, that domesticated cattle were introduced by the same new arrivals who brought horses and were received with the same awe. Leaping must have been commonplace, and probably part of a religious rite because of the prominent "horns of consecration" at the palace at Knossos, plus the odd sort of mounting block found in an open space in front of the palace that was assumed to be its venue.

Since no one seemed to know much or even had opinions, opportunity opened to guess that something basic had changed. The bulls, not long domesticated, could have been more like pets trained to tricks rather than prodded to ferocity and enjoyed the game like dogs do Frisbee. The leapers could have been larger and the bulls smaller than now; mind-altering substances could have energized the leapers and quieted the bulls. The paper was submitted but not remarked upon.

The pediment statues were a shoo-in; everybody knew and wrote everything—so I turned the usual presentation around a bit by sticking to the story of why these figures were together and who was up to what. That the tale attracted attention of a few other museum visitors and even a smattering of applause was exhilarating.

As to the Battle of Marathon, the presenter needed no help, the terrain moved the warriors and where the fighting took place but I sounded knowing enough when I said anything at all.

I could do these things with pleasure as every student there could. With the exception of oddities such as Aleta and me, these were scholars who had invested years to get here—a real coup for starting and continuing their careers. To an untrained eye, there was no need for the professors who nevertheless were putting a final luster on their dedicated.

Who and why would anyone hire me? It had not occurred to me that this would be my future life. At age 48, it was just too much and too late and home had changed since June. The almost daily funny, affectionate letters from Memphis scrawled on yellow legal pad were a magnet. But was I really a dilettante who could just walk away from these extraordinary gifts I had been given without doing anything in return?

Then Barbara Johnson, a PhD candidate at the University of Missouri, asked if I might want to join as a volunteer, which is what much of its work force was, at their excavation at Tel Anafa, a Greek site in the upper Galilee which had just started a seven-year permit. Good grief, I had expected to have to seek that out and here it was in my lap! Serious sweat-equity would be something. "Thank you," I said, "that would be good." And so it was for eight weeks a summer for the next five years.

The last week in the hinterlands was unique: swimming alone off the beach at the battlefield of Thermopolis with three curious dolphins; being boosted some ten feet in the air on the shoulders of two mighty young men and pulled from above into a lookout in the ancient Athenian defense wall against the Persians.

The Temple to Apollo on the high outcrop at Bassae in the Peloponnese was a well-preserved puzzle. Who initiated its construction on such an inaccessible site? Who paid for something so costly? Why the north/west orientation instead of the normal east/west? Was it the constraint of the site itself? Could the first introduction of a door in the sidewall be only to let the rising sun illuminate the cult statue which instead of a figure of a god was the oldest known Corinthian column? Pausanias, ancient travel writer and gossip, whose words have proved both sound and fanciful, said that there had been a statue of Apollo, but there are no markings on the floor to indicate such. The column was shattered during excavation and is sadly missing. But there are pictures. Puzzles, puzzles!

Andritsaina, mountain village of some 100, provided supper, sleeping arrangements, early morning coffee, warm yeasty bread from the public oven and wild honey in the shade of the sacred plane tree which spouted, waist high, a jet of pure and cool water into a drinking basin for men and beasts alike. Setting out on foot the few kilometers to the site, we paused to admire five young girls at a loom. The convenience of garish chemical dyes had driven out the lovely natural dyes but they still sang the patterns aloud as they had forever.

Up the mountain track, there was the temple, as wondrous to the world as to us. It is writ large on the World Heritage List, as well it should be.

Cabo San Lucas

Cabo San Lucas was a long way from anywhere—two and a half days of sporadic sleep was the line between two great wonders of the world—one manmade, the other the product of time, wind and the sea.

From Athens started the western swoop of the great circle route across the Alps, green land's end of Britain, then water, water everywhere to JFK. From there to Memphis in August, where we walked out of the terminal as into a warm sponge where sweat turned on like spigots. Through the cotton fields to Holly Springs' fixed-base airport and that low-slung red beauty parked out front, ready, willin' and headed for Brownsville, Texas.

Across the sad trickle of the Rio Grande was another world—the

Mexican highlands of mountains after mountains all greenish grey. If there was anyone there, they kept to themselves. Set the compass 220 degrees toward the out-of-range VOR at Torreon—all there was of communication, but enough.

At the airport in Torreon, the dusty jumping-off place, pay attention. Be sure not to arrive between noon and four; customs officers take siestas seriously. Go with the fuel truck with a twenty in hand for the driver; test the gas yourself before he leaves. Aviation gasoline you got here was the last until you got back without a detour halfway to California.

This was the only time we went into town (I couldn't stay awake) to a surprisingly elegant hotel where my first real Mexican meal was served to candlelight, fresh flowers, toe-wiggling music and the plashing of a fountain. The bed was turned down with a rose on each pillow. When and where Mexican talent and taste appears, it is world-class and more.

From here navigation was easy in the trailing morning sun. We held the same heading, checked the ETA for the VOR at Acapulco to the south. With mountains behind, green-grey changed to semi-desert brown and then the blue-blue Sea of Cortez in all directions. Hours passed in the calm air while he read and I navigated and watched for stationary objects. (If you see anything that doesn't seem to move, you are on collision course.) Then there the jagged-toothed rocks held back the mighty Pacific at the tip of Baja California. Veering north toward Cabo Falso, then south along the coast, Himself laid down his book to make the perfect landing on the runway, downhill, downwind, short by any standard, sand strip tucked in the shadow of the rocks. But first he buzzed the village a couple of times to alert Doc to come fetch us and the soccer players who shared the space to get out the way.

"Welcome, Sar!" with a crisp salute was shouted on a falling note as the engines quieted; "Welcome back, Sar," from the transport officer of Cabo. Doc, a British veteran on disability pay from WWII (strong and healthy as an ox) designed the job for himself out of curiosity, for hard cash and new audience to hear the village bad news—Mexico made him indignant.

In that 1968 there was only a dirt track from the US; yachts came, small private planes and occasional hitchhikers on local trucks. The Mexican Tourist Agency, like the Greek, hosted a series of hotels for the first two groups in difficult places of special interest. Like the others with the same name, this Camino Real was posh—open Colonial architecture of deep arches, red tile, lush garden with swimming pool and splendid dining room—lovely to see on the rise above the bay.

There were only three locals who spoke English. Doc was one and he also had a Jeep. Belying his disability status, he seized the two backpacks and couple of cases of books, good red wine and such trivia as unsalted butter for lobster and cold-pressed olive oil wrapped in dry ice. Off we went stirring clouds of dust, skinny dogs, chickens and beautiful children through the village to the last turn off toward the sea.

There a two-house-of-cards looking structure where a *porte-cochère* sheltered the road grader to smooth the rain gullies. (I never saw it rain, nor the grader moved.) Upstairs was the hideaway of a Mexico City politician, used for whatever infrequent purposes. Downstairs lived Chito, the dearest of men who could and did do everything, and spoke with the lilt of song.

A couple of hosepipe extensions away from the pump house rested a vintage house trailer with a thatch-roofed porch which doubled the space and housed a ferret of local species which kept the snakes and rodents at bay. An obsolete USPO mail truck parked nearby provided storage for diving gear. All was set about with mesquite trees where scooted small gem-green lizards lapping bugs, white sand, a picnic table, two Pawley's Island hammocks—one he gave me for Christmas and the other I gave to him.

Beyond a wire-and-stick fence began the cactus garden that is Baja:

> Bright before it beat the water,
> Beat the clear and sunny water,
> Beat the shining Big-Sea-Waters.
>
> H.W. Longfellow

La vita could not have been more *dulce:* up whenever, coffee water to boil, trot up and back to a rock painted "1 m.", warm bread from the bakery (a real mom-and-pop operation—the baby squirmed in its cradle above the dough board where it was sung to and rocked), local honey and smoked fish. Off to Señor Coberubias (spelling dubious), he of the only air compressor for hundreds of miles. Señor was revered as a member of a First Family of Cabo, which dated back to the days of pirating ships seeking fresh water after rounding the Horn, bound for California.

Rojo, the boatman, sat waiting behind the outboard, murmuring with Jesus, a gentleman of infinite age and rectitude whose life's last job was to hold the little boat by a rope then shove it off with his foot. After male *abrazos* all around, we swished out past the raucous herd of sea lions to the rocks and natural bridge where the Sea of Cortez and the Pacific Ocean met.

The yachts in the bay came for swordfish and marlin well out at sea, not SCUBA. There was no competition for the rocky holes up and down the coast where myriads of fish had swum since the beginning of time. Whatever other divers came, came to play with Himself—not me, who had chickened out early. In preparation I had gone to the YMCA to get certified and did fine until the final test. Told to go to the deepest part of the pool, release my weight belt, tanks, mouthpiece and goggles then to put it all back on, blow the mask clear and resurface, I panicked midway—which was just as well.

Here where the two great bodies of water converged, no surf broke, but swells often rose twenty feet and more. First rule: "Never dive without a buddy." Himself ignored it and I certainly didn't qualify. It was rational to stick with what was comfortable—track the bubbles from his tanks (one of the dangers in diving is getting lost from the dive boat) with Rojo, who didn't know how to swim. I brazened the deep by snorkeling nearby over those bubbles (in a swell, you bob up and down in place instead of being bashed about as in a surf), catching occasional glimpses of him, and swimming slowly in schools of mahi-mahi, barracuda or gorgeous-colored angel and parrot fish as big as dinner plates—hypnotic.

Days fell into an easy pattern: a couple of morning hours in the water, leave the tanks with Señor to refill and gather the news of the day, off to the bakery of delicious smells. Home again where Chito's niece, Jane, had come while we were gone. She always left the trailer immaculate, with warm tortillas wrapped in a cloth, and washed the sheets (with no air conditioning, sweat was a constant) to hang in the sun to dry.

There was almost always a visitor or two—usually the other two who spoke English. Jimmy Jeffries, like Doc, was a man with a disability pension. He and his dune buggy were supported by the San Diego Fire Department, AND he had a fallback position. He married a pretty, demure girl whose family owned several miles of beachfront. If they were not finked out of it by lavish resort developers, they must be as rich as guano.

He was big, handsome, about thirty, and made friends instantly—including with the indigini in the hinterlands. He was a sort of local anthropologist, who kept in touch with the museum in Mexico City. One morning, well before day, he took us (me, the want-to-be archaeologist, jumping with joy) to a remote compound where, in the cookhouse, the only light was the smoldering fire on the big stone that was both table and stove. There was bitter coffee and tortillas wrapped around something that was perfect for this time and place.

By full day we were on an ordinary dune overlooking the sea. I pulled the scruff from a random hillock and found something odd. Using a twig and lung power to clear the sand and dirt, we discovered a large horn: the suave curve of a mammoth tusk. I had only seen pictures of the huge extinct elephant-like creatures whose remains are also found in Europe, Asia and North America, from well before the cracking away of the tectonic plates.

What should be done? If we tried to move it, it would crumble. Jeffries covered and marked the spot. The next time I saw it was in a velvet-lined box in his house. He had contacted the museum; they had sent a hardening compound to inject before moving, told him to send pictures and site location, and to keep it for the present.

Oswaldo was raised in an orphanage run by New England nuns on an upper reach of the Amazon. How he got to Cabo, why he stayed, how he lived, was he married, *yo no sé*. About 35 years old, intellectually curious, educated, fluent in Portuguese, Spanish and English, a listener as well as talker, ingenious in getting things done and up on the news of the world; he would have been comfortable anywhere, but here he was.

These three formed a salon around that picnic table that would have done credit to the *Académie Française*. Hippies from the beach came to ask use of our solar shower—the long black hose coiled in the sun with nozzle thrown over the branch of a mesquite—luxurious!

There were not many, but the ones who managed to be there were interesting and welcomed.

Come lunch time, had they been invited to stay they would have said "no thank you" and departed. So more beer was passed and gradually there appeared, without silver or linen, a couple of fresh loaves, cold grilled fish and my ever-so-good mayonnaise. (Eggs, olive oil, wild citrus juice, a scrape of onion, salt and cayenne whipped up in the Cuisinart.) Oswaldo brought pats of *caso de casa*–zesty, smooth local cheese; Jeffries came with the wild citrus, dried desert herbs and fresh garlic to eat raw or roasted with the next batch of fish on the grill. If someone brought dulces, they appeared. *Voilà*—no mess, sucked fingers, and all heading home for siesta—no fifteen minutes but a couple of hot afternoon hours.

Later was for a leisurely swim toward the anchored boats—rarely more than four, maybe five. For you who have not snorkeled, never miss a chance; it is miraculous. With the flippers it is as easy as walking and faster. Through the mask fish appear as cohorts, the water stays out of your nose, and you make friends in unlikely places. For example: swim around any boat at a respectful distance, casually inspect and make minor adjustment to the anchor chain. Someone will show up on deck with thanks and invitation to come aboard. Regret and swim on, but if they seem interesting, invite them to come by when they are ashore. They almost always did.

The ends of the days were to be, not to do. To sit, ankles touching, on the still-warm sand breathing the enormity of the pink quietude of dusk was a wakening, an awareness of the evening star—Venus rising. The two billion bodies of our galaxy turning above to points of light were the same as seen from the moon-lit Parthenon in the beginning. What of the two billion galaxies beyond them? *Quién sabe?*

Good Things One After Another

Not just days but months and years fell into easy patterns: Late fall and winter were for quail, deer and turkey hunting, with me in lockstep watching, not shooting. The slightly improved four-room tenant house with a view of 1,800 acres of wildlife preserve in West Tennessee's Hardeman County was a paradise of sorts. For the fireplace and cooking stove there was wood stacked on the porch; for water: the rain barrel outside the kitchen door; for instant heat: an electric blanket; for hearing the turkeys talk with the owls at daybreak: the outhouse; for elegance and comfort: a few antiques, big hooked rug and guest room for visiting hunters; for spells of warm weather: a full front porch with cane chairs. It, with tents and a cabin in Wyoming, hooked me on small, warm dry spaces that need almost no upkeep, such as I have now.

In between, long weekends were for hiking chunks of the Appalachian Trail—the best of which was the Jefferson National Forest in Southwest Virginia. There, a new stretch included Mount Rogers, second-highest peak east of the Mississippi, and the old was maintained as the Iron Mountain Trail. Voila: a 40+ mile circle without backtracking.

The new part included a rainforest, some two miles of dense hemlock, balsam, forest hydrangeas, ferns and moss-padded stones caused by unblocked exposure to the prevailing northwest wind bringing much moisture. Several years later, I saw a picture of this once lovely spot— skeletons of dead trees and bare stones. The same winds of its creation had brought its destruction: the gathering pollutants from the industrial Midwest.

Eight weeks of summer were for field archaeology as arranged the previous summer in Athens. The University of Missouri, via PhD. candidate Barbara Johnson, expected me to show up at Kibbutz Shamir, Golan Heights, upper Galilee, Israel, June 15, 1969… hmmm. El Al flew me to Tel Aviv; hotel at the airport put me up overnight, fed breakfast and delivered to the interior airport next morning. After that—on my own.

JFK shunted El Al passengers through an underground tunnel armed with blank faces holding Sten guns to a Quonset hut on the outer rim where we signed papers and queued up for luggage inspection. A pretty, unsmiling Israeli girl soldier stood behind my small suitcase, took my ticket and passport, and examined the meager contents: three well-worn culottes, three long-sleeve cotton shirts, one knee-length cotton night shirt, tennis shoes, socks and trivia.

"Where is your other baggage?" she asked.

"That's it."

"It says you stay eight weeks."

"Yes, but I don't plan to be very well dressed."

She grinned at last and passed me through without commenting on the flat, broad-brimmed straw hat with poison-green silk ribbon streamers on my head. (I had been told of need for a hat to ward off the sun; this was what I owned.)

The plane was configured for the greatest number of people; I had to stand up to cross my legs, as did the two tall British B'nai B'rith girls who shared my row. There was scrambling during the night. At breakfast, I asked, "What are lox?" and a sudden herd of Jewish mothers gathered to explain. On landing in Tel Aviv, the lights of the airport were turned off except for the upside-down blue ones that marked one side of the runway in the dark. There had been a recent massacre in baggage pickup.

The hotel was handsome and there were sounds of gaiety by night in the atrium beneath my balcony—a wedding with group dancing to rousing *Fiddler on the Roof*-type music. Israel offered a sophisticated face to visitors; for its own needs, basics would do. The interior airport was a small but impressive clutch of tower and high-tech looking outbuildings; the passenger waiting area was a small frame house without seats, and when the flight was called, the stampede that followed belied the fact that all seats were reserved. The flight itself made clear how small Israel is; we had hardly taken off and gotten a splendid view of the Jordan River when we started our descent.

The transformation that took place on landing was impressive. Suddenly the mob that had rushed the takeoff became a group of people all of whom knew exactly what they were doing. However, there wasn't a lot of choice—vans were directed by a soldier with a clipboard who asked for destinations. "Kibbutz Shamir" was all I said, which was enough, and within minutes off we went. After several stops in out-of-the-way places all wound around with cyclone fences, Shamir appeared at the end of the line on a vast bare hillside with full view of the verdant valley. Inside its cyclone fence topped with razor wire near a swimming pool was Barbara Johnson. I was there—wherever there was.

The pool had a history. Jonathon Shiloach, eldest son of a prosperous Berlin family, was the chosen one, at age sixteen, to be smuggled to Palestine when the rest were doomed to concentration camps. After the war, the German government sent him compensation for family losses, which he gave to his new home—part went for the pool. We were about the same age, he spoke English, one of the very few; we became friends. He told me about the *kibbutzim* in general and Shamir in particular. This is what I remember:

At the end of World War I, the Treaty of Versailles imposed such an oppressive peace on Germany and its allies as to lead in a few years to World War II. The British were credited with the Balfour Resolution, by which Palestine was given as a homeland for the Jews, but had little enthusiasm for the transformation, which proved bloody. With the coming of Hitler and the new war, emigration accelerated with increasing belligerence.

Northern Israel, where we were, is a small tongue of alluvial plain squeezed between Golan Heights of Syria and the Naphtali Heights of Lebanon. But it has water. Two great springs bring together the water from the heights and the snow pack from Mt. Hermon (in Hebrew almost all names and nouns have the accent on the last syllable) to the north. Shortly they join to form Lake Kinneret (the biblical Sea of Galilee).

There were pictures hanging in the dining room of settlers with only wheelbarrows clearing the maze of rocks and building the intricate irrigation system on land which formerly had been for grazing sheep and goats.

The Israeli government saw to it that *kibbutzim* do not fail:
Criteria of population, support, diversity to supply a needed work force, etc., are met before formation. Shamir, formed after the Six Day War, 1967, got special attention as one of the few built on captured Syrian land—the Golan—of vital defensive importance.

Government research determined that it raise grapefruit and fish on assigned irrigated land in the valley with motto "sell the best and keep the rest"—low cost, high profit. It was a place of rare beauty and efficiency—the green/blue checkerboard of orchards and fish ponds operated in lockstep. Carp, (I don't think we have such—our carp are scavengers, smelly trash fish), plate-shaped like our crappie, are farmed thus: clean ponds about four feet deep fill with clean ditch water; slide in fingerlings by the thousand; blow concentrated feed in daily for about four weeks; net fish as pond empties, transfer to shipping water tanks, off to Tel Aviv; close ditch gates to dry enough for small forklifts to scoop out muck and apply to orchards (perfect organic fertilizer); close gates and start again—twelve months a year, all done by gravity flow and minimum labor.

Orchards were irrigated by overhead circling sprays. When they started turning in sequence at sunset, they were twirling white tutus that would become the Bolshoi.

Within the high fence, which was padlocked and patrolled at night, there was the main building, which included a dining room, kitchen, conference rooms, offices and a small factory for precision trifocal lenses manned by six trained residents. Amenities were comfortable cottages for the married, dormitories for the unmarried, volunteers and us (for a fee); an outdoor movie theater and, of course, the pool—constantly fed by an artesian well, the outflow drained into the irrigation ditch below.

At the center was the complex for children, both on the surface and underground—double guarded. From birth to high school they lived together with teachers, nurses and a separate dining room. (Parents stayed connected by direct telephone lines and permission to enter at any time.) For high school, they went together nearby to boarding school in Kyriot Shmona, the only town this far north. (Crushed hopes appeared in odd places, like the rusted, dangling road sign: "Future home of Holiday Inn.") Then came their two years of military training for both boys and girls. After that they went to one of the universities or technical schools according to their ability. Active military assignment lasted for several years, while they went about making a living. These years were not in barracks but at home or wherever, but when summoned, they could be fully armed quickly and travel to assigned zone by any means possible—including hitchhiking and public buses. Everyone of active military age was issued an Uzi, the VERY efficient small, Israeli made sub-machine gun which, if lost or stolen, they had to pay for a replacement. As a result, great care was taken by not letting it out of sight—they were carried everywhere, like sunglasses, and attracted as little attention.

Our crew gathered on Saturday evening (the end of *Shabbat*, their day of rest) for a cold supper since no one was supposed to work on that day. (This offered a real problem to the conservative settlements, which took it seriously enough to include fighting in the list of banned activities. It didn't take the Palestinians long to catch on.) Some thirty of us were welcomed by our director, Dr. Saul Weinberg. (Dr. Weinberg to his face, Super Sol, as in the popular detergent, out of earshot.) He was an urbane gentleman of many parts. He was recognized as a premier archaeologist for discipline, precision and particularly for recording and promptness of publication. A man of physical courage (he was one of the last children left lame by poliomyelitis) who scrambled up the unstable structure for overhead photography with his cane hanging from his hip pocket, he spoke Hebrew and French, read Latin and Greek, rotated in six-month periods with the curator of the splendid museum and professor at Hebrew University in Jerusalem, and, with it all, was very wry, attentive and generous.

Sunday morning at 4:30 (not 4:25, not 4:35), two crowded trucks pulled off to Tel Anafa with crew fortified by coffee/tea and biscuits (cookies for dunking). Getting aboard was a challenge—large rocks covered the floor to prevent being blown off the road in case of a land mine. Roads, such as they were, were paved on one lane only as a compromise between safety and expense—mines could not be set in asphalt and there was little traffic.

Self-Reliance or Else

There it was in reality, not just a mantra. I had taken what Vanderbilt offered in Classical Archaeology, started summer field work, the children were gone, Husband David sold our house and bought an apartment. His being a late riser/late nighter and my early rising left us pleasant strangers who could go for days without seeing one another. Next he bought a condo and moved out, and there I was, middle aged, and on my own for the really first time. Spooky!

Time took care of itself. I frequented bookstores—two excellent ones, Zibart's and Mill's—and cousin Mrs. Philips' music store, where she reignited my delight in the classics by turning me loose in her listening room and plying me with a little of everything. I studied sculpture at the Watkins Institute under Nashville artist Puryear Mims, lunched with someone almost every day, and developed the best habit of my life. Since Son David's marriage, I had seen him only in groups and knew him less and less. My solution: invite him to lunch every Friday and pick up the tab. It has worked for decades; he became by far my closest local friend.

Then a brochure for the Sierra Club grabbed me by the nape and never let loose—voila, a full-time conservationist to this day.

In the early seventies, when the clean air and clean water bills were passed by the Feds, an environmentalist was something of a joke. I was frequently a lone voice crying in the wilderness, demanding protection of drinking water and energy conservation in a room of assured male legislators making archaic decisions. The Sierra Club was so hard up for volunteers that two weeks after joining I was asked to take the job of program chairman. "Certainly not," I told them—I had only been to one meeting and had no idea of how to do that. Next week there was another call, suggesting I co-chair with someone named Bill Meadows. "Certainly," I said. Bill was in Alumni Relations at Vanderbilt; we had a good time and did a decent job. He became and remains Director of the Wilderness Society, one of the nation's best outfits. He is a splendid man and seldom-seen friend.

I hankered for something to do every Monday morning and there it was—the Tennessee Environmental Council. The malfeasance of the Nixon administration bestirred a hotbed of people, long on feelings and short on science, to clot into all sorts of volunteer groups dedicated to caring for our good earth. That the abounding energy needed focus into a common voice to be effective was obvious to a handful of wise men and at least two powerful women, Mary Wade and Elsie Quarterman. (Mary is gone now but Elsie is still around—older than I am, which seems impossible.)

Enter Dr. Ruth Neff. She of the quiet voice of calm and double doctorates in earth sciences was provided a beautiful office at Cheekwood and proceeded to do much more than hoped for. She not only provided the science and orderly thinking to some 20 or 30 statewide bunches of us tree-huggers, but also raised hard cash by contracting with government agencies to do much-needed research.

There I was at the start of a movement, searching for what I knew not. When my bookkeeping ability surfaced, I was acclaimed Treasurer. I stayed in that role for the next 17 years, then spent two as president before differing opinions with Ruthie's successor led me to different fields.

When thriving Cheekwood needed to reclaim its space, our office moved from the sublime to the less-so: a back room of the garage at UT Nashville just down the hill from the Capitol. Small, dark and occasionally cold, it was the convenient stomping ground for the paid employees and volunteers that swarmed around the vortex of miraculous Ruthie.

As I sit here this fair May morning thinking about her and the two other most imposing of humans—my grandfather and Lucius Burch (plus Mama in a different way)—who have led to my good life, gratitude flows.

All of this was laced together by long weekends of bliss tracking Himself up mountains, clod hopping across plowed West Tennessee fields shooting quail for supper, and further. The Sierra Club published "tote books" such as *Hut Hopping in the Swiss Alps* and *Tracing the Apennines* which we traveled with during the summer before I returned to work as an archaeologist. They gave us such directions as: "Get off the train at Montreux, walk around to the back of the station through a garden gate; the trek starts here."

Role of Middle-Aged Archaeologist

The second summer went well; it was spent in Jerusalem working six days a week at whatever Super Sol said. Arrival there was again as haphazard as having landed at the kibbutz half way up the Golan Heights.

This time it was again to Tel Aviv, not on El Al but Olympus for leg room and sleep—there was plenty of both. Charlotte Ford Niarchos had first class, and I had the caboose almost to myself. Her seventeen-piece matched floral tapestry luggage looked imposing beside my one small duffle bag on the loading tram. Dinner was good: roast lamb and *baklava*; my wine was *retsina*, she may have had a better vintage. Then all that was needed was to flip up three armrests and request a blanket and pillow. She didn't wake me when she got off in Athens and I went on.

The long haul up 2,000 feet from Tel Aviv to the Holy City via jitney was through a park where the military detritus of the Six Day War was left *in situ*—tanks, trucks, jeeps akimbo from explosives—as outdoor art. The taxi driver was a Frenchman who threw up his arms in horror at my destination and said, *"Mon dieu, Madame, c'est un monastre!"* Indeed it was: a huge stone building with pink/orange bougainvillea sweeping across the entry. *"Laissez moi voir votre papier."* which I was clutching in early stage of panic. (Dear Dr. Rochedieu would have been proud, I understood everything.) *"Ah, mais oui, il y a une autre porte."* We wheeled around the monastery through a dusty courtyard to a small open door framing Barbara Johnson.

Up two long flights of stone steps, the French Sisters ran a modest hostel. Supper was ready, as was I, for the simple meal of such finesse as only the French can conjure. Cohort Barbara Gordon was on hand while her husband Bob dined with the monks up front. They were allowed to share the gate house but not the dining rooms.

My "cell" was shaped like a cracker box standing on end—about eight by 10 feet—just big enough for a narrow bed, desk with chair under the window, combination clothes chest with glassed two bookshelves atop, and a wash basin. How such a small space could have charmed so completely was no mystery: the ceiling was at least twelve feet; the walls were immaculately whitewashed with a magnificent olive wood crucifix above the bed; the floor was of large polished red tiles; the one window of some four by eight feet set in the thick stone wall had weathered shutters pressed back against the jambs and in the huge unscreened opening sat a glass holding a great purple artichoke thistle. Beyond was Jerusalem the golden, settling in for the night. (Across the courtyard but near my window there was attached an unroofed enclosure where the monks showered. So much for modesty.)

"*Bonjour, Madame,*" came a voice from outside, and I dressed in one of the immortal divided skirts and Oxford cloth shirts that took me mountain trekking. The good Sisters were like the tooth fairy, rarely seen but omnipresent, and the warm smell of baking seduced like the scent of cheese to the mouse in the wall. Barbara filled bowl-sized white cups with black, black coffee and steaming milk. A pirate-sized knife lay beside the warm crisp loaf of country bread, sweet butter and pale honey.

Seven o'clock, straight up, found us down another long flight of stone steps and through a heavy door into a facsimile of Ali Baba's cave: a great stone room with trestle tables bearing stout brown boxes of all the sherds from Anafa. Smiling Dr. Weinberg, with Bob Gordon, was warm but brief in his welcome.

For a jigsaw puzzle fan, this was paradise. For a world-class archaeologist it was the next step in "reporting"—the timely written interpretation of the finds without which excavation is mere "pot hunting." They knew the drill from having done it frequently as Saul's young lions of graduate students; they were patient with me. They taught me to start at any box, separating the clearly important pieces into new boxes—each piece was numbered with indelible ink on the underside so they didn't lose their identity in the shuffle.

Sigulata, the easily-recognized fine red tableware so prevalent at this site and all over the Middle East, Greece and Rome, went to Barbara

Johnson, whose subject it was for her doctoral thesis and which she would teach at the end of the seven years of the excavation at the Ben-Gurion University of the Negev.

Rims, handles, bases and shoulders were further divided and pieces of similar color, texture and shape added to each. The arrangements went quickly; there was something magical about how easily the eyes could pick and retain these similarities. Frequently the desired complete interlocking profiles built up. Each of us tracked what others were constructing so that, if we saw anything similar, no matter where, it could be tested. Fitting sherds from separate trenches indicated different destruction patterns from those restricted to immediate areas.

At mid-morning the door opened for one of the most beautiful of humans—an Arab boy of about fourteen. Dressed in an ankle-length white robe, his beardless face, bare feet and hands of richest café au lait, he carried a bouquet of mint.

"*Allahu Akbar*," he said.

"*Allahu Akbar*," we replied.

At the niche in the wall housing a water tap and electric kettle, he filled a bucket and carefully slid in the nearest box to soak while he shredded the mint into the kettle. The mint smell permeating the cool, quiet cavern with sun pouring through the celestial windows high in the stone walls did aver that *Allah*, as well as much else, was indeed *Akbar*. For the rest of the morning as we went about our business while sipping the best of mint tea, he hunkered on his heels, cleaning the sherds and laying them out to dry on the floor in mosaic patterns while softly chanting to himself.

Variations on Many Themes
1971–1973

1971: Second season at Tel Anafa. Surprise! Surprise! I was assigned, like a pro, three stout lads to open a new trench at the base of the tel near where the slit trenches had been dug during the Six Day War. The nearby fish pond had been drained for cleaning; there were vestiges of settlement walls visible and the site was as dry as it would ever be. Had there been a glass factory as we and Corning Glass, our funders, hoped for and expected, this was the place.

Great was our excitement with the first few levels where there were promising surface finds. But it was not to be. Quickly the soil became damp and heavy, but we dug on under Dr. W.'s watchful eyes. When he finally called a halt, we were down about two feet sloshing up to the knees in muddy water. Over the passing years the water table had risen to drown whatever was there. That was that, and we moved back uphill to another trench which had been unopened this season.

That turned out to be spectacular. There was an ashlar block (a squared stone with one smoothed surface) of about 2.5 by 1.5 feet projecting from the balk (the wall of a trench) at an angle with the smooth side down that had appeared early and left *in situ*. (We never dug anything out of balk unless it became dangerous.) As we started again to excavate, it started to show unstable signs until Sol said to ease it out and to make sure to get out of the way when it came. It was no problem to ease out. Press with one hand—pressure of one hand and the soil underneath began to crumble, and there it came, tumbled over and landed face up. The sight was dazzling—the arid soil had sealed the colors for more than 1,500 years. It was a perfect piece of geometric border wall painting common for its day, Pompeian red, royal blue and gold. The gold was gold leaf, the real stuff, as bright as it had been the day it was laid. As we stood there staring, the hot air began to dry the moisture it had retained and the colors faded, finally stabilizing after the first exposure.

A few days later, the step trench provided an equal treasure: a great Corinthian capital, the most elaborate of them all! Tel Anafa was no simple *caravanserai* (a wayside inn) on the trade route between Damascus and the sea. Along with the lascivious oil lamp decorations, it just may have been what we called it, "The Playboy Club of the Upper Galilee."

Mid-August—house party at Dromahair. After World War II, Himself bought an Irish property containing the ruins of the castle and feasting hall of Tiernen O'Rourke, 12th-century King of Leitrim County. This came with hunting rights to 29,000 additional acres and a long stretch of the River Bonet. It was Yeats country, and as we approached the village of Sligo, there it was:

The Lake Isle of Innisfree

I will arise and go now, and go to Innisfree,
And a small cabin build there, of clay and wattles made:
Nine bean-rows will I have there, a hive for the honey-bee,
And live alone in the bee-loud glade.

And I shall have some peace there, for peace comes dropping slow,
Dropping from the veils of the morning to where the cricket sings;
There's midnight's all a glimmer, and noon a purple glow,
And evening full of linnet's wings.

I will arise and go now, for always night and day
I hear lake water lapping with low sounds by the shore;
While I stand on the roadway, or on the pavements grey,
I hear it in the deep heart's core.

—William Butler Yeats

It was joy unbounded to reconnect at the Shannon airport. The handful from Memphis included Charlie and Kay Newman, Mike Cody and Nancy, a Massachusetts journalist, Francis Gasner, Dorothy Reid from Nashville bringing me three silk dresses to supplement my well-worn culottes, Himself and me, mud-brown from the Israeli summer.

We headed straight for the nearest pub on the two-lane highway heading north where there were raw oysters and something long and fizzing from the tap. It must have been an old stomping ground because both Francis and Lucius were addressed by name by the barkeep.

Going north we sighted the Lake Isle, passed through the ancient village and pulled into the driveway of a large white oblong building. If it looked like an inn, that's because that was what it was built for, but it also fit a couple with four daughters and friends from hither and thither.

Resolute Mrs. McAlister shouted her welcome from the open back entry, directed the two lassies hauling suitcases like a sergeant major, and led us down a long hall to the drawing room where tea was laid. But that had to wait.

Through the front wet room where green Wellies lined up for instant use, the double doors swung open, and there it all was.

The stone walls, many up to the roofline, of a great feasting hall were draped in green vines.

> In elder days than these men sat at meat with the gods,
> Tearing the goat-flesh, jesting over the mead
> Till the rafters rang and the gold haired maidens laughed.
>
> Donald Davidson
The Tall Men

To the left and further up the grassy slope, half encircled with ancient trees, was what was left since the castle was burned some 800 years earlier. The stone walls were sturdy as they stood, some to the top of the second story; the Gothic arched windows and doorways were elegantly proportioned and rooks nested in the chimney pots. At some distance ran the River Bonet.

And this is what I remember: This was the family seat of the O'Rourkes, of which there were 19 successive chiefs all named Tiernan. The one who reigned here was the King of Leitrim County, a mighty fighter, who came to cross purposes with Dermot MacMurrough who, with an army of French and Welsh mercenaries, defeated him, burned his castle and stole his wife, Devorgilla. It was suggested that she may have gone willingly since her furniture and cattle went with her.

The latest of the clan leaders, also named Tiernan O'Rourke, was a London stockbroker. So much for continuity.

Days were spent following animal tracks through bogs in the provided Wellies. Bracken and gorse turned great swaths of the hillsides golden. We brought no guns, as hunting season was closed. Evenings were spent dining back and forth with a cluster of Irish friends whose houses had their kitchens and dining room on the ground floor, drawing room across the second and bedrooms above.

When our turns came, Mrs. McAlister the miraculous and the two lassies produced beautiful meals from a remarkable kitchen. It was a big room with a stone floor and a huge commercial-sized Aga, a gas stove of many eyes and ovens upon which one tea kettle reigned. Beside it was a neat apartment-sized electric four burner of uncertain vintage which surged with heat. To add to the magic, in the late afternoon that kitchen was full of black smoke which never seeped into the big dining hall or affected the taste of monumental meals of wild birds, fresh vegetables and desserts of much whipped cream. (One more note on the McAlister management style: when you climbed into bed later to the cold linen sheets, there was a hot water bottle. Delicious."

On our last evening, Himself had a party in a thatched cottage of whitewashed clay and wattles built aside the lapping waters of the bay. We were about twenty in evening clothes, comfortably filling the reception room over drinks in the light of many candles. In the dining room were two round tables, white clothed and properly set with the right wine glasses and, again, candles. My place card put me against the nether wall and him on the furthest, facing each other across the sea of faces. Occasionally our eyes would meet and he would grin before returning to carving the crown of lamb.

I had never seen a crown of lamb before, except in pictures. For you who are as ignorant as I, a crown is two racks of loin chops tied together backwards in a circle, with bones sticking up dressed in white ruffled paper pantaloons. Sprinkle with herbs and black pepper, roast until pink inside, and then fill the hollow with watercress.

He was so beautiful busying himself at such a chore and beguiling the table with good humor. How could I possibly have just spent eight weeks of my advancing years in Israel, of all places, and spent them so cheerfully?

Late August sent the two of us south to overnight in Brownsville, Texas, after the flight from Shannon. The next morning we refueled and passed through customs with enough daylight left to tempt fate according to his fateful words:

"There is only one island on the way out, Tres Marias. It's a penal colony for political prisoners where they live with their families—not far off our course. Let's see if we can find it."

We found it, and he explained the drill: "You are a famous news reporter for a renowned international periodical, so stick in your shirttail, take this notebook and put the pencil behind your ear."

When we landed and the props lulled to a halt, I pushed back my seat and he climbed on the wing and turned to assist me as if I were a VIP or an invalid. All smiles, he snapped to attention and saluted the fast-arriving Commandante, using manners left over from the Gulf Coast Military Academy, which had been his Alma Mater from age eight to sixteen. In lilting kitchen Spanish, he bade his peer good day and explained how fortunate he was to host such an important personage as I, who would bring him and his splendid institution world recognition.

El Commandante responded in equally polished English. He was polite, but would have none of it. He explained that if either of us put a foot on the ground, we should be prepared for a longer stay. He was backed up by six Jeeps, each of five *soldados* fully armed with submachine guns. After bows all around and good wishes, off we went headed for Baja.

Win some, lose some.

1972—A cog railroad chugged up the mountain from Domodossola to a village, the jumping-off place above the Simplon Tunnel, which connects Italy to Switzerland. How or why we got there, I have no idea. It may be that ignorance is an asset and we had gotten snowed out further north. Anyway, there we were again heading north, back to the full rising sun between the peaks on a most remarkably easy stone-paved track. Grazing cows came to nuzzle our pockets for salt. A pocket full of salt was the way the cowherds kept track of their beasts. We were told that it's hard to tell the herders from the smugglers who prospered here. But they were smugglers, not robbers, and just disappeared if we got close.

Suddenly, Lucius stopped and pointed down. "This is a Roman Road! Look at the ruts in the stones—just the width for chariot wheels. Hannibal must have passed this way atop his elephant on his way south to sack Rome!"

Sure enough it wound its way hour after hour until we came to the lip over a sharp ridge between north and south exposure where it disappeared under a ten or twelve-foot snow bank. When he put himself to an extended time of trying to climb it, the idea seeped into my head that he was completely mad and meant to try to go on no matter what.

While I was seriously thinking of what I should do, I turned and started back to an easier footing. It wasn't long before he was crunching behind and took my shoulder. "You were going off and leaving me, weren't you?"

"I was thinking about it."

"You should know me well enough by now to know that I had to look, but am no fool."

"I don't think I would have gone very far."

To backtrack is tedious, so we cut off at the next track, which led to a big lake and the business end of a funicular looping up the mountain. We were welcomed inside by two cheerful young watchmen drinking *grappa*, the fire water that comes at the end of the wine-making process from the discarded grape seeds and stems, and which is illegal in some places. They shared their lunch with us and we shared ours with them. Voilà with the aid of the *grappa*—an instant party.

As the afternoon wore on amid laughter and the mix of Spanish and Italian fused into a sort of sense, they advised us to follow the cable down to its lower barn where we could build a fire and spend the night, or walk to the nearby town to find beds.

The track fell quickly; snow disappeared and it began to rain lightly. By the time we hit bottom, the wind had picked up and the rain had become serious. The barn was a minimal structure of three stacked open-sided concrete boxes, with the bare side downwind toward the rise. The cable made its turn at the top; the rest was empty. We followed their advice, grabbed dead wood from the forest floor, built a fire on the bottom cement floor, made tea and put the soup pot on to boil. Knorr brand dehydrated soups of many flavors—I prefer the asparagus—is the Swiss gift to the backpacking world. It is delicious, and a perfect carrier for any other odds and ends you find in the bottom of your pack, including stale bread.

Followed by a goodly chunk of bittersweet Baker's chocolate, starvation was warded off and the cockles of hearts sang. Supper was only a Rossini overture to a night in that double sleeping bag with the lightning—snap, crackle and pop—sparking up and down the cable.

> "A man is rich in proportion to the number
> of things which he can afford to let alone."
>
> Henry David Thoreau

The morning was quiet, full of sun, when we walked a short distance to the village of Bel Paese, where that world treasure of soft, mild Italian cheese is made. I could have gone my whole life without sitting in that tiny cafe faced with an extra-large wedge, a whole loaf of crunchy bread, a bowl of *café au lait* and that grinning face, but I didn't. Bel Paese translates to "beautiful country." Indeed it was.

A bus ran through town and headed us off to wherever we were going—he to Memphis and I to the William F. Albright Institute for Archaeological Research in Jerusalem. The Albright was not nearly as imposing as its name—just an ordinary-looking residence with extra bedrooms on the main street of the Arab section of East Jerusalem near the Jaffa Gate to the old city.

It was very British, with a stash of Corn Flakes for every breakfast. Compared to the French Sisters, the rest of the food was bland. I shared a room with Barbara Johnson. Barbara and Bob Gordon were welcomed as they had not been at our earlier monastery, and allowed to sleep and dine together. We rode a bus across town to our Ali Baba's cave of artifacts. The collection had grown and had an orderly look, as was expected of anything under Saul's direction as we honed our work.

Living in the Arab section was expansive. There was a cinema open on Shabbat, a barnlike structure with wooden benches instead of seats. We munched on sack lunches of *falafel* (the delicious chickpea fritters in split pita bread, topped with salad and hot sauces, sold by push-carts on the streets) while watching exotic movies. A flight of stone stairs just inside the gate led to the top of the city wall where you could sit on the parapet in first or last light and watch Jerusalem turn golden. Looking east, there was the Mount of Olives topped by a small Greek Orthodox Church where we went on a few Sunday afternoons to hear the nuns sing *a capella*. It was rumored that the Abbess who entered the small sanctuary with great pomp was a surviving Russian Grand Duchess. She looked every inch the part garbed in heavy black silk habit with a ruffle train and a plain gold crucifix so big and heavy that it was a wonder her ancient neck could support it.

South of the holy site was a row of hideous grey concrete apartment houses built for the flood of eastern Jewish *émigrés*.

Wandering the streets of the old city and the open-air shops, I bought something that would cause something of a stir thousands of miles away. A *keffiyeh*, the male Arab headdress of a square of red and white cloth held on by a heavy dark woven cords and whatever the name of the white over-garments is, struck me as perfect Mexican attire for Himself. What I sent was gorgeous: a translucent Egyptian cotton embroidered square, machine made for the tourist trade, with gold thread and a size "huge" formless under-dress of grey and white striped mattress ticking-looking cloth. Along with the head dress, it was a hit!

The story went thus: An unsuspected visitor from Memphis flew in for a visit and went to the Camino Real for directions. At the desk, the attendant responded in a puzzled way, asked his name, and handed him a note. He said that some sort of a nun with a white beard, smoking a cigar had left it. He had been accompanied by *"uno hombre flaco con anteojos negrosy una muy bonita chicay una bikini rojo."* (A skinny man in dark glasses and a very beautiful young woman and a red bikini.)

Dick and Frau Rosen—no doubt—and Himself as the nun.

Later, when I got there, Cabo was almost still Cabo but noisy with cement grinders, hammers and shouting workmen. The bakery was locked, accused of being unsanitary, to be replaced with a glass fronted mom-and-pop tortilla factory grinding out poor substitutes. Trucks ground their gears, angel-eyed children were fenced in with the scratching chickens. But the thatched trailer in the mesquite grove behind the first dune was still a haven and the sea glorious.

1973—In June our excavation living quarters had moved from the Golan to a cyclone-fenced guest enclave as far north in Israel as you can go under the shadow of the Lebanese Naphtali heights and Mt. Hermon. There was sporadic fighting north of us, out of sight or sound, but heads looked up from the tel whenever a chopper sputtered over—a sign of the wounded being transported to Tel Aviv for treatment.

Other than that, things were the same as the dig exposed more and more of its past. It was definitely a rich Greek trading post between Damascus and the sea. The early surface finds of a temporary Roman camp and an Arab grave gave way quickly to pure luxurious Greek artifacts such as the great Corinthian capital and my gold-leafed stone wall.

Another season, the seventh, would wind things up and Saul would work his magic of "reporting"—writing the story of this one important site in the footprints of Alexander the Great's conquest of Asia Minor. There were rumors of Corning Glass extending support for an additional three years, but that prospect was crossed off during the last week.

Just at light, getting-up time, loud swooshing sounds followed by explosions, two of them, shattered the quiet. There was a long pause. Then Barbara Johnson got up, put on her bathrobe with a determined tug on the sash, and said in a normal voice, "Well, I'm damned well not going to be found dead without my teeth." She replaced her lower bridge and started to dress. Not another word was said as we four roommates followed suit—out into the cool morning to the dining room. Saul was there alone, humming and setting out the biscuits. The coffee and tea were almost ready; good mornings were said but conversation limited.

Breakfast arrived at the tel on time. Saul briefly announced that two Katyusha rockets had landed in an open field just short of Kiryat Schmona, the town south of us, that they would have been fired from a mobile launcher which moved on quickly to avoid detection.

Five days later, I sat in the airport in Tel Aviv for the four-hour wait for takeoff, counting the minutes and trying to face up to the fact that, here I was again—mediocre, a chicken—relieved to be heading out.

Monday, November 6, 1973

My 54th birthday was celebrated by adding the day to the weekend. Indian summer in the mountains, the warm spell after the first killing frost while the forests are at their most exuberant, is a gift like no other.

With me deposited in Nashville, he filed an instrument plan to Memphis International instead of Holly Springs—heavy weather was helling east through Arkansas. After a stop at Jack's Creek to top the fuel, he moved on. Dark settled with heavy rain and constant lightning which called for full dashboard lights to lessen the contrast as he followed the tower instructions to turn north over the forest at the end of the south runway. The altimeter bounced in the turbulence, but he was cleared for landing when he clipped the tree tops.

Seconds later, jammed in the seat with the wing section shoved into the fuselage, he couldn't move. The cabin filled with gas fumes; smoke or steam clouded everything. Had it not been pouring rain, it would have been smoke and flames. He later said he knew he wasn't dead because he was making too much noise yelling for help. The tower knew he was down; sirens screamed on the roads, but help would never get off the pavement into the woods in such weather; he kept yelling. Two flashlights bobbed through the woods with cheerful voices shouting, "Hey, dude, whacha doin'? Want a weed?" As they rattled the jammed door he saw the glowing cigarette.

"For God sake," he shouted, "put that out or you'll blow us all up." These two hippies camped nearby in their van did what was needed to cut the door open, get him out and on his way to Baptist Hospital emergency room.

It was a slow night. Two interns had about finished putting him back together, just starting on his feet, when the chief surgeon called in.

"It's pretty quiet," said the intern. "One old homeless fellow brought in pretty broken up, he may make it. Says his name is Lucius Burch."

On the other end of the line, the chief exploded: "Lucius! Don't touch him, I'm on my way."

My dinner was half over when the telephone rang, "Shirley, he went down." There was no doubt what Charlie Newman was saying. "He's still alive in surgery at Baptist."

"Charlie, where are you?"

"Cody, Gassner, Cates and I are in the motel in front of the hospital waiting for a call. They won't let us in."

"Don't leave, I'm on my way." I stuck my head back in the dining room, "I'll be back." Dorothy Reid, a good friend to have in odd circumstances, was standing in her doorway when I pulled in her drive. She piled into the car. Almost nothing was said until Charlie opened the door and handed us two glasses of something.

"Sit down," he said. "They're finished. He's asleep, will be out for a couple of days. We can't see him now or tomorrow. It missed his spine and head. We'll talk."

We reversed our tracks, keeping pace with the weather front that was still pouring through. Somewhere along the way, the clouds broke and the full moon shone through with the black and white glory of a Dürer print.

At mid-morning we talked. Lucius' voice was low, husky. "You came last night, Charlie says. When will you be back?"

"You tell me."

"Tomorrow. I'll get you a cot rigged."

Early next morning, when I walked in and pinched his toe, all I could think of to say was, "You look like a hammock. Think I'll have a swing."

His feet were elevated in a sort of trapeze at the foot of the bed and his arms were suspended at the top from another. All was covered with a white sheet crisscrossed with plastic tubes. He was so pale, so sheepish, so downright wan when I stood beside and he said, "Hang the 'no visitors' on the door."

Thus began seven weeks of gradually shedding tubes, casts and bandages, and a procession of friends including his children and Elsie. The savior hippies at first refused the offered envelope but finally took it. They said they were heading back to California, needed gas, their forest had become a f— parking lot.

I came and went, every day from Wednesday afternoons until early Monday mornings, until Christmas Eve. Then, packed in a van with wheelchair et al, curiously dressed, he headed home to Nashville, to Riverwood, to its lavish holiday party that had been held since well before the Civil War. When Miss Sadie placed her hand on his cheek, the affection that flowed between him and his mother was contagious—joy unbounded.

Mr. Ivory, the miraculous, drove. Miraculous he was—a study in black and white whose teeth reflected his name. Half Lucius' size and weight, he tossed him about like a down pillow and his word was good-natured law. His needed presence was longer than expected when hepatitis from the blood transfusions cropped up, adding more weeks in the hospital.

Winter, 1974, bloomed into spring. Mr. Ivory was gone, but his requested 45 minutes of increasingly strenuous twice-daily exercise continued, and walking was added as well. Soon Lucius was driving, allowing us to use his hunting country in Hardeman County as base camp for long weekends before he went home to Collierville and I to Nashville, to tend to what we each needed to do.

One fine spring morning he announced he had bought a single engine Cessna, which was slower than his old plane but more dependable and simpler to fly. He was going to take four months off over the summer to get back in shape.

"I hope you will go."

The summer before the crash, I had assured Dr. Weinberg that I would be back for the final season at the Israeli site. He said that he would arrange my next opportunity—possibly in Greece, which I longed for. There it was: the Robert Frost poem that I had taught in Athens, "The Road Not Taken," in which the last line is, "And that has made all the difference." Lucius knew this.

What do you think when Cavafy's words crowd you head?

"To certain people there comes a day
when they must say the great Yes or the great No.
He who has the Yes ready within him reveals
himself at once, and saying it he crosses over
to the path of his own conviction.
He who refuses does not repent, Should he be asked again,
he would say No again. And yet that No—
the right No—crushes him for the rest of his life."

What do you do when you ask the key question: "If I don't go, who will?" and you get back, "No one." What do you do with a man who sends a handwritten scrawl on your birthday with "for Sas on turning fifty":

"And you, my beloved, it is no April fire
That brings my lips to yours again. It is
No sudden springtime burning in the veins
That soon must slacken. This is the deepest flame
Ever given to man, the love of life
Summed up in you. For that which we have learned of God
Is not yet more mysterious, is not
More powerful a life than this we share.
Companions, lovers, in one destiny."

Donald Davidson
The Breaking Mold

Not Too Late to Seek a Newer World

May in Cabo was paradise for mending. Snorkel for hours each day in the cool lapping waters of the bay with a simple trident to spear small supper flounders, trail the huge rays gliding over the sand bottom with a minute flick of a wing, scrounge slipper lobsters from the rocks, soak up the sun, take long afternoon naps, plan our next move in this gift of time. Swelling left his ankles and feet as he toasted brown; breathing became steady and deep.

Jimmy Jeffries bounced us around in his dune buggy looking at "progress." There were even rumors of a traffic light. Oswaldo, bearing homemade cheeses, *dulces* and healing herbs to brew up for tea, told exotic tales of life on the upper Amazon. A couple of Memphis planes arrived and tents were pitched under the mesquites.

Then, there is was: the Mexican government announced the closure of the entire bay to fishing, including spear guns. Diving had become too popular and the huge grouper in the rock caves were fast disappearing. The largest one Himself ever took was so big it had to be lashed to the side of the boat to bring ashore. Weighed on the commercial scale at the fish house, it read 362 pounds. Rojo, the boatman, butchered it in front of his house and sold it at half price to get it out of the sun—a fiesta.

It was time to move on. The new law made it easier, but not much. Saturday was the assigned day: Oswaldo and friends arrived to build small, very hot mesquite fires on the ground to cook turtle stew in their own upside-down shells. There were a number of never-before-seen policemen who came to help. Who or why they were, I'll never know. Everything was for sale, for cash and instant delivery—including the postal truck. Lunch was served to all in a mild frenzy of pesos. Himself was left with a huge roll of tattered bills; his beloved toys of so many years were on their way out. The roll was divvied and handed with "*Gracias para todos y vaya con Dios*" and *abrazos* to Chito and Oswaldo—which cheered their doleful faces.

Dark caught us in a swish hotel in La Paz, halfway up the coast. "If you have to do anything unpleasant, do it as quickly, thoroughly and civilly as possible," is writ large in my mind's copy of "What Would Lucius Say?"

To find the border between Mexico and the US was easy; the smog line was up to about 5,000 feet rose and rose gradually heading north. As we passed LA only the tips of the tallest buildings were visible. Sacramento was for the jump off to Yosemite and a return to the mountains with backpacks, tent, sleeping bags and all.

The park was as awesome as its Ansel Adams photographs, El Capitan as regal—if you don't mind viewing it over acres of parking lots. An hour and a half of creeping traffic got us to 8,000 feet and Tuolumne Meadows, where most cars didn't stop. A hand-painted sign on the roadside in front of a barn announced, "Do it the easy way, rent a mule."

The proprietor rocked back in a cane chair, accurately spitting tobacco juice at the beetles in the dust. He let himself down carefully and, in a rolling walk, followed us inside where Lucius was emptying mice nests from a cowhide pannier.

"Talk to me, man," said Lucius. "I don't know anything about packing a mule."

"You don't have to. With Licorice here, you don't have to know, but I'll tell you. If you take gingersnaps, Licorice will do everything but keep an eye out for bears."

And so, after a trip to the nearby general store to lay in provisions, we were off.

The fairly flat trail that started at the back door took us six days across the huge valley, which still contained patches of snow on sprouting grass and glorious peaks. Walking without packs was a luxury. When mending feet hurt, he stood in the little creeks of melting snow until the swelling receded. Percocet was legal then, and a must if you believed that recovery lay by pushing through the pain threshold.

Camp was pitched for the night slightly off the trail where there was a patch of grass, a dry hummock and freshets for cooking and soaking his piteous feet. There was no dry wood for a fire, but the trusty Svea stove had plenty of fuel. The canned stew was sufficient with a crusty loaf, chunks of bittersweet Baker's chocolate, apples and tea laced with Jack Daniels.

Then, we had nothing to worry about but the bears, and Himself had known what to do since his late teenage summers in Alaska, when he hunted eagles for bounty paid by the Geological Survey. He laid the tarp near the campsite and stacked everything that wouldn't go in the tent on top of it—including the grub bag, because there were no trees tall enough to swing it from. He covered it with saddle blankets, and piled them high with everything that rattled, such as cooking utensils. Voila.

Sure enough, even before true dark, a grizzly sow with two cubs started to dig. Lucius poked his head through the tent flap and said politely, since there was a lady present, "Please, Mama Bear, take your children and go." She did not listen. Then, crash, bang—the challenge was on. Lucius let loose a tirade of curse words, known and unknown, and Mama—startled by the crashing cutlery and the screaming—herded her young 'uns back down the trail at a lumbering pace, looking back over her shoulder. Licorice glanced up occasionally, but never stopped grazing.

The next six days proceeded with a series of mile-long walks sprinkled with stops to foot soak in icy streams of thawing snow. Nothing much was said and progress was slow, but at the end of the week, the deed had been done and the trip to recovery underway.

World, here we come!

Quantas Airline

Quantas Airline led to a different world. Its ticket office was on a fashionable street of San Francisco, and its doors opened to reveal four handsomely-uniformed Australians celebrating the late afternoon with a jug of good red wine, a present from a grateful traveler. The place was empty except for us as we accepted seats behind the counter, glasses in hand, and bought tickets for five weeks in New Zealand and Australia. We arranged for round trip air fare plus unlimited car use, plus paid hotel reservations in interesting and/or posh places at a fraction of the cost of other airlines. Both countries were hungry for tourists, and made getting there as easy as possible.

When we boarded the plane, our only row companion rose, introduced himself and shook hands with Lucius. Dressed in a flawless medium-grey collarless Eton jacket, knee-length shorts, a white shirt buttoned to the throat, black tie, long black socks and polished shoes, he almost clicked his heels as be bowed slightly to me.

Tea was served shortly after takeoff from a real tea cart—real loose tea steeped in real teapots with painted roses, in real cups, with real lump sugar and real warm milk. Conversation flowed over the next many hours. Lucius told our young new friend about the boarding school on the Gulf Coast where he had learned to sail, and how his mother sold the hay crop to send him to London to bide with kin for a while and take on polish. He told of the day he saw a roadside sign that said, "Learn to Fly: 20 pounds." When he asked, "Can you teach me?", the answer was, "Have you 20 pounds?" So it came to pass that after three lessons at age 15, he had a document written on the back of an envelope affirming that he was a pilot who was adequate to obtain a license and renew it until he qualified years later for a multi-engine upgrade. There was more, such as how to sail a skiff alone in Alaska shooting eagles for government pay.

In exchange we learned of Ian's family, their 100,000-acre sheep station near Alice Springs, his walkabouts with Aborigine neighbors, his horse, his school and his mother. Indeed, almost every sentence was punctuated with "my mother." He was so beautiful with his blond hair combed back, vibrating with excitement at a home visit after a year in his English school.

Ian was nine years old.

It only occurs to me now how parallel were the young lives of these two long-ago transported Englishmen. They were raised on isolated farms, had close and constant contact with blacks, took joy in their mothers, and were sent to boarding school at the age of eight.

Something else occurs in remembering the letter written to Ian's mother praising her son, who had invited us to visit. Lucius may have been the world's last, best letter writer.

New Zealand

New Zealand was calendar art of a green and pleasant land. Once completely forested, the sheep, which outnumbered humans, trimmed it to look like an endless golf course. In 1974, great swaths of land on the south island were still open to homesteading by squatters' rights—squat and farm it for seven years and it was yours. (I remember homesteading on the Cumberland Plateau, and the Crab Orchard stone houses built by the government for each squatter that are easily recognized today.) A number of big men who stepped off the plane with sheep shears in their hip pockets seemed to have this in mind. We went together to an office to have our boots fumigated before leaving the terminal. (Flora and fauna introduced to new terrain can play havoc—think kudzu.)

The first order of the day was to find a sporting goods shop to arrange for a guide to hunt Scottish red deer. Introduced many years ago to "make things like home," they had grown to enormous size and were so plentiful as to be pests harvested by government hunters from helicopters, with a year-round open season.

A Scot with a brogue that nearly brought tears to my eyes insisted that this was not the time of year to hunt stag on foot—they were too scattered—but if Himself insisted, we should be in the hotel lobby at 4:30 next morning. Then began the process of renting a rifle, which was no small thing; New Zealand is not as cavalier as we are about who carries around a weapon so powerful it can drop a beast you can hardly see in the distance.

The hunt was painful. When his bones were reassembled after the plane crash, Lucius' feet were put off until last, and were given short shrift. His little toes were displaced, curling over the rest, which hampered his balance and the fit of his shoes. The sea at Cabo and flat terrain at Tuolumne Meadows had been child's play in comparison with deer stalking.

Red deer feed on mountainsides from which they can see predators (especially men) and move steadily uphill out of sight when disturbed. You have to climb to the top and hunt down; otherwise you can go all day and see nothing. Once, and only once, we climbed a similar mountain in Scotland to pitch a tent for a night. It was nigh-impossible to find a dry enough place; the turf oozed water. When we came down next morning, hundreds of feeding deer paid us no attention.

It is impossible to judge how miserable another person can be, but when asked, he let me carry the heavy rifle for a while—a wretched sign. After one day, stalking was not an option. The fallback position was to heed the little pamphlet, "Where to go, What to see," handed out by Quantas.

The British settlement of New Zealand, land of friendly Polynesian Maoris whose communities were still intact in 1974, and, I assume, still are—moved from north to south. We headed south; I drove, he took off his shoes and started to read: "Fumaroles at Rotorua furnish geothermal energy for a large percentage of NZ's needs. I don't want to look at fumaroles; they are the same as in Yellowstone. Let's hie toward the glaciers and see what happens." The first thing to happen was just down the road.

For a long while we had been seeing to the west maybe the biggest lake in the world (about 300 sq. miles), Lake Taupo, which in some places is so wide you can't see across. When we crossed the bridge over the Tongariro River, a major feeder stream, it was love at first sight. I had never seen a fly fisherman standing up to his waist in a river, casting a slow, sensuous line: there he was—it looked so easy. I could do that.

Wrong. It was a farce. Where we stopped at a fishing lodge for lunch, seductive pictures of grinning men holding BIG fish lined the walls. Lunch stretched to a search for a tackle shop for Himself to rent gear—waders, rigged rod, net et al. And as fishermen go, he went, leaving me with the proprietor who lent me a stout glass rigged rod, tied on a fly and pointed to the gravel shore at the back door. Off I went, light of heart.

Never have I been more grateful for being alone as when I cast my first line. As a longtime spin caster and bait fisher (New Zealanders used this sexless term instead of fishermen, bless their hearts), my first, best cast was a Nothing. I pulled out some line and tried again, and got a serving of pasta coiled in the gravel. Time passed and finally by pulling out about ten foot of line and giving a mighty side-hand heave, my line landed in the water, and, caught by the current, played out—I was fishing? Afternoon wore into evening; I was exhausted. When Himself returned, fishless, he looked like I felt. Our problems were nothing that could not be eased by a Beefeater's martini and fresh-broiled fish. The only remark: "This place will take time. We'll come back when it's warmer."

So it came to pass—trade SCUBA at Cabo for big flies on the Tongariro from Christmas through January (summertime below the equator) for next year. Before we left, Frank Harwood, owner of the tackle shop, introduced us to Phil, owner of the Creel Lodge next door, and we had a place to sleep for December 1975.

Wellington, capital of N.Z., is a city of parks, none of which we saw. The ferry was leaving for the south island and so were we—a few hours across Cook Straits to a simpler world. Or certainly it was in 1974. There was one main road which clung to the coast all the way around, with only branches leading to the few inland towns. We took the right turn west toward Milford Sound with visions of walking part of the Track—similar to our Appalachian Trail but not so long.

NZ has unusual advantages for visitors. It is so small that it can be sampled in short order, and its maritime climate means fairly moderate temperature year round—first-class skiing in the high elevations and tree ferns on sea level trails threading among the mountains. Unlike its neighbor Australia, it broke away in a tectonic shift off of South America so long ago that it developed no predators and no poisonous snakes. AND it is so beautiful that the entire lower part is preserved as a World Heritage Site.

We started slowly, stopping when tempted along the road, which was a one-lane paved track with frequent lay-bys where we drove for miles without seeing another soul. Soon there was a hand-printed sign with an arrow saying "grotto." A grassy lane offered a small opening into a wonderworld of rock bluffs dripping water into splurges of mosses, ferns and small pools. With the motor off, we heard the gentle plashing, felt the coolness of a cave.

"Sas, we must talk," he said. "Of matrimony."

"Yes, of course, but let me talk first." I had been sure this would come up. We both knew that in coming with him, I erased the rest-of-my-life plans. There had been time to perfect my speech.

In jerky terms my rationale unrolled. I had a dim view of marriage as a bludgeon to friendship, and legal sex a trap for young wishful-thinkers at the height of their reproductive urge. I saw husband-snatching, especially from a cousin, as untenable until it happens, mitigated then by the passage of time beyond the raising of children and the mores of each partner. Elsie had been more than generous not to interfere with my staying with him in the hospital; had a heartbeat of her own in England and had thrown him out earlier; he had shown inclination to being snatched; etc., etc. Anyway, here I was. I could never be myself in Memphis, and Nashville for him was inconceivable. Timbuktu was a possibility.

"I don't need your cash or social support as she might," I said. "Ergo, leave it for the now and we can talk again should a change arise.

"Besides, in your *Ascent of Man*, Bronowski expounds that in music, it is not the striking of the string but the interval of silence between that creates magic. Methinks the intervals of silence, the brief separations between us hold our own magic. Agree?"

"Yes. For now."

A charming old hotel at Milford Sound was on our paid-for list. It's the only one I remember seeing there. The dining room I remember best, its little tassel-shaded table lamps brightening the white/white tablecloths and providing a low light that didn't dim the view through the huge windows. Fiordland of the south island, at the mouths of its glaciers, has to be the most dramatic sight on earth. In moonlight bright as day sitting across the table from Himself with the question that had hung between us out of the way, fingering the cold stem of a Champagne flute, was paradise now.

The next day was again the first day of the rest of our lives and one again to test his toes—on to the famed Milford Track! We had seen a sign near a wee (how easily that word comes when thinking of NZ) house saying "lodgings, provisions." So that's where we went, were provisioned for a few days, slapped on the back, and told to come on back if it rained. We had read nothing and so treated it like the Appalachian Trail in the States—hit the trail wherever, no registering, no fees, camp where you like, on your own. Had we read of the high passes, the off-season avalanches, the treacherous footing, and the prohibition of camping anywhere along the trail, we might not have started.

That was not what we saw for the couple of days of about a twenty-five-mile trek. I really don't know where we were, but it was a wondrous undulating walk through lush, strange trees and understory with footing squshy as tanbark and mountains rearing up. Himself disappeared ahead almost immediately, a most excellent sign, and waited at an unexpected hut with cots, gas stove, outdoor WC, etc. We poked about a bit then moved on in the sunshine until dusk when appeared flying bugs that bit, vicious as deer flies. Up went the tent ASAP; cold supper was fine.

Next morning they were gone; the wind stirred and it snowed—heavy, wet. The lights in the wee house beckoned, we were invited for supper, the lamp lit in one of the "lodgings" which was hardly big enough for the one bed and heavy-duty down comforter. The next morning, rain pounded the metal roof when a knock came and the door opened to our host bearing a pot of tea, warm bread and jam just like in Peter Rabbit. We had had the sense to bring our clothes under the covers; dressing was quick. By the time we expressed our thanks and left cash, the sun was out.

Sheep Station

It was one-word signs in the middle of nowhere that made the south island such a success. "Guests" appeared at a gap in the fence on a long stretch of grasslands, followed by a dirt road winding through the hills to a neat house. (NZ will never be a destination site for its architecture.) The dogs barked and the door opened to a smiling host followed by three children.

"Welcome," she said. "You've come at a good time." Inside, a lady was seated, very erect, in the dining room at the informally set table, pouring steaming hot chocolate. "We're about to go feed the sheep." And so we did after a regular meal called "elevenses." Or at least the twelve-year-old daughter did.

There were a number of outbuildings scattered about, of which a big two-story barn was most ingenious. Built into a hillside with two large entrances, the front opened on the ground level and the opposite on the uphill level. A gated fence separated the two paddocks. At the front, a big flatbed truck parked tail-in was stacked with hay bales which loaded from the top through a big hole from where the hay was stored—no lifting required. The second story, where the sheep were sheared once a year by traveling Maoris, had a chute leading to the bottom level. Shearing is a competitive art, as we saw later at a country fair. With electric shears, they were peeled out of their wool like a lemon in a couple of minutes then eased down the chute. Voila—all shaven, shorn and back in the pasture.

Everyone except Mama piled in the truck, where we moved slowly so as not to lose the load or the daughter perched on the top. Within a couple of miles, the horn sounded long and loud; sheep appeared—hundreds, maybe thousands. Daughter snipped the cord and, with her foot, shoved each bale overboard where it scattered. Looking back over the long, long lines of feeding sheep was the essence of NZ

When we got back, it was two o'clock dinner time, and a mighty meal it was: roasted lamb cooked pink—just right, delicious. What else we ate is forgotten, but it was a leisurely time. Mama encouraged the children to discuss what they had learned in their morning home school—it was thus that matters of the world arrived in Eden.

After the strenuous morning, a nap was in order, then a walkabout before tea/supper, a much lighter meal, marked by urbane conversation, children at attention and then their formal good nights—cheek kisses all round. More conversation followed in the snug drawing room warmed by fire on the heath and *"portiere"* across the door to hold the heat and eliminate drafts. (No central heat but this arrangement throughout the house made it very comfortable.)

Our hosts (I cannot believe I have forgotten names) were university graduates—Oxford and the University of Canterbury in Christchurch (the south island's largest city) where the older children were now. Without being pedantic, they taught us New Zealand: its socialist government, free public healthcare, home schooling service for the scattered population, semi-free enterprise system, outdoor sports at hand—fishing, skiing, boating, etc.—and its problems. Most vivid was the success of welcoming strangers/guests as a means of bringing the world to their children and themselves. There was chamomile tea and cookies at midnight.

Morning started early with tea and scones on a tray in bed, and not much later a hardy breakfast—rashers of home-cured bacon, eggs, broiled tomatoes, toast, jam and COFFEE. We had been there less than 24 hours and had eaten seven meals.

"Sas," he said, "I've got to leave this place, I feel like a blimp."

Instead, armed with lunch in our backpacks, fully-rigged fly rods and proper flies, we followed a path uphill for a couple of miles to an unusually tempting spot—a dredge hole left from gold sluicing in the early days. Not really a pond, it was more just a hole in the ground of about thirty feet diameter and maybe fifteen feet deep, fed by a tiny stream of very clear water. The kicker was the fish—four huge brown trout somehow trapped, or maybe stocked, were clearly visible feeding at the inlet. Brown trout are different from others in that they never stop growing as long as there is enough feed. These were enormous—maybe thirty inches.

With great precision he cast to the mouth of the inflow—they moved aside—not just once but all afternoon. But he sure looked good.

"Tell me what you're doing," I said. "If we're coming back, I need to know."

"The trout in the Tongariro are migrants, coming upriver from the lake to spawn, feeding along the way. They're lazy like we are, always facing upstream, slightly off to the side of the main current, and just move back and forth to nab passing morsels. Browns spawn in the fall, rainbow in the spring and the crossbreds at any time—so you can fish all year round. The trick is to get your fly to look like either a morsel or an irritant trying to hog the territory—then zap, a strike. Your gut tells you when it's time to raise the tip of your rod—presto—straight up and there you have him.

"The problem is the way your bait gets there. With a spinning rod, which you are used to, it is exactly opposite. Forget everything you know. Now you are trying to cast a nigh weightless line and the only way to do that is to create tension by pulling it strongly in both directions—forward by the momentum of the moving line and backward with your left hand pulling the line taut.

"Don't read a book; watch a fellow like the one we saw near the bridge the other day. Just believe that it works and, like learning to ride a bicycle, once you get the rhythm, you'll never forget it. These blasted critters take *la dolce vita* too seriously. If there's a rise in this puddle at dusk, we may take one. So let's come up again tomorrow and spend the night." He handed me the wand that would double my life's pleasure.

So we did, bearing sleeping bags, lunch, supper and breakfast but caught nothing.

The day after, we fled, fearing obesity.

Australia

Australia was not so endearing as NZ, so big, so flat, so like ourselves fifty years earlier. Brisbane, where we landed, was a city of scattered multi-story hotels on broad, empty beaches—there was an infestation of biting insects. The play we saw the one night there was a very funny, disturbing comedy, the brunt of which was a US Colonel sent to teach the Anzacs how to fight in one of our many wars.

The next day, it was off to Cairns in northeastern Queensland to dive the Great Barrier Reef. There the man with the twang at the sporting goods shop said the law provided for only one single tank per person per day for diving—a nothing, but very wise. He recommended instead the oh-so-posh retreat on Dunk Island on the Reef, which offered snorkeling. There was only one place there, which held 36 guests and was oh-so-beautiful. Sean Connery, whom we saw at the bar, was beautiful, too, but not nearly as much as the trails through the rain forest or the flights of white cockatoos that came in to roost at nightfall.

There I was in the "something else" of advancing years—knowing in succession, without intent, three of the World Heritage Sites—the Greek temple at Bassae, south NZ's Milford Sound and Australia's Dunk Island.

BUT I had started learning the poetry of fly fishing.

AL-SUMUT

Al-Sumut, the ancient Arabic word for "the way," brings us azimuth, meaning a bearing on an arc that can be set at place of origin to a known destination with a protractor on an area chart. (I think—it's the best I can do.) This was the option in 1974: to navigate from San Francisco hundreds of miles to Williams Lake, BC, slicing over the Cascades and Canadian Rockies, which were barriers to the infrequent radio signals. With this occult knowledge, full fuel tanks and the portable oxygen tank as required for pilots of small planes at twelve thousand feet and above, we flew. He looked at my fingernails at regular intervals to see if they had turned blue. That was his job, mine was the harder—to hold that flying machine above the gnashing mountain peaks and glaciers snatching at our bouncing bottoms mile after mile after mile, and do the worrying. Surprise—there it was—so much for 14th-century Muslim wisdom when you need it.

(While we're here, let us remind ourselves that it was the Moorish conquest of Spain which, lasted until 1492—the year Columbus sailed the ocean blue—that brought the concept of 0 to Europe, without which we might be still hacking Roman numerals into rocks or clay tablets.)

WILLIAMS LAKE

Williams Lake, a town of frontier charm, was the jumping-off place to the wilderness of the Caribou and Chilcotin regions of British Columbia and Yukon Territory. Himself was no greenhorn; he had flown for years with his bird dogs sleeping in the back through Saskatchewan and the

Northwest Territory to hunt pheasant. He knew Yellowknife and Great Slave Lake. We went to the big outfitters, an emporium of wilderness travel agents, hunting and fishing licenses, weather reports, area charts, and provisioners in general, to get our gear.

Al-sumut was the way, this was the how. He talked with everybody and, when we left with a plan, we were equipped: chest waders of heavy rubber with a repair kit for snags, wading boots with felt soles, heavy leather belts to snug the waist—if you slip and fall unbelted, waders fill with water and you sink like a rock—vests for reels, flies, polarized glasses etc., etc. (That's one of the good things about fly-fishing—somewhere you have everything you need on you.) AND the hottest new Eagle Claw glass rods which converted from spinning to fly rods by reversing handles and changing reels, which are now as obsolete as a Model T.

Kleena Kleene

Here we were, after buzzing the strip to see if there were grazers, pulled up to tie-downs near the house. How he found it, I didn't know and didn't need to; I had not seen the clearing in the endless forest until we started to descend. There was a normal country house with a few outbuildings, one of which was to be ours, and a normal-looking man greeted us as if we were on a public square. He put our stuff in a wheelbarrow, led the way, and told us supper would be ready soon. They would ring the bell. An osprey flew slowly along the gravel lakeshore, weighted down by a great fish in his talons.

And the loons. Jack London's *Call of the Wild,* the reading of my youth, spoke of the cry of loons—a leitmotif from which I have never recovered—my call of the wild. "And when I get to heaven, I'm gonna put on my shoes and walk all over God's heaven"—that's what I want to hear when Himself takes my hand.

Jonathon, our host, was an engineer. Dot was a teacher, now a home teacher, from St. Louis. Their two young children were as well behaved and exuberant as their New Zealand counterparts. A few sheep grazed the paddock next to the big vegetable garden—both enclosed in heavy-duty deer fence. Supper was venison stew with garden vegetables, wild mushrooms and a splash of good Sherry, a fresh-baked loaf and wild blackberry pie. Coffee was by the lake in the coral afterglow. Wavelets lapped the shore, the air chilled, the potbellied stove in our cabin which housed a maximum-warmth down comforter soon died down. Quickly it was morning with thermos of coffee on the doorstep.

Following the dictum of breakfasting like a king, there was lamb sausage, soft scrambled eggs, sliced tomatoes, a handful of watercress, wholegrain biscuits and a side of cinnamon rolls. The canoe pulled up on the gravel beach by our cabin contained a lunch hamper that would have held us for a week. Off we went to test the new Eagle Claws, with me starting from scratch, in a lake packed with fish.

Days followed days, mixing my less-and-less floppy line with hikes in the forest primeval and evenings of worldly conversation. When Jonathon spoke of a small cabin on an island, nearby but out of sight and sound of the homeplace, we accepted.

There it was: great logs laid by a master, with a parlor where a purple velvet Victorian love seat beside the wood stove overlooked the lake. The bed, built into the corner, was equipped with the fattest of down comforters. Super that night was a package of the ever-delicious Knorr's lobster bisque, enhanced by trout from the shining lake. It qualified for Michelin Four Stars if anything ever did.

Outside at some distance was the outhouse, where oil lamps cast their lovely light and a bookshelf introduced us to Robertson Davies, the Canadian writer of the elegant, howlingly funny *Deptford Trilogy*. His Booker Award-winning play, *Eros at Breakfast,* is to be reckoned with if your aim is pure pleasure—try them.

Days passed until the promise of New Experiences sent us to Bella Coola with regret and promise to return—which we did the following summer, trailed by two more planes of trusting Memphians. We took to the greenwoods instead of the lake—it was splendid too but not to be compared with the cry of the loons on the lake.

Bella Coola

Bella Coola is an historic site never mentioned at Ward-Belmont. There on a great rock is writ in vermillion and bear grease: "Alexander Mackenzie, from Canada by land, 22 July, 1793"—11 years before Lewis and Clark, he had crossed the North American continent.[1]

At Williams Lake they advised us to set the azimuth from Kleena Kleene to Bella Coola, follow its *fjord* out to sea, then turn and come back upriver about ten miles to the Hagensborg airstrip. The terrain there is narrow and this was safer than dropping abruptly down from the mountains to the east. There it all was—flying the winding visual course at a few hundred feet between the mountainsides of the *fjord* was awesome.

The strip had aviation fuel, weather reports, and a helpful attendant who suggested we try a nearby lodge owned by the Sierra Club. Again things fell into place, allowing us to feel the human heartbeat of a wilderness paradise. Ben, an MD from Campbell River across the straits on Vancouver Island, had brought his car by ferry, and we prowled the dirt roads and trails together.

In following a feeder stream in search of a newly reported eagle's nest, we came on a group of some 25 Indians on the far side of the river. The men were spearing salmon which swam so closely together they almost formed a bridge. Smudge fires were burning and women were slicing fillets of dressed fish into long strips with the skin left on, which they dipped into pots of something that hung on the smoke racks over the fires. We later found out that something was honey and water cooked down to thick simple syrup.

We parked, got out to watch, waved and cheered at taken fish. They paid us no attention until one went into a wickiup, brought out a moose-willow basket of something, stepped into the stream, waded across

---

[1] But let us now remember Cabeza de Vaca, the Spanish Conquistador, who is credited with the first crossing in the 16th century. He was one of the four survivors of some four hundred who came to conquer North America but were slaughtered by the Florida Indians and swamps. For eight years he moved westward toward Mexico City in response to rumors of other Spaniards and GOLD. He did this almost naked—his clothes had been used as oakum to plug the holes in a ship which they tried to build in Galveston Bay. His fiery red hair and beard made him welcome as "the child of the sun" foretold by the shamans. A man of some medical knowledge, a faith healer of a warm heart, he was welcomed by the natives. The tribes he traveled with adored him and guarded him so closely that he couldn't run away. But he made it to the coast where there actually were Spanish settlements from whence he returned to Spain.

up to his chest, dodging fish, and handed the basket to Lucius. He shook Lucius' hands, then looked at me without shaking mine. Without ever a smile he waded back and picked up his spear. What he had brought was called squaw candy by the locals—the long strips the women were smoking—and delicious they were. We were stars when we passed them around at supper that evening

Another day was different: We were fishing another stream way up a timbering road when a tall, very thin, vague-looking hippie—there were a few scattered around—appeared out of nowhere to ask if we could give him a few fishhooks. He said his wife had just had a baby and was sick; they didn't have much to eat. When Ben offered to see her, we went to his cabin, which he told us, with some pride, that he himself had built. That was obvious. There were gaps between the skinny logs, a tarp swung under the unsealed ceiling and a dirt floor. One small, nailed-closed window gave the only light. In the stick bed built in a corner, wrapped in a couple of sleeping bags, lay a pale young woman holding a newborn. There was no sound from either; her eyes were watching. Ben put the back of his hand on her forehead and took her pulse.

"Lucius, there's an infirmary in town. Here are the car keys, see how far up here you can come. It's a four wheel drive."

How I'll never know, but all six of us got to town. Ben was known at the infirmary since he came frequently by the ferry from Campbell River to help out. He went in with her and the silent, wide-eyed baby. We took the father to wolf down a meal and gave him fish hooks.

Aspens turned gold, ice formed at night, court cases were set in Memphis, Ben located her family—Main Line Philadelphia, not unusual. Her father came to fetch her and his granddaughter in a medevac. We set the azimuth back to Williams Lake for aviation fuel, oil change and early morning start for:

Tennessee, the Beautiful

Tennessee, the beautiful, at the end of a smooth flight across the huge circular harvested wheat fields of central Canada, Nebraska and Kansas. With the prevailing winds pushing, we almost made it in one day, but not quite. When we stopped in a town somewhere, its harvest fair was in progress and there was no room in the inns. We got to sleep in the plane and got an early start.

At Riverwood, Miss Sadie was already bathed, powdered and pale lipsticked, and dressed in a lacy bed jacket when we walked up the hill from the little airport. Joy was unbounded as she hugged her big white-bearded, nut-brown boy.

"Step back, Child, I want to look at you," she said. "Yes, you have done what you said you would. You look splendid." Then she added, "Thank you, Shirley."

Breakfast was served in her bedroom. Then she put on her robe and was helped down in the elevator to the porch. They talked. I listened. All was right with this world.

After lunch, for the first time in four months, he was gone—until Friday. Our life began to reel with other themes and variations. Cabo was gone, to become rich and famous with the press of the tourist world; the promise of the Tongariro was a worthy substitute. The Appalachian Trail was eternal. The hut in Hardeman County was as tranquil, the wild turkeys as gleaming bronze, the deer as wary, the fires as warm. When I was home in Nashville during the week, long did I labor with my Eagle Claw on a grassy plot, reading and rereading the instructions that had come with the line. It explained in second-grade terms what to do with your left hand, how to build line tension and most everything else.

Tennessee was a nice place to come back to. It was like sliding under the dining room table at Longview at exactly two o'clock—there were smiles and continued conversation. They would be surprised if you were not there, but probably not notice that you had been gone for months. If I were not out in the beyond of the beyond, this was where I belonged—where I was used to being—certainly not Memphis. I was busy all day, every day. The best part of being a volunteer is that there is always plenty to be done when you show up.

Himself had done what he meant to do when he set out in the spring a semi-invalid and now he returned in the fall in full vigor. Our *modus vivendi* on return was much the same; the difference was that I had completely thrown in my hat beside his. The Appalachian Trail was glorious in the coming of October's bright weather. Added were long weekends at a splendidly funky place, Free Mason Island, a high place of maybe twenty acres in the Gulf off the coast at Mobile. This consisted of a fair-sized shanty built atop a sunken barge, outfitted with maybe the best of all Cajun cooks. Her husband lounged outside the kitchen window. His bailiwick was the road grader parked alongside, with which he tended the barely minimum 1,000 foot airstrip. You could stand in the surf, waist deep, and catch schools of sea trout, which she smoked and cooked into magical things. Sleeping quarters were four staterooms of a 1910 opulent wrecked yacht tamped halfway in the sand. On our last visit, Lucius mentioned that the strip seemed short.

Sure enough, half had eroded in a storm. So that was that.

The house in the cornfield in Hardeman County had collected an electric stove, refrigerator, kitchen sink and HOT and cold running water—downright palatial. The day the telephone was added caused only momentary confusion. The installer said the wire would have to snake through the front door and then under the rug. Himself fetched his rifle from under the bed where it was kept, laid it on the floor next to the baseboard at the proper place and pulled the trigger. Voila, a perfect conduit substituted.

Mr. Cossa and his pleasant wife lived and tended their garden in the two-story white house on the gravel road where she was the local beauty parlor. He did the farming, warded off timber thieves from the virgin white oak forest and raised some cattle. When he called them in each morning to feed, the wild turkeys answered. He, with Curtis, his second-in-command, converted the tiny unused house by the kitchen door into sleeping quarters for two huntsmen by adding a floor, lights and a bucket of whitewash. So with the guest room of a double and bunk beds, we could and did sleep six during hunting seasons...

On New Year's Day we shared a feast of Erlene's (his cook in Memphis) wild meat pies, cranberries with orange zest and pecans, homemade eggnog and fruit cake, good hard whiskey and cigars with SUVs of Memphians. When they frequently got stuck in the corn field, Mr. C. with his trusty John Deere stood by to pull them out, happily muddy for the first time since last year. Mickey Babcock brought white tulips.

David Halberstam came to spend a day of civil rights talk for his work in progress about the happenings in Memphis the day Himself had been in Federal Court to get the injunction lifted against Martin Luther King's attending the second Garbage Collectors march—the day that King was shot.

It was a rare opportunity to watch and hear those two men, lest we forget that life is earnest, life is real. But next day we were off to New Zealand as planned.

Tongariro River

New Zealand was the best for wild Rainbows and Browns flowing into Lake Taupo (next to our Great Lake Superior and Siberia's Lake Baikal, the largest of the world's freshwater lakes) at Turangi. Built about 15 years prior to our first visit for workers on the hydro-dam, this new town was shaped like the Stoa of Attallos in Athens: a very long portico with shops attached, broken in the middle and bent back at a right angle. The town was raw, but the river was long a playground for the rich and royal as property of the Crown. Prince Charles had recently been there to fish his very own Prince's Pool and was distressed that it was silting in spite of its royal name. But the Duchess Pool, named for his grandmother, whose favorite it was, had improved. Rivers move and change course for all of us alike.

Phyllis of the Creel Lodge and Frank Harwood of the tackle shop greeted us, helped carry our stuff to a cottage and fed us supper. We walked the thirty yards to the arbor footpath which followed the river for a long way along the series of pools. The first one upriver, the Major Jones, was the most famous. There, even at dusk, several men at regular intervals, all dressed alike and waist-deep in the water, stood casting their long, long powerful lines.

My gosh, it was at our back door!

Frank explained the protocol. The first arrival (who came when it was still dark) takes the head of the pool to have first go at the fresh fish swimming upstream toward the spawning beds. (Rainbows spawn in the spring, Browns in the fall, and crossbreds most anytime so there were always spawning fish moving up from the lake.) Next arrival steps in upstream, never downstream, with several yards of casting space between, and so on. You never step in until you are ready to cast—that's what determines your arrival time. By the time the sun is well up, there can be twelve rods fishing peacefully at five or six-yard intervals.

If the rod on either side takes a fish, its neighbors must wait until it's landed before casting. The drill is three casts, then two sidesteps downstream then three more casts, step—step. On no occasion cast to the place where a fish was just caught by your neighbor—that is his territory. You have only a few yards to cast from but your target area, since you are casting toward an outward bend, is larger and new fish are always moving in fast and deep along the bottom. Sophisticated devices are used, such as lead leaders on weight-forward lines which cause big flies to drop quickly and stay down in the heavy current. That heavy line called for a retrieval basket belted at the waist into which to feed the line instead of coiling it in your hand. It feeds out faster during the next cast.

There is a notion that where British royalty moves, civility and manners reign; the Major Jones was an example. In most other places it would have been chaos, a reach to be avoided, but not here. From before to after light, crowds of fishermen moved quietly, politely, seemingly on top of each other, catching BIG trout. I benefitted from it myself one morning just at light. Himself and I had arrived early enough to need flashlights held in our teeth to check the gear we had rigged the night before. There was no one in the water; I would at last be first on the line.

I was about to take my spot when, lo and behold, a very polite-looking man waded smack in front of me. He bade me good morning, and I returned his greeting. I gulped and then, in the same polite voice, said, "This is your first time here, isn't it?"

"Yes, it is. How did you know?"

"Oh, that was easy. If you had been here before, you wouldn't have entered just below me, you would have taken your place at the top of the line."

Poor man. He was just as embarrassed as I had hoped, and hurriedly retreated. When we crossed paths in town, he did a lot of bowing and scraping to both of our amusement.

Himself did well enough on the river to want to return early. He would roll out of bed before the alarm sounded into the dark, drink last night's warmed-over coffee, wolf a hunk of bread and slab of cheese and be out the door to be first on the water; I came mumbling after. It was hard work, small wonder there were no other women, and after the first day when I took one fish, my count was zero.

I again found another something else: Frank Harwood, one of our two friends, was a professional guide (Lucius would think it unmanly to hire a guide) who made a point of checking on us almost every day. One day I hunkered down beside him as he watched from the bank. We chattered nothingness for a while until I threw my heart ahead of me, "Frank, why can't I catch a fish or even get a strike?"

"Your fly is not getting deep enough quick enough."

"How can I do that?"

"I would have to show you."

"Frank, I am one of the world's greatest cheapskates, but I want to cut a deal with you. I want to give you $100 for one day of your time to do just that."

"When?"

"Tomorrow."

"Good. We'll go up to the Redhut pool at a decent hour. There'll not be a crowd."

It was again another first day of the rest of my life, and at 56 years it was only getting better. Redhut was a broader, less dramatic reach where a few were happily casting across to play the current downstream. There was one heavy splash of a hooked fish as Frank and I walked to the lower end of the pool where it narrowed.

"We'll cross here," he said. "Give me your rod and take firm hold of both of your wrists." He put both rods (his was a gorgeous bamboo that he probably made himself) facing backwards and pointing up, in his right hand, slipped his left arm through my crossed right and held his own wrists as we stepped in the current, totally secure. It was miraculous!

We sat on one of the rocks that littered the run.

"We'll re-rig your line," he said. "Pay attention."

With a Swiss Army knife just like mine, he cut off the lead tippet, dropped it in one of his many pockets, and pulled out a small spool of clear filament. He cut off about 16 inches, which he aligned with the tip of the leader from the opposite direction, and tied it in a plain knot, but wrapped it twice instead of once, and pulled it taut. He took one line in each hand and tugged in opposite directions till the knot snugged, then gave it a good snatch—it held. The tag ends were trimmed against the knot and he snatched again.

"Here. You break it. That's a surgeon's knot and that's a tippet. They will save you money in leaders."

I had seen pictures but never tried one, rather stood it awe at the thought. When I tried to break it, it held.

"Always do that," he said. "Testing beats a good strike snapping it off."

He stuck my big Red Setter fly, about two inches, on the sheep-skin patch of his vest and took a little black thing that looked like a wadded ball of under-bed sweepings the size of my little fingernail—a nymph.

"Here, you tie it on," he said. "That's good, a single clinch knot. Carry my rod and stay a bit behind and to my left. You're too big to fit in my creel. Now, forget everything you know and just watch."

We had been sitting on a rock in some 10 inches of water in a side cut off the river. He took a couple of steps upstream, cast about 10 feet of line so that the wad landed and started to slowly sink into a small pool. BAM. The rod shot straight up, arcing forward at the tip. A strike. He stood steady until the thrashing lessened, then waded forward to the pool, taking in line with his left hand, rod tip up and flexed, until he slipped his hand down the taut, agitating leader. He felt the hook and, with a flick of his wrist, released a big, bright shining Rainbow.

He never touched the fish nor took it out of the water. (To do this, the barb of the hook must be clipped off.) As we waded on up, he explained that the slime on a trout is fungus-proof and any handling with hand or net wipes some away and exposes the fish to trouble.

Just as suddenly as the first time, the short line again shot forward and another slightly bigger fish went through the same routine. By the time we had negotiated the slick rocks the distance to the main stream, he had taken and released another. That was three respectable fish caught and released without touching one.

The main stream came in from the left so that when we held in the calmer water, it was rushing at us. Handing me my rod, he took from his pocket a little flame-orange thing which he pressed together on the leader at some eighteen inches above the fly.

"This is a strike indicator," he said. "You don't have to use one, but where you cast may be too turbulent to see anything. You can see this and when you see it stop even for a second, it may be a strike, set your fly—quick.

"Take a natural stance like a boxer, left foot forward, toes a bit out, weight balanced on back foot, left side quartered to the current. Get steady. I have watched you cast—not too bad. Now look at those two rocks right there, with the space where the water Vs through and quiets on the downstream side. Perfect place. Short cast to the V, about ten feet of the line not counting the leader. Start instantly to retrieve the line as fast as you can, it'll come straight at you—fast. Drop loose line, it will float behind; don't try to coil it in your hand—that is too slow.

"Remember: short line cast to the V, watch the red indicator. If it even just looks like it stops—rod tip goes straight up, quick. NOW, GO!"

Nothing.

"Not bad. Again."

Nothing.

"Again."

"Blast, Frank, I've got a snag."

"How do you know?"

I was standing there with the tip slightly up, tugging, but I was stuck. All of a sudden a HUGE trout smacked the surface and was gone. Frank stood there grinning.

"You lost your tension," he said. "Remember, rod straight up with full tension on the line—quick. He spit the fly out."

"Come on, that calls for a beer."

Lucius had been watching from the other side and let out a roar. Off we went to town with me on the back seat vibrating. At lunch, all of the toasts were for me and once again, the first day of the rest of my life looked good.

After lunch, Lucius went back to the Major Jones, Frank and I to the easier Island Pool behind the cottage where we sat and talked. He suggested we put off my second half-day until the next morning, that he wanted me to think about what I had done, how to do it next time and PRACTICE. Asked what I remembered, I told him not much. I had been so excited that all was knocked out of my head except "cast to the V" and that when fish struck I had not been paying full attention. He said that was enough, that next day I would see what else I had picked up subconsciously.

He spoke of regretting that so much hocus-pocus was attached to fly fishing, especially for beginners; there was no such thing as secret holes, or special tricks to casting or devices. There was only practice, practice, practice. That's what it took to cast a straight line to the desired spot with the least disturbance. Once that was done, you simply had to maintain tension, pay attention, and think like a fish. Where would I be, lazy creature that I am, if I wanted to feed with the least amount of effort? He told me to get in the water, look around, and pick out places where I, a fish, would spend time. And then practice—a short line, no bellying out in the current, etc., and that he would fetch me at 8:30 next morning.

Himself was up again in the dark; I brewed fresh coffee and toasted our bread and cheese, then he was gone. Leisurely, I dressed for the day (the water was about 40 degrees) from the stack folded on the floor beside the bed where they had been shed the night before. First the usual, then, in order: snug silk long johns, flannel pajama bottoms, army surplus wool pants, socks—light cotton to absorb moisture and heavy wool for warmth and cushioning—a t-shirt, a light wool turtleneck, a wool shirt, a short lightweight raincoat/windbreaker folded in possum pocket on back of vest, the heavy rubber chest-high waders, tightly belted, and wading boots which had dried overnight on the porch. I removed from the vest the pocket-size flashlight and fingerless wool gloves—unneeded after sunup—and at last put on the inflatable fishing vest and brimmed hat.

At 8:35, Frank attached a walking staff to my belt at the end of a four-foot cord. We crossed the river at the end of the Island Pool and headed upstream a few feet, where he stopped and pointed—"There." I waded a couple of feet forward, dropped the staff, which floated behind, took a boxer's stance, released the fly from the little hook just above the handle, tested the knots, stripped a few feet of line and cast. Nothing.

"Again," he said. "Two feet further."

Nothing.

"Another three feet. You're in no hurry."

Pop, there he was. The fish was small, about fourteen fat inches, and we released him without touching the slime.

"Where there's one fish, there are apt to be others. You know that fishing upstream you are standing behind them; they don't see you as long as keep your shadow off of their pool, in which case they think you are an overhead predator and hide. Wait a minute, then give it a few more tries."

No luck.

There was a likely-looking pool in front of us, but small trees overhung the bank, leaving no room for an overhead cast.

"Now pay attention," Frank said. "This may be the best thing you'll learn: a Tongariro roll cast. Palm up, lower the rod to a point where it will clear the trees, then pull your elbow back. Wait until the line has time to drop absolutely perpendicular to the water, then strongly flip your wrist forward and over, and rock your weight forward while you cast. This is easy and accurate at a shortish distance."

It was both—IF I remembered to give the line time to drop straight down—then cast... It needed practice—a lot.

"Now for the most fun of all: dry flies," he said. "Here, I have a present for you."

He handed me an aluminum box, just small enough to fit in the upper vest pocket, and lined with white, stiff spongy-looking something. On one side, hooked on six upright strips, were a variety of textured and colored nymphs, little black terrestrials (ants and beetles) and pale mosquitoes, then ranks of parachutes (little crowns of white feathers, so you can see from a distance that the dry fly beneath is floating and when it goes under with a strike) atop a small variety of shaped and colored dry flies. On the other side, without strips, was a collection of larger flies—elk hair caddis, stoneflies, Adams, Wulffs, and Humpies and so on. Each was a small work of art. They would supply me for decades. (A beat-up fly doesn't put a fish off; after all, there are beat-up bugs.)

I could have wept.

"You tied?" I said.

"Yes."

"They are very beautiful. Thank you."

(Right now, 2014, they lay open to the sun in the window of my "retirement home" apartment, so when I stop to touch and gladden at the subtle colors, I am less "retired." A few are originals, many are gone, the rest are replacements from over 18 glorious years.)

"Come on, we'll go down to the Bridge Pool, it's smoother for this. You know how good Lucius looks casting those long, sensuous loops? That is a 'false cast,' which is for two things: to lengthen a cast or to dry a wet dry fly. Also, it's fun—exaggerates the rhythm and timing, which is crucial. Now, tie on a dry fly. You have some, remember?"

Dry fly fishing is the most seductive of all: two critters trying to outsmart each other. Now is the time when you are after A fish, not just any fish. You know it is right there by the tiny air bubble centered in a series of out-flowing rings. It has just taken and is apt to take again. It's up to you to lure him in his own element. You don't much consider that you are both predators.

Oh, psychologists, have a field day!

The rest of our time in Turangi was joyfully consumed by just being with Himself and practicing, practicing, remembering, remembering what I had learned, minding my manners by not invading the territory of the downstream fishermen, finding fishy-looking places where I could get in and be able to wade. We saw Frank frequently for a wave, some chatter and meals. He was a good cook, did trout like the native he was, and we staked out a spot in town that specialized in wood-choppers' spaghetti and served a decent red house wine.

One last evening before we left, he lifted his glass in a toast, "You have created something of a stir—a good-looking woman taking better than her share of fish by herself and doing it on the wrong side of the river and in the wrong direction. I would take odds that when you come back in five years, there will be a continuous footpath and some entries cut on the other side, and you won't be alone."

Lucius and I took to fishing the Bridge Pool frequently. There was an older couple, properly attired in their tweeds and fishing 15-foot handmade split bamboos, who came many afternoons. Their chauffeur pulled waders over his uniform to wade to a small mid-stream island with a wicker tea hamper.

Himself watched. One afternoon he said, "I have decided what I want to do in my old age—let's you and I just sit on an island in the middle of a river and have angel food cake with our tea."

GREATER COMPLIMENT HATH NO ISLAND THAN THAT!

Horses, Hitches and Rocky Trails

Horses, Hitches and Rocky Trails is the horse packers' wilderness bible, a masterpiece of rollicking drawings by Joe Back of Dubois, Wyoming,[2] pop. 869, elev. 6,896 feet, and located in the alluvial valley of the upper Wind River. The book is to be wary of unless you're not opposed to a new life. Lucius Burch was a natural candidate to take it on—lights, liver and soul—and I trotted right behind.[3] Having been smitten by Licorice, the burro hero of Tuolumne Meadows, this was the next move for such a dude as Lucius, who had about done himself in by plowing a hot red twin-Comanche into the mud and was determined to ignore the results.

Easter, 1975, found him armed with an invitation to lunch, a fine dressed wild turkey, a jug of Jack Daniel's and a sedate Cessna tied down on the airstrip of the bench above town.

Mary, Joe's instantly charming wife, welcomed us at the door and put the turkey on to roast while we went to the Episcopal Mission in town. She was in charge of the service, and told of the resurrection of Christ using her "chalk talk," a series of colorful pictures she drew rapidly on an easel.

Joe, a renowned Western bronze sculptor, and she, a painter, had met at the Chicago Art Institute years before. Their sturdy two-story log cabin on the bank of the Wind was full of their works—a veritable museum. The turkey looked like one I once cooked—pitiful with legs sticking straight up. But talk of horse packing in the back country glowed through the afternoon while Mary's bird feeding platform outside the studio window clicked with juncos and chickadees. Come dusk we went back to town, armed with her promise to find us a cabin with a paddock of green, green grass and a creeklet of running water for our horse.

Over the doorway of the Rustic Tavern a sign said BEST SALOON WEST OF MUDDY GAP and NO FIREARMS. Inside was quiet, with only a few people (all with their hats on) in booths that lined the wall;

---

[2] Originally dubbed Never Sweat, till it was changed by an embarrassed rural postman.

[3] Liver and lights is only cooked once in the fall, at hog butchering time. Lights are pork lungs and, with liver, are browned with onion and sage, cooked into gravy, and served over biscuits. —Ed.

the juke box was set low on western swing in the dance hall at the back. The barkeep was an aging lady with one too few front teeth and a thatch of blondined green hair. Martinis never would have done, but there was a sign on the mirror behind her: "Whiskey Sours $1.50," so whiskey sours it was. She took a couple of glasses and sloshed in ice, something from a jug, and a generous pour from the bottle, and stuck out her hand. I carried them to a booth while Himself settled up, plus a tip, which brought a wisp of a smile but nothing more.

(The drinks were fine, and became a late afternoon ritual for several years when we were in town—until one afternoon when she wanted $7.50. When reminded of the price, she said that she "didn't much like to make 'um.")

The Rustic Pines, the attached restaurant of white table linen and candles, served a powerful good rare roast beef, Idaho potatoes baked without tinfoil, green salad and strong coffee. It was spitting snow when we walked to the Twin Pines Hotel—itself an historical marker—which had sent a car to fetch us in answer to the telephone from the unattended hut on the airstrip. We talked of staying to get acquainted, but that decision was taken from of our hands.

Next morning the town was knee-deep in snow. All was quiet in the empty lobby except a coffeepot gurgling and fire hissing in the big fireplace—both of which we took advantage of. The cafe next door where a few men sat (hats on) smelled of sausage. "It's just pancakes this morning," was the proprietor's greeting. "The cook didn't show up yet, and that's all I know how to make."

Outside, the sun glared on the snow where car tracks laced the one paved street (also the main highway), but you could navigate the sidewalk in your boots. Lights were on in the newspaper office—a starting place. Cindy Boyhan, who had a soft North Carolina voice and was busying herself getting out the next issue, stopped to bid good morning and pour coffee. She urged us to come when the weather warmed, saying that the airstrip on the bench above town was a full 5,000 feet and that thought Dave Martin had a place that might suit us. He was out of town, she said, but she would call. Then she invited us to supper.

Next stop was the harness shop. Inside was a bear of a man, Jerry Rowe, hammering on something behind the counter. He laid down the weapon, wiped his hands on the seat of his pants and eyed Himself. It wasn't long before they were deep in talk of panniers, halters, cotton ropes, horseshoeing repair kits... I was attracted by a magazine rack near the front door. Two young boys, who should have been in school, sidled in with their eyes hitched on the stock until Jerry looked at them and they asked what time it was. He looked at the big clock right behind him and told them. They loitered a while longer until he eyed them again, then they left. The magazines were of a special sort. The only names I recognized were *Playboy* and *Penthouse*.

Jerry became a friend when we came back in May. Among other things, he took on the gear that had hung unused for a time in Lucius' barn. They were an unusual collection for the Wild West: English handmade Indian cavalry and a fine hunting saddle (which even had a name which I have forgotten) both in good shape except for needing new girths, a brad in one stirrup flap, a lot of saddle soap and neatsfoot oil. When Jerry was through with them, they would have had a prime spot in the museum at Churchill Downs. Such oddities caused salty comments from the outfitters we met on the trails. But I don't think I could have lasted a week in a western saddle, much less eighteen years.

Lunch at the Cowboy Café was big bowls of homemade chili, followed by a surprise that made Dubois memorable There was a lady in town who cooked pies for fun and cash; the Cowboy was her main outlet. A slate on the glass display case listed twelve choices, and the chocolate Kahlua with a two-inch-plus meringue leaped out as winner. The coffee steamed.

The afternoon was for getting a lay of the land. The two bookstores had a surprisingly wide selection and knowledgeable owners; the town library was a small building on an unpaved street, locked; the shop carrying Indian treasures smelled of sage and sounded of far-off drums.

The hotel shower was hot, and Cindy's house was within easy walking distance. She was not only a joy to be with (and a good cook) but so were her three civilized children. AND she was full of good news—she had talked with Dave Martin who did have a cabin with pasture he would rent.

Next day the airstrip had been snowplowed, and back in Nashville, spring was busting out all over. That was just the beginning.

A Long Time

A long time it was between Easter and June, but at last we headed west, as Thoreau says man's natural compass veers. We followed the sun as the sunflowers did on the dirt shoulders of the highway out of Riverton to Dubois—76 miles across the end of the eastern plains, through two million acres of the Wind River Indian Reservation, and into the mountains.

To this Southerner used to trees, trees and more trees, the road goes through desolation of treeless hills, almost waterless, rocks and scrub, sage, grey, brown. Is it a wonder that the US turned such as this over to the Eastern Shoshone and Arapaho tribes, mortal enemies, and then forced their children into boarding schools to teach them to farm? The mortality rate ran as high as 60%—such is man's inhumanity to man! Would my government, would we do that again now? If not, then the world is improving. When Lucius was asked how he could remain so optimistic, his reply was short, "My nurse as a child, whom I loved above all else, was born a slave. That wouldn't happen now."

The land rises without notice; a firstcomer's heart sinks until Crowheart Butte appears to lift the land. The Wind River valley, land of warm snow-eating Chinooks (warm winds) in the weather shadow of the Tetons, was so blessed with game that it was the hunting grounds of many tribes. But by the late 1800s, game was getting scarce—especially along the routes taken by the white men rushing west to the gold fields.

Chief Washakie of the then-powerful Shoshone took offense when the Crows continued to come after his warning them off. Here a battle raged with such loss of life that it was agreed to settle it *mano-a-mano* between the two chiefs. Washakie killed his enemy after a brave and bloody fight. To show his respect for courage, instead of scalping his foe, he cut out his heart, mounted it on his spear and rode out among his braves to show his respect for bravery.

Just imagine the two in full war-bonnet and little else, armed only with spears and small shields of buffalo hide, bareback on their sleek spotted ponies. (There were no indigenous horses in the Americas. These were the best of those brought from Spain by the *Conquistadores*, which had benefitted from the magnificent Arabians of their Moorish conquerors in the XII century. Of course that bloodline thinned long ago, but the finely chiseled ears and nostrils, bowed necks, lush manes and tails still appear among herds of wild horses.)

The butte is the gateway to the Rocky Mountains. The Wind River valley severs a mighty mountain range into two—the Wind Rivers to the south and the Absarokas to the north, which stretch 150 miles to the Beartooth Wilderness on the Montana border and Yellowstone Park—all ours, yours and mine. Blessed be the politicos who had/have the foresight to see that this is done.

Beyond starts the green of irrigated alfalfa (high-quality hay is one of the cash crops possible in this country of short seasons) and the first sight of the river running through Albert Winchester's place. Albert and his wife, with sons and Gussy, his henchperson (who was reported to have been born on a horse and refused to get off), ran a class outfit from the cluster of barns, hay sheds and cabins. At home, he and Hazel were perfect hosts who could and did tell of the West the way it was. And she made the best of all worlds' sourdough bread, and even taught me to use the "starter" to make pancakes.

Years later, when they moved on, the Nature Conservancy bought and holds their land and, with luck, always will.

From there to where East Fork angles into the Wind, the hills become serious and the cutbanks of the river dramatic. Chugwater formations of barn-red mudstone and soil slice open like cake and explode into the Badlands—several miles of mountain-high red bluffs which attract droves of geologists and photographers who line the roadside, especially at sunset, for this *Pousse-Café*: a narrow band of dark cottonwood green with snatches of deep river blue, a wider band of tender alfalfa green, and bands of glowing red that almost fill the sight but leave ample space for the incredible blue of the darkening sky. The suffused light overspreads and fills with such a glow! In remembering the West, it is the light that prevails.

But I dawdle. We had not come for the glories of Dubois. They were fine for three or four days to stow stuff, take a bath, wash hair/clothes, replenish grub, try the saloons, eat somebody else's cooking, sleep in a bed and other non-essentials. Cindy Boyhan found us a place to rent for the next three months, a cluster of three one-room cabins and a monumental outhouse of six graduated-size holes which had been the town brothel when Dubois was the tie-hack (a tie is the log stretcher which hold rails together and to the ground) capital of the world. The early 1900s were the time of building railroads, and mobs of Swedes and Norwegians who knew what they were doing took to these woods. They too enjoyed city life—occasionally.

We had come for the high country—the wilderness. Joe Back's book gave us a drop on how not to be dudes and assured us that it was easy.

The first outing was not a total success for me. We backpacked to the second crossing of Horse Creek toward Five Pockets with Cindy and her children. The youngest was nine and already a veteran. I alone was weary; it snowed. I waded the river (Horse Creek is one of the main tributaries of the Wind) according to instructions: remove boots, roll pants above knees, place socks in shirt front, replace boots, get up, grab staff, GO! When I sat on a wet stone to reverse the drill, there were lines across my shins gently oozing trickles of pink—my blood had met the skim ice. But heavy wool socks hold your body heat and all was well.

Close by, a grove of barely leafing trees provided a campsite of dry spots, downed wood, and the fire that Lucius started. Never, ever, has a goodly slosh of Jim Beam and creek water tasted better. Supper, provided by Cindy, was superb: thick T-bone steaks (I gnawed and sucked on my bone, threw it over my shoulder for the next critter—it was gone by morning), instant mashed potatoes, dried milk, creek water, plenty of butter from town and chunks of German baking chocolate with blacker-than-black coffee. The tent stayed dry, and a double sleeping bag is the joy of the world.

It didn't snow much during the night but the louring morning sky left it a no-brainer—go to town. Coffee was brewed while we broke camp and left armed with a couple of granola bars and an apple. Re-crossing the creek brought the same results: a thin sliver of pink on the shins. The rest was all downhill to the Cowboy Café for great bowls of homemade chili and chocolate Kahlua pie.

Cindy explained that spring snows came from the east and usually last only a few days. You just hole up in your tent, read your book, eat what you have brought for the occasion, nap and enjoy. Such snows could come anytime. Get used to them. Summer is August 12, from ten to two o'clock.

Lucius still had visions of Licorice. "We haven't scratched the surface and it's obvious we can't carry all our stuff on our backs for a very long time. We'll find a horse." And so we did. While poking about a side street, there he stood: white and proud, in a paddock by the river. He was very much for sale at $200.

When we had come at Easter, Himself looked for a rental car. There was none, but if you were in need, the filling station man would sell you one and buy it back on return. There was a great grey Charger, retired by the USPS, that only had 300,000 miles. For $500 dollars, a good grease job and new battery, we had wheels. And Jerry Rowe, our friend of the harness shop, found a discarded baby-blue two horse trailer, knocked the nails back in and repainted it fire engine red. Voila!

Snoop was content with the grass in his new digs, but he was still edgy without a friend. It was time to beat the rallying drum for stalwarts named Joe McCarty, Dana Fagan, and John Ellerbeck—all powerful walkers. They appeared with Quiche, the Malamute, and a gorgeous strawberry blond who could and did out-walk and out-work everyone else. Himself, bless his heart, was properly dizzily dazzled!

"But MINE, said the cat as she looked at the moon," as off we went to Brooks Lake beneath Washakie's Needles, where Snoop was packed with museum-quality panniers (a going-away gift from FedEx's machine shop) swung on a wooden pack saddle hauled up from Mexico. Two duffle bags packed with tents and sleeping bags rode atop, snugged according to the "the book" of Joe Back, and in the V between was the bag of heavy stuff separately bungeed. When another of Ellerbeck's friends, who carried a great timberman's axe as a part of his gear, asked to add it to the load and lead Snoop, his offer was accepted.

It should be remembered that it is tough for a person on foot to lead a horse—it wants to hang back to graze or to tread on your heels.

When we started down the trail with a new leader and a solitary horse as nervous as a Victorian bride, within a hundred yards all hell broke loose. Snoop panicked and slammed through the trees, shedding as he raced, with the panniers flapping, flying back to the barn. With nary a word, Lucius started hoofing back and was gone for some three long, long hours. We collected the stuff, broke out a deck of cards, listened to mumblings over the broken axe handle and waited for whatever next was to be. When the two came back Snoop's ears were on the alert, so we set camp and bedded down early.

Himself said that the wranglers, amid whoops of laughter, told him that western horses are herd animals and to take one out by itself is sure trouble. (It was my hope that we could just give him back and settle for less lofty ambitions, but I didn't mention that nor did it occur.)

By the next morning the stake was pulled and Snoop long gone. This time there was no trouble knowing where, and the drill was repeated. When they returned at mid-morning, there was a hurry-up meal amid some mewling over the axe and insurance until Lucius summoned John for a brief private talk. John called axe owner for a brief private talk. The axe reappeared in a private backpack and Peace descended. Who knows what was said!

It was hard to remain irritated, swinging along in that gorgeous country up Bear Creek and beyond and beyond. Snoop, renamed Spook, now wore his bridle, which Himself led by the bit. This way they could talk and ears relaxed. (Spook bore Arab features: fine shaped ears and nostrils, a lush white mane and tail, and an attachment to people. Later I was to ride Joker, a smaller, lighter-structured dapple grey who was never tied and munched the grass next to our tent—a lovely sound for falling asleep.)

Bless Cindy again, it was she who got us further off first base and made Spook's life one of joy. It was she who spoke sweetly to Perce, manager of the Walt Disney ranch which stretched up the Dunoir valley, possibly the most magnificent in the world, which was the view from our cabin. So we had a friend in Jacob, an unused burro lent for the summer. With Spook, it was love at first sight.

A museum piece from Himself's barn in Memphis was a Confederate Army mule saddle. (Mules have tender backbones and narrow withers—so the saddle has a slit down the center and is more triangular than a horse saddle which is flatter. I tell you these things because so few are horse people any more. Poor you!) It arrived and was put in the hands of Jerry Rowe 'til its leather glowed and brass fittings shone. Jacob had the presence of Winston Churchill and the strength of Godzilla. Spook was charmed, as were we all. The drill of ride an hour, walk an hour with never a heel tread upon was the absolute best. I have a picture of Lucius clipping along astride Jacob, his long legs clearing the ground by about six inches, leading Spook, whose ears are forward. (For you city folk, a horse's ears indicate mood like a person's smile or frown. Forward, all is well. Back, better watch out.)

The four of us—we invited Perce but he, the businessman, declined—struck out again for a week's stay in Five Pockets.

That I say "the four of us" calls for speaking of Joe McCarty, who came for the first trip and is part of this saga. This average-size, handsome (hope you're reading this, Joe) in his own way, establishment-type Memphis lawyer arranged a life of relative freedom. As a boyhood friend of Freddy Smith, he became General Counsel for FedEx at its birthing and stayed so until booted upstairs to guide its Eastern Rim from Hong Kong and later all of South America from Santiago in Chile. But this was early when he could take time as he chose. I don't think he missed a trip even unto the very end. (At least three people is the safest number in the wilderness. If there is an accident, there is one to suffer, one to take care and one to do something about it.) He knew and did what was needed, and, above all, he knew when to talk and when to be quiet better than a lot of VIPs.

Lunch at Five Pockets

Five Pockets is Shangri-La in Wyoming, a cul-de-sac off a main trail to the Yellowstone, some fifteen miles from the trailhead. The large sack meadow is all set about with aspen and lodgepole pine, and surrounded by five mountain peaks whose drainages form the headwaters of Horse Creek. The grass is lush and the creek full of brookies, those best-of-all-the-worlds little six-inch trout that you just gut, dredge in salted and peppered cornmeal, fry and eat whole—bones, heads, tails and all. (I don't eat the heads, the eyes keep watching.)

The hike up each mountain draw was a whole-day trip. One led to a wide treeless plateau where a great band of elk grazed on the opposite mountainside, another to a forested saddle into a long swale where, far in the future, we were to hunt for most of a day to find our stock which had followed a wayward mare into the night.

After the third and closest, we stopped looking. A beaten path led to a smallish lake where fishing for cutthroats was easy and Big Horn rams watched from their eyrie of rocks high above. With lunch and a paperback in the possum pocket of your vest and fly rod, this was enough.

Summer glided by, filled with us pushing further and further into the backcountry for longer and longer time. Occasionally, friends from Memphis came along, including the two interns who had put L. back together after his plane crash and were now full-fledged orthopedists. To watch Spook and Jacob was watching young love. When they were left alone during the day while we went off on foot, Jacob was tethered in the shade. (This was not cruel and inhuman. Horses that graze all day tend to want to wander at night—almost always back to their corral by the shortest route. So, if you don't want to find yourself afoot with a lot of heavy stuff, give them a long tether—say forty feet—in the lushest grass just before dark; they will be apt to still be there in the morning.) They would stand head to tail all day swishing flies off each other's faces, and when taken to water, they gamboled like spring lambs.

Later, we went to an all-day meeting of the Nature Conservancy at the T Cross Ranch, a splendid 200 acre in-holding in the National Forest belonging to Emily Stevens, who lived some 90 miles away in Jackson Hole. While I attended every session and listened to every word, Lucius and Joe wandered around admiring the layout.

There was much to admire. It was one of the earliest guest ranches, where families such as Emily's (her mother was a DuPont) from the East came for the entire summer. She was one among many girls who could not get the West out of her system and came back to marry. (The older sister of a friend at Spence School married in Montana—the family thought of it as a funeral.) She and Dick Stevens—one of the numerous Dubois' Stevens—ran it as a guest ranch for a while, but gave up. She, with her two young children, was using it as an occasional change from Jackson Hole, and she was generous in letting groups in which she had an interest use it for conferences and the like.

Dave Martin was making noises about using our cabin himself. I only heard one side of the telephone converstion between Lucius and Emily, but it was a legal textbook example of negotiation. In his most sonorous voice (it was really sonorous!), he introduced himself, said we had just come from the T-Cross and what a splendid place it was, and he wanted to ask her a favor... that she listen to what he had to say without interrupting until he finished... Pause! He told her that he had talked with Frank (Paladino, the ranch caretaker and to be a very special friend) who said that poachers of her part of Horse Creek were a problem, that he sure would be glad for some help and company.

Then he got to the point—that we would like to use the small cabin next to her house, and the corral and pasture for his few horses for the next summer for the sum of $x to be paid, in her name, to any organization of her choice or any other arrangement that she preferred. Long, long pause! She had never considered such a thing; she'd have to think about it, she said, and asked him to call her back in the evening.

It was a done deal! When we left in September, the panniers, saddles et al were in their proper place in the barn under Frank's watchful eye and Spook turned loose with her horses so that he did not miss Jacob, who had to go home to Disneyland.

The T Cross became the lodestar where we took root in Wyoming—he at 64 and I at 56. Life at its best fell into place with the precision of the sundial in the garden at Belle Meade: "Mark only the sunny hours." Mid-June to mid-September, the mountain wilderness was the heart; Christmas through January was fishing in Argentina and, later, the island of Utila in the Bay of Honduras, long weekends on the Appalachian Trail and hunting season in Hardeman County. Interesting people with something on their minds came and went, then came again.

South America Bound

Tennessee in the fall was for catching up with those whom you missed and getting on with what had been left undone in June. The house in Hardeman County had summered well. The corn crop was on the stalk drying, there were deer tracks aplenty and the turkeys were talking with the owls as always. Messages from Chito, in Baja, told of people pouring in with money and said we were missed. Frank, in NZ, reported that accesses were clear for upstream fishers and said we should come back in January. Aye, that was the rub. It was so far to New Zealand, and a friend in Chile extolled the fishing in South America.

An afternoon flight to New Orleans put us at Galatoire's to sup on soft-shelled crab, artichokes, chocolate soufflé and a splash of good Cognac in the coffee before catching American Airlines overnight to Santiago. There a good Captain Somebody (his name I forget) swished us off to his country club for Pisco Sours and congrio, a fish-like eel or an eel-like fish, their national treasures—both habit forming.

French culture hangs over Santiago enough to make you think of Paris with its wide boulevards separated with swathes of grass and studded by great bronze equestrian statues. The main one terminates at the railroad station of lacy ironwork as designed by Gustav Eiffel of the Eiffel Tower, which is much like our Union Station in Nashville.

Chilean buses which share the terminal with the trains are very different from ours. The overnighter we took down the coast included pre-dinner drinks served by a steward, a passable meal, reclining seats for air-conditioned comfort. But the fishing was tedious trolling on lakes and too-big rivers. Time to move on.

Across the Andes in Argentina, things were different. We awoke in the dark to ensure we could get seats, but need not have bothered. It was a filling station where we mounted with some twenty others bearing bundles tied in colorful shawls. Windows were open to breezes and music for tango, a mite scratchy, seemed to come from everywhere. The road was too narrow for buses to pass, so the road through the park where Volcan Villarica spewed peacefully was one way only, the allowed direction switching on alternate days. Pavement gave way to gravel as we mounted the foothills, and unpainted houses, as in the hills and hollows of East Tennessee, were sprinkled about. The only other traffic except us were carettas drawn by oxen flicked along by their gauchos' snake whips.

We lunched at a house beside the road on a fine meal of homebrewed beer, soup from the garden, the corn still on the cob and chicken still on the bone, in huge red bowls with bread from the adobe oven out in yard. Dessert was hot fried doughnuts swimming in warm honey and coffee so strong it about frizzled your head.

We woke once from *siesta* to get out and walk while the bus did its tricks. The road took a ninety-degree angle across a wooden bridge over a torrent crashing down its boulder-strewn course. No side rails interfered, and at one point in the turn the body of the bus was suspended over the void. After the bus safely passed over, we were a very quiet group on the bridge.

Chile and Argentina were then at crossed swords over the ownership of the tip of *Tierra del Fuego,* separated from the mainland by the Straits of Magellan. We made it through the Chileno frontier, traveling some ten miles of no-man land before reaching the Argentine frontier, where we were not welcomed. It took a couple of hours in the hot sun to produce passports, unpack all belongings and hand over contraband. They relieved me of a brochure of our inn in Villarrica. Himself was clean.

Mile after mile after mile we shimmied down the gravel road through what looked like the African veldt, all flat-topped thorn trees and scrub. On almost every fencepost along the road perched gavilans awaiting road-killed jackrabbits, which had been introduced long ago and, like many exotics, reproduced—well, like rabbits. Along the rivers that flow from the Andes all is lush green, attracting great flocks of Magellan geese and herds of guanacos, the wild llamas. Horses and sheep which grow to great size and strength on the lava soil seem to be the only cash crops.

I slept and sweated, only rousing when prodded to see a large ranch gate with Hostoria St. Huberto carved on the crosspiece. Next was a refueling stop in the small town of Junin de los Andes where Himself got off as I dozed.

"Wake up," he said. "We're getting off. There's an inn which caters to an assortment of famous fishermen just down the road by the river."

Traveling with a backpack saved a lot of waiting around. Within minutes we were in a small lobby looking at signed photographs of the great fishers of the world—so he said. The only one I recognized was Billy Pate, whom we had met at Islamorada with my ex-son-in-law. As well as being a great fisherman, Pate manufactured high-quality reels and had a factory here in Junin, where he had a house and fished trophy trout at the mouth of Lago Huechulafquen.4

What a spectacle! Five or six men stood in the water well above their waists where the huge lake tailed to the Chimehuin River. The drill was to spot the fish from a high bank, from where they were visible in the clear water, and then wade in. The footing was a rock shelf, but with a catch. There were potholes where, if you made a misstep, you were in deep trouble. It certainly was no place for me, so we walked on downstream. We didn't find a suitable spot, as the Chimehuin is a big river with hard approaches, and besides—it was supper time, well past ten thirty.

Arrangements were made for a guide the next day—a lot of time can be wasted in new waters just finding the fish. It was Jorge Trucco who came, and as with Frank Harwood in New Zealand, became an important man in my fishing life. They taught me how to think like a fish, how to see them or their marks. For instance, if there is an air bubble in the middle of a series of concentric circles that you easily see, a fish has just fed from the surface and is apt to again. Cast a dry fly. If the circles are there but no bubble, he's taking nymphs just below the surface, so that was what was called for. Take him gently and release under water as quickly as you can, he'll be far fatter and wiser the next time you meet.

Jorge went on to make a name for himself as a key to introducing "catch and release" to fly-fishing culture. Just imagine being able to do that! Until his idea took hold, it was the late-afternoon ritual to slosh through the bar toward the kitchen bearing the entire day's catch beaming and bowing.

Best of all, he took us some forty miles *[may not be accurate—Ed.]* north of the Malleo. When we turned in the ranch gate, on which was writ Hosteria San Huberto, glimpsed the day before, there was no clue of the infinite pleasure it was to give us for the next eight winters.

---

4 That's the way it is spelled according to the journal where I wrote odd things. Spanish is a simpler language than English in that sounds are consistent. If you once know how the letters are pronounced—that's it.

That western part of Argentina, upper Patagonia, is called the lake country because of the ten huge lakes fed by the Andean snows which spawn its great rivers. Of them all, the Malleo (pronounced "Majeo"—Argentine Spanish is different from the Castellanos taught in our schools and spoke in Chile) is the crown jewel for wading fly-fishers. It flows from Lago Tromen through some 20 miles of pools and riffles, canyons and quiet water on Estancia Tres Picos (Three Peaks).

Carlos Olsen, son of a Norwegian family which settled here early, married Carmen, a city girl from Cordova, the wine-making country to the north. She was not content to rusticate on her in-laws isolated, relatively-small 57,500 acre ranch. The young couple built their house by the side of the road, added a wing of eight guest rooms and called it a hosteria dedicated to St. Huberto, patron saint of hunters. The location was perfect for the Scottish Red Deer (the same as imported to New Zealand, probably at about the same time) and wild boar which grow to magnificent size on the mineral-rich lava soil. Only fairly recently had they set about to attract fishermen; the price was more than attractive—$25 per person included meals from the garden, hills and rivers, remarkably good table wine and private use of 20 miles of possibly the best sight fishing in the world!

We three were their guests for the night and had two too-short days on a dazzling variety of reaches, left with reservations for a month next season, and went on to St. Martin with visions of exploring southern Patagonia.

The paved road broke into gravel just out of town for the many, many miles to Chile Chico where a bridge over part of the Straits into the disputed land. (It only occurs to me now that the reason for the very wide, well-tended gravel road had to do with the passage of military vehicles should war break out—which it didn't.)

A half hour along, the few cars came to a stop. An oil tanker had jack-knifed on a downhill turn and a mosquito of a tow truck was trying to reopen the road. Miracle! It did. Such is the wonder of human determination with very little help.

Then the cars strung out on the flat plain beyond the foothills, where the only things that moved were the rheas, smallish South American ostriches that browsed the semi-desert, which resembled a moonscape. The car excited them, causing them to race alongside or off in all directions at easily 50 mph.

For some thousand miles there were only two small towns. The bridge to Chile Chico was locked—no reason given. At the last, there was an inn for fishermen, so we stayed a couple of days. The Reo Simpson was pale grey with volcanic ash, and the wind never stopped. You had to find a spot where it blew over your left shoulder and use a roll cast to get a weighted dry fly on the water, and sit facing downwind of a great rock to eat lunch. It is good to have seen but calls not for a return.

However, there was a happening in the middle of nowhere: a traffic jam of dilapidated cars, trucks and two gaily painted ramshackle buses. On top of one, being cheered by a crowd, stood a man with his right arm raised in triumph. In his left hand, raised as high, was a naked new-born held by his heels. It was a traveling circus, going who knows where, which had stopped to celebrate the birth of, I'm sure, a son—such a to-do would not have occurred had it been a daughter.

Westward Ho!

By mid-February, spring hiccupped into Tennessee—shirtsleeves one day, rain, or maybe wet snow, the next. Crocuses and daffodils stuck their heads up with yellowing forsythia, and a mite later, Japanese magnolias dared late freezes to batter them from pink to brown. We had missed the cold, cold spell that comes to remind us that winter can be serious and to mind the groundhog's instructions. When spring exploded, last year's experience taught that it was not so in Wyoming. But by late May when it was downright hot, the call of the wild was so strong that off we went.

The T Cross ranch, 15 miles up a gravel, then rocky dirt road north of Dubois, is a wide alluvial valley at more than 7,500 feet, pancake-flat, all wound about with Aspens and Lodgepole Pines and Horse Creek running through. Lodgepoles, relatively short-lived conifers, dominate. They fall in place to form a matchstick ground cover just right for building cabins, corrals, fences and the handsome furniture made by snowbound cowboys—now most seen in museums and other unchanging places. They warm the potbellied stoves, fireplaces and camp fires to make life not just possible but enchanting.

Frank Paladino watched from the kitchen porch; it was his job to know who was there and why. There was balm in his Gilead and he meant to keep it that way. When he recognized us, welcome gleamed. The lodge kitchen was warm and smelled of garlic, just as it should to go with his Italian name, and the pot on the stove was lunch. He was expecting us, had stacked firewood on our porch, cleared the pipes and turned the hot water heater on. We had brought red wine and pulled the cork forthwith. Pasta *bourguignon*, quasi-French bread warm, buttered and garlicked, cold, hard apples with very soft cheese and a jug of *vino tinto* were all polished off during the hours of becoming acquainted. Day became night and the double sleeping bag just thrown on top of the bed was far too good to resist. Coyotes sang to their beloved moon and all was right.

When the kitchen bell rang it meant that Frank was cooking breakfast. Thick-sliced peppered bacon, with the rind still on, and eggs fried in its grease were washed down with biscuits the size of butter plates by cowboy coffee from a pot big enough for refills the rest of the day. We hunkered down on the front steps in the sun and watched the moose which appeared each day jump the fence to scrounge hay from the barn. For the greenhorns among us, to watch a 2,000-pounder jump an eight-foot wooden fence is a happening. It walks up, sniffs, bends all four legs, then blump—over it goes and slowly walks on to nuzzle the bales. Think of doing this yourself!

In our one-room cabin, books filled the window sills, clothes went into the closet and rain gear hung on a pair of antlers. The Lodgepole furniture was put to use, with the desk taking on legal pads, pens, *grabadora*, extra batteries. The chest of drawers was stacked with wool socks, long johns, etc., etc. Three canvas captain's chairs crowded the two-burner gas stove on the front porch; the flag was hung with due ceremony; hummingbirds thought the red oil lantern was a feeder and crowded about. Then it was time for a beer and to town for lunch and laying in provisions to stow in a corner of the big walk-in refrigerator and freezer of the lodge kitchen. By sundown we were as moved in as we would ever be. Supper, prefaced by a couple of toddies, was a good-size chunk of beef cooked to perfection on the kitchen grill, potatoes baked without tinfoil, and salad of greens from the little fenced-in garden. (Lettuce was the only thing it ever produced at that short season altitude, but it was enough and, with replanting, lasted all summer.) The pair of North Face sleeping bags zipped into one was miraculously warm from the moment we crawled in, and the reading light was just right.

Next day, the time for idling was over. The horses ran loose in winter but came to the corral in the afternoons for hay to supplement the short grazing. Himself was suddenly no man to wait and Frank knew roughly where they had been recently staying and told us the way. Off we went with only a lead rope for our recently renamed Spook (*née* Snoop) past the picnic ground of an ancient flatbed hay wagon and big fire ring by the creek. The water was clear, which meant that the snow melt in the high country was yet to come. There was the footbridge built from a wobbly set of wired-together planks, with a single-strand hand rail. Watching him negotiate that, I opted to wait where I was. The belled mares were faintly heard; they couldn't be far.

Sure enough, within minutes, there he came riding gentle Spook with only the lead rope clipped around his neck. The rest of some 15 horses followed at a sedate walk and splashed through the knee-deep water with bells ajangle. He said he would ride on in so I scurried behind.

When they realized where they were, they hit a trot and then a full gallop toward the barn. He hung on for a few leaps; then there he was in a heap. I took off my jacket, tucked it over his shoulders and told him not to move, that I'd be back. He was much too pale!

Frank was on hand; I grabbed a couple of pillows and blanket but never thought to get the Percocet. He had not moved, had a tough time when he had to. I remembered the half bottle of Jim Beam in the glove compartment and handed it to him.

"Want this?"

To the nearest hospital in Riverton was 95 miles—an hour and a half. As I watched, his eyes closed, he took swigs from the bottle. It was empty when we helped him into the waiting room. Some color had returned to his face and he was four sheets to the wind—waving to everybody from the stretcher. Some fifteen minutes later the doctor arrived, booted, spurred and with his hat still on. In Wyoming, it is rare to get any man out from under his hat, but after he took a pulse, off his came as he helped push open the door to the x-ray room. As they moved out of sight, the doctors asked him how he felt. He replied, almost joyfully, "I don't know, but I bet better than you do."

When Doc came back (hat on) to report broken ribs, no head or spinal injury or evidence of lung perforation, he added that he had given a shot of morphine and wanted to let him sleep for a while, then he could go home. This we did, and, when I told him of the miles of rough road, he wrapped his chest with yards of Ace bandage and trusted me with a couple of more tablets of oral morphine.

Back at the ranch and him in the sleeping bag, the telephone rang. The good doctor said the x-ray had been reexamined. One lung was perforated and we must bring him back. When that message was delivered to Lucius, there was a long pause, then he said, "Forget it."

I feared he would be suffering from a mammoth hangover, but it just did not occur. Why, I can't imagine, except for the words of the wise that the Lord looks after drunks and fools. It was lucky—if he'd been hungover on top of ignoring the doctor's summons, it could have been dire.

We dropped back into the pattern of three years earlier, when his life had been much more threatened. He was medically informed from his father, who had even allowed him to watch surgery as a boy. And, as he said, had freshman algebra taken him less than three years to pass, he would have been a doctor instead of a lawyer.

For the first couple of days, not knowing the extent of damage to his lung, he kept the bindings on his chest and immobilized it by lying flat on his back 95% of the time. Gradually, movement increased, not to the pain level but just beyond; health was not discussed; painkillers and booze were dispensed with; he read for hours at a time, sometimes out loud to me or I to him; he dictated responses to his mail without mention of his disability and talked in a normal voice when Frank came to call. I took care of his diet, added multiple vitamins and large amounts of vitamin C. Within the week, we slow-started two walks a day as increasingly far as suited him. We laughed a lot, held hands, got the word out that he was in the market for another horse to take Jacob's place with Spook.

AND we planned (after seeking approval from Emily) a Fourth of July party to precede our first sashay into the backcountry. That struck me as letting our expectations far exceed our grasp, but it happened.

Giving a party at the T Cross in early July was a venture into the unknown. The rules:

1. Invite everyone you know. (Once invited, always expected.)
2. The number who actually come depends on the unpredictable weather. For example, if you invite 25...

If it snows a little, 12 or more hearties will brave the patch of bentonite[5] mixed with stones that formed the dirt road at the last creek crossing before the gate.

If it snows a lot, zero will come, safe for the three or six of us already there.

If it's a gorgeous early summer day, you'll get at least 40. Everybody brings their nearest and dearest, along with homemade

---

[5] A form of slick clay used in drilling and, at one time, to swab cannon barrels to speed the balls. Its greenish color appears in patches about the size of a big yurt. It acts like quicksand and can be recognized and avoided if you pay attention. Once we were taking an unknown, little-used pass, when I took a shortcut and hit a patch that sank Joker up to his shoulders—I crawled off on all fours to the edge, leaving him to fend for himself which, with much plunging about, he did.

dishes prepared for the multitudes.

3. A flexible menu is a must.

Our routine for the next 17 years was:

Lucius smoked the biggest turkeys from the grocery and six whole chickens overnight to perfection in the smoker, which was housed in the obsolete outhouse where the wind couldn't blow out the fire.

I waited until the morning to predict the number of guests, then fried four pounds of peppered bacon really crisp. I removed from the grease, then set aside. I boiled a big mesh bag of unpeeled Yukon Gold potatoes, chopped them into pieces with lots of onions, green and red bell peppers, a half container of coarse-ground black pepper (no salt, that comes with the best part), a rounded spoon of sugar mixed in with a couple of cups or more of cider vinegar (Lena said a bit of sugar to the sour is like salt to the sweet), then the crumbled bacon. Then, for the best part, I reheated the bacon grease until it almost started to smoke, and poured it in with everything else, stirring and turning upward to thoroughly mix—this partially cooks the onions and peppers. There you have it. The longer it stands, the better—best warm but good anytime.

We had Frenchish bread loaves from the bakery, lathered in garlic butter, browned crisp in the oven, kept warm wrapped in fresh-washed tea towels in the warmer over the stove for the right moment.

The season's first watermelons were omnipresent for hors d'oeuvre, vegetable and dessert, supplemented by a stack of German semisweet chocolate bars (from the bakery counter at the grocery store) on a butcher block with a mallet for chunking, and the beautiful pies which came with the guests.

Pitchers of Sangria (red wine, fruit juice of all sorts, lots of ice) and beer brought cheer on the Fourth for the next seventeen years. Indeed, Sharon Kahin once said it became Dubois' only "tradition." It did look festive laid out on the wagon bed with Mason jars of early wildflowers or huddled around the great fireplace of the lodge.

All of this just set the stage for Himself's favorite holiday, when he stood to retell of the march to Yorktown by the combined force of American troops under Washington and the French under Lafayette. The Conte de Grasse brought his French West Indies fleet into the Chesapeake to cut off supplies to the British and forced Cornwallis to surrender at the last great battle of our Revolution. His favorite detail: "The French Army marched south, magnificent in their freshly chalked white britches, with such discipline that not a single housewife voiced a complaint of the loss of a chicken." It makes me want to weep in gratitude not just for the French but for hearing these words in such a place.

Emily, with her young Julie and Anthony, came for the celebration and stayed for a while. She, tall, handsome, was as easily befriended as the children. Anthony, age about eight, sort of moved over to our front porch. I have a charming picture of him with his big English bulldog nattily dressed in Lucius' wool jacket and brimmed hat.

Word came from Ab Cross that he had a splendid horse that might be available for cash. When we arrived to inspect him, it was not a horse but a mare by the name of Pat. Emily rode and pronounced her acceptable, so off we went with what we thought was a longtime friend for Spook.

But here is note of caution to those with visions of becoming a horse-packer: avoid mares! It is no accident that alpha mares lead the bands of wild horses. They know what is best for all—such as that the green, green grass of near-home pasture is better than rock hopping above the timberline. This one was a wizard at getting loose from her hobble and leading the boys homeward.

Luckily they grazed along the way and Himself knew how to find them.

Big Ap

Big Ap completed the horse string coming off Cougar Pass. Heading home to Dubois, we crossed trail with another string led by a big Appaloosa which stuck out his neck and rattled Himself's stirrup. Greetings were exchanged all round, with fishing reports from Bliss Meadows. Some 10 minutes later in a little spring meadow, Lucius stopped and asked that we wait a few minutes, he'd be right back. As usual when he disappeared like that, we broke out our books and backed up to the nearest downed log in the full Wyoming sunshine.

Finally, there was too much noise for just one horse coming back down the trail and, sure enough, Ap, of the great leopard spots of black, brown and white, was led into the opening. Lucius astride was at one with the horse. Absolutely magnificent! That man and that horse were made for each other, one piece—Boss and Boss Hoss.6

He became not only the leader of our cult but the canary. Any tough spot on the trail that Ap would go over, under or around, everything else could, would and did. The only time we EVER turned around was on Marston Pass early one season. He put his foot down, the trail gave way. That was that. Everyone tippy-toed around on the narrow slide with changed plans!

In spring, July, there were still snow fields crusting patches of trails. Some were strong enough to bear our weight, but there were others that wouldn't. Which was which? Lucius would go first on foot, leading Ap with a long rein to distribute the weight; if it broke through, it was a matter of climbing out of two or three feet of snow, backing off and breaking another trail. It took a lot of time, a lot of huffing and puffing. I have a picture—there he is, fully loaded, up to his shoulders in snow with his head stretched out on the icy shelf resting, waiting for Himself to extricate him.

Once, coming out of Bliss Creek meadows, where Swan Creek trail came in, we saw a few horses tied up. The riders must have walked up the trail, but we never saw them. A horse was dead, his head stretched suspended by the lead rope tied in a slip knot. For whatever reason he had jerked back and that was that. Only ignorance, or even worse, carelessness, would ever put a slip knot on a horse's neck.

It was on that same Swan Creek trail, a very steep short cut from Bear Creek, that I had my nearest miss.7

---

6 Some time about the 12th century BC, a nomadic tribe moved from the northeast into Greece. Little was known of its origins in 1971 when I was there—probably because they took over the culture so completely. Credited as the bearers of the Indo-European language, male gods and the well-known shallow drinking bowl, the *kylix*, they made the Greeks the Greeks. They were credited with introducing horses for the first time, which so stunned the locals that they thought a man and a horse were all of one piece—the centaur of mythology. Incidentally, we have a sort of parallel in the introduction of the horse to the western Plains Indians which so disrupted the balance of power among the tribes. It was the escaped or released Spanish horses brought by the Conquistadores that formed our wild herds.

7 The National Forest Service did a good job of maintaining the huge trail system in the wilderness areas which permit nothing motorized, including electric saws. Early in the season, maintenance teams, usually volunteers, combed through the maze to repair blockages by fallen trees, washes and so on. But sometimes we were there before them, and always carried a Swedish Sven saw—rugged, light, foldable, safe. The washes were different; you broke a trail uphill to its head and came around whereever it was possible or, only occasionally, backtracked.

The wash that morning looked doable for Ap. It was about four feet wide, fairly level and solid footing. John Pritchard, Himself's eleven-year-old grandson, and Andy were behind. I came around Ap on foot, was handed the lead and told, "Just hold him, I'll be right back." Off the threesome went with the other horses, about 30 feet uphill, breaking a trail through the thicket. They crossed the head of the cut, went back down to the trail and far enough down to be out of the way. No problem. Ap watched, restless. With my trying to hold him, he inched forward on the narrowing trail. I tugged, he shook his head. It was obvious what was in his herd mind. As they dropped to the trail on the other side, Lucius looked back, saw what was happening, and yelled, "For God's sake, get out of the way, turn him loose." We were close to the lip of the much-narrowed, steep-sided trail. There was no place for me to get out of the way except drop sidewise into the brush, pull my feet to my chest, and grab for anything to keep from sliding under him. I pushed the pannier with one foot as it went by, shoving myself uphill deeper in the brush.

When he jumped, it was from a standstill. His front feet landed on the trail, but the right hind hoof slipped on the far lip and the whole mass disappeared within touching distance down the wash. Thuds and the banging of metal on rocks; then it was quiet. Lucius grabbed his pistol from his saddlebag and went sliding down the drop grabbing at branches and tree trunks as he went out of sight. (It is for just such disasters that a pistol is carried into the backcountry. If a horse breaks a leg, the only humane solution is to shoot him.) Andy and John were right behind him as I scrambled uphill to where the wash was crossable, then down to the trail and sat down, teeth chattering, eyes closed, waiting for the shot which didn't come.

The later description was graphic. Ap hung upright between the wedged panniers. When the lines were cut to release the load, he dropped to his haunches and slid the rest of the way followed by the whole mass of stuff, shook himself a couple of times and started grazing a patch of grass. The next sound was Ap lunging up the steep, with Lucius above with the lead rope. All this was done to a lusty sea shanty.

Then his hand was on the top of my head.

"Stay here," he said. "It's all right, won't take long."

I was not alone. There looking at me in the trail duff, almost camouflaged, was a deer mouse the size of a bantam egg with black shoe-button eyes and huge round ears. We sat and looked at each other and nothing more except that my teeth relaxed. Together we watched as that threesome muscled the 200-pound load, Lucius singing out "Blow the Men Down" as taught in Nashville's fourth grade at Ward-Belmont and using the ropes and the trees for pulleys.

When I came back after repacking, my mouse was gone. But I think of him as my mouse, a friend indeed even now when things get tough.

Himself took my hand and put it in his jacket pocket with his own, an endearing habit. "Let's walk a while." The trail widened down to a big flat rock where the two streams met. It was lunchtime with retelling of grass-eating Ap and my very own mouse—time for laughing and moving on.

Return to the Malleo

"CALL ME ISHMAEL." Those opening words of Melville's *Moby-Dick* sounded as we topped the steps to the bar at the Hosteria San Huberto, "and I shall call you Ernest."

"You'd be wrong. Call me Lucius."

This exchange opened a lasting friendship as soon as we arrived after the 1977 February night flight from Miami to Buenos Aires, over the Pampas to Bariloche, driven the few hours to Junin de los Andes and on up the gravel road for another hour. We were more than ready for a toddy and the 10:30 dinner for which he joined us.

This Ishmael Cardin, Brazilian-born-and-bred cousin to Pierre Cardin, *haute couturier* of Paris. He was educated at the Sorbonne, edited encyclopedias for a living and had a left-at-home non-fishing wife in an apartment overlooking Copacabana in Rio. Like many South Americans, and particularly those of French extraction, he was suave, educated, immaculately dressed, a fine upstream fly-fisherman determined to see with his thick bottle-bottom eyeglasses. But best of all was his droll, guileless humor and boundless enthusiasm for and knowledge in any subject that arose. His favorite was World War I English and American fiction, with Ernest Hemingway his idol.

Carmen, our hostess, must have told him of Lucius' resemblance. He was not disappointed, continued to call him Ernest and accused him of lying about his identity. When we settled down, he wanted to know if Himself had known the great man.

"Only twice. When I was sixteen, my mother sold the hay crop and sent me to live with our family in London for a while to polish my edges. I was left to entertain myself frequently and decided to go to Pamplona for the Bull Running. He was there with his cronies and took me under his wing as a green young fellow-American. He was very gracious and I'm sure that I saw and did things I could not have otherwise.

"The next time was years later when he lived in Cuba. I used to quail shoot down there. I just put my dogs in the back of whatever flying contraption I had at the time, stayed with a farmer, landed in his pasture, hunted his land. Birds were all over the place!

"Live pigeon shoots were the rage of the time. I ran into him one winter near Varadero Beach. We spent the day together, but he was demanding, furious when he was outshot, just unwell. It wasn't long before he shot himself."

Ishmael was the only other person who spoke English, so it was natural that we should fall in together—for the whole month. The drill was to breakfast about eight and drive through the farm road—very rough—a bit less than an hour to Tres Picos upstream in the shadow of the Volcano Lanin, where over the years we watched its snowcap recede with wonder, but no inkling that it was the beginning of climate change.

Most guests fished downstream, but we found that the further upstream from the hosteria, the better. There we spent the next nine hours in every kind of productive waters, admiring the next generation of Argentina's renowned thoroughbred polo ponies grazing across the river, lunching from a wicker hamper, drinking good red wine, taking *siestas* under the tree. The conversation between those two would have graced any Parisian salon until it was time to shower, drink single malt Scotch, sup by candle light, jump in bed before the generators went off at midnight and follow the Southern Cross out the window.

Carmen, the city girl from Cordoba, Argentina's second-largest city in the wine country to the north, was not only a charming hostess, but also the barkeep. If you wanted hard whiskey, you brought it from the airport—tax-free boozery. Excellent wine was on the house. AND she was the cook, all in a sweeping dinner gown. She had multiple sous-chefs to prepare everything, but come the moment of truth, she was it. The dish I remember best was a fluffy omelet filled with smoked trout in a cream sauce that stood about four inches high like a *soufflé*. It was served with a salad of her garden greens and some lascivious dessert.

Thursday nights were different. They started early while you were still in your fishing clothes—a classic Argentine *asado*—in the screened pavilion separate from the main house. On a great stone grill sizzled all kinds of beef, lamb, sweetbreads, blood sausage, chitterlings. But first there were *tapas*—traditional small dishes of most everything to go with wine and encourage conversation among strangers. No private tables here, but two long trestles with benches where you were expected to help create a general conversation. Everybody was there: the family, the guides, all of the help, everybody for maybe a hundred miles around (except the Mapuches on the reservation nearby) including Carlos' cousins from the 150,000 hectare *finca* across the road, whose horses we admired. Hands flew in the air and everybody spoke Spanish; I even told a few unsteady jokes and they were kind enough to laugh. There is nothing as effective as *vino tinto* to improve one's language skills.

At the first such happening when things settled down, I sat between Lucius and Ishmael attacking the meat and sopping juices with most excellent crusty bread. Ishmael told me how much he admired the John Wayne red bandana around my neck. As jolly as I was, I pulled it off to give to him but he demurred. Then his face lighted up and his bottle-bottom glasses shone as he pulled off his colorful scarf tied as an Ascot and said, "Here, maybe we can trade. Cousin Pierre sent this for Christmas. It's supposed to be very fine; he is *le dernier cri* in Paris these days." So the deal was cut; it was beautiful, I wore it every day and he the bandana. I think of it as a small museum piece with its discreet little label, Pierre Cardin, Paris.

Ishmael had come to the San Huberto ever since it had been devoted to summer stalking of the great Scottish Red Deer, before fly fishing took over. He knew the country and made sure we did too—over several seasons.

This was Argentina's Lake Country, headwaters of its famous rivers flowing from the eastern foothills of the Andes. Across the road the terrain rose to a high overview of one the lakes where we climbed the miles of rocks and thorny scrub just once to gaze into infinity over a pocketed sandwich. There were other treasures close to home.

He directed our way from the back seat of the car to a cave of primitive rock paintings of the pre-Columbian Araucaria Indians whose many tribes still compose about 1% of Argentina's population living on widespread reservations. It is a wonder that there are still so many; for years, the government paid cash bounties on the presentation of the left ear of each killed.

When we visited their reservation on the dirt road to Tres Picos, he spoke their pidgin well enough for me to buy roughly carved *pudu* (small indigenous deer) from some soft local wood. It wasn't much of a *pudu*, they were not much carvers, but I was assured that if it were put under the bed, fleas would be avoided. Mama, to whom I gave it, said it worked just fine.

The women of this tribe were weavers. They sat on the ground at a loom tied on one end waist-high to a tree; the other end managed by their feet. The colors of natural dyes glowed, but the seemingly endless strip was only about 14 inches wide. Puzzle, puzzle.

Ishmael explained the total absence of men, whom you never saw except riding at a distance. They did no work that couldn't be done from the back of a horse, so they were either gone or asleep in their huts. How they got away with that may be that they were so gorgeous in their black *bombachas* (baggy pants), crimson sashes holding *facons* (wicked looking knives) flat at the back, black broad brim, shallow crown, flat-topped hats worn straight on the head and knee-high boots (shades of Crete, with the same strut).

He led us to Lago Tromen, a favorite of his for reasons I cannot imagine. Tucked away in a bowl in the first serious Andean foothills, it is beautiful, as are all remote gin-clear lakes, and easy to get to, but no one caught anything. Lake fishing from the shore with a fly rod is fun for casting long but useless lines into the backing. Overlong lines have too much play to hold a fish even if it strikes. Unless there is a hatch-off that you can see or an infall big enough to find, you waste a lot of time.

However, there are other things than fish. While I watched Lucius walking around the beach, something big calmly walked out of the forest some 30 yards in front of him, ducked its head for a long drink. When it turned its profile, sat on its haunches and watched his progress, it looked like a cat. A cat! Good grief, a mountain lion; pumas live here. I yelled and gestured but it was too far and neither one heard nor saw. I could just stand and watch. When he stopped, turned around and sauntered back, the cat went back into the woods—no telling where to. I was a wreck when he got back; he had not seen or heard anything.

It was dark enough for headlights when we started home. Right outside the parking place, a huge pale mountain lion caught in the headlights and raced in front for a mile or so. It had to have been the same one; it was so close. Had it been stalking Lucius as we had the fish—for fun or for supper?

Would that there were more years to tell you of this younger earth when we didn't all speak English, and cruises didn't promise the world in ten days with free shopping bags.

What a blessing it was that Chile and Argentina were not melting pots! The cities display their Frenchness in the great boulevards separated by greenswards, formal gardens and bronze equine statues of long-dead heroes who saw to it that the natives were brought to their proper place of poverty or death—just like us. The railroad stations were of decorative wrought iron and the restaurants fine.

Bariloche, in the west, is Swiss with high pitched roofs and clear view of the enormous resort hotel atop the nearest mountain, where Olympic skiers hone their talents all summer.

And the Italians left their stamp on the old *cascas*, the home-places of the enormous farms. I knew only three, widely apart, and just one from the inside, but they look like they were all built by the same people: unadorned Roman red brick villas, perfectly proportioned. The one I knew best had been built years earlier as a sort of home/fortress/country store. There were no outside windows in its single story but very high-ceilinged rooms with tall windows opened on the open atrium which centered by a great sculptured fountain. Pliny the Younger (or Elder) would have been quite at home. But the topiary garden at the back was the giveaway. It must have taken generations of Italians to trim to such perfection the arbors and the cypress trees, some thirty feet high, shaped into spirals and lace, and to rake the river gravel walkways.

Dinner conversation the one evening we were there was with a handful of men from the Wilderness Society, a US environmental organization much concerned with the hydro dam planned north of Bariloche. On completion it played havoc with three major rivers, displaced thousands of the Indigenous people, and destroyed for years a major source of income for the region. All of this was foreseen that evening. Beside all that, it leaked from the beginning and was abandoned after completion.

So much for progress.

Next day, we set off to float the *Aluminé* for some days in a couple of sturdy pontoon boats. Lucius and I went first with the guide. Two people could easily cast—he stood in the center facing the bank and cast overhead; I sat facing forward straddling the prow with feet hanging overboard, side casting. Ishmael, with a second guide and camping gear, tucked right in behind us. When we came to a riffle, we got out to wade, and here I learned the magic of riffles that stood me in good stead the rest of my fishing life.

Good trout rivers are similarly beautiful; it is small things that identify them. Of this one I remember, when asking for a drink of water, I was handed a cup with a puzzled expression and told to help myself. Imagine drinking water without harm from a river about the size of the Cumberland!

When we were set up for the night and supper started, I watched the guide slosh out a coffeepot on the bank and fill with the same river water. When he had added a double handfull of peeled garlic buds to simmer on the open fire, libations passed around. When dry milk and a sack of stale French bread were added, the mixture was allowed to cool enough to where he could squeeze the mass to mush. Then was added bit of salt, black pepper, and a goodly ration of butter from an insulated box. With two each of the smallest (about 12-inch) trout we had caught (the rest were released) rubbed in oil, sprinkled with herbs and spitted on sticks over the open fire and with the best of all red wine, that meal with silken-smooth garlic soup would have brought a fortune anywhere in Paris.

To add mystery to the night while we were in our tents, there came a single loud bark. Next morning, Ariel, our guide, told us that that had been from one of the few remaining wild native dogs—very rare, almost never heard, very fierce.

Thus we spent January for several years, until all changed.

Frontier Outfitters discovered this idyll and fellow Americans poured in—nice enough, but the same ones you saw at the country club on Saturday nights and "who knew whom" was the chief subject for conversation. Prices multiplied and Argentine guides bitterly resented the gringos taking over their territory—rightly so.

Ishmael's wife, Gilda, arrived—he must have been too glowing in his telling of the fun. Here she came, a bit too shrill in making her presence known; pickings were slim for her during the day. No one was left at the hosteria and nine hours sitting on a riverbank, even with a book, must have been a crashing bore for her. The result was that we started fishing closer to home so that she could join us for lunch and siesta. There was much rushing about, arranging and rearranging, and forced conversation. She spoke only Portuguese.

Lucius and Ishmael corresponded for years; their letters back and forth were reminders of other precious things, like Cabo, which could not hold.

Then Summer was A-Comin' In

UG! was the first sentiment expressed and became a name for the colt that stood with its momma Pat, side by side in the greening grass of Wyoming July—possibly the result of immaculate conception. What could have fathered this strange creature, with his oversized head, ears, knees, feet and unworldly mottled coloring of red, grey, black, yellow—all the colors of dirt and gravel. What could be done with him all summer? He would just have to take his chances like everybody else.

But Pat was a perfect mother: When Ug frolicked too far up the hillsides (building powerful legs) a low nicker brought him to heel. When hunger called, he circled around in front of her, she stopped, we waited, he suckled, then off we went. When she was tied off, he laid right behind her hind feet where her tail swished away the flies; had she stepped back an inch, he would have been mush.

There was one frequently-used creek crossing, shallow except close to the bank, where it dropped off. She would pause at the brink, then jump the three-feet-deep part to the bank. He did the same and continued to do so well into manhood even when he could easily have waded. They were so content with one another!

Only on one occasion did he reveal another self: a dandy at heart. We passed a posh outfitter out of Cody, who brought dudes to the back country with all the comforts of home and more. The pompous "Crossed Sabers" haul all sorts of stuff in on a double line of perfectly matched white burros whose huge ears would not have dared to flop back and forth in anything but unison. Ug was thrilled; they were just his size and ever so elegant. He dashed out to greet them by winding back and forth through the line. The disruption was minor in comparison with the scowls of the wranglers and leader of the cult while things were set aright.

Leaving them behind, we carried on until the usual 4:30, then set up camp on the bend of a creek with good grass. An hour later, they stopped near the same spot and set up a couple of hundred yards upstream. It may have been their usual place, but there was no sign of it, and so this was a breach of wilderness manners. Lucius looped a lead rope around Ug's neck, the first time he had ever been so restrained, and tied him off without incident next to Pat.

Within an hour of their bringing forth folding canvas chairs for the dudes, serving them sundowners, pitching a thicket of tents, the honcho crossed the pasture. That very nice, well-dressed man did not "hello the camp." It was obvious we were there, but he arrived with his right hand extended. Lucius, the perfect host, formally welcomed him, offered coffee or a drink, which was refused with thanks. It turned out that all of their matches had gotten wet, and could we spare a few?

Yes, of course. The Ziploc bag was extended, from which he took a modest handful with thanks. He walked to Ug and stroked his flank. "Strong looking colt," he said, "why don't you turn him loose?" His manners had improved, but you never fool with another man's (person's) horse without permission. His white hat was clean; he was obviously new at the game—a clean white Stetson is for Sunday church, not the wilderness!

For anyone interested in childhood education, that summer was classic not just to watch momma and son, but to watch Lucius gradually turn Ug into a mountain horse. By August, he was almost full-size, with very strong legs from frolicking hither and thither.

A horse's back, the bridge between his fore and hind legs, is the weakest part of his body; saddles (including pack saddles) are built to distribute weight to each side to clear the spine. From the very beginning, Lucius would occasionally lean on his back with increasing pressure, followed by a piece of horse cake. (Pressed molasses and alfalfa was candy to this baby.) As time passed, he flopped a soft saddle blanket on and then leaned. Then came a rope halter, just like momma's, which bothered him not at all, and so became permanent. In late summer, while we were in camp, the pack saddle went on. Later the panniers—empty, except for a batch of rocks that rattled. Then he was carrying a light load.

It was not until the following summer, when he was full-size, that the saddle went on, lightly cinched, and Lucius, all 185 pounds of him, mounted. All was peaceful; they calmly moved out to join the rest. From then on his name always began with a capital U.

My Horse Joker

When Lucius handed me Joker's lead rope, I thought about Mama—of the hours, patience and expertise she and Charlie Hatcher had spent on me years before. What she would have said of my living in lovely sin with this inevitable man, I would not have asked. But she sure would have approved of that horse—dappled grey with black mane and tail, the chiseled nostrils and alert ears of an Arabian, and the strong chest of a Quarter Horse. He was small enough for me to throw the English saddle over his back without help and easily mount. He was much more than a friend and convenience. I was easily smitten and he, like many males (and females) conformed to ancient knowledge that the way to the heart is via the stomach; there was always horse cake in my pocket to sneak a piece or two when least expected as well as morning and evening. He knew it. I was a horse person and he, like many Arabians, a people horse. He didn't have to be tethered; to hear him chomping grass outside our tent at night was a lullaby. Anyone could ride him, and did, but he was all mine; the yellow slicker and extra sweater strapped to the back of his saddle belonged to me.

The drill of "ride an hour, trade, walk an hour" is a most efficient and agreeable way to cover the backcountry. The quiet hours through the waves and waves of grasses and flowers in the open and the shade of groves of conifers or aspen, I remember as a sort of meditation. And all I had to do was to look up and there was Himself setting the pace.

Mountains are where you are most aware of the succession of blossoming, starting in the river bottoms; they explode in the spring and gradually move up in increasing profusion higher and higher so that they are always there until snow. Great pieces of meadows wave with sun-loving bluebells and lupine next to patches of pink wild garlic. Yellow seems to prevail on the mountainsides next to the forest, sprinkled with huge, knee-high from a horse, stalks of white clustered cowbane—deadly poison in self-protection—spicy orange of I know not what, an infinity of everything—waves at a distance but as individual as friends close up.

In the forests, you have to look for the bushes of tender lavender and pink wild hollyhocks. Once I found a small bunch of white lupine in a spread of the usual blue. Ron Mammot, who knew everything about everything, explained that we were looking at evolution in action—a gene had flipped over and there was a mutation.

Another time, I saw a splash of purple gentians clinging to the scree of Whiskey Mountain by six-inch stems. When asked, Dwane Howe—as excited as if it were a new mastodon—explained it would be an alpine variety which he had never seen. He asked for directions, that he might photograph the rarity. Alpine flowers are the small, six-inch stem adaption of a number of common varieties to their environment of constant wind, sparse water and cold above timberline. One day I counted 27 varieties that I could name; there were many more.

It is said that a catastrophe is a terrible thing to waste, and in the wildflower world that holds. Almost immediately after the Greater Yellowstone forest fires of 1988, in the Greater Yellowstone ecosystem as the earth cooled, fireweed took over in the most dramatic explosion of resurrection one is apt to see. The earth was black, the spikes of zillions of trees in every direction were charcoal, but the upheaval of waving pinkish red triumphed. Only later did the other colors reappear, and by the next summer, grasses and the ubiquitous evergreen Lodgepole pines were waist-high. The pines' future was assured; their seeds only germinate when subjected to fire.

And so it was that summers rolled on in harmony with the earth and friends who thrived in this place with this man. Time interfered only casually.

Young Andrew Carter, the sack boy at the grocery store whose guileless chatter made shopping a pleasure, became, as he said, the highest paid wrangler in Wyoming. There was one kicker—he was relieved of a goodly portion of it every evening after supper, by wagering on who could shoot the most rocks off a log with the emergency pistol.

He graduated from high school and love kicked him in the face; he was headed for matrimony and pumping gas in Dubois as a career. Somehow, he found himself at Sewanee on a DuPont scholarship, with the honor of wearing his academic robes with his cowpoke boots and clean Wyoming hat. Law school led to his advising elderly widows as to how to handle their handsome inheritances, a proper wife and the right number of children in Memphis.

I am beholden to Andrew for many things, but most for his help in nurturing my granddaughter, Meredith, with whom I was closely bonded by spending much time together in her extreme youth. At age eight she lived in Aspen, about an hour's flight due south of Dubois. She was the only person I ever asked Lucius to invite to the backcountry; he was by far the best judge of that as evidenced by a couple of dismal failures of the few who asked to come and left in a hurry.

"Of course, yes, as long as she comes without either parent. But if she has a friend, that's different. She can bring her along."

Traylor, who turned out to be a he instead of a she, was nine. After a slow start, they followed Andrew around, fetched firewood, toted water, and gutted and ate their own fish. Most memorable was when they balked at getting up in the mornings and he unzipped their tent, grabbed up their sleeping bags and dumped them into the ice-tinged grass. All progressed with much yelling and laughter, and she became strongly self-confident, a horsewoman and fly-fisher—a joy to be with and a thoroughly decent human being. Plus now she is the mother of my two great-grandchildren who are moving along somewhat the same way.

Lift Up Thine Eyes

In May, we came to Wyoming planning to take to the backcountry on July 5th, since by then the streams would have cleared of snow melt. (Drowning is the greatest cause of death in the backcountry, on foot or horseback.) Except for broken ribs and the punctured lung, which no longer seemed a factor, we were late but ready. I was silently leery, but should not have been.

Joe McCarty, our to-be constant companion, arrived from Memphis, with the first in a line of establishment-type lovelies, to set up in the empty bunkhouse. There was a long line of those magnolias, who when faced with such a future, had second thoughts, but the last of the line, Mickey Babcock, hung in and they had happy years together. He left his august FedEx position; she sold her business and off they moved to Buffalo Valley north of Jackson Hole. Her tale of his introduction to the wilds was this: "The trail is marked with big white blazes. Don't get lost, keep up, do your work, and don't whine." With that he disappeared, not to be seen again for a number of hours when she staggered into camp, where he handed her a cup of tea. TEA?!

Cissy Akers, my ever loving/much loved niece, came for her first thrust into the back-country. That she had never before ridden, nor handled a horse, didn't occur to Lucius. He treated her like an old hand by tossing a lead rope of one of the pack horses into her ungloved hand. Pretty soon she showed him her palm, where the skin had been shorn off. He glanced at it and suggested she apply snow, of which there was plenty, and use the other hand.

It was a tough day, on beginners and everybody else, but she was relieved of the packhorse coming down the face of the Lynx Creek, where the snow still held except along its trickle. When we finally got to the bottom, into the upper reaches of Yellowstone Meadows, there was the tangle of streams where the Thoroughfare, Yellowstone and some smaller streams joined to pour into Yellowstone Lake. That meant some wading, but the loss of altitude and joining the southern exposure of full sunlight warmed the air. I told Cissy to just follow Himself's horse, which she did. Just before she climbed out of the stream, to my horror, she stepped in a hole, lost her footing and was quickly washed downstream. He reached out with the crook of his walking staff and hooked the shoulder strap of her backpack, then held her steady until the current swung her around to the bank, where she scrambled out.

In the meanwhile, I was afoot after Joker and I stupidly took a short cut across a switchback. The snow was deeper than it looked, about his shoulder high, and there was a trickle of blood dripping on the snow when we rejoined the trail. Joker had taken a hidden stob in his chest. I got off to lighten his load, crossed behind Cissy, and we walked together, soon to dry in the warming sun.

Lucius watched without a word and turned off to a grassy knoll encircled by pines and a streamlet. Hawks Rest was in sight, several miles across the huge Yellowstone Meadows, so a night's reconnoiter here was something of a good notion. Eric Gioia, neurosurgeon from Memphis, tied Joker's left hind foot up against itself to keep him from moving, broke out his surgical kit and sewed up the hole in his chest. His audience included a pair of black bears, with a cub, which watched from the tree line and retreated to the forest as Joker, released, stood quietly to pull out all the stitches with his teeth and then proceeded to graze.

John Ellerbeck, and his Malamute, Quiche, whom we had met on our first hiking trip into the Mission Mountains offered by the Wilderness Society (he was the guide), lived a day trip away in Logan, Utah, and frequently joined us.8

---

8 That trip warrants an aside in that it was our first into the Rocky Mountains. It is

We took off, following Lucius on Spook, leading fully loaded Pat and prepared for as long as fish kept us fed and the afternoon toddies held— say a couple or three weeks or so. We passed the cut-off to Five Pockets to go up and through Twilight Basin, then up, up and up over Cougar Pass at about 10,000 feet, where you can almost always see bands of Bighorn ewes with lambs lolling on grassy shelves. The long haul into Hidden Basin put us in a lodgepole forest of the three musts for a camp—water, wood and grass.

The first order of business was to tend the horses. Two hefted and held up the panniers while Himself unhooked the leather slings from the packsaddle. Pat was turned loose to roll in the grass while her hobbles were fetched. (Hobbles, as you may or may not know, are leather anklets for the two front feet. They hold the legs about 10 inches apart, allowing for forward motion like a circus pony but not enough freedom to start home.) She drank from the spring branch and grazed while Spook, relieved of his saddle and bridle, was let go to do the same. We knew he would not leave her side.

Meanwhile dry wood was fetched. (One of my favorite pictures of Lucius is with a rope over his shoulder in a drizzle dragging in a load of wood as big as a small cabin, dressed in his long yellow slicker and his beat-up hat, smoking a cigar.) Fire blazed, water was put to boil. Two of the few camp rules started right here: no booze until after at least one cup of tea with lots of sugar and milk. Everyone carried their own whiskey, rationed it as they chose, with no borrowing, begging or whining.

Pitching a tent was a one person hurry-up job, while sleeping bags

---

memorable for the quality/quantity of blueberries along the trail and the assigned leader of us twenty greenhorns. Most were charmed, except Lucius who was mortified at having to follow the EIGHT YEAR OLD DAUGHTER of the family that owned the ranch where we spent the first night.

She handled him like a magician when he showed any sign of questioning her ability or giving her helpful advice. It was hilarious! I know not why it took him so long. He had told me that he helped his mother make paper roses for the parades of Nashville women who opposed suffrage when the final decision was being approved in Tennessee's legislature. He claimed he was puzzled since he knew that his mother was just as smart, if not smarter, than his father.

The pair became fast friends, and he took an early step in realizing that the weaker gender is multi-purposed. This conviction culminated, to my satisfaction, decades later, when I overheard him tell Bob Buckman that I was a better fly fisher than he!

Himself

were spread on the grass to loft in the remaining sun. Then it was tea time, the most civil of times to breathe the pine-scented air, the wood smoke, and welcome the fact you had come to where you had cast your eyes and beyond.

Chores were minimum effort, maximum results. First night menu (because the meat was fresh and it lightened the bag of vegetables) was a big pot of stew of prime beef, carrots, red and green bell peppers, onions and garlic, real mushrooms and potatoes. Brew thus: brown the cubed tenderloin in olive oil, add vegetables already washed and chopped, bouillon cubes and water to match, then a package of dried brown gravy, stir with the wooden spoon. Simmer long enough while sipping your Sierra Club cup of spring water and the strongest whiskey available—the stronger, the less used, so the longer it lasted. Silence ascended as we waited with backs to a log, the raking shadows of the setting sun swept the huge basin, and we were released to our thoughts as a near-full moon rose to lighten the night.

Bliss Meadows

Tom Bliss was a horse-thief—one with a plan. He gathered horses in Dubois, drove them the some hundred miles through the mountains to Cody where they were rebranded and sold; then he reversed the drill. It seemed wise to delay the process by holing up out of sight while people forgot whose were whose. He did this for years until he got careless and tried to sell someone his own used-to-be horse. A posse tracked him to his hideout. Tom was no man to take lightly, so they waited until dawn when he came to his front door "to relieve himself," as the chronicle reported, and Tom was no more.

Eons earlier the south fork of the Shoshone River started sculpting the meadow where Bliss Creek, falling from a high ridge, joins the flow. Silt built an alluvial plain of a few hundred acres to become a rich, treeless pasture for moose, elk and for us. These waters were so filled with native brook trout that Game & Fish placed no limit.

We settled in to the middle camp at the bottom of the canyon through which we had come. Its spring, abundance of firewood, soft forest floor and makeshift outhouse, illegally left standing, were irresistible.

These camp sites were licensed by the year but only used in the late fall and winter when hunting seasons opened. When unused they were supposed to be totally cleared except for stacks of firewood and the tree houses built to store the kill out of reach from bears. In later years, the rules were changed to allow their use year-round and some wall-tents could be left standing.

The change of rules brought a Happening. One late summer afternoon, a small pack string came up the trail from Cody led by a taciturn cowboy (most of them are) and trailed by a handsome young woman, with long copper-colored hair and an Australian twang who took charge.

Of course, they were invited to supper. He drifted home early; she stayed late and told the story of her life: she was the recent widow of the camp's license holder, who had been accidentally killed in the previous season. To say that all male ears pricked up would be an understatement. As alpha seeks alpha, she staked out Lucius, who even shared his hitherto private horse-pannier seat. She was a storyteller, her tale graphic and accent beguiling. Before he walked her home, we were expected for breakfast.

Our trails met, to mutual pleasure, several times each summer for a few years and the two of them corresponded regularly. To know of her progress in running a successful hunting camp—maybe a first in the macho state of Wyoming—was gratifying. However, let us not forget that Wyoming had the first woman governor, and her statue, with that of Chief Washakie, are the two to represent the state in the Capitol rotunda in Washington.

Days in Bliss Meadows were just that. Whoever roused first built the fire and put water to boil. Remembering the sound of someone breaking sticks for kindling while still swathed in a double sleeping bag brings a grin to this ancient. The smell of coffee pulled heads out of tent flaps like possums from under a wood pile. Walk out to the whinny of horses accustomed to chunks of horse cake from your jacket pocket (never leave home without it) at this time of day, scratch an ear, stroke a velvet nose steaming the air. Joy unbound!

Breakfast was what and when you chose. (Trout are convenient fish; they get active only when the sun strikes the water, so don't call for pre-dawn waking.) There was granola, instant oatmeal, nuts, seeds, warm reconstituted milk, and makings for devils on horseback, which takes a bit of doing. Fry the best ever bacon—thick sliced, rind on, lots of lean, until it crisps to a crackle. Add a slice of bread with a large hole pulled from middle, crack egg in hole, brown, flop over until it's as done as you please, add Parmesan cheese and a dollop of hot, hot salsa. (Eggs and bacon kept well when packed in hard plastic cartons and wrapped in jacket atop the load.)

Fly fishing is best done alone. With company, you think about which holes to take, which to leave for friend; chatter is best left for another time. Here the South Fork is still a creek; you can wade anywhere to dark holes, below riffles, cut banks, behind rocks where your best chances lie. You fish wet, meaning without waders, when you have the warmth of the well-up sun. Here you are also pot-hunting; the usual catch and release procedure in trout fishing is canceled. Even to feed just five people (Quiche carries his own food in two soft bags strapped on like panniers) takes a lot of six or seven-inch fish. None were ever wasted: just cook them all and with any left, make a fish salad for lunch.

There was one place where I could catch 35 or 40 in a couple of hours. Downstream a bit from camp, caught on a riffle was a small downed tree that backed up a hole about the size and shape of an overgrown bathtub fed by a trickle from a beaver dam. Stand on the opposite bank, cast a short line (about twelve foot) with a #14 peacock herl, bead-eyed, nymph (the only ones I tied) which sink quickly and flash the sun. There was about a yard opening for a cast. Give it only seconds to settle, retrieve by lifting the rod-tip before the current carries it into the brush. If there's not that exhilarating tug, try again. There will be.

They are my favorites and I want to tell you more about brookies. First off, for the non-fisher people among you: trout don't have scales to cope with. Just keep your Swiss army knife sharp, especially at the tip. Lay the fish in your palm, belly up. Starting at the anus, stick the point in and move the blade just under the skin, straight up to the v-shaped cartilage under his mouth. Snip the cartilage—the whole works come out in one piece, neatly wrapped. Throw that into the bushes (organic fertilizer). There's one capillary of blood, easily removed by the back of your thumbnail, from the back of the hollow where his gut was. Some people leave the head; I cut it off—don't want that fish looking at me when I'm about to eat it.

Since we've gone this far, let's finish. Have a sack of plain white cornmeal, flavored with lots of black pepper and a smidgen of salt. Drop in the fish and shake well. Put in one layer in an already sizzling half inch of oil (or better, saved bacon grease), don't let it smoke, turn only once—takes about five minutes. Crunch the whole crisp thing, bones, tails and all—four or five for the ladies and who knows how many for the men.

Tel Anafa

Tel Anafa was so beautiful. Everything was beautiful as we jostled through that lush valley at first light. But the tel was awesome, tucked under a forest-size ficus tree and topped with tender pink blossoms of wild caper shrubs, resprouted since last season. Huge white storks stood on one foot waiting for fish to show themselves in the pond just below—landscape painting at its best.

That this one was special had been revealed when slit trenches were dug during the Six Day War three years before. The mass of glass sherds unearthed alerted the military (every other Israeli is a born archaeologist) and things came together. They alerted the antiquarians, who alerted Dr. Weinberg, who alerted his wife, who just happened to be a world authority on ancient glass and who, a few years earlier, had investigated a Roman glass factory at nearby Haifa. She alerted Corning Glass Co., which funded this seven season dig to start within months of the end of the war. This quick action was spurred because glass to the ancients was as rare and valuable as gold, and such abundance and diversity of shapes raised hopes of a factory.

I was in hog heaven, except for Hat. It had shown perversity since dawn with no sign of weakening. Of course it had to ride in my lap in the truck and struggled to sail off on its own. At the tel in a light breeze, the brim snapped back, and left me clutching.

There is a movie, *The Red Balloon*, about a little French boy given a balloon with a mind of its own which pulled him stumbling all over Paris. It was obvious from the start that Hat had no notion of protecting me from sunstroke; the label inside the crown which read *"faite en Paris"* should have been an omen.

I just mentioned that Dr. W. was an observing man, and sure enough, before we went up the hill, he handed me a kibbutznik special—a washable khaki hat with a deep crown and downturned protective brim that stays on in a gale and rolls up to go in your hip pocket.

"Here," he said, taking Hat, "let me put this brat in the office. Get it at lunch time."

It was forthwith hung on the wall of my four-cot dorm room, where the green ribbons shone like Christmas as the only touch of color. One late afternoon a young teenage girl approached with a note in English which she hesitatingly read asking to see Hat. Off we went to call. When offered, she took it slowly, put it on her head, turned toward the one small mirror and looked at herself—she was gorgeous. After that when she shyly approached, we went back to call and, at the end of my stay, I gave it to her with a quiet ceremony. What of Hat's life with that young woman?

That, with other such intimacy with Israelis leaves me empathetic, but as Jonathon expressed at the time, until and unless settlements built on acknowledged Palestinian land cease, peace is a dream.

The term "dig" for an excavation is short, convenient, snappy and inaccurate. To dig indicates a hole and makes a modern day archaeologist's blood run cold. The drill was this:

During the first season the entire flat area was cleared, surveyed with transits, marked off in four-meter squares and a datum point set to measure altitude. Depending on the number of workers available at about four per trench, squares were visually assessed and five selected as potentially most productive. They were stringed off in three-meter excavation trenches with one meter left unexcavated for balks and walkways. All had been dug to about three feet, with the exception of the step trench down the side, which was a must. Here the entire habitation age had been determined. Anafa produced artifacts at the bottom level in the Neolithic age, estimated 3,000-2,500 years B.C., which further assured its importance.

This lovely morning, while some reran transits and checked the datum point for accuracy, work started where it had left off last summer. I was the only beginner, but the technique was easily taught by the very experienced and pleasant professor from the University of New York at Stony Brook. (I can't believe I have forgotten his name.) Armed with a pick the size and shape of a hammer with a round pointed head, dust brush, dustpan and rubber bucket, I hunkered down, holding pick as instructed with a limp wrist. I swung the head sidewise, parallel to the ground through a couple of inches of soil. If it stopped, I stopped, and swept loose dirt into pan and thence to bucket. Located hindrance was not moved or even touched; it was probably an artifact. I repeated over small area which exposed more, then as a beginner, called Boss to identify and measure depth by a series of strings related to datum point. He entered the info and marked the site on map in his notebook. Repeated layers of dirt were removed until the object was fully exposed when he picked it up, marked with ink on the concave side an identity number and placed it in a collection bucket while I watched.

We found mostly pottery sherds, so when the first piece of glass appeared it was a physical shock—so beautiful. Glass, as it ages, oxidizes to form a thin, thin outer layer of translucent rainbow color, like a soap bubble, which is easily smudged. It also loses thickness to become sharper and more fragile. It was handled with care, and placed in assigned box. Bless Boss' heart, after this procedure was repeated a few times, he left me on my own except for significant finds.

The process was repeated for some three hours in the cool of morning until breakfast was called. This exotic meal was brought by Jeep and laid out under the big tent which served for all sorts of things out of the sun. The adage for good health of breakfasting like a king, lunching like a prince and supping like a pauper may have originated here; no one was too fat or too thin. Colorful platters of raw vegetables (tomatoes, cucumbers, onions, sweet peppers), small fish (pickled, smoked, grilled), local cheeses (soft, hard, from creamy to zesty, with smelly varieties which were delicious), bagels, whole grain bread with herbs, and scones stood up well to our appetites. There also was warm cereal that looked like, but didn't taste like, grits, hot milk and grapefruit blossom honey. All was stitched together with serious coffee and fresh mint tea, and salted with excitement.

Gradually we left the tent, to sit in the mottled shade of the giant ficus tree, washing the finds in a metal bucket of clear water from an artesian well.

Back at Shamir, we showered in individual stalls under sun-heated water, then pushed our sweaty clothes into a bucket of cold water with a miraculous detergent which called for no scrubbing or rinsing—just leave during lunch time then hang on the line in the sun. *Voilà*.

Lunch was undistinguished but filling, and was followed by the precious rite of this pre-air conditioning southerner—a blessed two-hour nap. The rest of the day took care of itself with supper and an outdoor movie preceded by superb rendition of Japanese Noh Theater by Jörg Schmeisser, who performed as the only character, the chorus and all of the musical instruments.

He was very tall, very thin, very young, and very authentic with straight black hair, eye-corners taped up in a slant, speaking made-up Japanese, robed in a kimono straight from Kyoto where he had taught engraving at their Fine Arts School the preceding winter. Jörg appeared at Anafa the first season as a green volunteer (just like me) until Dr. W. got a glimpse of his drawing—he drew on every scrap he found—and immediately pronounced him excavation artist. He was probably the best in the business.

Summer slipped by with no lessening of enthusiasm—rousing at first light and spending hours of strenuous mental and physical work suited me. An ancient culture was slowly being unearthed and to walk around to see the goings-on in the other trenches, puzzling over how the pieces meshed—fascinating.

So were the packets of daily scrawls from Memphis and Baja, which were again in the offing.

Loose the Hounds of Change
1969 - 1973

Cabo, which we wished would be eternal, was in the path of road paving bounding down the peninsula from San Diego/Tijuana to San Jose. The dusty village some thirty miles east was almost ready with a huge new landing strip to replace our old one, which had been leveled to build a fish processing plant whose pipes poured rotting fish innards into the bay.

With George Grider, Francis Gasner, Memphis architect (a Frank Lloyd Wright aficionado and painter of wistful watercolors, some I have and see every day) landed behind us in a split-tail Bonanza. The fine new strip was huge and freshly paved, but nothing more—no building, no vehicles, no outhouse, certainly no telephone. We found it only by super-skilled seat-of-the-pants navigation. An uneasy hour passed before the dust line appeared in the west as Doc jolted up the dirt track in his Jeep, and somehow layers of people and luggage were packed aboard. I straddled the gear shift.

Spirits rose bouncing toward the magic of Cabo primed by a housewarming bottle of tequila (the real stuff—the bottle had its *gusano*, the grub of its agave origin). Talk was overcome by wind, dust and rocks in the road until the final turn, when joy was unbounded. Gasner, an old hand, began to pitch his tent and air his sleeping bag under his usual mesquite. Plump Grider looked dubious and murmured about relocating to the hotel. He was assured that he could leave if he wished, and that the postal truck was at his disposal if he wanted to go. The thought of arriving at the swish Camino Real in such a vehicle must have been too much and his tent was pitched.

He, a constant orator with an interesting past, was an Annapolis graduate who captained a celebrated submarine during WWII and co-authored its biography *War Fish*. Later he was elected to Congress for a few years, in the aftermath of the Crump machine in Memphis. But with these other two who had helped him getting elected, he was just one of the boys.

There was a club of Japanese free divers at the hotel who arranged a parley to discuss usage of the point, a favorite spot for all divers that was essential for their unique hobby. With nothing but string bikinis, goggles and spear guns they dove 15 or 20 feet and sat on the bottom, plucking the strings of their weapons to entice fish from their holes. They could sit there many minutes before resurfacing—with fish—to breathe deep before submerging again. With polite gestures, they invited us to join. I avoided the invitation, but the men were obligated to give it a try. It was not a success—on with the tanks and putter down the beach.

The new Finisterra Hotel, built on the rocks that had protected the first air strip, was spectacular. Roughly trimmed native stone, weathered wood and glass of the lobby and dining room were visible on the horizon, but barely so. Glass walls overlooking the bay on one side and the Pacific on the other magnified the view and supported the inconspicuous roof so that it seemed to float on its own. Guest rooms nestled into the side rocks were approached by catwalks. To watch the Pacific surf roaring eternally over a fine meal and good conversation was indeed a happening and walking home on the dirt street where the beautiful children and skinny dogs played created a beguiling contrast of textures.

Two brothers arrived in yacht with crew from San Diego wanting to dive the Middle Ground, an uprising about thirty five miles offshore of black coral at a do-able ninety feet. They needed someone who knew the waters; Himself was their man. Off we all went to the middle of nowhere, bringing fine meals, white linen, vintage wine and plenty of ICE.

Later, after we left, they disappeared. Search teams found one floating deck chair with the boat name imprinted; the rest was silence. They probably struck a basking-shark which frequently came inshore. The second-largest fish in the world (for a whale is an aquatic mammal, not a fish), they move slowly and feed barely visibly just below the surface.

The change was gradual. That year, yachts and hotel guests came for marlin and swordfish well out to sea; diving was still uncluttered. Then, there it was—the dirt road from San Jose became a highway and the one street of town was paved. The angel-eyed children sat on their thresholds behind barbed wire and stick fences after one was killed by a fast moving car; hippies poured onto the beach with accompanying litter; the shark hunters' camp down beach disappeared; a gay bar was built at the waterline and disposed its waste directly into the surf; the fish house was demolished for a wharf for ferry loads of noisy revelers.

Hawks Rest

Hawks Rest is acclaimed the most remote place in the U.S. outside of Alaska. It was a magnet, an axle to which lead six major trails coming from all directions with the nearest paved road 38 miles in Turpin Meadows. From the back gate of the T-Cross, across the Divide, to the headwaters of the Yellowstone, then the some 20 miles of Yellowstone Meadows was considerably further. The Sirens' song of Bliss Meadows might have held us without promise of this more remote paradise.

As Sigmund Freud said, "Runs of unkempt nature serve the culture not unlike fantasy serves the individual."

Down the South Fork there were double blazes that call for a left turn. Along the way was the only remnant of Tom Bliss—a gate post, some two feet square by nine as firmly planted as the day he set it. From there on was seriously uphill, and our progress slowed. Camp was pitched for the night at the upper end of a meadow where we watched a small band of elk bed down in the grass at the lower end. We watched them; they watched us, and peace was in the valley.

Next morning started the crossing over into Eden. Marston Pass eased upward, turned to sharp switchbacks, then a long section of scree (loose rock fragments) covering the slope with an angle of repose so steep that the trail needed constant repair but got it only occasionally. I was grateful to be on foot.

Crossing that stretch many times never lessened my fear. The first time on Joker, I dropped the reins on his neck, dismounted, crept uphill behind him and smacked his rump. He crossed without hesitation. I walked.

Himself waited at the first switchback to remind me that a horse has four feet and I only two, and that Joker was smarter than I and knew when to go and when to not. All of which was true, but that didn't mean I didn't dread even the thought of it. Still do.

One time, I worked up the nerve to look down. There a band of elk was crossing, hundreds of feet below; one was pure white, an albino—a great rarity. Echoes of L.'s admonition, "Never let fear deter you!"

At the top of this rise, the terrain flattened to a grassy, gentle lift to the Continental Divide. Ferry Lake glimmered in the bowl below; the Grand Teton, more than a hundred miles away, pointed into clear air.

On the other side, the trail led down, down, down to the Yellowstone through Woodard Canyon—hikers' and bears' delight of wild blueberries and currants. Bears, especially grizzlies, are timid creatures except when riled; they just move away from the scent of humans. Until the great forest fire in the Park in 1988, I never saw one—plenty of tracks but no beasts. (Their tracks have the pointed claw prints, whereas blacks show none.) Blacks show up frequently in odd, familiar places; my first sighted were two adults standing on the side of the gravel road into Turpin Meadows like hitchhikers.

Yellowstone Meadows stretches some 25 miles from the foot of the canyon to the park boundary. At the end of another day's walk after crossing the upper reach of its great river (one of the only big western rivers left undammed) there is Castle Creek, a lacing of rocks which shift from time to time to form new channels.

Fish in the wild spawn where they were born and, if that is blocked, they wait. So well after season, the bright red mating color of amorous cutthroats still flash in the fast-moving current: a late afternoon challenge for supper.

A September 1, 2001, *Economist* article, "The Trouble Is, People Get There," has this to say about Bridger Lake, which is enfolded in that V:

"This lake is small, clear and surrounded by shores dotted with bluebells and trees... The mountains above, which look like giant pin-cushions of green velvet... protected by Congress from the chainsaw and miners' drills... But remote, nowadays, does not mean untouched... Others less polite say it reminds them of Grand Central Station. No fewer than 41 local outfitters have permits to run pack trips or hunting camps. In 1997, the last year for which figures are available, some 106,000 people visited this wilderness... Mules loaded with gear and riders with sore behinds crowd the trails alongside the hikers... Isolation no longer means peace and quiet... With Walmart selling hand held GPS at $99 and ubiquitous cell phones, hordes of people take to wilderness without a clue as to how to care for themselves. If you get a blister or tired, call 911, they'll come get you; there's even the story of a call for a hot chocolate. The vital system of medevacs was thrown into such chaos that there is now a huge charge where it once was a free service of mercy for those between life and death."

There is not much good to say about being ninety-four except when you consider the alternative, but I am forever grateful that I knew the West before it was so inundated with people dragging their urban stuff (and Greece before its sanctuaries had to be protected from people by cyclone fences). A great fun of it all was to see how good life can be with a bare minimum of civilization.

Since we had closed the back gate of the T-Cross, except for the Australian and her solemn wrangler we had not seen a single soul. Luck held. A couple of horses lifted their heads in the fenced-in pasture around a ranger's cabin. There was no smoke from the chimney, but there wouldn't be in the middle of the day.

Choosing a campsite for some days must include the usual water, wood and grass plus a private place to dig a latrine. Ellerbeck, erstwhile professional guide, volunteered. With the multi-purposed trenching tool, he dug a slit about three feet by 18 inches, as deep as the roots allowed behind a good size log, left the shovel stuck in the dirt nearby with the roll on the handle covered with a plastic baggie in case of rain. All the comforts of home in about twenty minutes; remember to use the shovel for a layer of dirt laid atop. All very tidy.

At the tip of the V, where the lake feeds into the river, was a spot with added charms. A pair of white trumpeter swans with four cygnets, nesting on the shore line some thirty feet away, paid us no attention as they taught their young the ways of the world. Up and down and all around they swam, as quiet as golf carts, in single file with the wee ones in between for safety from turtles below looking for supper. Occasionally an early flying lesson would be marked by the flapping of wings, which was no small thing. The adults were surprisingly big and awkward out of the water. I read that these are the largest native American bird and the largest global waterfowl. Whatever, they are beautiful, and so fierce when approached that even Quiche kept his distance.

A resident cow moose stared us down from afar. Moose are the most socially adroit of wild animals. Long, and I mean long, they stand and look before easing away. But don't push your luck; be as polite as they or you can end up dead.

She taught her calf to swim and feed on underwater greenery one morning right before my eyes. It was a "mama do, baby do" operation. The pair approached the shore in lock-step and browsed the moose-willows. Mama put her foot in the lake; baby stopped. Mama put in the other foot; baby watched. There was more munching. Mama stepped in with all four feet; baby watched. Mama waded out another step, stretching the bond. Mama drank; baby put one foot in water and pulled it back. Mama waded another step; two small hoofs followed. Time passed. The process took a fascinating hour, until at last the deed was done—babe was paddling behind mama swimming to the next cove where both heads went under and reappeared with dripping mouths full of bright greenery.

(The Wildlife Museum in Jackson has a splendid bronze fountain depicting such a scene, where the water trickles down grasses dripping from the raised head of a life-size moose.)

"Hello the Camp!"

"Hello the Camp!" shouted from a distance, was the greeting that preceded entering any camp. Just after first-night supper, this came from Gordon Reese, a ranger-icon. We had been under his supervision all day without laying eyes on one another, and maybe since we closed Emily's back gate. (The T-Cross is an in-holding of the National Forest.) The area is so huge and personnel so sparse, I never got it through my head what was what, nor needed to. The topo maps in Lucius' saddle bag were rarely read.

The federal government has a way of getting things done, usually well. There were thousands of miles of trails that you took for granted would be passable—an overlooked miracle. The blazes were easily seen above the snow line—it was almost impossible to get lost. As head ranger, Gordon Reese traveled these many miles for days at a time. He talked with everybody he saw about where they had been, what had they seen. He had that gift of instant friendship. We saw him many times over the years, and told him anytime we saw anything that needed reporting. If everyone he saw were equally beguiled, he had hundreds of eyes. Beyond that, he was constantly able to take the pulse of public opinion: the hot subjects of the time were whether or not to feed the bears in that time of drought and the whirling disease that was devastating the trout. He always came after supper, to which he was invited but never accepted, and never took an offered toddy. What he did do was to reinforce the recognition of the fragility of this Eden, and our responsibility to it, just by talking with love in his voice.

August in the Wind River Range

August in the Wind River Range was warm enough to go jacketless. But be sure to wear two shirts, or the mosquitoes and an occasional horsefly will feed on your shoulders, savoring your salt and blood. Don't be lulled into rolling up your sleeves or shedding your gloves—your skin will look like mine. Keep your cowpoke hat on; it is not just for show. You are so close to the sun and there are some 6 million acres more to explore.

Glacier Trail was a gut-buster from the time the horses backed out of the trailer. These were newer mountains than the Absarokas, and start just north of the river. The streams slicing them were fast and slippery, like Trail Lake Creek which comes helling over its great rocks 30 minutes up the switchbacks. Blessedly, the Forest Service built a sturdy bridge of retired railroad ties, which appears just when you are most seriously huffing and puffing. Then it was up, up and up to a forested plateau for a short distance, then more of the same steep rise to Sheep Flats. From here you see again the Grand Teton pointing to heaven over Jackson Hole some hundred miles west. The windswept flats extend gradually to a cairn of stones two or three miles south which head you in that direction anyway you want to go—there were lacings of trails across the expanse of gravel and broken stones sparsely covered with Alpine flowers, clumps of grasses, trickles of clear, cold water. (In elder days than these you never carried water or filters—just a cup clipped to your belt. Now you should not dare!)

Beyond the cairn was more of the same but slanting downward, then switchbacks down, down and down to a small meadow of enough grass for two horses for one night and a creek ran through. The repeat of Jim Beam and branch and beef stew was just as delicious if not more so; the sun did not fade sooner than we. Next day came in a flash, when sleep was interrupted by the murmuring of, "The day shall not be up so soon as I, to try the fair adventure of tomorrow." There again is Shakespeare when you want him.

From the foot of the sleeping bag, I pulled on my still-warm woolen pants and soft leather camp-shoes with sheepskin linings. I pulled on my down jacket, which had been my pillow, and crawled out. Naturally I kept on my moth-eaten cashmere sleeping shirt. Some kind soul had already built the fire and left coffee steaming. Back at the tent the Cheshire cat grin rose to my folded legs and a sweatered arm reached for his cup.

The topo map spotted Philips Lake, half a day away, which was reported to have Golden Trout, called "the fish from Heaven" because there's nowhere else they could have come from. They are a subspecies of Rainbows (as are native Cutthroats) which thrive above timberline lakes. How they manage to be there is an ancient puzzle: there are no intakes or outlets so are totally isolated, and yet they are found in many such lakes and all have the same red and gold coloring. The most reasonable explanation is that they go back to the end of the last ice age, about 13,000 B.C. (the one that permitted Russians tribes to cross the Bering Straits to evolve into American Indians.) As the ice covering receded, the deep lakes remained as did their isolated fish of exotic coloring. Exactly what the benefit of the gaudy coloring is still remains a question.

Yesterday's huffing and puffing was just a test. The trail flattened out as we mushed on at a better pace into a narrow valley of wildflowers, Box Canyon. Supper was about ready when up the trail strolled revered and ridiculed wildlife biologist, John Mionczynski, with a friend and three domestic goats—Billy, Nanny and Kid. After a couple of good shooters, he fetched his huge accordion from one of the goat panniers and softly played as he told of living on Long Island by working a truck garden. One afternoon when he could stand it no longer, he strapped his piano atop his car and headed west to go as far as it and his ready cash took him.

The car gave out and he settled in to Atlantic City, Wyoming, population 27, 18 miles on the dirt road between Lander and Muddy Gap. He got a job with Game & Fish researching the Bighorn sheep which inhabit the rocks and crannies of mountain peaks, where a pack horse would have starved. When he went to their kinsmen, domestic goats, to haul his equipment, he became the acknowledged father of goat packing which, not much later, became very popular with dudes.

Atlantic City was once a busy community which served the early settler and seekers of the California gold fields going over the mountains through South Pass, a comparably easy route. It was a late night, but when we rolled out, they were gone. Where and how they had slept was a question—I envisioned them dropping the waterproof ground cover, zipping up their jackets and cuddling, man and goat together, for animal warmth. I'm sure it was better than that: both men carried heavy packs and the accordion only took up one goat pannier, which left three for gear.

According to John, they were living on goat's milk, warm and abundant from Nanny, and in their packs they carried fish hooks and line along with nuts, seeds, dried fruit. Gesturing toward the sparsely covered rocky terrain, he said, "Almost everything you see there is not just edible but good and filling." They left a thank-you gift: a big pot of fresh milk!

When we were breakfasting, there came two figures up the trail: young women with oversize packs, full of smiles. They propped their loads against a tree and accepted coffee, and said they had already had breakfast. They were trail-keepers, Forest Service volunteers out just for the fun of it.

They didn't stay long and when Lucius, ever the gentleman, rose to help them pull on their packs, he had a hard time picking them up. Later, he swore they weighed at least 75 to 80 pounds, which included heavy duty mattocks for grubbing up small trees.

(Theoretically, anyone can carry 20% of his own weight without noticing it. After that, every ounce makes a difference—I even cut off half of my toothbrush handle. At my 130 pounds, a 30 pound pack was heavy and 35 a burden.)

What these two young women in their early twenties were doing was about the same as I had done in the Galilee, but in a different way at a different age. They were trading eight weeks of their sweat for the privilege of immersing themselves in the untrammeled earth, with people of like mind and longing.

Dinwoody Glacier

Dinwoody Glacier on Gannett Peak was as overwhelming as the other two we had seen. Those were the Franz Josef at Mitford Sound, New Zealand, which we saw from the ground, and Edith Cavell in British Columbia, which we looked down on from one thousand feet overhead. This one we saw from its milky side stream, and it consumed the horizon. (Never confuse snow packs with glaciers.) This mighty frozen river was moving forward, taking part of the earth with it.

On our way out, Dan Kinnerman greeted us with, "Hey! I've been meaning to look you up." Bighorn sheep professional guide that he was, he had his life worked out. He was married to one of the best looking ladies in town, who was the boss at the bank and on the school board. His clean, open, pleasant, handsome face had the attributes of a good horse trader and friend.

"Heard you bought Pat," he said. "How do you keep up with her?"

Back country conversations, particularly about horses, are extended, and often fruitful. An hour later, a deal was struck—I don't remember exactly what, but whatever it was, it worked. By the beginning of the next summer, Pat was back to a more controlled life, Ug had good work experience, and I had a new and faster horse.

This meeting also lead to Himself's first and only legal experience in Wyoming. The Fourth of July was celebrated *con brio* in Dubois, a jolly affair when the town law of no-open-bottles on the street was suspended.

Ladies with feathery hats and large bosoms waved like Queen Mary, with palms facing inward, from an ancient convertible touring sedan. A prewar fire engine with brass a-shine cruised up the street. A pick-up truck of school musicians tootled and beat out patriotism and pop. Horses galore slowly pranced and side-stepped, short-reined by their sedate riders. But, most glorious of all were the *coureurs du bois* (runners of the woods: French fur traders like the ones who came first to this area) and Eastern Shoshones—dressed in breechcloths, beaded sandals, feathers and little else. The Shoshones carried long knives and tomahawks to the competitions at the town park, and they pulled a cannon which exploded at short intervals to shoot forth rolls of toilet paper to festoon the world.

Mighty and accurate was the hurling of weapons at posts set deep in the ground: wagers were made with shouts of victory and prowess. Brother (and even I) would have had a field day with an icepick.

We had hardly gotten back to the T-Cross when Dan called for help. Town fathers had arrested the *coureurs* on the grounds of violating the no-open-bottles law. He knew his right, and called on his attorney.

Since there was no jail, they were locked in the fire engine garage, which was vacant at the moment. In their scant dress, it threatened to be a cold night. Calls went out to wives and girlfriends for surety bonds if they wanted their loved ones back before dark. That must have been discouraging if many of the responses were similar to one, "$100? Keep the son-of-a-bitch!" And besides, it was already past supper time; all were released to their nearest and dearest on their own terms.

Next day when court convened and formalities were completed, the crowd heard an elegant dissertation on selective enforcement being contrary to provisions of the Constitution of the United States of America. Thomas Jefferson could have done no better; everybody went home for lunch—some more pleased than others.

Kinnerman came with us back across the divide to the north face of the range, which we hit at sunset. From high above the world, looking across the streak of alfalfa green of the Wind River toward the infinity of the Absaroka Range, the setting sun struck the Badlands—the huge bluffs of barn red and pink Chugwater soil cut by the stream. The universe inflamed; the pace slowed to a stop as we stared. No one said a word. The sun died behind the Tetons; dusk took over like a closing curtain.

Dan turned to go on about his business and we went home in the dark.

October's Bright Blue Weather

October's bright blue weather is a joy almost everywhere, certainly including Tennessee. Nights cool enough for a blanket and mild, dry days are a relief after the summer heat, and are an atavistic preparation for winter. Sight in the shotguns, un-kennel the Setters after their summer's ease, tramp with them the fields of soybeans and corn, watch for deer tracks—follow them into the woods. Where are they bedding at night?

My children thrived during the summer in their own ways. Friends, more constant than I, struggled to preserve some of nature's earth. It was a good place to come; my work was cut out. Bookkeeping soothes my soul, especially when it is in the black. Numbers are so clean, concise. If there is a mistake, it is my fault—find it! In its early days, the Tennessee Environmental Council prospered, and even had a surplus. We formed as an umbrella group to coordinate and amplify the voices of a number of groups with common agendas. (The concept is now re-circulating under the term "collective impact.") Guru Ruth Neff more than supported it by contract work with federal agencies with a staff of one (Mayo Taylor, a minor genius on her own) and an ardent clutch of volunteers.

With the advent of the Reagan administration, all of that came to a halt almost overnight. Salaries went in arrears; the jig was up until Lucius stepped in, got us a foundation grant to cover back pay, and the Conservation League (the hunters and fishermen outfit he helped form along with the Tennessee Wildlife Resources Agency for which he wrote the Model Law to keep the state from politicizing the license funds) to share its office space.

Things changed as things do. Ruth was invited into the Alexander administration—a good place for her extraordinary talents. Mayo Taylor took over as Director until she moved to Murfreesboro with her husband. A gung-ho young man was hired, while I was in Wyoming, bound to bring government to its knees. He started by disposing of our two industry board members, Bowater and Rhone-Poulenc. Furious, I walked out of the board meeting which approved the motion.

But I do digress.

Summer moved into fall as smooth as warm honey. Christmas was coming, hunting seasons opened. Himself was like a lad expecting Santa Claus with ancient rites going back to the Neanderthals in their caves painting bison on the walls to assure their coming.

Deer hunting is not for the impatient or weaklings. It is autumn; fallen leaves crunch under foot unless it rains, so it is futile for much of the time for stalking. That called for the less exciting but surest way to fill the larder—hours, from well before light, of sitting motionless in a tree waiting for them to come to you—which they will.

The drill was this. Turn off the odious alarm clock; ready the coffee pot; put on everything you have with special attention to head, toes and fingers, plus a flame orange vest to keep from being shot. Pour coffee, with lots of sugar and milk into covered vacuum cup. Drink as you walk by flashlight to one of the blinds, of which there were three overlooking the cropped field nearby—one for him, one for me. The third, which we could share, had a bench, where he sat with me backed up to his knees and he had to shoot over my shoulder.

Deer don't look up, so a four foot square platform up in a tree won't spook them. Climb the cross-nailed planks and squirm to get you back to the trunk and be prepared to wait, and wait. As the light sneaks in, birds chatter and feed. Their scratching in the leaves sounds much like approaching hooves, which they just may be. You can move your eyes; but if your nose itches, let it do so. The Jays perched nearby watch; if you don't move they accept your being there and go on about their business.

Once there was a patter of feet along the farm road below and there trotted a great red fox. As he passed, I gave a short low whistle between my teeth. He stopped, looked around. When he set off, another whistle, a bit louder. This time he sat down on his haunches, facing the tree but not looking up. The next time he seriously started to depart, I let forth a full blast which really stopped him. Again he faced the tree, scratched his ear, stretched out full length watching and waited several minutes, ears on the alert. I did not whistle when he finally got up again and went jogging along in his original direction.

Fox gone, attention back to the open field. I saw does at some twenty yards, browsing the beans. (Soy beans are left unpicked until late when they are completely dry.) Magic, I had neither heard nor seen them come, but there they were slowly feeding—one head always up as a lookout.

Flame-oranged Lucius had not moved on the other side of the field. He couldn't have seen them, and besides this was stag season. When a shot sounded, shortly followed by a second, but no third, I scrambled down and the does took back to the woods.

In the time it took me to cross over, most of the field dressing was done. The magnificent seven-pointer was laid with his head angled for the stream of blood from his slit throat to gush away downhill. With a sharp-pointed bowie knife, Lucius cut a circle around the anus, then a long slit just under the skin (like gutting a fish) in the belly to the slit in the throat. He avoided puncturing the digestive track, pushed the legs apart with his foot to open the cavity long-ways, and rolled the now-free intestinal sack out of the carcass. He pushed that neat package downhill with his foot—it would be gone soon to the wood critters' delight.

All this took sweat, strength, know-how *and* a head-shot. (If it had been a body-shot the intestinal sack would be penetrated and field dressing one long messy, smelly ordeal.) He got the vehicle and wrestled the carcass, now only weighing about 400 pounds, to the lowered tail-gate with the assistance of me and a pulley rope attached to the spare tire. He took it back to the cabin's front porch, attached the ankles to a winch and swung the carcass up, then washed the cavity with full blast of hose until the water ran clear. He wired the tag he got with his license to an antler spike—a dead deer without a tag can call for a lot of conversation with a ranger and a *big* fine.

If it was coming dark, he left the beast winched well off ground, away from the varmints, knowing it would keep fine over the cold night. First thing in the morning, off we would go to the check-in station and wild meat processors 20 miles away in Bolivar.

Then it was tea time. Build up the fire and put the kettle on. A lot of people were now assured of winter meat—some who count on it, others who merely savor. Tea was never better, nor the toddies that came afterward, the simple supper, the warmed bed of the electric blanket and eider down comforter that his mother had had made years earlier from most of the other comforters in the house, encased in waterproof canvas for her adolescent son going off to Alaska, alone at 17.

Time encases and entwines small joys of yesterday, which we took for granted and too frequently abandon, even though they can be most delicious in ancient age. Let it not happen to you!

Spider Silk

Spider silk is said to be, relative to size, the strongest of all fibers. 1973 to 1989 was a time for such spinning life to the lees, from the wilds of Wyoming to the charm of the Andean foothills, with spring, fall and in-between to pay our separate dues for the privilege.

Lucius reduced his law practice to, as he said, "the interesting and lucrative." Yet when he died in 1996, more than 70% of the firm's clients were listed as his. 15 years after his departure, Burch, Porter & Johnson is still known for taking on the tough landmark cases that others won't touch. His third floor office in the restored Tennessee Club facing Court Square in Memphis is now used as a meeting room, with his memories still there on the walls in the same cases where they had been placed years ago.

An interesting lot they were. The first day he took me there, I looked at the black-and-white pictures, all inscribed with endearing messages, that covered the wall. Circling the room, gazing, wondering what I could say, the only one I recognized was Martin Luther King.

At one end of the room hung paintings of naval battles with inscriptions blurred by cannon fire, glass-topped tables of ancient, military buckles of every size, a sword and scabbard—these from the Armada warship of Tobermory Bay and these from the Spanish treasure ship, *Nuestra Signora de Atocha*, of the Florida Keys. But most exciting of all—the photo of the dedication at the Memphis City Hall of one of the three cannons from the Bay of St. Eustatius which he and his scuba friend, Thane Muller, had found and retrieved. They fired the first salvo at a U.S. vessel during the Revolutionary War.

With the spinning went time and change. In 1986 the T-Cross sold to a consortium, which included Ken and Gary Neal, that intended to re-establish it as a guest ranch. Changes were made within the limits allowed by the conservation easement legally held by The Nature Conservancy and things rolled on much as usual.

Walter Kerr, literary critic for the *New York Times*, once said "Every age brings its own lantern." That was true. Interesting people, writers and pundits came, along with dudes in aloha shirts, to knock at our door and pontificate at length. How sad the conversations are lost.

We took Ken into the back country to introduce him to the wilds he had purchased—a bit of fun that later turned out to be a matter of life or death.

1988, time of the great fires in Yellowstone Park, was the last of our splendid years, and splendid they were. Early in 1989 all changed. Age snapped at Lucius' heel after 77 years of walking away from three airplane crashes (one upside down in a bay off Cuba), a heavy round of hepatitis C from transfusions and three types of cancer. He only mentioned it in saying he could use a smaller horse. When Ken, as a sort of joke, offered a big burro from his string, who called to mind the still-bright loving memories of Licorice and Jacob, off we went.

It was a perfect bunch setting out through the back gate for leisurely days to Hawks' Rest with layovers in Bliss Meadows and Castle Creek along the way—Ellerbeck, Dana and his wife, John Noel and Melinda Welton, and Joe McCarty—all experts—on foot with backpacks. We had been blocked the previous year to east of the Continental Divide by the forest fires, so there was the excitement of homecoming, and Ug was packed to the gunnels for at least a three week stay.

Joy unbounded went along with wisecracks about Lucius and the burro which, after hours of uphill pull, was ready to head home. Strong words and my leading Ug followed.

Overnighting at the mouth of Twilight Basin on a bench above the rocky headwaters of the creek was lovely. First night out stew, French bread for sopping and hard black chocolate with coffee sat well on the foundation of Jim Beam and branch water. You cannot forget how close the stars and the near-full moon are at 10,000 feet.

Lucius once observed that it made no difference how long we stayed up or how early we rose, starting time was always nine o'clock. After breakfast John and Melinda headed up the long valley toward the switch-backed rise to Cougar Pass—she had never seen the Bighorn ewes and lambs that loitered there and couldn't wait to do so. The rest stayed to douse the fire and replace the sod before they followed.

I had to hold the bit while Lucius mounted and he and his burro started arguing about where to go—downhill toward home or uphill to the mountain. As I got up and adjusted Ug's lead rope, everything happened at once. Lucius smacked the burro's rump with the flat of his hand and off they bolted down the steep drop to the creek. It was just seconds before the animal slipped on the rocks, scrambled up and ran off, leaving Himself on his back on the rocks with icy water running below. He was so quiet when I put my wool jacket across his chest, his eyes opened once then closed again with a wisp of a smile.

"Lucius, don't move," I said, "I'm going for help."

He didn't respond; there was no choice but to leave him alone.

I remounted and started yelling. Everybody else had disappeared over the rise. They started back at a run, and I pointed back towards Lucius, racing on to catch John and Melinda who were now out of sight. Even in panic, I knew I had to get back to the ranch to call for the medevac from Jackson Hole. It seemed forever before I spotted them and got their attention.

Helling back down the draw, I spotted the burro grazing in the distance. It was obvious that decisions must be made and I had damned well better settle down. The chopper was first. If I went back to Lucius, my herd-bound horse would raise cane at leaving the rest, but now he was moving and heading for the corral. John and Dana, both professional guides, knew first aid. John Noel had been in a similar situation in a recent lighter-than-air plane crash and knew, first-hand, about trauma.

I pumped my fist overhead as I passed.

Mama and Charlie Hatcher's fifty-year-old drilling, "Never run downhill or toward the barn," was clear. For the next four or more hours we hit a trot as fast as the terrain allowed. I started yelling for Ken at the second gate, and he met me with, "What is it?"

"Lucius at Twilight Creek," I said.

As I leaned forward to dismount, my knees gave. I would have been head-down in the dirt had he not grabbed my shoulders as I fell forward, pushed back and lifted me to the ground.

"Sit here, rub your knees hard, then come to the kitchen," he said. When I wobbled in, he was shaking his head. "This is Sunday afternoon, things are slow in Jackson."

Dialing another number, his face brightened, and he said, "Need you now, old man. Got problems. Pasture in front of lodge, T-Cross, Dubois."

We sat cross-legged in the pasture as I explained exactly where and what had happened. He knew the spot—he had been there with us—and I told him there was a good landing place for the helicopter. He had the good sense not to ask other questions. I could not have answered, and would probably have come apart at the seams at any sympathy. A calming voice goes a long way.

The chopper only had room for one person besides pilot and medic, and that had to be Ken, who knew the way to Twilight Creek. I let them go, and set out on the 85 miles to the hospital. Of the trip, I remember nothing until entering the ER where it was warm, where there were lights, and where people in pastels moved about talking in normal voices. And there he was—eyes brilliant, some color in his face and a sickly grin. No telling what he had been given, but it was enough.

Of the next days, weeks, there are only flashes of memory. I watched him sleep. No one suggested that I leave. I took off my shoes, rolled my jacket for a pillow and wrapped in our sleeping bag which had reappeared, laid on the floor between his bed and the wall, and struggled for sleep. Noiselessly a gurney was rolled into another alcove in the semi-dark with a patient flat on his back, hat on his chest and boots stood at his feet. I knew where I was.

Strangely, there was no orthopedist at the hospital in Jackson Hole, an outdoor sports center of the world. (They must mob in during ski season.) He was in the hands of an internist to be stabilized until able to be medivaced to the nearest center to meet his needs. Days melted together.

It was suggested that I take a walk while they started draining the fluid from his chest through a hole punched between his ribs. A gallon size beaker of pink something gradually filled under his bed with a tube snaking up under the covers when I came back. His expression never changed and his eyes were glazed but there was a slight squeeze when I settled in for the coming hours of hand holding.

The good doctor told me that I just could not sleep on the ER floor, that I could come and go as I pleased and that there was a motel across the street. I had already figured what was coming and spotted a my-size gap behind the sofa in the waiting room for night two. That also would not do. There was a usable overnight room for insomniacs available with reclining chairs. After night three faced with a television as wide and high as the sky and volume set for the elderly, I opted for our vehicle in the parking lot. Then it rained; my sleeping bag got wet (there is nothing colder than a wet down sleeping bag) and I took Gary and Ken's offer of their house in Moose.

Weeks passed, how many I don't know, before he was moved out of intensive care. X-ray showed two vertebrae between his shoulders crushed to triangles which could not support his upper weight and there was nothing more they could do there. That the spinal cord to his brain was not affected was evidenced by the battery of communications with the insurance company which held that they would only pay for his being moved to Salt Lake City for further treatment. The policy said "the nearest'" medical center with the "needed facilities." However it also contained the term "best needed." At Baptist Memorial he was a regular; Memphis it was.

The difference in the way he was handled for the next months was awesome. Starting with the uniformed crew that fetched us to the sleek private jet at the Jackson airport, he was treated as a neonate or ancient Chinese porcelain, not a cowpoke with hat on chest and boots at his feet. Within a few hours we were in a jungle of flowers, and I had a cot, small but mine own—with a reading light.

Physical therapy started almost immediately, the likes of which I had never seen before or since. Strapped to a board from shoulders to hips which attached to a bar at the center, he could be rotated to standing position and told to move whatever he could. Next the board was submerged in a tank of tepid water; the straps from waist down were loosened so he could move his legs and arms—twice a day and each for an hour.

Slowly something called a clam shell cast contoured to his torso in two removable pieces for sleeping (even I could remove and replace it) gradually allowed him to pull himself to a seated position by an overhead bar. How much or if it was painful, he never said and I didn't ask. That was a silent agreement between us.

Visitors were limited to Elsie and his daughters, one at a time, then gradually expanded to all sorts of interesting people. Again it became a sort of salon. When we finally moved to the executive suite in Germantown where we had been after his plane crash, visitors became a mild problem but were still welcomed. Home physical therapy consumed an hour in the morning with a pro, and in the afternoon with me armed with instructions and determination. Evenings were quiet with reading, and after *Are You Being Served* on the tube, lights went out for nights without pills.

Of all engraved pictures, the keenest was his last day of therapy when the doctor removed the brace for good. His deformity was little improved, but he was up and moving.

"We have done what we can," said the doctor. "The rest is up to you."

Summer was for convalescing. "There must be some place you would like to go where we've never been," he said. That question was repeated as we clod hopped down the dirt road at the T-Cross on our afternoon walk. For years I had refused to answer that; anything that he suggested was way beyond my imagination. But this was different; life was too quiet for this man. He needed action.

"Yes," I said. "I would like to go to Alaska and catch rainbows."

Copper River is a salmon spawning stream off the sea-sized Lake Iliamna, northwest of Anchorage. Just getting there was an adventure. We flew over the plains of Saskatchewan to the Yukon's White Horse, turned left, and leapt the mountains to the coast. The plane's oil needed changing, so we over-nighted in the dreams of my childhood—the setting of London's *Call of the Wild*. Anchorage was just another city, but not so the Iliamna airport. Men with great beards heaved moose racks nearly the size of VWs; seaplanes dodged in and out like mosquitoes. Ours splashed into an enormous silence while we watched the canoe come to fetch us.

I had guessed right. This was the place for him at such a fragile time.

Gin-clear water smoothed to the steep steps up to the porch of the lodge, which he climbed without comment. In the great room in front of a river-stone fireplace, with four-foot logs roaring away, sat some eight or nine men who would have been just as comfortable in three-piece suits—lawyers and merchant chiefs. They rose when we came in, politely ignored the fact that I was the lone female, and offered seats and drinks. I rose to the occasion by asking for single malt with a splash of hot water.

Dinner, fish of course—delicious—was served at one big table with everybody present. The manager, a bear of a man, and his wife were up to running this place with discreet flourish. They were worldly people—no telling how they got here. Luck, I suppose.

Dessert was coffee and homemade fudge in front of the chunked up fire; bedtime was early. It had been a good day.

October meant frosty nights and sunny days—trout fishing time. As Alaskan trout migrate for spawning, they swim just below the salmon, close enough to bump the hen's bellies to make them drop their eggs on which they feed. This place is the end of their road where, if they are to reproduce, they must come.

The migrating salmon are so dense, it is almost impossible to get a line through to the trout until most die off. Then there they are, visible in the clear waters, smelling to high heaven of dead and dying fish. Flaubert, in *Madame Bovary*, says that no woman can be truly beautiful without one flaw. That smell is the single flaw of fly fishing for trout in Alaska—it is so bad that many of the lodges close in August as it starts. However, don't panic. By October it is like swimming in a sulfur water pool: as soon as you get in, the rotten egg smell disappears. So it is with dead fish in paradise.

Fishing was leisurely, easy. A guide took the three-man boat upstream whenever we chose, well after the sun-up, then we took the rest of the day floating back, stopping at the many pools. We pulled the boat ashore on the gravel beach, climbed out, waded in and had at it. In the clear water, fish were visible so we were usually casting to a particular fish, not just random.

This was bear country. The Alaskan browns (which are the same species as our grizzlies but with different coloring) are solitary creatures except where there are fish, and that was here. It was prudent to stay near the boat so that if a bear appeared, you could move on.

This arrangement suited us. Lucius' casting was as accurate as ever and the wading was easy. The problem was in leaning over to release a catch—his balance was off. We stood close, alternating his casting downstream with that long, sensuous curl and I upstream with my shorter arc into the current. When he brought it a fish, I turned and released it without ado. Just right.

Three weeks glided by. On the final afternoon, civilization smacked my face while he snoozed, face up to the setting sun, cradled by the life-preservers in the prow of the boat. It had been our longest day on the river, a good one.

The mouth of the Copper where it joins Iliamna is a great V of deepening, faster running water. The guide had handled me out to a depth where I would not have gone alone. The fishing was terrific—casting long line downstream gave a feeling of omnipotence even if he did have to stand right behind to break the rush of the current. The fish were big, the strikes heavy, and it was tiring even with light equipment and exuberance.

When finally side-stepping toward the shore, we saw for the first time that a small seaplane had landed not far upstream. Pulled up on the shore, it had unloaded three fishermen—a "fly-out" from another lodge—with a guide carrying a high-powered rifle. Of necessity, they were spread out over about a hundred yards.

There was a small island in the stream and on its shore reared a bear (average standing height is 9 feet) rocking back and forth which must have looked very threatening to the men on the opposite shore that he faced. From our safe distance, it looked pathetic. All bears are very near-sighted, for which they compensate by the rocking motion to establish perspective.

Where he had come from or was going, who knows? We hadn't seen or smelled him as we came through, but he obviously wanted to cross that river and was blocked by whatever it was that faced him. The guide had the rifle at his shoulder but didn't fire; at that range he would have easily dropped him.

What happened next is totally erased. But when I think of man's inhumanity to man, terrorism, etc., and consider that humans are the most successful of all predators—including me—that picture flashes up. There that fellow creature was, that solitary bear, probably taking a nap, suddenly roused with strange noises invading his territory, trying to find a way out. And there was I, gleefully snagging those fish just for the fun of it.

Shakespeare, as usual, has words for it in *King Lear*.
"As flies to wanton boys are we to the gods; they kill us for their sport."

Rage, Rage Against the Dying of the Light

This he did not do. He ignored it or, at least, kept it to himself, and so allowed me to. From eating too many hazelnuts, crashing airplanes, hepatitis, downed from horses, three breeds of cancer, leaky heart valve, etc., he had managed to walk away, little changed. I expected no less this time.

When you are in your ninety-fourth year, death thoughts do crop up. I agree with Woody Allen who said that he didn't mind dying, he just didn't want to be there when it happened. How do I handle it with dignity and self-reliance when I, for convenience sake, have grown into a trap even with all good intentions?

Since Himself died in 1996, I know that nothing else is ever going to be worse—maybe as bad, but not worse. I have coped without him as he suggested—pleasantly enough and productively. Indeed, from lack of anything else to do, I think life since then has been my most productive in the seemingly fruitless effort to convince great numbers of people that:

> The earth does not belong to man, man belongs to the earth. All things are connected like the blood that connects us all. Man did not weave the web of life; he is merely a strand in it. Whatever he does to the web, he does to himself.
>
> Chief Seattle

As to dying—Thomas Mann, literary icon of my youth, in *The Magic Mountain* (a novel set in a sanitarium in the Swiss Alps for patients dying of tuberculosis) includes thoughts on the mistake that healthy people make in expecting the mortally ill to think as they themselves do. I may go whoopin' and hollerin', but I hope not. As soon as I finish this opus of several years and quit trying to convince mankind that we cannot continue to befoul our earth and expect to survive as a species—I'm ready to move on.

As to death itself? Lucius said in a paper to a literary club, and I agree with him: "It has always seemed strange to me that an allegedly intelligent people, whose existence biologically has the duration of no more than a twinkling of an eye in the life of one indescribably insignificant planet, can believe that it is singled out for special treatment after death."

Socrates, in his *Apology*, considered all alternatives that can possibly ensue from death and found them all good and desirable: "Now if you suppose that there is no consciousness, but a sleep, like the sleep of him who is undisturbed even by dreams, death will be an unspeakable gain. If a person were to select the night undisturbed even by dreams and were to compare it with other nights of his life and were to tell us how many nights were better or more pleasant than this one, I think that any man, I shall not say any private man for even the great king will not find many such nights.

"But if death is the journey to another place where all the dead abide, what good, O my friends, can be greater than this?"

If it is, and that man is waiting for me—Hurray!

Mushing On

For such a strong man lacking much instinct for self-preservation, he was somehow fragile. We spent a lot of time recovering from near-tragedies, but spent them well. He was still comfortable flying (had an active pilot's license the day he died—for 69 years since he was 15). His suggestion of leery me taking flying lessons, concentrating on landing the thing, which I managed once, was, like long ago SCUBA lessons, not a great success. It was obvious that we would be better off if flight control talked me down in case of need, rather than thinking I knew what I was doing.

By summer, 1990, life in Wyoming was a bit slower, which suited me fine. Friends were the same. There was more time for afternoon naps, for reading, barely touching from hip to ankle, backed up to a log, and this beguiled me. It was unneeded evidence that we had literally grown together, yin/yang. Fishing was reduced for him to when he saw a rise. I never asked how he felt, lest he say "rotten"; he never said anything. As long as he slept and ate well, life in the outback was good. Boss Hoss Ap was packed and Ug, a bit smaller, became his horse of choice. Andrew was absent, with law school back in Memphis, but his absolutely splendid father, Bill Carter, came along to do what was needed.

Quail shooting in the fall sadly halted. It was such a vigorous sport, hopping the clod fields of west Tennessee in November cold. But it was less sad, or much sadder, because over the years the wild birds were almost gone. Planting of Bermuda grass as a main cover crop had exposed these ground-nesting birds to predators, and heavy use of toxic pesticides and herbicides killed them off. Deer hunting from a blind thrived and kept larders full. But nothing will ever be as good as those quail browned in an iron skillet in a half pound of butter, then covered to steam in a splash of blackest coffee, served on toasted French bread soaking in the gravy.

In a turkey blind in the middle of the bean field within easy walking of the cabin, we sat for hours watching for the bronze flashes to come out of the woods. You could be reading along, glance up and there they were—twenty or thirty—bright as hammered coppers, breeding colors dazzling. The gobblers, their most attractive with spread tail fans aquiver and wattles swinging like heavy black silk, competed with one another to attract the indifferent hens pecking away, fattening for the coming winter and the next clutches of poults.

Argentina, like Baja, had become infested with over-dressed, over-equipped Yankee fishermen and the cost had become a joke. We tried the islands of Roatan and Vieques, and even built a small house on stilts on Utila in the Bay of Honduras. The bone fishing was fair wading off the beach, but for SCUBA, Himself was no longer able to swing the heavy tanks.

Enough was enough. When hunting season closed, we became content to settle for Spring Valley, a small lodge tucked in southeast Missouri on a spring creek. Fishing limited to guests, the reaches varied, the food good, the bedside reading light just right. The adjacent Mark Twain National Forest was good walking, and maybe best of all, there was so little hassle getting there. It was about an hour flight from Memphis to Mountain Home, Arkansas, where he left the Green Machine, an ancient gas guzzler bought in town for almost nothing, which was big enough to haul us and sundry friends who trailed along in their own Cessnas most weekends.

Come July, the Fourth was celebrated with the usual verve on the front porch of the T-Cross. (It didn't occur to me that it would be the last.) Jane Whitson, over from her cabin in Turpin Meadows, taped the ceremony. I am forever grateful to her for being able to replay it every Fourth since.

The days of summer unrolled in the same back country until Ug stepped in a nest of ground-dwelling hornets and, terrified, started bucking. There again was Himself on the rocky trail, white-faced and silent. We were some quarter of a mile from an opening in the forest where a Medevac could land, but he had to get back on that horse to get there. With the help of Percocet, he did. Bill Carter set out to the ranger's cabin at Hawks Rest, five or six miles down the way. In this we were lucky, as Gordon Reese's cabin was the only one in the thousands of miles of wilderness. It had a short-wave radio with the headquarters on the highway some 35 miles away. However it was locked down, with a note on the door saying he would be back that night or early next morning.

There was nothing to do but wait. We got Lucius as comfortable as possible with his deformed back and whatever this latest insult had added. He said nothing but, when he dozed, his pale face and moaning spoke for him. Bill went back to the station; it was early morning when the chopper arrived with all its blessed efficiency but no place for me. We headed the couple of days back to the ranch.

When I finally got to the Jackson hospital, an orthopedist was with him discussing his condition.

"Mr. Burch, I can't tell you much," he said. "To look at your x-rays is like looking into a rock crusher. Every bone in your body seems to have been broken at least once. I recommend that you stay here for a few days, move around as you can, then go home to your doctors for therapy as soon as possible. And stay away from horses. I am reluctant to mention this, but try to realize that you are in your eightieth year."

It was a pleasant room, as such rooms go, with a place for me. Within a couple of weeks he managed to dress and Joe McCarty arranged for a FedEx executive jet to deliver us to Memphis.

That shack in Hardeman County was a home, really the first one I had since leaving Belle Meade—both were equally pleasant. The two setters were gone but Bear, the dog of Lucius' youngest daughter, who had recently died under sad, sad circumstances, took the place in front of the fire. Interesting people streamed through. Mr. Cossa kept us provisioned, we took an occasional wild turkey for roasting and gradually he was planning summer without horses.

Salmon fishing seemed a sedentary sport worth trying under the circumstances. Off we headed to a chartered boat on highly recommended Desolation Sound between Vancouver Island and the mainland. The day we planned to leave, he took an offer for his "for sale" flying machine without a whimper—to my silent relief.

Victoria, the waterfront capital, is by far the most British city in North America. History hovers over it like a halo; a few day's stay is a must, even for fishermen. Three recommendations:

1. Stay at the historic hotel. I think it is called the Princess Elizabeth. Its bar is straight out of Kenya, with zebra rugs, a leather shield, carved spears, masks, and animal racks to pound the heart of any conservationist. Try a gin and lemon and breathe deep.

2. Give at least three hours to the huge Butchart Garden: some 50 acre of recycled rock quarry that shows what dreamers of the world can do.

3. Maybe best of all is the 60 foot long, 12 foot beam, intricately carved Haida (called the Indian Vikings) war canoe hewn from a single tree displayed nearby at the Royal Museum. It is so big that the room where it rests had to be built around it.

Campbell River, a much-sung town and harbor for salmon fishermen, was just that—a town and harbor. The chartered boat was small enough for three people but suspiciously sleek, as was its captain in his white naval uniform with Commodore's cap of gold filigree. He was also the so-so cook and steward, showed us where to fish, rigged the gear, almost plumped the cushions as we nosed into some of British Columbia's magnificent fjords with trolling lines dragging behind.

Trolling has got to be the most tedious of ways to catch a fish. You sit in a seat while the boatman takes you where he chooses. He does most of the work, including tossing your lure overboard, and putters along at one mph. If you happen to snag something, it will be big and deep. He will leap to action, armed with a great gaff to snag it by the gills after you reel and reel something that feels like a tree trunk. He alone pulls it aboard, offers to take pictures, then up-ends the gaff to slide it back into the water. If there is blood, you know it cannot survive.

The week's trip was at least five days too long, but the country had much charm, as had dropping anchor in a quiet cove for the night without another soul in sight.

Campbell River was also the ferry terminal for Quadra Island, a second home haven for the idle rich to rusticate in privacy. We found a pleasant house isolated on its own cove, with four widely spaced guest cottages to let. No guest meals were served, but we were invited for supper frequently, and there were other serendipities, like the bait bucket hanging from our small private dock, which was kept supplied with thumb-size clams to steam in a slosh of sea water until they popped open.

We would retire to the recliners on the hillside, libation in one hand, throw the shells on the beach, and make a meal with ripe tomatoes from the garden and be grateful. We could watch two eaglets hopping up and down, exercising their wings to fly from their huge nest atop the dead tree snag across the way. I am told that after they are fledged, they never return to the nest. Be prepared!

A few miles at the end of the island, a marina attached to a small hotel rented outboard fishing boats and, if you accidentally caught something, they would filet and cook it on the grill of the outdoor dining room. The martinis were frosty; the setting sun blossomed pink and green and on the way home, a roadside shop sold homemade ice cream cones!

One night with the moon streaming bright through the windows, he asked if I could hear a wheeze in his chest. I said that I could but that it was nothing new.

"Dr. Apperson keeps trying to sell me a pig's valve, says I need it," he said. "I've had this thing ever since I can remember, even as a child—never paid it any attention. What shall I do?"

"Lucius, I don't know what that means. But, please, don't ask me what you should do. Do what you think you should do. Whatever that is, it's all right with me, but I can't answer that."

Life moved on smooth and sweet. Through hunting season there was venison and wild turkey for the delicious meat pies that Erlene, his ever faithful cook, sent from home to fill the larder. Weekends the sleeping house out back was used mainly by Andrew Carter, permanently moved from Dubois to be a full-fledged attorney in Memphis, and the head mechanic (I cannot believe that I have forgotten his name) at FedEx who had built the museum quality bear-proof panniers which were required after the fires in Yellowstone. He always brought a big pot of chipotle and took over many kitchen duties.

Spring Valley was close, convenient and the fishing good all year.

The law business thrived, he still reserved for himself the most interesting and lucrative cases. But he had become discouraged with the business, said that lawyers had become time-card punchers instead of friends who sorted things out, that had he his life to lead over he would be a teacher.

In the 1995 summer return to Quadra Island, the novelty had worn off and the fishing from a small boat was almost no fishing at all. The only way to find them was to watch where the birds congregated—usually too far away to bother. We got in the habit of taking our books along to while away the long intervals of inactivity. He sat with a life preserver to cushion his back against the motor, and I sat between his knees on the floor, with his hands on top of my head. That called for a lot of scrambling when there was indication of fish nearby.

"I would like to go back to Yellowknife to see how it fares now that it calls itself the diamond capital of North America," he said. "Used to fly up there for wing shooting grouse and pheasant."

We bade our hosts goodbye and off we drove and drove and drove. Across the Sound by the ferry to Vancouver, then north to Whistler, site of the 2010 Winter Olympics, which he declared the least inviting place he had ever seen. From there on northeast almost to the Arctic Circle, we passed through open country.

After the sign saying "Northwest Territory," the pavement stopped and it was gravel from there on for some five or six hundred miles. Very few cars but huge trucks churning the dust and throwing up gravel. Occasionally small herds of woods bison sunned across the roadway. The drill to get past was to drive up close to the nearest and stop. Soon the alpha male (he could weigh well over a ton) would get up, stretch and wander down the embankment into the trees followed reluctantly by his harem. They were like our buffalo, but bigger, and not to be fooled with.

Come suppertime, when things didn't look promising, a large tar papered frame building appeared with a few parked trucks. This was it. Inside was an empty dance hall but at a lone round table close to the entry were seated eight or so men the size of the bison. Cold beers were set in front of us without asking.

Lucius had a knack for blending with whatever company he found himself. His whole vocabulary changed, he talked and laughed louder. With his trimmed white beard and ancient hat sporting its black and white eagle feather stuck in the brim. (Illegal, but presented to him by a befriended Haida of comparable size with these few words, "Me sachem, you sachem.") He looked like the fastest truck driver north of wherever we were.

It was enormous fun. I wasn't expected to say a word, but was addressed as ma'am, and no raw stories were told. They talked of little except the diamond spike which had appeared seemingly out of nowhere a few years earlier, and how Yellowknife was thriving. When bedtime came, there was a low building at the end of the parking lot, where the architectural admonition of form following function was carried to perfection. Our room was just the right size for two cots with enough room between to walk sideways. There was one window, one light bulb on a wire from the ceiling, a door—that was it. The conveniences down the hall were co-ed. But the moon was bright and breakfast the next morning sumptuous.

The monster trucks were gone when we got up. Petrol was available; we were advised to fill all the way up and take sandwiches. I drove most of the day, he catnapped. I don't think we saw another soul, but more herds of basking bison on the road, until early afternoon when Yellowknife gradually emerged on the horizon—an ordinary looking town of high rise buildings and many construction cranes. The last few miles of road were paved.

There were traffic lights and the multi-storied hotel was pleasant, with people coming and going, many in business suits. Our room had a spectacular view of enormous Great Slave Lake sprinkled with islands, stretching forever.

He stood long at the window, then picked up the telephone with the little well-worn booklet in hand, his Michelin Guide to odd-ball offerings of the fishing world.

"If it suits you," he said, "let's poke around here for a day or two then head out to catch some of the local monsters."

That was followed by a soaking in the bathtub's hottest, and thence to the quiet bar for a couple of martinis, a decent dinner and on to long, hard sleep.

The drill the next day was the usual in new towns: find the local museum, arrive at midmorning when the thin, straight-backed curator is still waiting for strangers to tell her story. Lucius' well-modulated voice, perfect enunciation, four syllable words and obvious interest charmed that lady to produce tea and give her four star spiel:

In 1990 the diamond spike (the term spike is used because it describes the shape of the ore site where it reaches the surface through the earth's crusts via occasional faults) had been discovered on one of the near islands, and was now being mined by the big boys of the business. Testing indicated other spikes close by, so prosperity seemed assured forever. (I googled in 2011 to find that two other spikes have been opened and testing suggests that there are still others. It is now the next most productive diamond area in the world, right behind Africa.)

She was equally charmed by the fact that he had last been there 40 years earlier, before she was born, when it was an Indian village. After being invited for a walking tour including the ancient village, she locked up and we lunched on grilled fish and French fries with malt vinegar (shades of fish and chips) in a hole in the wall. It was what she called the village, but he recognized nothing.

The open Chris Craft pulled into the public wharf at the same time as we. A Lucius-sized man with a short black beard and a flame orange, thigh-length anorak threw a line over the mooring and raised his arm in greeting. They met as a couple of old friends, and he gallantly dropped our backpacks on the stack of supplies in the back and gave me a hand to board. Off he swished through the maze of small islands due north, guiding the boat with the tip of his fingers from a standing position. When we hit the deeper water, where the islands were fewer and the vision better, the wake deepened and the prow rose for some thirty minutes until we slowly nosed into the mooring of a small island.

A tall, copper-colored Indian with an identical young boy at his side moved down the ramp to shake hands all around. Lucius said something to him that I didn't understand and it brought forth a reply with a slight smile. They unloaded the cargo into the only house and the boy went to the nearest walled tent with our packs. The captain welcomed us in, seated us at one of the two raw wood trestle tables, set out cold beers and explained the drill.

We would be the only guests, until possibly next week, and could work out any schedule we wanted. The fishing was very good at the moment, and if we wanted to take some when we left, that was possible if it were smoked, which they could do. He asked that we not approach the sled dogs staked a little way off. They ran the Iditarod and the fewer human scents they knew, the better. But beautiful they were—Malamutes and Samoyeds and some crosses. It was a great temptation to scratch behind the ears and look into those ice-blue eyes.

Lunch was a great bowl of pasta, fish, really well seasoned and topped with *parmigiano reggiano* scraped from its own wheel—the world's best had come to Yellowknife along with the diamonds. Dessert was hot fried doughnuts drenched in dark honey and pine nuts, and black, black coffee brewed by an expert.

Then he was gone with a sweep of the boat that seemed to be waltzing, and we took to our tent. It was a cozy place, with a wooden floor and waist high walls finished out with a tightly stretched white canvas, inset with netted window openings covered by rolled flaps like Roman shades. At least twice the size of our accommodations at the dance hall, there were shelves to hold stuff and a little potbellied stove with a basket of wood chunks in the corner.

Lucius chattered away with the pleasant-looking middle aged Indian woman, in what suddenly dawned on me must be pidgin-English, something he had had use for 65 years earlier when, at age 18, he summered in southeast Alaska shooting eagles for bounty.

I lolled behind them examining the flowering ground cover and stunted trees common to the far north. When I stuck my head in, they had moved the two narrow beds together in the middle of the back wall with a blanket rolled to fill the gap. They had put the side table, which held a kerosene lamp to one side, and raised the flaps to the mild breeze. He was propped on the pillows with his eyes closed; the grin on his face was as broad as mine. No fishing today.

But there was fishing tomorrow, in abundance, and the next day and the next. Pike and lake trout—big, five or six pound fighters, almost too many, but not quite. The lake was huge, disappearing over the horizon; fish were for taking anywhere but very sporting on our light tackle. Lunch alone was worth the trip. Rajik had a favorite spot where we went often. From a distance, it looked like the rest—a big flat rock canting into the water, backed by a small hummock lush with moose willows. In the middle of the stone slab was an unnatural cauldron-shaped depression about two feet deep, straight sides, visually a perfect circle, unsoiled and perfectly polished. His voice fell as he pointed: "What made?"

To the side he laid the contents of the possum-pocket of his anorak, a sack, neatly folded paper packets, a more than adequate long knife and a small file. An armful of dead willow branches was supplemented with four long green switches. Hunkering down on his heels, he whittled toothpick-sized dry sticks to cover a pinch of duff, held the file close and scraped it quickly with the back of the knife blade. Sparks shot out, the duff smoked then blazed, the toothpicks caught, he stood up and fed the small stuff first then added the rest. Voila!

He filleted a lunch-sized fish like a master chef, pressed in all of one packet of crushed herbs with a piece of the oily skin, spiked the pieces on the green switches and wove together the tips to form a coverless tent-like structure which later straddled the fire when it died down. He broke out beers for us from a bait bucket tied to the stern. He merely cupped his hands for a long drink from the lake.

With remarkable skill, he pushed the fire around into two circles of embers, fixed the bent switches of fish low to catch the heat, tore the sack open to become an instant plate and folded in the Yukon Golds. They had already been baked and stuffed, with butter kept frozen in an insulated box sunk in the permafrost outside the kitchen door, wild onions and other treasures from the woods. He skewered them to the skin of the fish, then placed the neat package on the second, cooler layer of embers to heat. This was lunch every day for weeks; it always tasted different.

The neatening up was a ritual. He burned the paper in the cauldron, then placed on top of the ashes the retrieved guts, loose bones and whatever else that was left, covered the stack with the remnants of the skin and carefully arranged the bone skeleton on top. Then we left at once. Every time we came to this place, the ceremony was repeated, and each time we returned, the site was immaculate.

Days rolled into weeks, no one else came, the sun set earlier, fingerless wool gloves were a constant, we read the Robinson Davies and Patrick O'Briens left on the bookshelf in the dining room by earlier fishermen. It was time to leave. Back down the gravel highway, with an eye out for the dance hall, there appeared a miracle. A Holiday Inn type motel had sprung fully functioning from the earth. Neither of us had seen any such a thing on the way up, but there it was, smelling new, with the usual hushed carpets and smiling room clerk. Only a few people were in the dining room where the service was good and dinner all right. Next day we drove straight to the Vancouver airport for an afternoon AA flight to Memphis, into the heat.

Nashville was much the same, my self-reliant children fine. And I took advantage of one of the best things about being a chronic volunteer: there's always something that needs doing when you show up. Then it was back to Hardeman County for long weekends and October's bright blue weather in the country. But things were not the same. Lucius was not out in the woods, finding where the deer were bedding or seeking out the turkey scratchings. He was rearing back in a chair on the front porch, watching others.

One afternoon was for sighting in the guns. This consisted of shooting at targets some 20 yards away, then walking down to see the results and making adjustments. I noticed that he had pulled the ancient vehicle around so that he could sit, awaiting his turn. Andrew and our master mechanic were with him, but he came in early and flopped on the bed, breathing hard, exhausted.

How could I have been so blind, so totally unaware? On the island we had taken very little exercise. The numerous trails out of camp were hard walking, like treading on the stones of a dried stream, and the scrub woods uninteresting. He had fished only in the mornings. For a while I went out in the afternoons, but the magic of that faded without him.

Andrew stuck his head in to say they were going to beat the bounds, and would be back by dark. I propped up beside him in the quiet.

"Lucius, you asked me what you should do and I begged off," I said. "Now I want to tell you. If it were I, I'd do what Dr. Apperson says. Let him sell me that pig valve. I understand it is not an uncommon operation, and has a history of success."

There was a long silence, until I thought he had fallen asleep. Then he said, "Yes. I have been waiting for that." With that, he got up and went into the living room, to the telephone. I couldn't hear what he was saying, but when he came back and lay down again, he said, "Well, that's a done deal. Monday morning."

The rest of the afternoon, until dark, was the most tender of times—like 27 years earlier, at the Grand Bretagne in Athens overlooking my solitary coffee table in Syntagma Square, the crossroads of my being.

"We'll check me in tomorrow and you'll get home before dark," he said. "Come back on Thursday. Newman will stay in touch."

And so it was.

Charlie didn't call until late afternoon. "Things didn't go as well as hoped," he said. "When they sewed him up, he continued to bleed. Had to open him again." He called several times to report, but by Wednesday morning the phone was not enough. I had to move.

There was a chart at the entrance, so I knew where to go. I just walked into Emergency without being stopped. It was silo shaped room, with the nurses' station in the middle and cubicles all around. A nurse came to see what I wanted. When I told her Lucius Burch, she asked, "Are you Sas?"

"Yes, I'm Sas."

"Come with me, he keeps asking for you."

It was dark in his cubicle. The only light was from the shaded center, but I could see that his hands were strapped to the guard rails and there was something in his mouth that looked like a beaten biscuit cutter.

"What is all this?" I said.

"That's to help him breathe. The restraints are to keep him from pulling it out."

"Undo his hands, now. Please. I'll be here; he won't do that."

To my eternal relief, she removed the ventilator, released the straps, and brought a straight back chair which barely fitted the space. Its lack of comfort was the only taste of reality for the next few weeks.

When I was able to pull that chair up to the head, and make my way through the witches' thicket of tubes to run my hand up through his sleeve and rest it on his shoulder, he moved his hand to cover mine. I almost dissolved. To avoid a scene, I sat still, propped my feet on something, and watched the streaks of light dash back and forth on the monitor. I had no idea what they were tracking, but the bright green was a focus.

When Charlie Newman came in at about nine, Himself was in a drugged sleep that the nurse said would last the night. I followed him home where Kay gave a great welcoming hug, a Scotch and set out a light supper, which was just what I was up to.

Well before light, I was back. He was awake; we just looked at each other. I couldn't, didn't speak, nor did he. I just pulled up the chair, walked my hand under the gown to his shoulder, which he covered with his own. Hand holding has got to be the most intimate of all human gestures.

How long this was the drill, I don't remember, nor does it matter. Fall rolled into winter as he graduated from Emergency to Intensive Care to whatever was the next step, where I could have a cot. Somewhere along the line, we changed hospitals to an over-decorated, garish-colored room for therapy and rehab.

Psychiatric evaluation was a hoot. A serious lad arrived, spouting acronyms and four-syllable terms, only to leave much later spouting words of undying gratitude for advice on how to deal with his new wife and step-child. We never saw him again.

Physical therapy was altogether different. At first, it was with only one or two other patients. A few times there was only one other—a very pretty sixteen-year-old girl. They talked together in normal voices of many things, and became fond of one another. He was very quiet when we got back to the room. Her problem was an automobile accident; both legs were cut off at the groin.

The therapy was intense and painful: one hour sessions three times a day with rest periods between. He repeatedly asked his doctor for marijuana. He explained that he was very familiar with its properties from being in Mexico, that he was unlikely to become a dope fiend and, if he did, it couldn't possibly matter. No dice.

"Lucius," I said, "I know you can tell me how to get it off the street."

"No. I don't want to muddy the water any worse than it already is."

Days passed, as days do, and, when it was time to leave the hospital, the question was. "Where to?" It was obviously going to be a long haul, even with continuing professional home care. I had gotten fairly adept at wrapping a belt around his waist, chocking his feet with mine and, with a mighty heave by both of us, getting him to his feet. He could even take a few steps, but it was tenuous and, should he fall, impossible. He really wanted to go to Hardeman County. He said we could get help, work it out. I would have none of that, wouldn't even discuss it. In retrospect, I wonder if that was a mistake. With just the promise of getting "away," his spirit would have lifted; the result would probably have been the same.

Early February, I think the 4th, a Sunday, we drove through the virgin grove of great white oaks to the white columned antebellum house: his home, where I had been only a couple of long ago times. Under the *porte-cochère,* where they rolled out his wheel chair, the van radio gave the temperature: 14 below zero. How they got that load up the steps to the front porch, I cannot imagine. But they did.

For those of you who have not lived in an old house, there are certain minuses for all the plusses. They were built for summer cooling—high, high ceilings, open stairwells, big windows, air sucking chimneys—not 14 below. Casual, seldom used central heat didn't stand much chance.

We had passed the library with its glowing open fire, but his pale face showed that we needed to get a lay of the land. He directed the way to the downstairs guest room, where they parked the wheelchair and bade us good-bye. It was cold, and it was dark. The half tester bed, with silken swags, didn't mean a thing. There was room between it and a window, but with the side table for a lamp and a nearby dressing table, the wheel chair had to be backed in. There was no way to get him onto the bed without propping him against the side while I moved the chair out of the way. There was nothing to do but laugh.

The bed looked short of covers; it was a relief that it was an electric blanket, which heated while I took off his shoes. His badly deformed spine left little margin and a good bit of exertion. When the job was done, his eyes were closed as his breathing dropped back to normal.

Turning on the lights threw a nice glow. The bathroom had an electric heater which groaned as it did it best to warm the tiled space; the fireplace behind its embroidered screen showed that this was a summer room—no fire was laid.

When Elsie knocked to say that supper was ready when we were, our greeting was near seamless. My heart flopped over with tinge of pleasure to see her—so little changed since Longview, the same firm stride, strong gestures, long black hair rolled in a bun at the nape. Of course I had seen her number of times at the hospitals and apartments, but not in her own house, under such irregular conditions.

Because it was Sunday, Erlene's day off, Elsie had cooked supper. The meal was good and the open door to the library quelled some of the cold. His wheel chair slid under his place at the head of the table. Elsie did most of the talking, and there was some familial laughter. It was a scene straight out of Tennessee Williams.

The electric blanket fought a losing battle against the 14 below, and by mid-Monday morning, we had to be back for the third time at Executive Suites in Germantown. Home care and physical therapy reappeared on a regular basis, and soon he was even taking a few steps. Colleagues and mutual friends appeared. Charlie Newman and Andrew arrived with a huge desktop computer, the latest thing, to keep him in touch with the office. It took up the entire dining room table, its wires writhing together like snakes hatching under a rock. After a long series of tutorials—endured with infinite patience on all sides—Lucius announced that until the computer was gone, he was never, ever going to set foot in that room again. It left.

Next came Dr. Tom Morris, who decades before as an intern had put this bearded unknown back together. They talked of accelerating physical therapy and even a treadmill which was so big that it had to be set up outside on the little covered porch. And, glory be, there came a miracle child physical therapist in a crisp white uniform who took charge.

I had never before met anyone from Lapland, but she of the chiseled cheekbones, ice blue eyes and platinum hair was the visage of the vast, untamed wilderness of northern Sweden where he had never been. He was smitten. He would have been smitten in any case, but for a man who had been crimped on his back in bed for four months, he was really smitten. She was offering him a way out, and he responded—he did (or tried to do) everything she said. From my perch in the other room, they sounded like two children on long skis heading north.

Sunday, May 22, 2011: Today as I write this, I feel fragile, like leaf-thin glass, something I have never felt before. If you popped me on the head with a spoon, everything would collapse in a sand pile. Not depressed, just fragile.

At lunch, Sister Allison swallowed something wrong and choked to the point that it came back in her napkin. She got up and went to the bathroom, waving me off. When she came back, she finished her meal and that was that. I felt the urge to burst into uncontrolled tears, as I once did fifteen summers ago as I pulled off the highway on a lay-by atop Togwotee Pass, Wyoming. I knew she was all right, but the same urge was there.

Saturday, March 11, 1996: Moon Child was coming six days a week and this was to be a special day. It had rained during the night. The cedar thicket dripped leftover drops and let off the glorious smell of Christmas trees. The mourning doves cooed their spring song over and over and over. Today was the day when he was going to walk the treadmill on the porch, for three whole minutes, on his own for the first time. I was invited to watch. The deed was done to much applause and martinis before lunch.

Waking from the afternoon nap, he was having chest pains for the first time. He called his cardiologist, who instructed him to stop all therapy except bed exercises. He picked up whatever book he was reading. Long before he had asked me not to ask how he felt; it was a quiet evening.

Sunday, March 12, 1996: It was raining, and cold enough for the porch door to be closed. We woke to the smell of coffee in the automatic brewer. I rolled out to fetch the usual morning cups and the newspaper from the front door, and climbed back in bed.

"Sas, I have asked you over and over what can I leave you, and you keep saying nothing," he said. "You have spent years of your life nursing me through one blasted thing after another, and now this mess. There must be something—for my sake."

"Lucius, think about this. You give me this magnificent journey, as well as your loving self. Your take me into the wildernesses of the whole earth long enough, close enough, to know them in my bones. You give me a tutorial of almost three decades that Socrates himself could not have bettered—how the world works and how to deal with it. From you I learned to care, to give a damn, to really give a damn. And to do something about it, get something done. Think about this."

After breakfast, he called his secretary to ask her to bring his first quarter tax return and a check to sign. By eleven, when she hadn't appeared, he called again, his voice controlled. What she brought called for prolonged discussion and a promise that it would be posted the next day, postmarked with that final date.

In late afternoon Elsie came and I, as usual, left them for private conservation by going into the other room. There was much talk, with some raised voices and occasional laughs. Somewhere along, a loud voice interrupted whatever I was reading: "Sas, will you please come in here and sit down." Which I did. We talked of nothingness, and it was not forced. We all knew each other too well for that. When she finally rose, I walked to the door with her, exchanging pleasantries.

Coming back, I looked at him. How could this vital man have laid propped at an angle, almost perforce motionless, for four months, under such control? How long could such a thing last? Was there balm in Gilead?

The balm was his grin, as I pulled my chair as close as possible to his head of the bed. How could this earth survive without grins?

"How would you feel about a couple of really first class shooters to warm the cockles of our heart?" he said. "And lock the door!"

As I put ice in the heavy cut crystal glasses that Uncle Rogers had given me, poured the Beefeaters and splashed the vermouth, how elegant they looked—how posh, how civil. There were even two cocktail napkins, made of lawn and handmade lace which Mama had included in my long-ago trousseau. They frosted on the handsome 18th century silver tray that Nancy Houghland had given me as a wedding present.

"You look just like Hebe," he said—the daughter of Zeus and Hera, cupbearer to the gods.

One was not quite enough, but two just right for sleep, such as Socrates described as "undisturbed even by dreams." I must have gone first. I remember his last words, spoken in a clear, normal voice: "Nothing mean or small."

IV

CAST A COLD EYE ON LIFE, ON DEATH

*Behind the darkly woven colors of sensuality
will be a friendship so profound
that we shall become bondsmen forever.*

Lawrence Durrell
Justine

Sunday, June 28, 2015, 5:04 a.m.: Surely this is the first day of the rest of my life and long past time to...

Monday, March 13, 1996: When I woke, you were dead. How or when I don't know but there it was—the long loneliness of the unseen presence in an empty room—with me clinging to your arm where I found your stilled pulse. I could not move for what seemed a long while, but finally it was past time. I called Charlie Newman and then Mike Cody, your once-young lions, but messages had to be left. All that remained was to dial Home Medical Service for instructions. Seams were unraveling, and my words were monosyllabic when they said to call 911. I told them that that was not possible—they would have to do it—and hung up.

It was so quiet until sirens howled in the distance, growing louder and louder until men in great yellow slickers, flapping boots and strange hats crammed in through the open door. I had had no thought of what to expect, but certainly not this. I was frozen until I saw our green field jacket, with which I covered your face against the swirlings around your head. I heard the scraping of the gurney through the narrow door mashing your fingers, jostling your body, but the great pressure hole in your back and endless struggle to move were gone forever. I now had to leave you to them.

Back in the living room, crammed in the corner of the sofa with the pillow in my lap, a saner man appeared, wearing a dark suit, white shirt and black knitted tie like you wore to court. To the questions he asked, I could only stare and nod yes or no. Then, I remembered the black book of your medical records which your doctor had sent. I watched as he read, closed it with a nod, shook my hand and departed.

It was then that Charlie and Kay and Mike appeared to take me to their pleasantly lighted sitting room where a drink and supper was offered. I took only the Scotch, even though it seemed that I had not eaten for years. Later, upstairs in the room where I had slept before there was a cot for me in your hospital room, I swallowed the two and a half Valiums left from November when, as you said, they swapped a pig's valve for your wheezing heart.

Monday, March 13, 1996 was surely the first day of the rest of my life, but it's one I scarcely remember. My ability to close doors when separation is the only solution may have seemed cold-hearted, but that is beside the point when it allowed me to operate, survive. Kay, your daughter Edith, and I returned to neaten the apartment, turn off the lights, lock the door. Late lunch was good, the sun appeared and Vivaldi was cheerful but the closer I got to home, the more hideous was the thought of walking into that darkness after so long a time. But when I got there, the lights were on and white tulips glowed in a crystal bowl. Elizabeth Queener had remembered, and Jane Whitson put down her book as I walked in.

"Drop your stuff," she said. "We're going to David's for supper."

In front of the warm kitchen fire he handed me my usual child-sized martini, and said, "Ma, we're going skiing at Vail at the end of the week, got a condo. Go with us. You can bunk in with Bethea and we'll leave you alone to do whatever you want."

And so there it was that I slept and fed and slept again. The last day in Vail, I hired a guide, rented waders, bought a license. The stream was narrow, waist deep with slick rocks. The guide was skilled and the fishing good, but I will not fish that stream again—ever.

The time of nothingness settled in solid and hard, but you left me, as I asked, the use of your fund at the Memphis Foundation. That was it, and it has and does make all the difference in the years that followed—a generous pot into which to dip when critical needs of our earth appear.

I made an offer to Ben Pierce, of the Wyoming Nature Conservancy: I would invest whatever was needed most at Red Canyon Ranch in exchange for a place to stay for the coming summer. His answer was typical Wyoming: "No problem." He added that the crucial need was native grass seed—lots of it. So now much of the green on that 35,000 acre spread is yours and mine. In return, I had a place to put one foot in front of the other which is where it always must go.

In early spring, Son David drove me to Memphis to lunch with Charlie Newman and Mike Cody, and my few other friends to get my part of your ashes. Now, if luck holds, when the time comes we will go off together in some clear, friendly stream, into the wind or wherever.

Before our starting home, Charlie told me that your office files were to join the legal ones in the Mississippi Valley Collection at the University of Memphis, alongside those of Mayor Edmund Orgill and Edward Meeman: fellow heroes of Civil Rights in Memphis. Archivists were in short supply, he said, and the process might be delayed. How would I feel about doing the job?

"Yes, of course," I said—again the refrain of our life together.

At the desk in front of your great arched window, surrounded by cases of artifacts from diving expeditions all over the world, the days clipped by as some patient soul from the University showed me how every page was to be checked. All duplicates, metal clips and staples were to be removed, placed in acid free folders and fitted in the long red boxes of history.

All duplicates were free to rest with the ones that I already owned, but not for long. John Noel and Bill Coble called from his eyrie above the Cumberland River on a Sunday afternoon—the sort given to tapping a jug of good red wine—and said, "Let's you do a book so when we want to know what Lucius would say about most anything, there it will be."

Two years later, there it was. On the most stunned day of my life, Peter Honsberger handed me the first printing of my *Lucius: The Writings of Lucius Burch*. And at the request of Texas cousin Bill Polk, my original copies moved from the Jack Daniel's box in my closet to the archives at the University of the South at Sewanee—founded long ago by your kinsman, Episcopal Bishop and Confederate General Leonidas Polk.

Whither Away

With you gone and me still gasping for life, the Nature Conservancy, as promised, produced the miracle of summer in an unknown place. Red Canyon Ranch was, and I hope still is, a testing ground for management practices, proving that cattle can coexist in a 35,000 acre environment dedicated to the diversity of wildlife. It starts just below 11,000 feet at the headwaters of the Little Popo Agie River, and hurtles from the red cliffs into prairie grass laced with a few small streams.

Turning west, as Thoreau says natural compasses always swing, and we had been done for 23 seasons. I had become an ancient of 76 overnight. I was on my own again and there was no need to change. It was cold for such a late spring morning, but Vivaldi again poured from the spheres and dogwoods whitened the Interstate to the Tennessee River. Home was left behind. My accustomed truck stop produced two sausage and biscuits, black, black coffee and a topped gas tank for the long haul.

This time I was armed with a brand-new, second-hand forest green Jeep Cherokee with 16,000 miles and a three year extended warranty. I asked for a four wheel drive and standard shift. Son David produced a two wheel drive with an automatic shift, saying, "Ma, wherever you need a four wheel drive, you got no business being."

The steps to the driver's seat reminded me of the cattle truck I once (only once) drove: really sturdy. As a feminine touch, there was the tape recorder and a bunch of new tapes. All that was lacking was you, but that was the way it was, and maybe best so. You had used your allotted years while some of mine were left for the gods to gather as they and I choose. The windshield wiper scraped away the dispersing fog and it was time to start talking. I figured you listened as only you did, but this must have tested even you. I talked and talked and talked, lulling myself into the future.

This went on for another 1,200 miles to Rawlins, where we turned due north toward Muddy Gap. Some miles along, the way steadily rose to the brow of a hill, where the curtains went up. There it was: WYOMING. Up until now, it has been a backdrop, a picture in a book, but here it was as far as you can see, the land of wild horses left from the Conquistadores!

Mickey Babcock, following behind since we pushed off in Memphis, said it was just as hard to keep up as not run me down, as I unknowingly sped well over the limit then slowed to a crawl. She was patient then, just as she was when she followed me into the chugwater light that gives Red Canyon its name. (Chugwater is the deep red sandstone and silt formation which turns parts of Wyoming, Montana and Colorado aglow every dawn and dusk.)

A Sunday night party was in progress. We waded into a mass of strangers, where Lynn and Bob Budd, my summer hosts, handed us plates of something and found us chairs as we chattered with these to-be friends. Included were their two silent young sons, wearing pressed jeans and clean white Stetsons: formal wear for the area. But the star was Maggie, the five-year-old with golden curls, somebody else's cowboy hat, which almost covered her eyes, a frilly white dress and red hand-me-down boots.

Next morning, I went with Mickey off to Buffalo Valley, where the staff taught me about range management in high country by the planting of the native grasses our money bought. First we took to the sloping tableland of Cherry Tree Creek to count the plant species as a baseline to evaluate change over the years. Everybody on the ranch, including Maggie and town volunteers, were given a nine foot cord knotted at 12 inch intervals, and four stakes to form two foot squares at intervals to form a wide grid. Hunkered down in our squares, we counted the species and entered the number on a chart, then leap-frogged up the line. There was serenity in all this as we quickly covered such a vast area. Afterwards there was a splendid ranch dinner of wild meat, the garden's vegetables and deep dish dewberry pie.

My only serious gesture at becoming a range manager was when Bob invited me to try the tiller, a many ton monster that did everything at one pass: opened the sod, dropped the seeds and covered them up while we sat in air cooled comfort with Wyoming Public Radio soothing our souls. But there was a hitch. Whenever a rock wedged between the blades, there was a screeching stop. The solution—to rock that baby back and forth until it came out—was beyond my capacity or courage.

But there were choices like transcribing those tapes on my brand new electric typewriter with its built-in printer, a sort of forerunner of the coming computer. The pages rolled slow and steady under my hunt-and-peck, and they could have become raw material for an epic poem called some such like "The Anatomy of Grief," but it was not to be. As summer moved on, page after page was stored in a sturdy box which I later lost—*sic transit gloria*.

Other times, we walked after supper: a two-mile stretch of the shortcut to the South Pass highway. There was again a hitch—to avoid the pigmy prairie rattlesnakes that slithered across the road from the dry cliffs to the creek below for water. They were small, swift, and super-poisonous. (Sometime in the 1800s, Oregon fur traders heading back to St. Louis turned south at the Yellowstone, where the Indians were riled. It was they who discovered this broad high saddle of prairie, containing a parting of the waters between the Pacific and the Atlantic, to be known as South Pass. It later became a part of the Oregon Trail.)

On the east side was Atlantic City, a near-ghost town with a population of 27 and most of the houses long-closed. It was a potent attraction to the locals. Halfway up the overlooking hill was the Episcopal Mission which could have modeled for any New England Christmas card. The minister welcomed its tiny congregation— two Presbyterians, a couple of Mormons, one Arapaho and a couple of strays—every Sunday. When he and I became friends, he invited me to services since I lived only about 30 miles away, in a land where distance means nothing.

I met him at Lander's vegetarian restaurant, which we both frequented. The Tennessee license plate on my Jeep had caught his eye: originally an employee of Wyoming Game and Fish, he had become an Episcopal minister via a correspondence course arranged by the University of the South in Sewanee, Tennessee. He had never seen his alma mater, or a Tennessean, and was theologically curious.

We lunched now and then, and a couple of summers later, when Wyoming Game and Fish invited the Lucius Burch Wildlife Habitat Center to set up business at Trail Lake Ranch in the Fitzpatrick Wilderness, he was one of our contacts. So I had two friends in Atlantic City.

The second was John Mionczynsk, a New England truck gardener and ethnobiologist who, when he could stand it no longer, strapped his piano to the roof of his car and drove as far as his money and gas would take him—namely Atlantic City. Do not think of these two as hermits. John's jazz band, the Buffalo Chips, was the hottest thing in Jackson Hole and the rest of Freemont County. And he worked for years, maybe still does, for the University of Wyoming, researching the early death of Bighorn lambs, which were dying of a withering disease affecting their hind legs which increased the population of Mountain Lions in the Wind River Range. For this he had to get his gear into the mountains, where horses or even burros could not survive, so he walked and packed three goats: the nanny which supplied milk, her kid and the great horned Billy saddled with a pair of canvas panniers to carry John's accordion on one side and everything else on the other. They slept cuddled together on the ground, proved you could not only eat but enjoy just about anything you saw growing, as long as you had a few fish hooks to tie to an adequate line.

There were trips to bread broken with the few new friends in Lander, and odd chores for the Conservancy of which I was a longtime member. And there was Jane Whitson at Turpin Meadows and Mickey Babcock and Joe McCarty in Buffalo Valley who welcomed me most every weekend.

The Fourth of July, 1997, was celebrated at Lily Lake in the up-country above Joe and Mick's house. I picnicked with libations, watched the fish turning while listening to the tape of our last celebration with you at the T-Cross and stayed until well after dark.

When I passed back and forth through Dubois, our home for so many summers, I looked neither left nor right, until there was no way for me not to see the resurrection of a great stack of logs next to the museum. By late summer I worked up my nerve to stop there. A special friend and museum director, Sharon Kahin, was always there seeing to the job.

She was a wondrous one-of-a-kind. She had gotten several grants from the National Endowment for the Humanities and for the Arts to use film and oral histories to document the customs of the Sheep Eater tribe (the Tukudika, as they called themselves. Who could forget a name like that?) of the Mountain Shoshone Indians, who were fast dying out of old age. At the museum, she told me the story of the lodge.

The pile of logs had once been a charming little house, called the Dennison Lodge, which was built years earlier by an affluent New England family for their black-sheep son to entertain his friends in the outback, or so it was said. It had served well but, when all were gone it became, according to Wyoming Game & Fish, "an attractive nuisance," for lightning strikes or for wanderers to set afire. So it was offered to anyone who would move it to town—otherwise it was to be control burned. Sharon came with her hands out, trusting that somehow the moving cost could be covered. It was.

The treasure was sawed into three pieces. The first two moved the 23 miles to town on a flatbed truck, but the larger middle piece was too heavy. The truck bed collapsed, and all was in a heap. Not to be deterred, Sharon had the logs logs numbered and moved in separately. Now, reconstruction was under way. Here was the opening for my next summer.

Cash came in, just as Sharon had expected, from hither and thither. Fremont County (the largest in the U.S.), the feds and well-heeled summer residents all chipped in for the reconstruction. Leota Didier turned the kitchen space into a first class *atelier* for Anita, who had come from catering to the rich and mighty in D.C., and now put Dubois on the culinary map. The huge river stone fireplace, which had collapsed in transit, was reconstructed from the same river rocks, and my blessed son, David, has his name attached on a small plaque as the underwriter. Former Tennessee governor Ned McWherter supplied the big professional-size screen and the three great flagpoles out front. And enough hard cash came from your Wildlife Fund at the Community Foundation in Memphis to have it carry the name of the Lucius Burch Center for Wildlife Tradition.

Mid-September was time to retreat. Light snow began, doors closed, fires were lighted, trucks slid on the main street and hunting season opened. Once, we'd have braved it, but for me it was time to get home while the getting was still fairly good.

The 2 million-plus acre Wind River Indian Reservation starts some six miles east of Dubois. It's where I spent my last few days and is the site of the last traffic ticket I have near-missed. Here you can drive seemingly forever without seeing another soul, but not that morning. There I was purring along at a few miles over the speed limit when a revolving green light came out of nowhere. I stopped. The highway patrolman rolled up, and said through my lowered window: "You were driving over the limit."

"Yes, I guess I was, but mighty little."

"I see you've got Tennessee plates."

"Yes, I'm heading home right now."

"I'm from Morristown."

"Morristown, Tennessee?" He nodded. "Well, it's mighty cold. Why don't you come around and get in?"

He did, and told me his tale. He'd come here to attend the University of Wyoming, and had never left. He wanted to know what I was doing on my own on a road where 85% of the many wrecks were single car accidents—especially with snow on the ground. He didn't give me a ticket, but told me to be careful and to turn south at Lander where it was clear.

It was just one of those small pleasures that crop up to make life what it is. Imagine that,

Morristown. What an odd summons but there it was—a bit of an overshot but there just the same. Snows had started in the high country, the first moisture since June, potbellied stoves sighed and dudes like me were departing.

Home, only 1,600 miles away, was where I would sputter through the glorious fall doing odds and ends and making reconnections. It was not until wintertime parties that another future opened.

Yuletide Was A'Comin In
Celtic folk song

Bill Forrester, a local treasure of a bartender for the ladies of Belle Meade, while working his magic at Alyne Massey's Christmas party, asked her sister Elizabeth Queener if she had seen the film of Vic Scoggin swimming the Cumberland River. When the answer was no, he described the ordeal.

The river starts in southwest Kentucky, where Clover, Poor and Martin's Forks creeks converge within twelve miles of the headwaters of the Tennessee. They form the double strands of gems that connect the west flank of Appalachia to the Ohio River, gathering strength from the fourteen main tributaries. Midway along the river's path, in the Middle Basin, is Nashville, a fertile land where game flourished and bread came easily to the table, leaving time and energy for wider thoughts. My 1859 copy of Parton's *Life of Jackson* describes the city as a southern Philadelphia with "brick walks and ante-bellum homes nestled back from the streets which bore such quaint names as High, Vine, Spruce and Summer," while Harriet Arnow in her *Seedtime on the Cumberland* deems it "more glamorous than New Orleans."

Framed in a video camera hand held by his wife and friends following in a small boat, this man swam the whole thing—all 697 miles – through stretches of uncanny beauty and islands of old cars and mule carcasses solid enough to hold yapping dogs, past straight pipes from the banks oozing raw sewage. Although he wore a full wetsuit, at the end of his swim a rash completely covered his body. Why, you can only imagine.

This got the party talking about the state of the river, which clearly needed help.

"What are we going to do?" asked one guest.

"I don't know, but we'll do something," answered another. "Come for coffee with Shirley Caldwell-Patterson and me in the morning and we'll talk. We are meeting with a rep from the Southern Environmental Law Center to explore the possibility of their opening an office here."

Starbucks was quiet that early Sunday and we sat long enough for Bill to retell the Scoggin saga. Somewhere along the way, someone mentioned

When the Compact Began

the size of the river basin: 17,014 square miles. Jay, our host, spoke up: "That sounds like the Ace Basin project in South Carolina. A few years ago it was nothing but three rivers which don't even touch, but the name sounded good. It's now 350,000 acres, containing two Wildlife Management Areas, a research reserve, outdoor activities from bird watching to hunting, and is designated a world class ecosystem by the Nature Conservancy's Last Great Places program."

It was then that we pointed at each other, grinned and spoke the name "The Cumberland River Basin!" There it was—bigger than Connecticut, Massachusetts and two Rhode Islands with an annual population growth of some 12%. We named our group the Cumberland River Compact, at the urging of historian Charlie Howell to commemorate the Cumberland Compact, the first legal document issued at Fort Nashborough and a precedent for our state constitution.

Within a couple of weeks, lists were made, and invitations were sent to the caring and generous to gather and decide what the *something* should be—who, why, where and how. We started at the First Amendment Center, guests of the Freedom Forum at Vanderbilt, thanks to John Seigenthaler, its honcho. On a snowy January night, 163 of us sat in a triple circle to speak our opinions, all in turn, uninterrupted and fully heard. Later the sign-up sheet passed for those who could and would "do something." It contained 36 names and formed the steering committee, which pledged to meet every third week for as long as it took.

At our first meeting it was obvious we had many opinions but little knowledge. However, we had friends who knew, and if we wanted their help, we would do well to mind our manners. So we did and so they did. For 15 years our Water Quality Advisory Committee, consisting of reps all the way from Metro Water through the US Geological Survey met every month to vet the accuracy of our pronouncements and keep us abreast of news that we otherwise would have missed. That they can trust us to treat them as friends—rather than as someone whose chain had to be rattled—was not just a joy but an imperative.

For many years we met at the Ellington Agricultural Center, which had once been Uncle Rogers' "Brentwood House." When I turned into the driveway, I breathed deep and thought like the cat: 'Mine,' he said as he looked at the moon." It is so beautiful, and I almost see my two young ones, now approaching 70, racing out of the front door after their long visits. I am beholden to Uncle and Aunt Margaret, who so happily helped me give my children civility, a sense of place and responsibility. These their roots and wings, for which I am pleased.

And I, a denied heir to the place, agree with Uncle when in his advanced age he said that he was grateful that things worked out as they did because, had it gone rightfully to us it might not still stand on the brow of that hill in the shade of its own great trees.

As to the Compact itself, after we met here and there for a while, Bill arranged for the use of the parish house at his elegant Episcopal Church on Lafayette Street, whose towers were used by the Federal troops before and during the Battle of Nashville. He poured us fruit punch while we pondered our mission, and new people appeared as if made to order.

Arleen Decker, Coordinator of the Vanderbilt Oncology Clinic who volunteered in writing to act as coordinator. (It had never occurred to me that we needed such a thing!) Without her we would have been in trouble. She arranged with Alan Jones, head of the Tennessee Environmental Council, for us to share her office space their office where she operated a volunteer telephone information service, and to use his clerical staff at $12 per hour, to start a database and to get letters out which started, "Send money—$50 for the Cumberland." And, bless Bess, many did just that!

Pete Kopcsak, retired CEO of the Ingram Barge Co., who knows our river like the palm of his hand, organized our advisory committee. He took the task seriously, and it stuck. And it was he who persuaded Margo Farnsworth to join the team as its fearless leader.

Eileen Hennessy, a Yankee sophisticate with not-for-profit experience (and, incidentally, a first class fly fisher) tried hard to better organize this group of people set on doing their own things. When she failed, she departed, but when she was on hand she was a whiz.

Andy Walker, Director of the Tennessee Nature Conservancy, pulled us back together when a rupture threatened. Without him, the Compact would probably be long-gone.

There were those who pulled out their wallets such as Dan Canale, the Lucius Burch Wildlife Habitat Fund in Memphis, and Paul Sloan, who underwrote a powerful piece written by Michael Sims titled "Strange Bedfellows Unite to Guard the Cumberland" which filled an entire edition of Bruce Dobie's *Nashville Scene*. They, along with many others, helped answer, "What can we do?"

We lost some stars too, such as Vic Scoggin, the swimmer, who found some of our decisions too non-combative and set up his own organization. But we remain friends and he still shows his soul rattling film when asked. We should watch it every day.

In a fairly short time our mission of the Compact was real: "To protect and enhance the water quality of the Cumberland River by education and promoting cooperation among us, the people, businesses and agencies of Tennessee and Kentucky." That means different things to different people, but its need increases with every dawn, every sunset if the River is to remain the vein of life for my homeplace.

Spring 1997

Spring 1997 was as lovely as Tennessee springs are, full of rain and daffodils poking their heads through the winter earth. By late May, I could stand it no longer and headed west to a different summer. Instead of heading out to the back country with you, I sat at a desk or put my hand at restoring the Dennison Lodge, as it became the home of the Lucius Burch Wildlife Habitat Center. Along with the local supporters whom Sharon corralled were a number of Tennesseans. The most miraculous was our Memphis fly fishing friends: Bob Buckman and his wife, Joyce Mollerup. I had written to Beaver Creek, where they summered, to tell them that I was only a few hundred miles north, and invited them to come fish our Wind River. They came, but not for fishing.

Bob brought two IBM laptops—one for me and one for Sharon—and said, "Here, you two, learn to use these." And so I was introduced to the future. Hours were filled with his instructions on a wall size blackboard. "Shirley, you sit down and listen. Sharon, you start. What do you all need? Begin at the top and write a few words as to the why and the give or take cost." The list started modestly but with his prodding climbed up, up and up until it was almost a joke as Sharon squeezed things in at the bottom. Then he said, "Go take a nap, we'll see you at the Pines at six."

The Rustic Pines was as close to posh as Dubois provided, offering rare beef, wine and candles. Conversation flowed on the ways of the world, the joys of the West, friends at home and remembrance of you. When fishing was mentioned, he said maybe next time, but that he and Joyce had to confer and they would meet us for breakfast at seven. Nothing was said of yesterday's talk until we walked out of the Cowboy Café, where he put his arm around my shoulder and said they would fund the whole project. Send invoices, he said, and they would stay in touch. They turned south for home on Main Street as Sharon and I just stood there and stared.

Dennison Lodge was a miracle. It put Dubois on the map as a place that kept the West the way it was. In summer, the spokes of the wagon-wheel lights that hung from its ceilings were painted blood red, and there was splendor in the second or third-hand overstuffed sofas and armchairs upholstered in purple, navy and dusty pink plush. Before the river-stone fireplace was a pair of cowboy settees, cushioned in the winest of red, and in between stretched a rare *Bijar* runner which must have come from Sharon's grandmother. As a touch to bring tears were the end tables of red and white spotted calf-hide panniers from the T-Cross barn. Add an ancient upright piano, which had cheered saloons of the past, Sharon's museum quality Indian bead work on the walls, a couple of small bronze models of Joe Back's museum pieces and later the pigment-infused bronze model of Chief Washakie which we saw introduced to the Rotunda of the Capitol in Washington by the Wind River Reservation's chanters and dancers.

Even if there were world enough and time, let's stay with the opening day at the Dennison, when James Trosper, Medicine Man of the Reservation, came to exorcise the evil spirits by waving a ten inch black iron skillet, and a smudge fire of sage, sweet grass and pine by the front doors, in full regalia and at a half-crouch, to the beat of drums and tramping of feet. With his eagle pinion he whisked smoke into the corners of the great room, the back hall with the His and Hers, and the kitchen rigged to perfection by Leota Didier who well knew the best, then into the dining room of companionable round tables, long-ago patched quilts and memorials to Dubois when it was known as Tie Hack Center of the world and later the South East Gate to Yellowstone Park. But that is not where my story lives.

That began later, when Wyoming Game & Fish told Sharon another sad story of having to find a takeover for Trail Lake Ranch, the homestead school in Torrey Valley at the gateway to the Fitzpatrick Wilderness a few miles east of Dubois. Since the University of Wyoming and then the Audubon Society, tenants of many successful years, moved out, unattended fires abandoned by wanderers threatened to turn into forest fires and again a controlled burn was in order. If the Lucius Burch Center would take over, another landmark could be saved and so it did—for a while.

Since remembering, people have come to experience this wilderness at its best, but they came and left. Time caught the Becks but not before they built the stone library with its welcoming fireplace, the clutch of cabins with potbellied stoves and ceiling-high windows to clear the winter snowpack. Who planted the cottonwoods in the trickling irrigation runoff where they thrived, I know not, but there they were and still are. Something else caught the University of Wyoming and the Audubon Society which came but then departed.

Then the Lucius Burch Wildlife Habitat Center moved in with bounding hope.

Now I am going to quote from an editor of the *New Yorker* who was my luncheon partner at a garden party in Vence, France. He was a charming man and, unlike others, asked what I did. I said I was a professional volunteer for environmental causes and had been for nearly 50 years, had founded four not-for-profit organizations and was working on a fifth to improve the water quality of the Cumberland River Basin, which was about the size of Connecticut, Massachusetts and two Rhode Islands.

This set him off on a subject which I should not have neglected until now. He said he was raised in the City, but because of his position received conservation publications which called up the small, medium and aging boy in him with the pictures that let him feel the clean sand of creek bottoms ooze through his toes. He longed to be a part of the scene. They told shocking stories about the state of the environment, and pled that he write to the powers-that-be, which he might have done—had they told him exactly who that was, given their addresses and provided some supporting facts that he could pass on with confidence. Let this be a lesson to every volunteer.

EPILOGUE

On a Saturday afternoon a few days before Christmas 2006, Allison's husband, B.F. Byrd, died at the reasonable age of 87. He was a good friend forever and savior of a sort. As member of the clan and a doctor to boot, he was the one who was called to sew up various members of the hotbed of 13 nieces and nephews and assorted cousins living nearby. For a long while trips to Vanderbilt emergency were routine, what with falling off of bicycles, off roofs, out of trees, and stepping on broken glass. Doc always beat us to the hospital where, armed with needle and thread, he put one of the bloody small things to rights with a minimum of confusion and howling.

Caldwell Memorial at Mt. Olivet Cemetery

After the standing-room-only funeral at the First Presbyterian Church, everybody went home except those of us who made our way to Mt. Olivet to honor this longtime friend.

Mt. Olivet, like all cemeteries, is a mute history of a place. We drove the web of roads up the hill to the virgin trees, where the pre-Civil War families cluster in Greek Revival mausoleums, thickets of crosses and stele pointing heavenward, scrolls and tablets of pious thoughts—the Kirkmans, Carters, Craigheads, Burches, et al. There my great-great grandmother, romantically named Phoebe Galion, lies next to her daughter Margaret—Mrs. James Erwin—for whose husband Papa was named.

Across the hill, the place where many or most of us shall look to eternity is, as Papa said of Longview, "always held as a home to all the children, to come to and be assured of a bed." The one monument is a double life-size marble figure of a woman in the swirling robes of the same *Belle Époque* style as the Peace Monument mentioned earlier and created by the same sculptor.

Her bared right arm extends forward. The hand, broken off by vandals at play, leaves its gesture a mystery. Does its palm face downward in blessing? Do its fingers point forward to the future? I hope both.

Immediately behind her, a thick frame of trimmed cedar is atwitter with the horde of little brown birds distressed by this intrusion at bedtime. In front, the trimmed grass is regularity punctuated by headstones bearing only names and dates where Blue, the red-haired child longed for by Mama in her grandchildren but never gotten until now, played hopscotch in her bright pink coat and leggings. For some of the gathered, these occasions are more reunion than funeral—a time to trade stories with kin. As we share more-than-occasional laughter, the figure stands on a low inward curving marble wall, on which is inscribed:

FOLD THEM, O FATHER, IN THY LOVING ARMS
AND LET THEM HENCEFORTH BE MESSENGERS
BETWEEN OUR HUMAN HEARTS AND THEIRS.

As our good friend and kinsman is lowered into the precious earth on this short winter day, the setting sun and smog turns the sky a darkening red and the words of Tennyson, left some fifty years ago from Papa's funeral, echo.

Sunset and evening star,
And one clear call for me!
And may there be no moaning of the bar,
When I put out to sea,

Twilight and evening bell,
And after that the dark!
And may there be no sadness of farewell,
When I embark

Shirley's Family

BACK ROW
*David Patterson, Libby Patterson, Bethea Patterson Schoenfeld,
Richard Schoenfeld, Meredith Gardner, Sheppard Speer, Peter Gardner*

FRONT ROW
Caldwell Gardner, Griffin Gardner

APPENDIX

*Cooper Creek Tape, recorded by Lucius Burch
on the porch of his cabin in
Hardeman County, TN Sept., 1995*

My name is Lucius Burch, and I am 83 years old. I was raised on Cooper's Creek and lived there until 1936. When I was a boy and big enough to get out by myself in about 1920 with a few others boys, some black, some white, sons of people who worked on the farm, and my cousin Delamer Cooper who lived with us, I spent almost all of my daytime hours in the creek and Cooper's Bottoms. The place was so remote then, no houses within several miles, it wasn't necessary to supervise children about anything. We just roved like Indians all over the place, and my knowledge of it is so intimate that I remember every bend in the creek and everything of significance about the Bottoms.

The land has been related to the family for many, many years. The first was William Frierson Cooper in 1835. He was the great uncle of my mother who was Sarah Polk Cooper, who married Dr. Lucius Burch in 1881. So the family has known the land, and lived there until about 1950.

Cooper's Creek is a lovely little stream that rises up where the old Shelby Golf Course used to be, which has been closed for many years. It flows on down where it enters the Cumberland River. Back in those days there were always one or two houseboats permanently moored at the confluence of the creek and the river. The people who lived there were fisher people, made their living by running trot lines and basket traps and then walking into Nashville with their fish. They would always pass our house with fish to sell. I remember the great variety of fish that don't exist there anymore. Sturgeon were very common, but most were rough fish such as drum, buffalo, carp, lots of catfish.

Where Cornelia Fort airport is was woods then, part of the farm. Right beyond it was shallow pond that was very fertile, had a lot of fish. It had been created in the early 1830s when the brick clay was dug there which was used for the construction of Riverwood, the house wherein I lived all those years, where the Coopers had lived since 1835.

It was a fascinating area for boys. We lived in the creek, learned to swim in the creek. There were all kinds of signs of previous civilizations. There was a very large Indian burial ground right at the confluence of creek and the river. The last time I was out there, a house had been constructed, the south side of which was on the north side of the burial ground. It was large and evidently a pretty advanced culture, the dead were buried in graves that were lined with slabs of material that seem to have been made from baking or burning mussel shells, which was unusual.

We were too small to do any digging. It was a terrible shame, there was one pothunter who had discovered that place, and he was there every weekend and took out all sorts of stuff. Sometimes he didn't recover the excavation and there were a lot of bones left lying around. There was another large burial ground right across the river on the Two Rivers property, the McGavock property, a very large area. Because it was a very rich area where the hunting was easy, all open land, there undoubtedly had been people living there since the Indians first moved into the area.

There was no sort of traffic then on the river that was significant, except the rafters going down with logs to the sawmills at Nashville. They were a picturesque bunch of people, fascinating to us boys. They lived on the raft, had a little lean-to, three or four men with sweeps to keep to the middle of the river. There was still some steamboat traffic. The two principle large vessels that were left were the Joe Horton Fall and the H.G. Hill.

During World War I, my father and brother were off in the army, and my mother was running the farm, and it would have been impossible to get the wheat crop into Nashville any other way. There weren't many trucks and not much fuel. I remember the steamboat coming out and mooring right below Cooper's Creek. The wheat which had been threshed by an old-fashioned steam powered threshing machine was carried on the boat by the roustabouts. I thought that was great to see. Of course, in those days there was no such thing as a combine. They just ran the wheat through the thresher which winnowed out the grain and threw the straw into a large stack. It was a great time of the year for kids to play on it.

I remember a big flood in about 1927. One of the steamers which had not been used much, or at all, in recent years, broke loose from her moorings at the River Rail Terminal and drifted down and went down opposite Cooper Bottoms. She stayed there for years, and years, and years. I expect the boilers may still be there.

The Cornelia Fort Airport was built much, much later. I lived in Memphis at that time. I went there in 1936, and it was a great convenience to me because I could fly up to Cornelia Fort, then walk up the hill to my home place there, Riverwood. It has been a busy little airport ever since and still is.

There was no access to Cooper's Bottoms at that time except for farm roads from our house, except there was a road, unsurfaced and unimproved, that ran through a part of our pasture right above where the old riding academy was. At that time it was still covered. There were planks on the abutments long disappeared, but there are abutments still there to this day. It never was much used, but the land on the other side of Cooper's Creek had been owned by William Frierson Cooper's brother and was still in the hands of their family. That road was meant for their use to get out that way, but it was so much easier for them to go out Maxey Lane it was never used although it was a public road.

The center of all this, the center of the world as far as I was concerned, was the residence Riverwood, in which the family had lived for so many years. It had been built by a man named Porter back in the late

1820s or perhaps the early '30s or possibly before that, because the original brick house was the first brick house built in Middle Tennessee. The oldest other-than-wood house I believe was Rock Castle. It was a fairly simple house at that time, just the basic farm house plan of a parlor and dining room downstairs and a couple of bedrooms upstairs, and a kitchen ell out the back.

William Frierson Cooper bought it in about 1835. He was a person of considerable means, one of the most distinguished lawyers that the state ever produced. His books that are collected when he was Chief Justice of the Tennessee Supreme Court are known as Cooper's Chancery Review. They are very much respected to this day for their scholarship.

He was the one who rebuilt it along the style generally known as the Greek Revival. It was done about the time that the state Capitol was built. It was said, although I don't know that this is true, that William Strickland, the builder of the Capitol, was the architect. One thing that adds credence to that is that the trim is in the Egyptian style that was favored by Strickland and much used in the Capitol.

It was situated on a high spot, I guess 150 feet above the bottom and about three quarters of a mile from it. It was surrounded completely by a lawn and enormous tulip poplar trees. It is difficult to imagine the size of those trees. It was a pasture, never was cultivated.

I remember in 1929, my mother, in an earnest but vain attempt to make of me a cultured individual, sold the hay crop for $700 and sent me to spend a summer with an aunt of mine in England and in France. $700 went a long, long way in those times; it was hard to come by.

During the war years, the first World War, my mother had a desperate time. Both my father and older brother were away in the army. A powder plant had been built across the river at Old Hickory and they were paying such wages that it was impossible to get help. So my mother was there with a large herd of fine Jersey cattle and very little help. She learned to drive the milk truck to make the deliveries of the milk to Nashville. When that was over she never drove a vehicle again for the rest of her life. She lived to be 96 and always had a chauffeur. I think that truck driving had worn her out on that side of travel.

For the last months or so we have driven some 7,000 miles, most of it in Canada. It gave a pretty good perspective on the advance of the country. It made me realize, for the first time, the nature of the trip that my mother and father took with Sir Henry Thornton, who was then the president of the Canadian National Railway. They joined him on his private car in Montreal, and went all the way across the continent on an inspection trip to Vancouver, stopping along the way at Lake Louise and Banff. It was a perfectly fabulous trip.

The relationship between my father and Sir Henry commenced, I suppose, about 1888.

Football was just a game that was just developing. It was not a game that was widely played, and didn't have much of a following. Indeed, the president of Columbia University was quoted as saying that "the institution would not finance sending 20 young men 300 miles to agitate a bag of wind," but the game was taking hold.

My father was a magnificent athlete, and for five years was a star at Vanderbilt. Henry Thornton, as he was then, an American lad, and also a fine athlete, had been a star at the University of Pennsylvania. He came to coach at Vanderbilt, which was the beginning of the acquaintanceship with my father. The years went on, Thornton completed his education as an engineer, went to Canada, and, in due course, became president of the Railway. My father developed his medical practice, had career as a teacher, and became Dean of the Vanderbilt Medical School. In about '23 or '24, through the instrumentality of my father, Sir Henry was invited to come down and made the Commencement Address at Vanderbilt.

I have left out a part that I will insert here of how he became Sir Henry: When World War I came on, he went to England and took charge of the British railway system, and kept it functioning in a very fine way throughout the war. For his efforts he was knighted, became Sir Henry Thornton, and then returned to his post as president of the Canadian National.

He and Lady Thornton stayed with my mother and father, and mighty preparations were made. We had a long gravel driveway through the lawn which, in preparation for Sir Henry's coming, was covered with asphalt. They occupied the downstairs bedroom, which adjoined my father's study. It had been mentioned that Lady Thornton had a bad back, and liked to sleep alone. A foldaway bed was installed in my father's library. I know now that there was more to the story than that. Anyway, as a result of their old friendship and a relationship that was renewed, my mother and father were invited on this inspection trip which extended all the way across Canada, which must have been a marvelous trip.

Sir Henry's life in the end was not happy. He and Lady Thornton were divorced. There was another lady who, I think, had been one of his employees. Then Canadian politics became very much involved, and the rivalry between the Canadian National and the Canadian Pacific railroads became one of the hot political issues of the day. Sir Henry's star was in decline. Indeed, a book was written about his life, *The Tragedy of Henry Thornton*. I have read it but don't know where the copy is.

For years a buffalo head hung at the Belle Meade Country Club which was a present from Sir Henry in recognition of the courtesies that had been extended to him.

The happening of this tape was a Saturday afternoon in September, 1995, hot and dull. We were sitting on the porch in Hardeman County awaiting the evening breeze and the coming of the deer to the corn patch. Suddenly he said, "All right, let's talk about Cooper's Bottoms. Where's your machine?"

I had been talking to him about doing this for several weeks to no avail. I was doing a series of oral histories on the natural area being developed by Greenways for Nashville named Shelby Bottoms which includes Cooper's Bottoms. His natural resistance to recording the past had almost caused me to give up the notion, although his recollection was important to the collection—the machine was at hand.

This was becoming a crucial time of his life. We had traveled all summer—by car. He had an asking bid on his plane and sold it the week before we set out—much to my relief. As said earlier, we covered some 7,000 miles to Vancouver Island, Prince Rupert Island—and caught big fish. Then east across the Canadian Northwest Territory to Yellowknife and Great Slave Lake for pike fishing—several hundred miles by gravel road. The only hazards were buffalo sleeping and kicking up dust on the right-of-way. It was cool, cold, and these were places of his youth.

Now we were home, sighting in rifles with Andy for the coming deer season. But he came in exhausted from the heat and the short walks to check the target. In the tape, you can hear the shortness of his breath. We had talked and retalked of, "Dr. Apperson wants to sell me a pig's heart valve," to which I could give no advice.

ADDITIONAL VOICES

David Patterson

What is a dutiful son to say about his Mother's book? Besides the obvious, let me start past the petty hurrahs.

Her family is one that, at a time, rose to iconic heights in the pantheon of commercial and financial success. The biggest in the South. Two Pulitzer prize novelists wrote about it. Robert Penn Warren's second novel *At Heaven's Gate* and Peter Taylor's Pulitzer Prize winning *A Summons to Memphis*. Like a Greek tragedy, it took its tumble. I need go no further here as it is scripted in detail in the three part title. What I appreciate most are things that I never knew, many before my age of three. Perhaps the most significant revelation is the relation I had with my great uncle Rogers Caldwell. His story is the second leg of her book. Again, let the book tell the story.

As the first born of a family's next generation, I perhaps was beneficiary of some special attention. This is especially true as it came to my relation with Uncle. Basically for the first twenty-six years of my life there were three important people in it. First my mother and then, and not necessarily in this order, my father and Uncle. As it happened my great uncle and aunt were childless, whereas my own grandfather went on to have thirteen grandchildren. Uncle still had an enticing home as well as the inclination and desire for a larger family. I first recall spending Saturday nights at Brentwood Hall when I was very young, maybe around the age of three. My father and mother were starting out simply as most young couples do. The exception was that we lived on land that my grandfather had given to his children and sons-in-law to build their first houses, as part of the original farm now known as Belle Meade Plantation. As to Saturday nights, my parents were ever too ready to have a night off at the invitation of free babysitting by my Uncle Rogers and Aunt Margaret. What Mama's book reveals, that I was not aware of, was that this started at my age of six months rather than three years, when I was handed over in a handbasket rather than on a tricycle. For a childless couple, this is a different experience, for obvious reasons.

As I now approach the fourth quarter of my own life, having been fortunate to have achieved a modicum of success, I reflect on the importance of both genetics and environment in one's early development.

In my life's experience, I (we) could have been the beneficiary of a great fortune had it not been for events of the late twenties and early thirties. As I have said many times, mainly to family, we inherited the best: genetics, environment, and no money.

Of my eleven first cousins and my sister, everyone has gone on to live successful lives, some exceptionally so. So much for the old saying "shirt tails to shirt tails in three generations." That ain't us.

From times prior to my first memory, till the last night I spent in the Franklin house, and writing a personal check for the last services of his cook the night before the burial, my experience with my Uncle Rogers has cast a long shadow in my existence.

He was never more to me than a loving grandfather. His earlier iconic success was before my time and he never looked back. As I entered my teens and went off to school, upon returning to town I would spend Saturday nights with him as I had always done. Whereas in my earlier youth many experiences with him were subliminal, as I approached late teens and early twenties, especially during college, his influence became more discernible. Not to steal from the book, but his late life style was one-of-a-kind. His luncheons are chronicled by many who experienced them as... I can't think of the proper word. I was fortunate to always have a seat at the table, and as I was about to enter the real world of responsibility post college, my memories of the important people and things going on in the Nashville community and beyond are still vivid. To recall just a few: the first jet landing at BNA, we drove out to watch the Boeing 707 land; the Jimmy Hoffa teamster trial in Chattanooga where his regular lunch guest John Hooker Sr. (or could have been Jim Neal) was the principal attorney. One lunch was interrupted so that John Seigenthaler could take a conference call as to the proceedings. I have a vivid memory of the early formation of Nashville's iconic Hospital Corporation of America, HCA, and its original cast. There were others, but these stick in mind.

As for the rest of Mama's book, the title almost suggests a trilogy, and that is the way I am reading it. It was long anticipated as she worked on it for years, which I felt was timed for her own finality, as it happened. My greatest regret is of learning of the recent passing of Bob Thomson, one of the two important collaborators with her on the book. The other is my cousin-in-law Will Akers, husband of Cissy who was perhaps her favorite niece. Both these guys have been around the block many times in the literary sense and their accolades for SCP's writing is touching. The soothing news from Will was that Bob had recently had the opportunity to read the proof copy of the book. I only wish I had been able to present him a final copy and have the opportunity to chat about it.

With the exception of the part about Uncle and Caldwell & Co., the rest is prior to my existence and after I had left the roost, so I am reading it as are others. I can say that she lived by the creed of her grandmother something to the extent of "for those to whom a lot is given, a lot is expected." She was the recipient of both National and Presidential commendations for her environmental work and one of her many ongoing legacies locally and regionally is as a founder of the Cumberland River Compact.

So for those reading the book, as they say in restaurants... Enjoy.

Sheppard Patterson Speer

I was lucky enough to watch my mother transition from a mid-twenties, traditional, married wife and mother into a globetrotting, fly fishing, environmentalist who absolutely believed in the Gaia Principle. She was intellectually curious, had the capacity for deep attachment to certain people, could muster small armies of enthusiasts to achieve her environmental projects and loathed political conflict. She asked in-depth questions and knew when to be quiet. Her legacy to me was permission to follow my own path into a meaningful life without the boundaries of confined expectations.

May this be a generational gift to all her female offspring.

Meredith Speer Gardner

Shirley was many things to many people but, as a grandmother, she was an advocate, a cheerleader, a sounding board, and a voice of reason. She pushed those she loved to be their best, constantly reminding us that, "From those to whom much is given, much is expected."

Together we drove cross country, wandered in the woods, tried to elect a President, and broke a few rules along the way.

Shirley was a mighty force who decided to live her life her very own way and did so politely but unapologetically.

Meredith Caldwell, III

Many of my favorite childhood memories, that I still reflect on even today, revolve around the times spent with Uncle Rogers. He had no children, and as families are prone to do, my cousin, David Patterson, and I were often left with him for weekend babysitting. He lived in Brentwood House, the home he built in 1928, which is now the State of Tennessee's Ellington Agricultural Center. It is a fairly large home and when we were there, David and I pretty much had the run of the house and the surrounding farm. Since Uncle and his wife, our Aunt Margaret, were normally the only residents, it was very quiet, except during monthly family lunches that Uncle often hosted. They were grand affairs attended by the Caldwell family adults and children. As an example, his dining room table was set with 24 Queen Anne armchairs and was usually filled to capacity. The children, typically 8 to 10 or so, were served on the back porch with a view of the farm's thoroughbred horse barn off in the distance.

Of the many meals enjoyed with Uncle, our Saturday morning breakfasts were my favorite. His bedroom was large enough to resemble a hotel suite. Harry, the fellow that worked many years for Uncle, would awaken David and me and instruct us to dress in our robes and meet downstairs for breakfast. After delightful conversation, Harry could be heard rolling a breakfast table from the kitchen to the bedroom where we proceeded to enjoy a wonderful English breakfast. To this day, when having hotel room service, I often recall breakfast at Brentwood House.

Surrounding the house were the beginnings of the Crieve Hall subdivision, and for a period, the roads were all that had been developed. David, a year older than me, started driving at around 12 years of age in Uncle's 1953 Ford. I can't remember if we had his permission to go driving, but the good news was if we ran off the road, there was nothing to hit. David finally taught me to drive a couple of years later.

I was probably in my late teens before having much understanding of Rogers Caldwell, the businessman and founder of the investment firm Caldwell & Company. As I grew older and more aware of the history of his business years, I began to realize what a high profile and complicated life he had lived before my arrival. I am still surprised how I separately remember the two men I knew; the one from the press reports and books on his business career and the person who continues to be one of the finest men I have or will ever meet.

Cissy Caldwell Akers

As a child, there was always Aunt Shirley. We grew up in a neighborhood surrounded by cousins. Shirley told me she came home one afternoon and a group of the cousins had found a gallon can of paint and were outside making a big mess. She said, "Well, that looks like fun. What did you paint?" A quiet, little voice responded, "Cissy." And there I was, covered in green paint. At that point, Shirley called out, "Cissy, time to go home!"

As an adult, more importantly, there was Shirley, my close friend. She was open minded, engaging, and always interesting. I remember all the fun we had together and think of her often.

One summer I expressed a desire to go hiking in Wyoming with Shirley and Lucius. I was told that Lucius had to meet me before he would commit to an invitation. He was coming to Nashville and Shirley arranged for us to meet. We hit it off splendidly from the get-go. When you're on a three week camping trip, mealtime took on a whole new meaning, especially with limited supplies. When you're hiking, your meals and your shower are your life. I struck a deal with Lucius: I would cook every night if someone else would clean up. I didn't know you could prepare trout seven different ways... it helped that I had brought a Ziploc with herbs from Nashville. Shirley was doing breakfast and I took the orange peels. That night after dinner, for dessert I gave Lucius a plate of *crêpes* with an orange syrup I had made. He spoke about that for days and told me I was invited to go with him, anytime, anywhere, he ever went.

Even though you weren't supposed to shoot guns in Yellowstone, he would occasionally race off and come back with a duck. The ultimate culinary prize was a canned ham we found strung up in a tree to keep it away from bears. No telling how long it had been there. It didn't even have a label anymore. We feasted for days. It's a wonder we didn't all die. Our obits could have read: "Cause of death—Ham in a tree."

A few days into my first trip to Wyoming, Shirley told Lucius I'd never been on a horse. He quickly saddled up two and announced to the group that we'd be back in about five or six hours. He took off at a gallop with me following with arms and legs flapping like I was trying to fly. My dad told me once: it's amazing what people will tell you if you'll just ask them. That day, as Lucius and I rode along, I asked him about everything. His work and personal life, and that set the tone for our future relationship. At the end of the day, he announced that I was an old pro.

The next day, when he decided to go over the Continental Divide, instead of around it, he put me on a horse and gave me the lead of a pack horse. What he didn't know was that we were going to run into six feet of snow. I still have a scar on my hand from where I was pulling the horse behind me. When I showed my torn up finger to Lucius, he said, "Really? Put some snow on it." That same day, Shirley's favorite horse, Joker, impaled himself on the top of a small tree and tore his chest open. Luckily we had a neurosurgeon with us and he was able to sew him up as best he could and gave him some antibiotics. After a few weeks, he was well. I think that was the only time I ever saw Shirley really mad at Lucius. Why he had to go over snow covered peaks and didn't take the sunny trail, didn't seem like a very good idea to her.

Lucius and Shirley were liberal and open minded. They didn't sit around and tell you what to think, or what they thought. They wanted to know what you thought and what your generation was thinking. It was always Lucius' first question whenever I saw him, "What are you thinking?"

Considering the way my dad and Shirley were raised, I was always amazed and pleased at their lack of interest in material possessions. Or social stuff. I remember Shirley telling me when she got to be in her forties, she could either go to the Club every day and play bridge and probably become an alcoholic, or she could try to figure out something a little more interesting to do with her life. That's when she began to go do the archaeological digs in Greece.

I adored Uncle Rogers. He had a keen intellect and a whimsical sense of humor. When I drove to Franklin to wish him a happy birthday, he took me aside and asked, "Shall I take this cake personally? Shall I begin my weight loss regime?" It was a beautifully iced cake but the inside was styrofoam. We all had a big laugh.

When I joined him at his well known luncheons, he would sit me opposite him at the far end of the table. He would throw a question out, wink at me, and smiled contentedly as the lively dialogue ensued.

One of my earliest memories was spending Friday nights at Brentwood Hall with either Rogers or Edie, and Uncle and Aunt Margaret. A table would be set up in Uncle's bedroom and Harry would cook us hamburgers and wonderful french fries. We had dinner while we watched *Gunsmoke*. My cousin David would often appear on Saturday and would pile us kids in the car with him and drive around the farm. I doubt if he was older than thirteen.

One inside game we delighted in playing could be named "Is the Upstairs Haunted?" On a big dare, you had to run solo up the back stairs, touch the sink in every bathroom, and charge down the front stairs before something big and scary got you.

We never saw much of Aunt Margaret. But I do remember her breaking a mirror. Being superstitious, she threw me in the car and raced down the hill to throw the pieces in the creek. When finished, much to her horror, and my tears, she realized she had shut my finger in the door.

What to do? How could she make up for this grave error? She devised a plan and drove directly to May's Beauty Parlor to have my hair coiffed. I remember it was a splendid afternoon.

At Sunday lunch, the extended family would convene and the children would sit on the covered back porch and misbehave. Each week, two kids were picked to eat in the dining room with the grown ups. A small table was set to the side where the kids and one adult would sit. The reason was to teach the children good manners. We all dreaded when it would come our turn.

At the end of lunch, Uncle would often have his farmhand bring one of the horses up and, if you were lucky, it would be your turn to go for a ride. One particular Sunday, the horse rared up and knocked me to the ground and stepped on my arm. I remember it was very painful. But Doc Byrd determined nothing was broken, and I could still go for my ride. With a horse footprint on my arm, I was the envy of the kindergarten class at Overbrook until it vanished.

Thomas Byrd

In my adult years, Shirley was one of the most remarkable women I knew. As was my mother, Shirley's sister, so it must be that common strong Caldwell gene. In my childhood, Shirley was a larger than life figure. Three brief stories come to mind.

Legend has it that Calvin Houghland, another larger than life Nashville figure, ran a brothel while attending college at Vanderbilt. Once discovered, Calvin went into hiding to avoid arrest. Shirley rescued the day, whisking Calvin away from town before the police could catch him. It may have also precipitated his joining the Navy.

When I was little, Shirley would suddenly appear at the Byrd house with small gifts for the children; usually having just returned from an archeological excavation in Egypt or Israel and then quickly moving on to fly fish in the Patagonia area of Argentina or Chile. Dressed in boots, with the appearance of Amelia Earhart, except with long flowing blond hair, it was always an unforgettable moment.

Lastly, one day during medical school, I was riding alone in the back seat of the car with Shirley and my father (BF Byrd) in the front (I think they dated before he married my mother). Spontaneously, in reference to the norm of the racial inequity of the Old South of their young adult years, Shirley leaned over and said, "BF, we were so unenlightened," to which they both nodded.

A remarkable lady on every level, I also felt special when she would call me up in the middle of a workday and say, "Let's have lunch." Although, I knew she made many people feel special this way.

Andrew W. Byrd

How can one describe Aunt Shirley in a few words?

She was made of love and service to others. Ms. Caldwell-Patterson was a person of action.

Aunt Shirley joined her family business as Treasurer of the Nashville Stockyards. She was the original Treasurer for Nashville's first pro hockey team, the Dixie Flyers. The Byrd family ended up with a lot of tickets to a very physical game. I would see her at the Tennessee State Capitol monitoring legislation for Common Cause and the Sierra Club. She was one of the founders in 1976, along with Nelson Andrews, of Leadership Nashville, Nashville's premier leadership organization. She personally started the Tennessee Environmental Council. She talked with her family and friends to fund the TEC each year.

She later started the Cumberland River Compact, where she recruited my brother Barney and me as Founding Members. The entity is a tremendous, non-confrontational success, incorporating volunteer professionals from all across the governmental, environmental and business spectrum. Next with her creative imagination, she developed the thought that a park was needed across the river in East Nashville, and in conjunction with the Metro government, she helped to create the Shelby Bottoms Park.

She later received the Lifetime Achievement Award from the U.S. Environmental Protection Agency.

Aunt Shirley and I would have lunch every six months. Her indomitable spirit was like a fresh breeze every time we ate. She always looked to me to share about my children, my mom, and my brothers and sisters as well as the inevitable business update. She also loved the political fray where we would share commentary on politicians, legislation and geo-political developments.

We were kindred spirits.

In my mother's final years, Shirley reached out and included my mother in her sphere of friends at Richland Place, a Nashville assisted living facility.

All this in no way expresses that love she shared on each occasion with her fellow travelers. People always knew that she cared about them and their feelings. She was a leader in love for the other person. This gave her the aura surrounding her, and her Grace descending from the Almighty.

Warmly Remembered over time.

Paul Sloan

"Whatever you can do, or dream you can, begin it, because boldness has power, magic and genius in it." The words are Goethe's; their embodiment is Shirley Caldwell-Patterson. Take power, magic and genius; add wisdom and charm, and you can understand the force that was Shirley and appreciate why she was and continues to be an inspiration to those who were within her orbit.

A conversation with Shirley could be a baptism by immersion. The opener: "Tell me what's on your mind." Don't think for a moment you can get away with a flip response. She doesn't suffer fools easily. It's substance she's after. She's just read the *Sunday Times*, the *Economist* and a newly published book of esoterica, and she wants to know what you think. It's not one-upmanship. It's an honest inquiry. There is a hint of impatience – not with you but with time's winged warrior pressing her with the urgency to restore and renew Nature's wild places and her treasured rivers and streams.

Shirley preferred to be out front where footprints are scarce. She was among the first trustees of The Nature Conservancy in Tennessee; co-founder of the Environmental Action Fund; among the founders of the Tennessee Environmental Council; among the first to suggest the creation of Leadership Nashville and the first to organize a Tennessee watershed association, the Cumberland River Compact. Much she accomplished was as an octogenarian proving that energy and focus can grow with age. She was a problem solver who showed by example that listening, understanding, and collaboration will trump conflict every time. Shirley insisted there were enough people who want to solve problems not to be distracted by those who don't. She was proven right time and again.

Along the way Shirley accumulated a boatload of awards and recognitions for her work, including the President's Volunteer Service Award in 2007. But to dwell among these recognitions would be to trail far behind. Shirley had little time for them. She was up ahead, on to solving the next challenge.

With these pages and the loving efforts of Cissy, Will and William Akers, Shirley has given us a gift of her reflections. Though these will provide clues, I suspect the alchemy that produced such an extraordinary person will continue to elude us, but every clue is nonetheless a treasured gift.

Joe McCarty

In March 1981 Shirley and I sat before a large fire at the Hosteria San Humberto in Argentina, drinking tea and comparing our fishing successes earlier in the day on the upper Malleo River. Lucius refused to come back to the lodge despite the early fall chill and wind. She and Lucius had arrived about a week before me by bus over the Andes from Santiago. I arrived from Buenos Aires with vague instructions to "Meet us in Argentina."

I had learned during the previous six or so years of traveling with them, that the less asked about arrangements the better, because they prided themselves on general or nonexistent itineraries. If I pressed for details, such as "Where in Argentina do you want to meet?" the reply was generally, "Do you want to go, or don't you?" In this instance, like many others, I was given the name of a fellow to contact and the name of a town and not much else. I did rent a Fiat, later named "*el Raton*" and after two towns and several tries, did find them at the San Humberto.

My conversations with Shirley, which lasted until her passing many years later, always left me scrambling for more information, facts she kept at hand and my requests to explain the incomprehensible to me such as archeology and Greek poetry. I was at best a poor student, but she tolerated my questions. That afternoon before the fire, she explained why she had earlier "run away from home," as she tells in this book.

In the mid 1970s I had been invited to hike with Lucius in the area near Mt. Rogers, Virginia, near Abingdon. We flew into Nashville and picked up Shirley and that was the start of a deep lifelong friendship (and my love affair) with the most interesting woman I ever knew. On the return trip to Nashville to deposit Shirley, she insisted we go to lunch at the Belle Meade Café and then drive through the grounds of Belle Meade Mansion, then in state hands. She delighted in pointing out the optimal windows to escape undetected.

Our adventures over many years ranged from the Appalachian Trail, the Caribbean, and Argentina to all the wonderful years in Wyoming. In Shirley's telling of the early trip to Dubois—pronounced "duboys" by the cowboys, not the French equivalent—she omits the details that we were trapped there for three days in May with snow higher than the wings of the plane. The locals belatedly informed us that summer began on July 4th.

The delight for me traveling in their wake was to meet and befriend a universe of interesting, sometimes eccentric, and usually fascinating people. They were as apt to chat up a nine year old or wrangler as a famous architect or author. They were generous with invitations to family and friends to join in, even some folks who would bail out on the first day of a long trip. Some friends today can be traced to our years of adventures. I think Lucius and Shirley knew every one of the Dubois inhabitants and a large part of Wyoming, or so it seemed.

Shirley understates her abiding love for the Wyoming horses. She could calm the fractious ones and bond with her own Joker and Ap the packhorse that was the Zen Master of the pack. Through all the horse wrecks, people wrecks and dangerous passages, Shirley could be counted on as a steady, knowledgeable hand. The horses knew they had a pro with them with Shirley—while sometimes "iffy" with Lucius.

The years after Lucius passed were bittersweet for us. We took a few Wyoming backcountry trips with friends, but neither of us could generate much enthusiasm for what seemed a pale imitation to our earlier adventures. Shirley became a generous supporter of the Nature Conservancy in Wyoming and we would some times meet at Red Canyon

Ranch which was run by the Conservancy as a working ranch education center.

In later years we visited whenever I was in Nashville. We'd drive out to Loveless' for coffee and biscuits before the touristas hit and sometimes walk Radnor Lake. We more regularly connected in later years when I began teaching part time at Vanderbilt Law School. Shirley would invite me to see her at "the home" as long as I didn't overlap with her Tai Chi class. I last saw her at a delightful lunch with son David and niece Cissy at the Belle Meade Club. She looked beautiful and happy that day and I will always remember her sitting in the sunlight.

Charlie Newman

Shirley was one of the most remarkable persons I have known.

Over several decades, I spent long periods with Lucius and Shirley in the outdoors in situations that challenged us physically—and sometimes mentally—and you get to know somebody that way.

Lucius and she combined extraordinary, adventurous minds, furnished by the best of Western literature, with an intense, almost overwhelming love for the outdoors, the "country," vigorous and often dangerous physical activity.

They shared a devotion to the written word. Reading was at the center of both their lives. Both were deeply educated.

Even when he was "in town," he rarely spent more than four days a week in the office, and whenever possible he was gone for weeks, sometimes months at a time, outdoors with Shirley. Often way outdoors, at the ends of the Earth, refusing most of the conveniences of life, holding themselves to standards, ethical and physical, to which few aspire.

When Lucius was 14, the head of the Gulf Coast Military Academy, W.T. Lowery, sent a letter to his parents saying:

"Dear Sir and Madam: With very deep regret we are sending Lucius home."

He said 25 boys had run away from campus and when they were caught Lucius and another boy stepped forward and "asked that they be given the whole penalty,' saying they had organized the rebellion and were responsible for what the other boys did. When told his punishment would be confinement to the campus for the night, while the other boys would be attending a banquet in Biloxi, "Lucius remarked that we would just as well get ready for it, because he was not going to stay on the campus that night." And sure enough he left.

Mr. Lowery said Lucius "is a boy of considerable influence, [but] "his influence has been against discipline." "He is capable of making a great man. We... expect that he will do so, but we must maintain the discipline of the institution."

What was the probability Lucius would have found someone to share the last decades of his life who equalled him in so many ways, willing and able to accompany him on his adventures, physical and intellectual, in the way Shirley did, defying authority and convention, but adhering to principle throughout their lives, turning their great talents to large causes?

John Noel

Who do you know, born blue of blood, preferring the trail and a tent to soak up the planet's natural wonders and intelligently organize the necessary protections for it to thrive? Those who traveled the trail with her were motivated and awed by her keen tenacity. She made a difference and we the people benefitted.

Vic Scoggin

Sometime in 1997, I was contacted by Shirley Patterson. She had read the newspaper articles on my swim down the Cumberland River... hence my 501(c)3 organization Save The Cumberland. Leon Alligood, the senior writer at the Nashville *Banner*, had written all the stories throughout the 65 day, 696 mile swim to save the river. His first article was April 30, 1996, the day before I was to enter the river at the Poor Fork of the Cumberland in Harlan, Kentucky.

There were many articles written, and plenty of news coverage all along the Cumberland River. Most towns covered it, even a television show called *Inside Edition* from New York City came to Nashville. Shirley told me she had seen most of the articles but not the *Inside Edition* piece or the self published documentary I had created from the first 125 miles of the swim. She asked if I would show her these films and would I like to meet with her, Bill Forrester, a few others I can't recall, and John Seigenthaler, chairman *emeritus* of the *Tennessean* newspaper.

We all met over in Mr. Seigenthaler's office to discuss the awareness I had brought to the river, and I guess, to have Mr. Seigenthaler's blessing for what Shirley had in mind. After I gave my spiel about what I had seen, and why I did what I did, I believe everybody came away from there confident of what Shirley wanted to do.

From that point on there was a series of meetings which I had attended to help in the process of helping Shirley move forward with the Cumberland River Compact. If my memory is right, I even wrote the first check to her organization, which was, I think, $50.00. I'm sure there were other donations, and I would assume Shirley had some at stake... but it was just a small gesture of my support from somebody actually outside of Shirley's circle.

Sometime after these meetings Shirley asked me to help write a mission statement for the Compact. I did, and sometime later it was changed to be non-confrontational.

Shirley called me many times over the years until her final days asking me to help with organizing watersheds throughout the state. Karen Smith was leading this charge. I was traveling to different towns to show my film and motivate local citizens to form watershed organizations.

In later years, I would meet Shirley over at Starbucks in Belle Meade Plaza to discuss other strategies concerning the environment, and talk about the old days in Nashville. She was kind and gentle and strong... the last of old Nashville. She cared deeply about the river, and the people that settled here.

I told her I would never say no to anything concerning the river. I always stayed true to my word, and continue with that today. Whatever she asked me to help with, I always obliged. Looking back over those 20 years, I wish I had met with her more and listened more closely to her words of encouragement and support of the river, and that crossing of paths, as the Cumberland River met Caldwell Lane.

Bill Forrester

I had an assignment [as a private investigator] to catch someone doing illegal dumping. I went down to the river, mosquito bites and everything, and filmed the dumping. A man was swimming down the river and interrupted my footage. You can't go the courts saying, "Dumping is hazardous and not good for the river" if somebody's swimming there.

The river is the greatest natural resource that we have. I talked to some scientists at TSU and they said, "That's an investigation that's going to be too hard to do anything. You're talking about something that's impossible... why don't you just turn it over to the EPA?" That was that, or so I thought.

About a year later, I ran into a friend who said, "Hey are you still investigating the river? There's this guy who has a film about saving the Cumberland River."

"What's his name?"

"Vic Scoggin." I put two and two together that it was the guy swimming in the river with the little boat with a "Save the Cumberland" banner on it. I met Vic and saw his film *Save The Cumberland*.

Then, I ran into Mrs. Elizabeth Queener, Mrs. [Alyne] Massey's sister. I told her, "There's nothing I can do with my footage, but I've seen an amazing film that does more than what mine could ever do." I explained to her what it was about. My whole concern was to inform people, to educate people, not only of the devastation, but what the value of the river is, its value in terms of vegetation, in terms of animal growth, soil. Mrs. Queener said "Bill, I'm having breakfast with someone who could really help. Her name is Shirley Patterson. You should know her." She invited me to come join them for breakfast the very next morning at Noshville. As a result of that, Shirley got involved.

I said, "We need to do something, and what can we do?" That was the question. It was like something spiritual, a strong pursuit of "Who do you contact?"

It was the perfect match because Shirley didn't want anything that was going to be confrontational. She knew who to get to, to talk the people at the EPA. The water quality people. The soil percolation people. The conservationists. She knew where to go. She knew the people in the state government, in the local government, and the federal government. She'd say, "Why are you talking to someone on the state EPA? You need to be talking here." She wanted to make sure we branched out, and talked to the stakeholders in other communities, to people downstream and upstream and involve them with what was going on with the Compact.

Shirley was different. If she didn't care for you, she wouldn't speak to you. She was tactful, but she was brutally honest. She would just come right out with it. I mean she was honest. If you asked her a question, she's going to give you what she thought. You might not like it initially, her response, but it might take a minute before you thought, "You know, she's probably right about that."

The main thing about Shirley was that she was she was so similar to my mother and my grandmother. I learned diplomacy and tactfulness and respect from my mother and grandmother, Momma's mother, who told me, "Son, you've got to always leave room for the other person to save face." I mentioned that to Shirley, and she said, "Right. You never know when you're going to have to go sit in that person's office and beg for some money or some help." You don't need any enemies and she taught me that.

It was easy for us to have meetings at Holy Trinity [Episcopal Church on 6th Avenue South], until it wasn't feasible. Shirley said, "Bill Forrester, you're going to have to come up with a bigger space. How well do you know John Seigenthaler? Do you think he'd let us hold a meeting at the Seigenthaler Center?" She knew that John Seigenthaler and I were very close. I was very comfortable in calling John Seigenthaler "Dad." Of course, she knew John Seigenthaler very well and could have made the call herself, but it was important for her to get others involved. This wasn't a Shirley Patterson production. There was total involvement.

I'm not sure if the Compact's doing totally what Shirley or Mrs. Queener wanted to see done, but the Compact is doing totally what I wished for.

Wendy Smith

I met Shirley at a crossroad in my life. I had been a video producer for ten years and I wanted to get back to doing conservation work, which was and is my calling and passion but I wasn't sure how to ease my way back into that world.

John Noel, that wonderful connector of people and causes, introduced me to Shirley because he said, "we ought to know each other." I remember Shirley looking me up and down with those intense eyes and frankly I felt a little scared (and for a girl from Detroit that is rare!) Before I knew it, we were having tea and she wanted to know my life story. During that first meeting I could feel her intelligence, passion and spirit. I love the way she zeroed in on the essence of a group, an idea, a process—whatever it was, she didn't have much patience with noodling around, she was a woman of action and that I respected.

In 1998, the Board of the Cumberland River Compact chose to hire paid staff to expand the reach of the Compact. I was fortunate to share the Director position with Rob Skinner. We were a good team; our very different backgrounds and beliefs balanced each other. Shirley, as always, was rarin' to go; sometimes it was hard for the two of us to keep up! After Rob left for another job, Shirley sought the advice and counsel of other board members and friends as they looked for someone to fill Rob's shoes. As it turned out, my new partner came with her own shoes and new skills that were exactly what the Compact needed. I know that Shirley was pleased with this new partnership, understood our skills and helped us nurture and develop those skills. She often referred to us as The Swan (Margo) and the Red Cockaded Firebird (me).

In 1999, I was offered a job with the World Wildlife Fund; it was a dream come true. Telling Shirley was difficult. She had come into my life at a time when I was low. She stood me up and pointed me in the right direction. For that I am grateful.

She was supportive and proud of me. I don't know if she ever knew the role she played in my life. I regret not telling her. One word of advice from this Red Cockaded Firebird, if there is someone in your life that supported you when you were down and helped you believe in yourself again, tell them. You won't regret it.

Margo Farnsworth

I witnessed Shirley in action before I knew her, which was fortunate. At the formative meeting she had conjured with Elizabeth Queener and Bill Forrester, I saw her collect and conduct a great and varied amalgam of Middle Tennesseans to watch a slideshow on the Cumberland River and discuss next steps. Some she knew personally. Others, like me, were there because we were active in some aspect of environmental protection or education and were curious.

As she noted, Vic Scoggin swam the entire length of that grand yet troubled river, which snaked its way from its modest tributary beginnings in southwest Kentucky, down through its heart in Nashville. From there it slowed and spread before emptying its contents into the Ohio River.

If the river's heart could be personified it would easily be embodied in Shirley. Her bright eyes varied that night in Nashville, from twinkling when she greeted dear friends to snapping flames as she viewed raw sewage being carried along the river's erstwhile healthy waters. Her entreaties to those attending to "sit in a circle" was one she carried to gatherings for the rest of her days; so that everyone could have an equal voice in whatever challenges arose. Those days Nashvillians thought of the Cumberland River as something "out back."

I had a plateful of environmental work at the time of Vic's show so did not see her again for almost two years. She showed up at my park to extoll the virtues of a new organization, The Cumberland River Compact, and asked me if I might get involved in some way. A couple of months later another board member, Pete Kopcsak, "he with the great booming voice" as Shirley anointed him, called to ask if I might want to work for The Compact as Co-Director with Wendy Smith.

Dubious but hopeful about their new way of doing business through collaboration, I had coffee with Pete and the next cup a few days later with the great lady herself. She was forthright and earnest but full of fun and mischief. It leaked out around the edges unless she was either very serious or in full play mode when she called us to be jolly, throwing her head back in delight. She was not a woman of half measures.

After joining the Compact under Shirley's leadership as Chairman of the Board, we began galloping to work. When confronted with troubling situations, she would analyze the predicament and decide, "I think he just needs a little petting and stroking." It's true she was both persistent and insistent; but always with her "call to arms" she would also urge, "Let's make joyful noises!" Her sense of fun was as big as all outdoors.

After the first Annual Meeting of the Compact she was particularly pleased, pulling Wendy and me aside to congratulate us. In doing so she pronounced Wendy her Red Cockaded Fire Bird. She then turned to me. Still early in our acquaintance, I thought, "Good grief, what is she going to say?" when she stated, "And you are my Swan." I contemplated the incongruity she lay before me when she added, "Have you ever seen how they can just beat things senseless with those wings?" I think it was a compliment. I'm still not quite sure.

In the following years the Compact was awarded the Southeast Natural Resource Leaders Award at the 2001 Southeast Watershed Forum, the prestigious Aquatic Resource Preservation Award (Citizen Division) from the Tennessee Department of Environment and Conservation (TDEC), and the 2002 Conservation Organization of the Year Award by the Tennessee Conservation League. In 2003 the Compact won with TDEC again, receiving their 2003 State Civic Volunteer Award. Shirley and the band of board members there at the time were largely the reason for all these accolades.

She was a force—but one always pointed in the direction of good for the Earth whether cajoling a government official or looking for support. One early e-mail she wrote to Katherine Luscher of the international organization River Network began, "Dear Kathy, I had a friend who said no one ever called him unless they wanted something—so here I am."

There she was, indeed! Years later after we partnered with them many times, she was awarded River Network's highest honor, the James R. Compton River Achievement Award for her dedication to conserving our nation's rivers. We had built watershed groups, engaged builders and developers to grow Nashville and the surrounding communities in a more water and energy-friendly way, engaged local officials to do the same and put together the Catfish Out of Water City Art Festival by partnering with Greenways for Nashville and the Parthenon and hatching the largest outdoor art exhibit in Nashville's history.

The combination of the last three drew Washington D.C.'s attention. As a result, one fine day the Administrator of the Environmental Protection Agency came to town. They came to visit us at Morgan Park Place (our first partners' water-friendly building project), award us with a sizable grant and present Shirley with the President's Volunteer Service Award.

Preceded by a bevy of Secret Service minions, Administrator Johnson arrived expecting to conduct the show. Shirley, ignoring security, approached him with, "I want to talk with you . . ." The poor man hadn't known it, but it was never his show to conduct. She successfully deployed a charm offensive and he was clearly smitten, which made for a jolly balance to the day.

Her persistence was also evident in many of her sign-offs. When she thought a meeting had gone on long enough, especially if it had been filled with bumps and challenges, she would invoke a close to the gathering with, "Let's mush on."

But as sure of herself as she was, she constantly sought the advice and counsel of those she considered wise. She never thought she knew it all—but once she had sought advice and done her homework, she was steady at the helm. The helm was where she was most comfortable and there she got much done for our Cumberland River Basin and the lands in the Southeast.

Later in our time together, she would tell stories over many cups of tea—stories of outings in her patent leather pony cart as a girl, of how her own mother faced the Great Depression and when speaking of travails working for water quality, of her grandfather James E. saying, "Anything of value is the seat of war."

Over the years the river evolved from something out back into the front door of our community. Her eyes had never left the basin as a whole, but as The Compact accomplished more, her gaze shifted toward land purchases—actions which would serve to preserve special places and filter waters to strengthen the heart of the river by strengthening its arteries.

SHIRLEY CALDWELL-PATTERSON
Nashville, TN

Conservation icon, mother, and staunch friend, Shirley Caldwell-Patterson was born on November 6, 1919 to parents Meredith Caldwell and Ellen Thomas Caldwell. The second of four children, her family was rounded out by brother, Meredith jr., and sisters Allison and Ellen. She died May 17, 2016. Shirley was the last member of her generation of the descendants of her grandfather, James E. Caldwell, family patriarch and founder of the Cumberland Telephone and Telegraph Company, which became Southern Bell. Making the most of a blissful childhood—Shirley grew up next door to her grandparents home, Longview, at the corner of Franklin Road and Caldwell Lane and their adjoining farm, Elysian Fields.

Shirley's lifelong ability to fight for what she believed in was inspired by her grandmother, Ma May, who raised the money for the Peace Monument that now stands at I-440 and Granny White Pike. Shirley wrote, "to consider what she accomplished makes me grateful for the pattern she set—not just for the adage 'to whom much is given, much is expected' but the joy, the fun of getting things done that need doing—things of more import than self."

A serious young rider, Shirley started showing horses at age seven, and through her childhood showed all over the country with her mother. At the Tennessee State Fair, she and Papa, her close friend and grandfather, entered the Parent and Child Ride. Side by side they rode into the ring, he in his farm riding clothes and she in her formal riding habit, complete with lapel gardenia, kid gloves, and top hat. Shirley wrote, "Round and round we went at top speed, passing the more sedate couples as if they were tethered." They won, hands down, a blue ribbon and a trophy. Years of riding gave her self-confidence and a love of travel, both of which fueled her all her days.

Often she would ride the Longview property with her grandfather, James E. Caldwell. Their discussions taught her about horses, cattle breeding, the evils of smoking, and especially, how to care for the land. These lessons stood Shirley in good stead the rest of her life. Her feelings for Longview and Elysian Fields, combined with her grandfather's ideas on looking after them, provided the foundation for her interest in conservation.

When she was 15, she went to New York City to take college preparatory classes at the Spence School. With visits to art museums, opera in Mrs. Andrew Carnegie's box every Friday night, and stimulating classes built wholly on discussion, her high school years are an example of how good teaching can impart intellectual curiosity and enthusiasm in a relatively short time. Shirley graduated in the class of 1937 and went on to Vanderbilt, where she majored in French and graduated *Magna Cum Laude* in 1941.

She married David Patterson at Belle Meade, on Harding Road, in 1942. The Meredith Caldwells were the last family to live at Belle Meade, which they sold to the city of Nashville to become the Belle Meade Plantation. Shirley and David had two children: David and Sheppard. She joined the Junior League and fueled her love of reading from Moon's Drug Store's lending collection. She took a correspondence course in bookkeeping, kept the books at her family's Nashville Union Stockyards and rose to the office of Treasurer and Vice President. At the behest of friends, she began to travel to Greece, where she took classes, taught English, and then began going on archaeological digs in Greece and Israel.

All her life, she crossed paths with Nashvillian-moved-to-Memphis Lucius Burch. Their time together was spent traveling, hunting and fishing, and always, always, eating well, reading deeply, and enjoying the company of friends, friends, and more friends—an outstanding accumulation of extraordinary people far too numerous to name.

Besides her family and friends, Shirley had a great and unquenchable love for the outdoors. Her desire to protect the environment was born from these trips and a lifetime spent enjoying nature. She said, "I'm a fly fisherman. I have a particular affection for rivers."

In 1997, at the age of 79, Shirley saw Vic Scoggin's documentary about his swimming the entire Cumberland River and she was appalled by the river's condition. With two friends, she started the Cumberland River Compact, dedicated to enhance the water quality of the entire 17,000 square mile watershed of the Cumberland River.

Shirley's particular brand of environmental work was driven by her mantra of "education, cooperation and communication." Like everything she did, Shirley's approach was unusual, personal, and successful. Her way of working with people instead of against them is part of what made her brand of conservation great, and, because of that, she created one of the very first watershed organizations with a collaborative model. The Compact was the first to partner with developers, when no other environmental group was willing to work with them, and this led to a grand shift in sustainability, benefitting rivers, habitat, and landscapes. Because of Shirley's framework, the Compact was held up as a model across the country and, because of her leadership, they were welcomed into offices where, with another leader, they never could have ventured. Because of the Cumberland River Compact, her work has benefitted more than two million people who depend on the Cumberland Basin.

At age 87, she was honored with the highest volunteer award given by the U.S. President, the President's Volunteer Service "Call to Service" Award, for nearly 6,000 hours of volunteer service.

She was also a Charter Member of the original board of trustees of the Nature Conservancy of Tennessee, helped establish the Tennessee Environmental Council, was its treasurer for 17 years and president for two. A member of the original Environmental Action Fund, she was a founder of the Lucius Burch Center for Western Tradition in Dubois, Wyoming as well as the Lucius Burch Conservation Funds of Nashville and Memphis. Shirley was a founding member of Leadership Nashville. She received the Z. Carter Patten Award from the Tennessee Conservation League for her outstanding contributions to conservation in Tennessee. She was awarded River Network's James R. Compton River Achievement award. She initiated the Gaia Fund at the Nashville Community Foundation, worked extensively with Tennessee Parks and Greenways, and the Tennessee Department of Environment and Conservation awarded her its Lifetime Achievement Award.

When asked how she found time and energy to pursue so many environmental battles, she quoted Nathan Bedford Forrest, "I get up in the morning, put on my boots, and start fighting." She often said, "One of the best things about a chronic volunteer, there's always something that needs doing when you show up."

Continuing the family writing tradition, begun with her grandparents' memoirs: *Recollections of a Lifetime* and *A Chapter in the Life of a Little Girl of the Confederacy*. in 2003, Shirley edited and co-authored *Lucius*, the personal papers and writings of Memphis environmentalist and attorney Lucius Burch, and, at her death, was making final updates to her family biography and autobiography, *The Patriarch, Caldwell & Company, and Me, Shirley.*

Shirley stayed interested and interesting until she left us. When speaking of her childhood, and this could be applied to every aspect of Shirley's life, she said, "If you were ever bored, it was your own fault." In recent years, when asked how she was doing, Shirley delighted in answering, "As I please." This hard-won statement applied equally to her incredibly satisfying, multi-faceted life and her smooth passing from this world.

Shirley was preceded in death by her parents, siblings, former husband David Patterson, and companion of 28 years, Lucius Burch. When asked about her own impending and unavoidable death, Shirley said, "I may go whoopin' and hollerin', but I hope not. As soon as I convince at least some of mankind that we cannot continue to befoul our earth and expect to survive as a species —I'm ready to move on."

Shirley was a great woman who will be remembered by her friends and family for her indomitable spirit, her crackling intellect, and by future generations for the green mark she left upon rivers and the land.

So many unforgettable things to so many people, she was Shirley, Miss Caldwell, Mrs. Caldwell-Patterson, Mama, Boss, and Sas. She will long be remembered and long missed.

Editor's Note by William M. Akers

For seven years, Shirley's book has been my off to the side pleasure. Everything writing-related I do is about earning money. This has been for fun and I will miss it.

It was a delight to work with my son William, who line edited. Even Shirley needed a smidgen of smoothing out.

Thank You

Cissy and her family, including Shade Murray, Went Caldwell, Langley Granbery, Paul Sloan, and especially David Patterson. Son Caldwell for thoughtful notes and bottomless support.

Vicki Moore at Chromatics and Jami Awalt at the Tennessee State Library and Archives. Marc Stengel for access to his father's photograph collection.

Everyone who contributed to the Additional Voices, especially Bill Forrester, for whom the light bulb switched on that became the Cumberland River Compact, which will improve Tennesseans' lives for generations to come.

The late Bob Thomson, a fervent encourager who helped me keep Shirley on her writing path. Pam Casey and Jackie Karneth, for immaculate proofreading. S.A. Habib and Leah Agler kindly designed the cover. John Balkwill of Lumino Press, who did *The Life and Times of a Soldier and Sportsman* by Meredith Caldwell, Jr., was a constant pleasure to work with.

Most of all, to Shirley for two of my life's finest compliments. She asked me to help with her book and offered to teach me fly fishing.

If you are curious, the Battle of Nashville Monument Park is at the corner of Granny White Pike and Clifton Lane.

www.ingramcontent.com/pod-product-compliance
Lightning Source LLC
Chambersburg PA
CBHW022024290426
44109CB00014B/730